WAGSTAFF:

BEFORE AND AFTER

MAPPLETHORPE

Also by Philip Gefter

Photography After Frank

WAGSTAFF

A BIOGRAPHY

BEFORE AND AFTER
MAPPLETHORPE

PHILIP GEFTER

LIVERIGHT PUBLISHING CORPORATION

A Division of W. W. NORTON & COMPANY • *New York London*

Frontispiece: Sam Wagstaff at Warhol opening at
Leo Castelli Gallery, 1964. *Photograph by Billy Name*

Copyright © 2015 by Philip Gefter

All rights reserved
Printed in the United States of America
First Edition

"You're the Top" (from *Anything Goes*), words and music
by Cole Porter, © 1934 (renewed) by W B Music Corp. All rights reserved.

For information about permission to reproduce selections from this book,
write to Permissions, Liveright Publishing Corporation, a division of
W. W. Norton & Company, Inc., 500 Fifth Avenue, New York, NY 10110

For information about special discounts for bulk purchases, please contact
W. W. Norton Special Sales at specialsales@wwnorton.com or 800-233-4830

Manufacturing by Quad Graphics, Fairfield
Book design by Barbara Bachman
Production manager: Julia Druskin

Library of Congress Cataloging-in-Publication Data

Gefter, Philip.
Wagstaff, before and after Mapplethorpe :
a biography / Philip Gefter. — First Edition.
    pages cm
Includes bibliographical references and index.
ISBN 978-0-87140-437-4 (hardcover)
1. Wagstaff, Samuel J. 2. Wagstaff, Samuel J.—Friends and associates.
3. Art museum curators—United States—Biography. 4. Art—Collectors
and collecting—United States—Biography. I. Title.
N406.W34G44 2014
709.2—dc23
[B]

                                          2014029920

Liveright Publishing Corporation
500 Fifth Avenue, New York, N.Y. 10110
www.wwnorton.com

W. W. Norton & Company Ltd.
Castle House, 75/76 Wells Street, London W1T 3QT

1 2 3 4 5 6 7 8 9 0

For Richard Press

Stare. It is the way to educate your eye, and more. Stare, pry, listen, eavesdrop. Die knowing something. You are not here long.

—Walker Evans[1]

#I – 5TH – 27 – 107

White night.
White dog, white cat,
White room, white dress, white floor, white sky,
White you, white me, white him.

White powder, white champagne, white light, white stars,
white teeth, white skin, white eyes, white feet,
White windows, white uphigh, higher, higher,
whiter, whiter, high and white.

White hands, white fingers, white nails,
White salavia [sic], spit, sweat, come,
White clouds, heat, sun, beach, sand, foam,
White ice, fluid, liquid, moisture,
White rain, white hair, white stallion, white sheets,
White hot liquid melting night.

—For Sam Wagstaff, by Ruth Kligman,
June 17, 1976[2]

CONTENTS

A
S A CURATOR, COLLECTOR, AND PATRON, SAM WAGSTAFF
played a more influential role in shaping art history during
the second half of the twentieth century than is widely understood, but
his influence is often obscured in the glare of his notoriety as the lover,
mentor, and patron of Robert Mapplethorpe. In fact, Mapplethorpe was
only the last and most conspicuous of Wagstaff's distinctions.

As a curator of contemporary art in the 1960s, Wagstaff set a standard at two leading American museums, the Wadsworth Atheneum and the Detroit Institute of Arts. In Hartford, he mounted several landmark exhibitions, among them "Black, White, and Gray,"[1] the first museum show of minimal art, in 1964, and, two years later, the first museum show of artist Tony Smith.[2] In Detroit, he brought the New York avant-garde to a conservative institution, creating not a little mischief in the process.

Wagstaff provided support and friendship to a roster of sometimes young, often unknown, artists throughout the 1960s whose names today constitute a pantheon of the era: Andy Warhol, Ray Johnson, Tony Smith, Agnes Martin, Richard Tuttle, Michael Heizer, Mark di Suvero, Walter De Maria, and Neil Jenney, among countless others. Mapplethorpe was the last in that long line—the only one with whom Wagstaff had a romantic relationship.

As a collector, Wagstaff sought the idiosyncratic and underappreciated, from Dogon African sculpture to Native American Mimbres pots, from photography to nineteenth-century American silver. Photography, though, remains his crowning legacy. Wagstaff began collecting photographs in 1973, when it was still considered a utilitarian medium—a bastard child of the arts. To his delight, his new enthusiasm surprised his art world friends, only further prompting his impassioned advocacy of the medium: "Gustave Le Gray made pictures in the 1850s. He's the greatest photographer of all, the best that there has been, and the textbooks hardly mention him," Wagstaff told *The Washington Post* in 1978. "It's like leaving Rembrandt out of a history of Western art."[3] Tireless in his defense of the medium, Wagstaff sat on museum committees, appeared on panels, lent works from his collection to museums, and wrote articles about photography. His activities brought increased curatorial attention and art historical recognition of the form. He was instrumental in establishing the international marketplace for photography in the 1970s, for better or worse, attracting other collectors into his circle. In 1984, three years before his death, he sold his photography collection to the J. Paul Getty Museum. His was one of three founding collections of that museum's photography holdings, now regarded among the top institutional collections in the world.

Wagstaff's glamour had preceded Mapplethorpe. He was tall, rich, and considered very handsome. Invariably, his good looks garnered comment from almost anyone who knew him. Springing heartily from the repressive atmosphere of his patrician upbringing in New York, his formal education at Hotchkiss and Yale, and the social circles he inhabited in Manhattan while in his twenties and thirties during the 1940s and '50s, Wagstaff would embark on a personal transformation throughout the next decade that appeared in direct conflict with his background but in perfect harmony with the era. In the 1940s he had been cited in society columns as among the most desirable bachelors in New York; in the '50s, he was living a double life as a proper Madison Avenue professional by day and embracing the gay demimonde by night; in the early '60s, he was a Jamesian weekend guest in the grand houses of the British countryside; by the end of that decade, he was tuning in, turning on, and getting ready to drop out. In 1972, when he met Mapplethorpe, a young, unknown artist half his age, Wagstaff was still the man-about-town.

Mapplethorpe would be instrumental in Wagstaff's absorption in photography to begin with, just as Wagstaff would be pivotal in Mapplethorpe's ascent in the art world.

As cultural history, the narrative of Wagstaff's life parallels a number of concurrent strains in the history of the last half century: one is the evolution of the gay rights movement; a second is the elevation of photography to an equal among the arts, becoming, finally, "the art of our day." Both are potent elements in the mix of contemporary life and, not surprisingly, intertwined in the context of Wagstaff and Mapplethorpe's relationship.

Wagstaff found a way to apply his excellent education and social cultivation in the pursuit of an authentic life on his own terms. In the process he left a legacy as a collector and tastemaker that benefits the generations that follow. Perhaps there is no more fitting description of this legacy than an observation in a eulogy delivered at his memorial in 1987 by Pierre Apraxine, then curator of the Gilman Paper Company Collection, arguably one of the finest private photography collections ever assembled, acquired by the Metropolitan Museum of Art in 2005: "Collector or beachcomber, Sam taught us all his life that it is less the object at which we look that gives value to our experience, than the intensity with which we look at it. It is the intensity of the pure act of seeing which illuminated Sam's life, and which now reflects ours."[4]

Sam was the most beautiful man. He had the

bone structure and lanky grace of a patrician.

He was as handsome as Gary Cooper.

—BARBARA JAKOBSON[1]

PART ONE

PROVENANCE

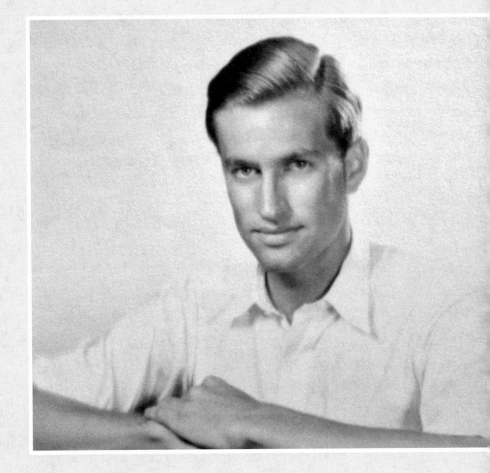

Samuel Jones Wagstaff Jr., Yale, 1944
Courtesy of Thomas L. Jefferson

DRAGGED MASS
DISPLACEMENT

O N THE MORNING OF MARCH 18, 1971, SAM WAGSTAFF STOOD before a crowd on the lawn of the Detroit Institute of Arts (DIA), waiting for a massive chunk of stone to hit the ground. This immense granite block was dangling in midair from a crane near the formidable Beaux Arts building on Woodward Avenue. The curator of contemporary art at DIA, Wagstaff had shoulder-length hair and was wearing a brown leather woodsman's jacket. Standing next to him was Michael Heizer, twenty-six, the artist who had planned the installation. While a crew of twenty workmen gawked from below, there was not a trace of apprehension in Wagstaff's expression, in his bearing, or in the authority with which he guided the workers that his own career was riding on that thirty-ton stone. Getting to this moment had been a marathon of political and logistical calculation, not least of it involving the transport of the granite from a quarry in Vermont. In the days before, Wagstaff had appealed personally to Governor William Milliken, with whom he had gone to school at Yale, for a variance on the freeze-and-thaw regulations in Michigan that prevented flatbed trucks on the freeways in winter—the only way the granite block could be transported from the railway station to the museum. Despite that logistical triumph, Wagstaff's enemies and skeptics were watching: the trustees, the patrons, and the citizens of a city perhaps not entirely ready to embrace the desecration of the landmark's lawn in the name of the avant-garde.

Among the trustees of the Detroit Institute of Arts, the case against Samuel Jones Wagstaff Jr. had been building long before this installation. When he had first arrived in Detroit in 1968, museum officials and wealthy patrons were captivated by his charm, his savoir faire, and his expertise, but over time, as he had taken on the more visible countercultural affects of the period, their allegiance began to waver. While an increasingly strained relationship between venturesome museum curators and the more staid board members was hardly anomalous, not even Wagstaff's long hair, beads, and recreational pot smoking were as damaging to his reputation as his hauteur. Although art history would judge him favorably, the city fathers at that moment were looking for an excuse to send him packing.

Wagstaff had commissioned the Heizer piece and authorized its installation on the front lawn for "Michael Heizer: Photographic and Actual Work," an exhibition that would open a week later.[2] Wagstaff later recalled that the idea of the lawn piece was "to see the remains of the action of something such as a rock dragged through the earth, to see the remains of that action visibly . . . you know it's like scraping your hands through the pie and you can see what you have done to it."[3] The fate of the stone, and the impact of the exhibition, would propel him out of the state, back to New York, and, finally, into the most productive and fervent stage of his career. But, on that day, at that moment, the museum's staff were gathered on the lawn along with several stalwart museum trustees who had challenged the project all along. The ominous piece of granite, which measured twenty-six feet long and four feet wide, was finally lowered to the ground and situated horizontally. It stood at the height of the workmen's shoulders, who began attaching the great mass to two bulldozers idling nearby.

Some people who had gathered began clapping as Heizer climbed into the cab of one of the bulldozers. Then both vehicles began to move in tandem, pulling the slab slowly across the museum grounds behind them. It was the artist's intention for the granite block to dig slowly into the ground in front of the museum, and, eventually, sink until it was level with the grass. A trail of churned earth was to remain behind it as an integral element of the installation.

BEFORE WE LEARN THE FATE of the granite slab, more biographical context is needed. Indeed, it had not been until Wagstaff's arrival in Detroit at the age of forty-six that he would undergo the transformation from a dashing man-about-town to a social renegade. He had already distinguished himself as the curator of painting, prints, and drawings at the Wadsworth Atheneum Museum of Art in Hartford from 1961 to 1968, organizing several landmark exhibits. For a while in Detroit, Sam retained the aura of his aristocratic upbringing, despite a growing defiance of the very conventions he seemed to exemplify. The dualities that accounted for his glamour in the art world of the 1960s and '70s—aristocrat and iconoclast, pillar of society and obdurate bohemian, eligible bachelor and unrepentant homosexual—were exactly what tarnished him in the eyes of the trustees. The disarray of Wagstaff's office, for example, and his general disregard for orderliness, did not escape notice. "A Monet would be on the floor underneath the table," Ann Perron Spivak, who would later become a trustee of the museum, recalled laughingly. "As a museum volunteer, I would occasionally go in there looking for something. I'd see the framed Monet and I would pick it up and put it on the table and lean it against the wall. And, of course, the next time I'd come in, it would be back on the floor again."[4]

As Sam's assistant, Susanne Hilberry came to observe in him the quirks and discrepancies often referred to as the eccentricities of the rich. "When you first saw Sam he looked immaculate, as though everything was perfect, perfectly this and that," she said. "Well, it couldn't have been further from the truth." She described his oxford shirts, which were often frayed at the collar, and his loafers, which might have had a hole in the bottom. "It didn't matter," she said, "he was always the most elegant person in the room, regardless." She would insist that he go to Saks Fifth Avenue, just down the street from the museum, and buy some new shirts, asserting that his slovenliness was an affectation. He always dismissed the suggestion, telling her she sounded just like his mother, who had always accused him of being so handsome that he thought he could get away with anything. "And he was," she said.[5]

Still, his curatorial leadership had, until this juncture, been unquestioned. Soon after Wagstaff was hired by the Detroit Institute of Arts, he received a call from Hawkins Ferry, chairman of the Friends of Modern Art, a group of collectors and supporters who endowed acquisitions for the museum, asking Sam's opinion about the possibility of the museum's purchasing an Andy Warhol *Self-Portrait*, a large screen painting. It seemed to augur well a climate in which Wagstaff would have likeminded support and be given full artistic latitude. "I not only approved but felt the painting was of the very, very highest order of excellence at that moment," Wagstaff recalled some years later. "Andy Warhol is for me one of the greatest artists of the twentieth century. I think *Campbell's Soup Can* is, undoubtedly, up to now, the single greatest image in art painting as we know it at this moment."[6]

A STROLL THROUGH THE modern galleries of the Detroit Institute of Arts today reveals the significance of Wagstaff's curatorial judgment in his brief three years there. He facilitated the acquisition of the museum's Robert Rauschenberg, its Ellsworth Kelly, the Roy Lichtenstein, the Donald Judd, the Mark di Suvero, the Claes Oldenburgs, and the Robert Morrises, among other works. *Gracehoper*, the looming black Tony Smith sculpture that Sam brought to the museum, is still situated on the lawn looking as much like a geometric creature of the primeval ages as a majestic sentinel from the future.[7]

Most impressively, Wagstaff was able to reverse the impulse of the trustees to perpetuate the museum's traditional past, specifically bringing the New York avant-garde to Detroit and in the process transforming a regional museum into a platform for the most contemporary thinking. Of course it was one thing for Sam to encourage the trustees' pride about the socially important and visually arresting *Detroit Industry* murals painted by Diego Rivera in the 1930s. It was another to expect them to embrace the disruption of their manicured lawn in the process of installing Michael Heizer's big chunk of stone.

Wagstaff's pedigree—Hotchkiss, Yale, the Institute of Fine Arts at New York University, the Wadsworth Atheneum—meant far more for an aspiring Midwestern city like Detroit than it would in New York. The museum and its trustees naturally anticipated that a man with such bloodlines would fit in quite well. Upon arriving in Detroit, Wagstaff had taken an apartment in Lafayette Towers, an international-style residential complex completed in 1963 by Ludwig Mies van der Rohe. The two identical twenty-two-story steel and glass apartment buildings bordered Lafayette Park, three miles from the museum. From there he made his way with ease to the elegant mansions of Grosse Pointe and Bloomfield Hills. He could charm the very stylish and sophisticated Florence Barron, who lived with her husband, Brooks, in a modernist house designed for them by Minuro Yamasaki[8] and who, in the early 1960s, had turned a request by Andy Warhol to paint her portrait into a commission of his first self-portrait series; or he could be happily entertained by the very wealthy and adventurous Anne MacDonald, the youngest trustee of the DIA.

At the time Anne was married to Richard Manoogian, president of Masco, an industrial goods company. He sat on the board of directors of the Ford Motor Company, served as a trustee of the Detroit Institute of Arts, and resided for many consecutive years on the Forbes 400 list of the richest people in America. Much younger than her husband, Anne was voluptuous, fun loving, restless, and wild. First as a volunteer at the DIA and then on its board, she had become one of Wagstaff's closest allies, a true co-conspirator. In 1970, with her help and that of Ann Perron, Wagstaff had orchestrated for the benefit of the Friends of Modern Art a "happening" of unparalleled cultural cachet for the Motor City: they imported the entire Broadway cast of *Hair* to Detroit for a gala performance. An enormous hit with unprecedented full-frontal nudity, a "be-in" at the end of the show in which the entire audience was invited on stage, and several songs that became anthems of the antiwar movement, *Hair* was a persuasive theatrical metaphor for the spirit of the age. Add this *grande jeste* to the list of visionary—and entertaining—feats that should have secured Detroit's loyalty to Wagstaff.

There was a period when Anne Manoogian and Sam were going to lunch three times a week at the Traffic Jam, a restaurant near the museum. She described what it was like walking back from lunch with him, his eyes scanning the street and the sidewalk for junk—cans that had been run over, paper wrappers, any kind of discarded object—and collecting them in his hands. "He would pick up things like a little kid," she recalled. "You wanted to say to him, 'Put that down.' But his eye picked out the beauty in each one of the things and by the time we'd get back to the museum he'd open his hands to show you and you went, Oh my god, together they were just beautiful."[9]

An encounter with Wagstaff often left the women of that social set starry-eyed. "He was such a dazzling figure," Ann Perron Spivak said. "Handsome and gorgeous and certainly charming when he wanted to be. I didn't know anyone else like him in Michigan." Sam, whose idea of preparing a meal for himself consisted of cooking a hamburger directly on the burner, would take advantage of the welcoming hostesses and manicured surroundings of Bloomfield Hills and Grosse Pointe, in which he found refractions of his own self-consciously glamorous and emotionally distant mother. The handsome curator would set up house visits with trustees to look at their art collections at 5:30 or 6 p.m. coincidentally, Spivak recalled, just in time for cocktail hour. She would offer Sam a drink and bring out hors d'oeuvres and he would invariably feign surprise while accepting a last-minute invitation to stay for dinner. "He would make the rounds in Bloomfield Hills," she said, where he was assured of a well-prepared meal and excellent French wine. "We joked about that among our friends."[10]

Wagstaff had endeared himself to the patrons in part by exposing them directly to the art and artists he intended to promote. Not only did he bring well-known artists to Detroit, he initiated activities and field trips to inform and educate the local art community about contemporary art. In early 1969, soon after he had arrived in Detroit, Wagstaff organized a trip to New York for eighty members of the Friends of Modern Art, that group of patrons' first large-scale, out-of-town excursion. Wagstaff knew the New York art world as a true insider. Andy Warhol had been a friend for almost a decade and Sam had spent a great deal of time at the Factory even before it became such a cultural phenomenon. He had included Warhol in exhibitions and he had bought Warhol's work for his own collection. He also knew well the circle of artists who had attended or taught at Black Mountain, an experimental and influential college in North Carolina in which the study of the arts was at the foundation of the liberal arts curriculum. These included John Cage, Merce Cunningham, Robert Rauschenberg, and Ray Johnson, all of whom lived in downtown Manhattan and also, like Sam, happened to be gay. He was close to any number of gallery owners, such as Klaus Kertess, of Bykert Gallery, who also lived in Wagstaff's building in New York. He knew other curators, as well, such as Henry Geldzahler at the Metropolitan Museum. For the Detroit patrons hoping to peek inside the New York art world, Wagstaff would be the consummate guide.

Wagstaff had kept his loft on the Bowery for regular weekend art-viewing trips. On the first evening of that trip in early 1969, he threw a party for the Detroit collectors and patrons. He invited his art world friends, as well as New York collectors and prominent artists. Andy Warhol, Robert Morris, Robert Rauschenberg, and Tony Smith were all there mingling with the Michigan collectors. While the presence of these artists reinforced the cultural glamour and art world heft that accompanied Wagstaff's reputation, the out-of-town visitors couldn't quite compute the discrepant and unconventional disarray of Sam's bare-bones loft.

"You'd walk into Sam's loft and there'd be an eighteen-foot-high Oldenburg doll," said Judy Linn, a photographer who had grown up in Detroit and would meet Wagstaff in the 1970s. "You know, some totally ratty weird thing hanging from the ceiling, and the place would be just filled with boxes. I remember him telling me that people would come over and say, 'Oh, did you just move in?' and he would say, 'No, I've been here for years.' But it always looked like he had just moved in, or he was about to move out."[11]

And when the patrons wanted something more polished to buttress their thoughts on contemporary art with some historical context, Wagstaff obliged, taking them to see the old masters on a viewing excursion to Brussels, Paris, Milan, and the South of France. His personal, privileged access to curators and collectors, museums and private collections, was a treat both exclusive and edifying. He could organize a private tour with a curator of painting of the French school at the Louvre, who would walk them through the galleries on a day the museum was closed, stopping here and there to give an impromptu discourse on *The Raft of the Medusa*, by Géricault. He could arrange a cocktail party in their honor in the home of a private collector along the Bois de Boulogne, a Delacroix on one wall and a Georges de la Tour on another.

Frank Kolbert, an assistant curator at the DIA whom Wagstaff had hired fresh from Yale, was among the fifteen people who went on one such trip in 1971. "The Vicomtesse de Noailles had died several months before, and Sam managed to get everybody into her house on Place des États-Unis," Kolbert said. "The Vicomtesse de Noailles was the great patron of Cocteau. She was the first person to commission Diego Giacometti to make furniture, and Jean-Michel Frank decorated it. . . . It was a great trip and an extraordinary group of people. Sam just knew all these people and he was able to call on them to do things."[12]

Although Wagstaff was well acquainted with the "fancy pants" crowd—a term he often used to describe the members of his social class, who relied on traditional measures of wealth and position to define themselves—the art world was his primary interest, and local young artists provided a nourishing counterpoint to the more formal obligations of his job in Detroit. When Wagstaff first got there, people were surprised by how passionate he was about exploring the city's nascent art scene. He was quick to find his way to Cobb's Corner, the scrappy local bar in the bohemian Cass Corridor district, where struggling young artists and students lived and worked. "I kept hearing about this guy at the museum," said Ellen Phelan, a well-regarded New York artist who grew up in Detroit. "There was a lot of excitement about Sam because he was the first person who ever arrived there and said, 'Where are the artists?' " [13]

After high school, Phelan had worked at a coffeehouse called the Cup of Socrates, where she fell in with a group of young artists and musicians, and, then, moved to San Francisco, where she met Jim Gurley of Big Brother and the Holding Company. She returned to Detroit to attend graduate school at Wayne State University and took a job as a curatorial assistant at the museum, where she got to know Sam. "He was a tremendously open person to some things and not others," she said. He had a great many fans, and while she considered him original in his thinking she was also struck by the way he could be totally dismissive of people who didn't interest him. If he was asked by a local resident to describe the meaning of an artist's work, for example, his response was often a rebuff. "Great art needs no explanation," was one of his standard refrains, and it put a lot of people off.[14]

In the 1960s, Detroit, home to the American automotive industry and Motown, was germinating some of the purest avant-garde impulses in the visual arts. Wagstaff wasted no time exploring this new community, which he found vital, exotic, and fun. At Cobb's Corner, he would listen to the homegrown bands. "Detroit introduced me to contemporary music," Wagstaff said, pointing out the many nationally recognized musicians the city had spawned: Aretha Franklin; Diana Ross and the Supremes; Martha and the Vandellas; the MC5; and Iggy Pop. The Grande Ballroom, the venue where these acts and many other nationally known groups performed (including Cream, the Grateful Dead, and Janis Joplin) was, in Sam's own words, his "musical nursery. It added an enormous amount of pleasure in my life."[15] Another favorite place of his was the New Bethel Baptist Church, where Aretha's father, Bishop C. L. Franklin, gave sermons with his "million-dollar voice" and led the gospel choir. Sam loved the music and he would tell visitors to Detroit that there was more life at that church during those gospel services than anywhere else in town.

Sam's home away from home, nevertheless, was the Cass Corridor district, and its community his brethren. The story of the Cass Corridor artists begins with the launch of the Artists Workshop in the early 1960s.

A collective founded by John Sinclair, its manifesto declared that "what we want is a place for artists—musicians, painters, poets, writers, filmmakers—who are committed to their art and to the concept of community involvement to meet and work with one another in an open, warm, loving, supportive environment (what they don't get in the real world)."[16] Young local artists rallied. Ellen Phelan, along with other artists like Nancy Mitchnik, John Egner, Michael Luchs, Gordon Newton, and Robert Sestok, had studios in the Cass Corridor and they all took part in Artists Workshop events.

The MC5 were founding members of the Artists Workshop and it seemed only natural that the collective would bring musicians into the Grande Ballroom, including Ornette Coleman, John Coltrane, Miles Davis, and Charles Mingus. Sinclair, a poet, who for a time also managed the MC5, considered Coltrane's music an influence on his own blues poetry: "It was our constant inspiration—we started to *breathe* with and from that music," he said.[17]

The Artists Workshop would evolve with the 1960s themselves, reflecting the creative impulses of the artists, the drug use, and the political tensions that came to define the era. The collective first changed its name to Trans-Love Energy, and, then, after the race riots that tore Detroit apart in 1967, the Rainbow People's party. In 1969, John Sinclair founded the White Panther party in response to a challenge by Huey Newton for more white people to voice their support for the Black Panthers.

But then, after Sinclair sold a joint to the same undercover police officer for the third time, he was arrested and sentenced to ten years in prison. A very public court case ensued, followed by a series of appeals over several years. A movement was begun to "free John Sinclair." This culminated in the John Sinclair Freedom Rally, a 1971 concert at the University of Michigan that drew John Lennon and Yoko Ono, who performed a song Lennon had written for the occasion called "John Sinclair." Stevie Wonder also performed at the concert and some of the most famous countercultural figures of the era spoke, including Allen Ginsberg, Jerry Rubin, and Bobby Seale. Sam Wagstaff attended that concert, driving up to Ann Arbor with Ellen Phelan and sitting on the gymnasium floor with thousands of students and followers of Sinclair. "Sam just loved it," Phelan said.[18] The rally succeeded in bringing about Sinclair's release from prison within days.

It was this kind of support that endeared Wagstaff to the Cass Corridor artists. Frederick J. Cummings, executive director of the Detroit Institute of Arts during Wagstaff's years there (and later the director of the museum), would write, "By breaking down such traditional barriers, Wagstaff made it possible, even after his departure from Detroit, for the museum to continue to reinforce his encouragement of the Corridor community."[19]

DURING HIS TENURE IN DETROIT, Sam was also seeking out new artists through his connections in New York. Among them was the man who, that day, would stand by Wagstaff's side on the DIA lawn, waiting for the calamitous stone to fall: Michael Heizer, a twenty-six-year-old living in New York, would later gain international acclaim, as well as respect among the most important artists of his generation, but at that time he was little known. Heizer had begun going out to the desert in Nevada and California and carving monumental geometric forms directly into the mountains of the Sierra Nevada. He was creating an entirely new kind of artwork in direct relationship with the landscape—earthworks that recalled the megalithic structures of ancient civilizations—and the press was beginning to take notice. At the time, other than Robert Smithson and Walter De Maria, very few other artists were utilizing earth and soil as an essential medium for art making on so grand a scale. The new movement, of which Heizer would be considered a pioneer, was being called "land art."

Walter de Maria introduced Wagstaff to Heizer in 1968, during one of Sam's frequent trips to New York. Heizer recalled, "Sam would come in on weekends and call me up and come down to the studio. Every other weekend he'd come by." When Heizer began traveling to the Mojave Desert, Wagstaff made it a point to stay in touch and follow his work. "Sam never bought anything," Heizer said. "He was not a collector of my work. He would come talk to me. We might go to dinner in Chinatown."[20]

Sam had developed a particular interest by this time in mentoring young artists, which resulted in a number of romantic infatuations, some realized, others not. In Detroit, his homosexuality was an open secret among the trustees as well as in the Cass Corridor community. He didn't discuss it, but neither did he hide it. During the first months of his tenure at DIA, Wagstaff got involved with a twenty-five-year-old artist named Jim Crawford. At the time, Crawford, a graduate student in the MFA program at Wayne State University, was doing work with neon that Wagstaff found compelling. Crawford recognized Sam's passion about art immediately, and he was drawn to his knowledge, his imagination, and his strong presence and sophistication. An eager student, he wanted to keep up a serious intellectual dialogue with Sam about the ideas swirling around the art world at that time.

One night Sam invited Crawford to a gathering for the museum's Friends of Modern Art in Bloomfield Hills, and they began an affair. "Interestingly enough, on that drive back from Ann Perron's house, the situation was electric—I was a needy kid and he was a greedy [significantly older] kid—and I don't know whether I put my hand on his leg or he put his hand on my thigh or what, but, we were sexually charged and attracted to each other," Crawford said. "I don't know if sex was on my mind but that's what happened. We went to his apartment. He had his mattress on the floor. And we had a very mutually exploring situation."[21] Crawford began spending time at Wagstaff's apartment.

For the Friends of Modern Art party in his New York loft, Sam commissioned a neon work comprised of six pieces by Jim Crawford, with whom he was still involved. He placed them alongside work by Tony Smith and Oldenburg. It was a way to show the collectors that a young Cass Corridor artist was making work that deserved a place in the New York art world. Interest in Crawford's work was further abetted when one of the guests, a tall, slender African-American dancer, leaped through the loft, crashing into—and breaking—three of the neon pieces.

Nevertheless, Crawford was respected among the Cass Corridor artists and several of the Detroit patrons had already bought his work, even before his involvement with Wagstaff. By placing the work in context of Smith and Oldenburg, Wagstaff was able to give Crawford a kind of exposure in New York, adding to his stature among the Midwestern visitors. This was one way Wagstaff was able to provide support to artists.

Six months after they met, the enterprising and intellectually curious Crawford embarked on an extended trip through Europe on his own to look at art. In the fall of 1969, Sam was in Paris for business, where they spent the week together. While Sam introduced him to several people, including the influential art dealer Ileana Sonnabend, Crawford was in a period of depression and Sam was less than sympathetic. That was the end of their relationship. When Crawford returned to Detroit, he took a job as the visual arts coordinator for the Michigan Council of the Arts, a position he held for twenty-two years. He never stopped making and showing art.

Their paths crossed one more time, in 1970, when the DIA's Junior Council undertook a fund-raiser. Because Wagstaff was interested in promoting the involvement of local young artists, he authorized an installation for the evening organized by trustees Mary Denison and Mrs. Walter B. Ford III. They commissioned Crawford for two "happenings," in which he used shattered ice, dry ice, and recorded soundtracks. These "happenings" occurred in prominent places in the museum, which was unprecedented for a local artist: one at the Woodward Avenue entrance, and the other in the museum's Diego Rivera Court.

Soon after his own return from that trip to Europe, Wagstaff was introduced to the work of Gordon Newton, barely twenty years old, who had come from Port Huron, a small town on Lake Huron in Michigan. A scrawny, scruffy postadolescent wild child with high cheekbones and sandy brown hair, Newton happened to be Wagstaff's type: Sam was often attracted to young, thin, and unpolished men. Assuming the role of Newton's mentor gave meaning and focus to Sam.

John Egner, another Cass Corridor artist, taught painting in the graduate program at Wayne State University during that period. He had arrived in Detroit in 1966 after obtaining his MFA from Yale. Egner was the one to bring Newton's work to Wagstaff's attention, inviting the curator across Woodward Avenue to the Wayne State campus to look at his student's drawings. It was because of Sam's immediate response to Newton's work that Egner concluded the curator to be the real thing. "The son of a bitch had an eye," Egner said of Wagstaff, citing the little gem of a painting by James Ensor in his office and the Pollock Sam had acquired, *The Deep*, as one of the artist's best paintings. "He bought good stuff. Like so many smart, classy people, he knew that his own enthusiasm could create value in a work of art."[22]

Newton's work was fierce and raw. His materials were industrial, from scrap metal and rubber to machinery parts, as if they were discarded directly from assembly lines and reimagined with the tools he had at hand—hammers, power saws, and drills. His assemblages were in tune with the conceptual ideas and attitudes of artists as diverse as Dorothea Rockburne, Mark di Suvero, Robert Rauschenberg, and John Chamberlain. When Wagstaff introduced Newton to Tony Smith, for example, Smith said that he had not seen work with that kind of energy and originality since Jackson Pollock.[23] Everything about the young artist seemed to whet Sam's appetite on a deeper, more primal level. It didn't matter that Newton was heterosexual.

Wagstaff invited Newton into his private passion for collecting. The two of them spent a good deal of time together in Detroit, often in Sam's barely furnished modern apartment, where they would sit on the floor barefoot, getting stoned together, looking at drawings one by one, sometimes in silence. Or they would fondle the wood-carved African artifacts from the Dogon period, which Sam collected, and he would explain what it was that struck him about this piece or that, why it was meaningful to him, why he considered it important in context of its tradition in art history. Newton's academic ignorance along with his visual intelligence sparked Sam's keen encyclopedic knowledge of art history. "He used to collect postcards, too," Newton said. "We would sit there on the floor and he would make you go through piles of postcards with him, one after the other."[24]

Wagstaff turned to Newton's drawings with the same obsessive

drive he brought to collecting the things that interested him, one species of object at a time. In a sense, collecting always seemed like the
ultimate organizing principle for Wagstaff's passions, going back to
what he claimed to be his first collection—cacti, on the island of
Majorca—when he was thirteen. As his tastes evolved, he would collect
Italian Renaissance drawings, nineteenth-century French lithographs
from the booksellers on the quays along the Seine in Paris, Native
American Mimbres burial pots. In contemporary art, it was the pop art
paintings out of the studios of his friends Andy Warhol, Jasper Johns,
or Roy Lichtenstein in New York; he turned to each one with the
monogamous—if serial—intensity of an infatuation. But, always, he
was in pursuit of some "collectible" form of art.

According to Egner, Newton was a country boy with his hands in
his pockets all the time and his shoulders hunched over, someone who
did not even have to utter the words "Aw, shucks" to leave that kind of
impression. While he rarely went to class, he was such a good artist that
school seemed utterly beside the point.

"Whatever intensity Pollock had, Gordon had as much of it," Egner
later said, echoing Tony Smith's observation.[25] "You name me an
expressionist artist through the ages and Gordon had as much of that
intensity. And style—I don't mean a style, I mean *style*. He was so
purely himself—I mean, he could be sloppy and coarse, and he could be
an abusive and violent person—but he had such integrity as an artist."

Newton's spontaneous reactions and comments provided exotic pleasure for Sam. Sam found in him a kind of native purity unencumbered by
the layers of knowledge and sophistication that he himself brought to
looking at art—as well as to living his life. In Newton's rough-hewn
simplicity he detected something about nature and spontaneity that was
truer than anything he could have found among his own peers as a young
man. For Newton, Wagstaff was as much a mentor as a peer: "Sam had
his nice office just crammed with crap," Newton said. "Piles. He was
into witchcraft and stuff. He had good luck charms and he was coming
to work in Levi's and a cowboy shirt. At the time he was into the hippie
thing. All of his friends were hippies. He loved to smoke his dope."[26]

Egner remembered once, in Convention Hall, where he and some other Cass Corridor artists had studios, Newton was making a large piece out of molding, sawing it in a violent, impulsive way. Egner could hear the buzz of the chain saw down the hall. Suddenly, there was silence, followed a few minutes later by a horrendous bang. Bob Hanamura, an architect whose studio was next to Newton's looked down to see a hammer poking through the wall of his studio and a hole growing in the plaster before his eyes. Then Newton's hand poked through the hole with an electric cord, which he plugged into Hanamura's outlet. Newton had blown the fuse in his own studio and thought nothing of breaking through the wall to continue working.[27]

The bold primitive shapes Newton drew in his works on paper fit into the dialogue in contemporary art that Wagstaff was instrumental in identifying in one exhibit after another throughout the 1960s. Newton's work was also in some evolutionary dialogue with the Mimbres pots and the Dogon sculpture Sam was collecting. "Sam started buying my work in 1969 or '70," Newton said about his drawings.

Today, buying and selling art comprises an international commercial industry, and museum curators have to be vigilant about maintaining immunity from encroaching market forces. A curator's choice to show an artist's work—and thus ordain him in the museum context—is watched closely in the marketplace because it invariably provides for the artist a substantial pedigree. Artists tend to have complex relationships with the museum world, often enough relying on their galleries to serve as intermediaries. But 1970 was a more innocent time, and Sam could buy work from the artist on the spot. With Newton, he would walk over to his studio at lunchtime and look through his most recent drawings. He would choose a dozen of them, roll them up, put them under his arm, and, then, returning to the museum, select a couple to buy for himself or the museum, and sell the rest to collectors or trustees. "If he said buy it, they bought it," Newton said. "The other curators were jealous . . . because he had this huge momentum. He was high profile."[28] Drawings, at that time, commanded very little money, but Sam would give Newton whatever amount he collected from the sale of the drawings for the young artist to live on.

"At some point, when Sam came along, all of a sudden Gordon started signing and dating every mark he made," Egner recalled, describing one way that Wagstaff instructed Newton about the importance of his work in the art world. "In other words, if he did a sketch on the back of an envelope or on a napkin or something, he would sign it and date it. That was something he had been consciously taught by Sam."[29]

Wagstaff made a point of taking Newton with him on his gallery trips to New York as well, paying his way and putting him up in his loft for the weekend. During those visits, they would follow Wagstaff's standard routine, walking all day from one gallery to the next, looking at art and chatting up the gallery owners. In those days, most of the galleries were on Madison Avenue north of 57th Street. They were elegant little showcases, hushed and carpeted, the people who walked in and out well dressed, often in jacket and tie. Conversely, Sam would then show Newton another arena altogether, dragging him downtown to flea markets set up in empty parking lots, the mélange of makeshift tables or blankets displaying old books and the occasional rare print along with stacks of old postcards. They would march through antique stores and used bookshops, where Sam was always looking for something unexpected to buy, mining for gold in what would seem to most people only barren terrain.

During those weekends, he took Newton to meet Warhol, already then quite a legend, as well as Oldenburg, Richard Tuttle, and Tony Smith. "Once we took the train down to New Jersey," Newton said, "and spent the day with Tony and Jane"—Smith's wife. "Sam would get so involved with a person. They were just as close as you can get, just like best friends."[30]

Then Newton and Sam would return to the Bowery, then known by reputation to be a grimy part of town. Newton was struck by the absence of furniture in Wagstaff's vast loft, as well as by the mattress on the floor at the end of the room. But it was the art that captured his attention, especially *Throne*, the Tony Smith sculpture that Sam had commissioned—a "big black *steel* thing with flat black paint on it," as Newton described it admiringly, "made to actually fit the room. You had to walk through it."[31]

While Wagstaff was giving Newton the kind of education and access

usually reserved for students in the finest graduate schools, he also reso-
lutely concealed his attraction. It thrilled him to have a receptive audience for his own ideas and observations about art. But, equally, he
experienced an almost kindred identification with Newton's youth. A
strain of adolescence persisted in Wagstaff's personality, at times surprising his friends; while it fueled his own youthful enthusiasm about
the things he liked and it directed him to prefer the company of younger
people, it was infused with eroticism.

Wagstaff could be quick to laugh, and eager to amuse, but he had a
provocative streak, challenging the status quo sometimes playfully but
also at times arrogantly. That and his impatience or boredom in conventional social situations—which would sometimes be construed as
haughtiness—created enemies on the board. "There was jealousy on
the part of these trustees, or homophobia," Ellen Phelan surmised.[32]
Because Wagstaff was urbane and handsome, he could "get away with
anything," at least for a while. An analogy can be drawn with Truman
Capote, whose talent, originality, and wit made him the so-called darling of New York society for over a decade. His homosexuality served
him well with his "swans," fostering a level of social intimacy that made
his set of rich female friends feel comfortable and which drew them
close, often to the exclusion of their husbands. But, then, Capote's flash
of impatience resulted in "La Cote Basque, 1965," a short story he published in *Esquire* in 1975 that betrayed the confidences of his prominent
friends and displayed his own contemptuous disaffection, if not his
self-destructive inclinations. Wagstaff would not intentionally set out
to make anyone feel bad, nor would his breeding predispose him to
plotting such revenge. His own "flashes of impatience" were not borne
of contempt, but rather disappointment: "somewhere i have never
travelled,gladly beyond any experience," wrote E. E. Cummings,[33] an
apt way of describing Sam's intellectual curiosity, hunger for surprise,
and, perhaps, his expectation of any new situation that might have been
pitched with more erotic intent than the reality often satisfied. He could
get bored. Not that he was a vindictive person; he did not intend to
insult people. It surprised Sam whenever he was told that someone in his
presence had been offended by something he said or did.

"My wife remembered a dinner party for some art collectors and Sam," recalled Gil Silverman, a DIA trustee who lived in Bloomfield Hills. "Sam brought a boyfriend of his and they smoked pot in our house. That never happened before and it has never happened since. Lila, my wife, was kind of put out by it."[34]

THE MICHAEL HEIZER INSTALLATION, then, was thought to be the biggest provocation of all. The block of granite slid across the lawn all morning without even making a dent. The men attached and reattached the ropes, hauling the monolith back and forth. Heizer and Wagstaff paced alongside, waiting for it to sink. The stone was dragged until 300 tons of earth had been displaced, forming a pile of brown dirt eight feet high that stretched at least forty feet in front of the museum. Still, the rock did not sink.

The crowd, which had swelled throughout the morning to almost one hundred people, now chattered persistently behind the curator and the artist. From time to time their laughter turned into outright heckling. Heizer called the project *Dragged Mass Displacement*, but in the end the chunk of granite was a dragged mass that left the museum lawn appearing like a very messy construction site. "Well, it was a typical Michael Heizer production," Wagstaff said years later, "which always takes its toll in money, anger, revolt."[35]

"I'll tell you why *Dragged Mass* failed," said Gil Silverman, the trustee who, with his wife, Lila, would later amass the most important collection of fluxus art in the world, which they sold to the Museum of Modern Art in New York in 2010. "The dirt here has too much clay. I told Sam. I warned him. The piece was conceived to sink into soil that was dirt. The grounds here are clay. The granite wouldn't sink, no matter how many times they dragged it across the lawn."[36]

Ann Perron Spivak recalled the trustees' reaction as swift and overwhelming. "Certain people on the board thought this was a desecration," she said. "They didn't see it as art. Almost immediately, they took their indignation directly to the mayor."[37]

That, along with a hostile reaction from the press, prompted the museum to demand that Wagstaff remove the piece from the grounds and restore the lawn at his own expense. Wagstaff would also end up paying for the storage of the granite. "There's a whole Detroit establishment from car money," said Judy Linn, who was seventeen when she left Detroit to attend Pratt Institute in New York in the mid-1960s. What it boiled down to, she surmised, was that "he ruined their lawn. It was the land of the lawn. The money there is suburban money, and it's your *lawn*! And the fact that Sam could do that was shocking to them."[38]

On October 14, 1971, the *Detroit Free Press* duly reported the many problems with the work, including a "recalcitrant soil composition" and the resulting "howls of derision" from the public. One member of the city's Arts Commission was quoted anonymously: "I was very much opposed to hauling that piece of rock onto our nice lawn that we had just seeded in preparation for the opening of our north wing. They left a mess."[39] Wagstaff, according to another *Free Press* article, conceded that a better explanation about Heizer's artistic intentions might have softened the public reaction, but ultimately he came off as unapologetic: "Art," he said, "especially when it's very new and ahead of its time, is going to look ugly or messy or tough to almost anyone who doesn't lean over backwards to try to be more sympathetic even than he thinks he should. I don't want to seem unsympathetic, but I frankly don't think art needs explaining."[40]

Still, by the end of the summer, the silent powers of the museum board had already formed their conclusions about Wagstaff. He could feel the change in climate and he knew it was time to go. His resignation letter of September 8, 1971, was cordial, if pro forma. He was aware that it would be circulated among the members of the Founder's Society and the Friends of Modern Art, two groups of DIA patrons he had become quite unpopular with.

"I had a huge going-away party for Sam after that," Anne Manoogian said. The Manoogians lived in a Grosse Pointe mansion and Wagstaff's good-bye party was a spectacular affair. They hired the Peter Duchin Orchestra, which had played at Truman Capote's famous Black and White Ball at New York's Plaza Hotel in 1966, as well as at various White House dinners during the Kennedy and Johnson administrations.

She invited the entire board of the museum along with many other guests—the young artists of the Cass Corridor, for example—who had never before been invited to a party in Grosse Pointe. They mingled uncomfortably with the wealthy regulars, who felt right at home in black tie and evening gowns. The hostess remembered many of her guests getting very drunk and smoking a lot of marijuana, which she had provided in abundance. "A few trustees had to be carried out to their cars and god only knows how they got home," she said. "Anyway, it was a proper send-off. I can remember many moments that night looking at Sam and catching his eye and smiling. I'll never forget it."[41] Some years later, in a letter to Anne, Wagstaff wrote fondly, "I always remember that crazy good-bye party with miles of lobster in Detroit."[42]

Within days, Wagstaff left Detroit and returned to New York, but his uncertainty about what to do next affected all his actions, even when it came to a question about what to do with Pollock's *The Deep* (1953),[43] which he had bought for himself with the idea that the Detroit Institute of Arts should raise the money to buy it from him. Only recently he had written to his good friend Tony Smith seeking advice about the Pollock: "*The Deep* may be slipping away," Sam began. "I have been offered $225,000 for it. I paid $190,000—but I wonder if it isn't worth even more. Should I keep it? I don't need the money though of course I could always do something with it. I don't want to denigrate the picture or the artist. Any ideas?"[44]

In his resignation letter to the DIA director, he wrote that he was looking for a new direction altogether. While he had been disillusioned by events in Detroit, his interest in going "somewhere he had never traveled" had not wavered:

> As discussed a short while ago, I wish to resign from my position as Curator of Contemporary Art at the museum.
>
> For some time I have been considering the idea of "dropping out" of the art world to begin a new life of self-employment of a nature whose structure I haven't completely determined yet, but which will allow me to branch out into fields beyond art in the strict sense of the word.[45]

THE CROSSING

You're the top! You're the Coliseum.
You're the top! You're the Louvre Museum.
You're the melody from a symphony by Strauss.
You're a Bendel bonnet,
A Shakespeare sonnet,
You're Mickey Mouse!

—COLE PORTER[1]

A MAN WITHOUT PORTFOLIO, SAMUEL JONES WAGSTAFF JR. returned to New York in the fall of 1971, aged fifty and humbled by his contretemps in Detroit. In the following summer he was still seeking relief from what he had come to refer to as "my tiresome exile in the provinces."[2] The question confronting him now was what to do next.

Current events provided some distraction. It was a presidential election year and the Vietnam war remained the most persistent preoccupation of America's youth movement. While President Nixon had several soaring achievements in 1972—a historic diplomatic trip to the People's Republic of China and a meeting with Soviet leaders that led to the beginning of détente with the USSR—the spectacularly idiotic, if also illegal, miscalculation that came to be known as the Watergate scandal would bring about his humiliating resignation halfway through his second term as president.

The lessons of world events are writ large for anyone who is paying attention. Sam had returned home to contemplate his own rapid rise and fall in Detroit, so the news of the President's hubris and decline must have resonated. Sam's departure from Detroit left him at sea, wondering how, after his own substantial achievements, he had arrived at this juncture. He considered the Heizer commission his finest moment, yet it had almost inexplicably become his downfall. *Dragged Mass Displacement*— indeed, in the end, he was the one left displaced.

The possibilities for a new direction were plentiful, but to pursue a consequential course would mean, first of all, liberating himself from his family background and the obligations of his social legacy. Yet he still craved, paradoxically, the respect of the same society he felt compelled to reject. While he embraced its impulses to preserve the best of civilization in terms of art, literature, music, and fine craft, he grew up in that world in which politesse was often mistaken for emotional intimacy and ritual for genuine experience. Now he was seeking emotional nourishment and meaningful experience in some new form altogether, on his own terms. Still, his ambivalence about his background would always be a factor.

"Sam was sort of a George Plimpton–like figure, a gad-about-town, proud of his social life, very well connected," recalled George Butler, the director of *Pumping Iron*, the 1977 film about bodybuilding, who was first introduced to Wagstaff in the late 1960s by his own very social mother-in-law, "Oatsie" Charles, a grand Washington, D.C., hostess. Sam had gotten to know Charles while on a fellowship at the National Gallery of Art in 1960.[3] "He was very proud of his family. He always said they used to have a farm in Central Park, owned by someone named Colonel Wagstaff."[4]

One branch of the Wagstaff family dated itself back to the arrival of Colonel Henry Filkins in America in the late 1600s, another to Chretien Du Bois, a French Huguenot of questionable royal descent who arrived in America in 1675 and whose children were the first settlers of Ulster

County, New York. Yet another branch of the family dated back to the 1700s and the Long Island dynasty of Major Thomas Jones, for whom Long Island's Jones Beach was named (the great American novelist Edith Wharton was descended from this family as well). The Wagstaff family once owned significant pieces of land in Manhattan, in fact including a farm in the middle of what is now Central Park, and another along West 59th Street on what is now Central Park South. Furthermore, in 1881 the estate of Alfred Wagstaff, Sam's great-grandfather, sold seventeen lots between West 76th and West 80th streets in Manhattan, adjacent to the construction of the Museum of Natural History.

Alfred Wagstaff Jr., Sam's grandfather, was a Civil War veteran forever known as the Colonel, who became a New York State assemblyman and later a state senator. He had inherited from his father an estate on Long Island called Tahlulah, which stretched from the Great South Bay northward about two miles in the town of West Islip. Dr. Wagstaff had bought Tahlulah in the early part of the nineteenth century, bequeathing it with a Native American name meaning "leaping water." The Colonel raised his children, including Sam Sr., on this estate, where he was host to two U.S. presidents, Grover Cleveland and William Howard Taft. When the stately country home that had been in the Wagstaff family for three generations was almost destroyed by fire in 1913, an article in *The New York Times* described it as "one of the great showplaces of the South Shore."[5]

The specter of Sam's grandfather hovered over the entire family. Butler recalled a story Wagstaff often told about the night in the late nineteenth century when a fire erupted in the theater where the Colonel was seated. Colonel Wagstaff stood up from his chair, told everyone to be calm and directed the crowd to leave the theater without panicking. "Of course what that means," Sam would say, "is that sometimes you have to take charge in life and tell others what to do, and you have to be very commanding to do that."[6]

The Colonel was described in an 1867 book about New York State Assembly members as a tall man with a "commanding stature, and dignified presence." He possesses, the book went on to say, "a vigorous, cultivated mind, and a retentive memory; he has a keen sense of the ludicrous, and a bright wit, which, together with an unending store of pleasant reminiscences, render him a most agreeable and entertaining companion; and is possessed of an unwearying activity, intense energy and perseverance. Mr. Wagstaff is a ready debater, is quick at repartee, caustic in sarcasm, and laconic in his arguments."[7]

In later years the Colonel became clerk to the Appellate Division of the Supreme Court of New York. In 1911, however, he endured a bit of public humiliation when, as president of the American Society for the Prevention of Cruelty to Animals, a campaign was launched to bring about his resignation. The members of the board of the ASPCA wanted to hire a paid employee to take care of the day-to-day needs of the office, believing that the Colonel did not devote enough time to the organization. Their campaign to remove the Colonel from his elected position reached the public in *New York Times* reports, an episode that ironically strikes the same humiliating note as Sam's own departure under pressure from the Detroit Institute of Arts.[8] In the end, the Colonel prevailed, staying on as president until 1921. But in 1972, Sam had no such vindication with which to find comfort.

Sam's father, Samuel Jones Wagstaff Sr., graduated from Harvard in 1908 (as a member of the Spee Club)[9] and, like his father before him, attended Columbia Law School. Once established as a prominent Manhattan attorney, he was listed in the *Social Register*. In a 1954 article in *American Heritage*, Cleveland Amory examined the exclusive world of New York's private clubs, like the Union and Knickerbocker clubs of which Sam Sr. was a member: "The gentlemen of New York's 400 belonged to not one but many clubs and wore them like ribbons— actually wearing them, in fact, on neckties, hatbands, vests, garters and suspenders."[10] These clubs were so exclusive that women were only allowed in certain rooms and accompanied by a family member. Anti-Semitism was a given, to the extent that one member of the Union Club, complaining of such bigotry, asserted that he wanted a club to which he could bring his friends without having to produce a birth certificate, blood test, and marriage license. Only in these exclusive rooms, wrote Amory with wry disapproval, did a man find "sanctuary and his four freedoms—freedom of speech against democracy, freedom of worship of aristocracy, freedom from want from tipping, and, above all, freedom from fear of women."[11]

Samuel Jones Wagstaff Jr. would inherit some of the lingering anti-Semitic sentiments and racial prejudices of his parents and their circle of socially prominent friends. Well into the 1970s and '80s, many of Wagstaff's friends and art world acquaintances, some of whom were Jewish, witnessed his occasional ethnic slurs, finding them offensive and uniquely discordant with his otherwise enlightened approach to so many other aspects of his life. These prejudices were the residue of an aristocratic background that he tried so hard to shed in some ways and yet had remained surprisingly unexamined in others.

WHEN SAM'S FATHER MARRIED his first wife, Pauline Le Roy French, niece of Elsie French Vanderbilt,[12] in May 1908, *The New York Times* reported that the wedding "opened the season" in Newport, Rhode Island. The senior Samuel Jones Wagstaff and his bride settled in at 405 Park Avenue, a prestigious Manhattan residential building, to pursue a life in New York society.

But Sam Sr. and his wife were not impervious to scandal. Pauline's sister, Julia French, eloped with the family chauffeur. The family issued a statement to the press: "Miss Julia French was married Wednesday to a man unknown to her family. There is nothing further to add."[13] As if it were a tragedy equal to a death in the family, the Wagstaffs drove up from New York to be with the French family, for whom, according to the *Times*, "much sympathy is felt because of the notoriety they are now suffering."[14]

That wasn't the last event to test the family's respectability. Divorce, at that time, was a serious transgression. According to the *Social Register*, Pauline French Wagstaff filed for divorce in 1917 because of ill treatment and neglect by Sam Sr. Worse, however, was another *Social Register* article in which Sam Sr. was accused of not paying Pauline's expenses for three years, until the divorce was granted. It seemed Sam Sr. was, in the Dreiseresque lingo of the 1920s, something of a cad.

In 1920, right after the divorce came through, Sam Sr. married Olga

May Piorkowska Thomas, an exotic, stylish young divorcée. She would give birth to Samuel Jones Wagstaff Jr. the following year, on November 4, 1921. This marriage, too, was not entirely sanctioned by society: the headline of the wedding announcement in the *New York Tribune* read, "S. J. Wagstaff, Divorced 2 Weeks, Weds Divorcee."[15]

Born in New York but raised and educated in Europe and the Far East, Olga was not a member of society in the strict sense. However, her prosperous family had exposed her to other international cultures and the finer things in those societies. Her father, Arthur Emil Piorkowski, was born in Leipzig, Germany, and had trained as an engineer at the Polytechnic in Dresden. He entered the Royal Seton (Saxon) Army as an officer of the artillery in 1864, seeing action in the Prusso-Austrian campaign of 1866. He would become the American military representative of two German matériel manufacturers, Krupp in Essen and Stahlwerks-Verband in Dusseldorf. He married Mary Auguste Bryant, an aspiring opera singer from Boston, in 1881. Olga would not be born for another thirteen years.

Olga's father's job required him to travel throughout Europe, Asia, and the United States, and he moved his family from continent to continent frequently. Known to venture into remote precincts of China, he sometimes arrived as the first Caucasian those populations had ever seen. Piorkowski's position brought him into contact with the power elite of an emerging military industrial complex. In 1909, for example, he delivered a speech to the National Civic Federation in New York before an audience including Louis D. Brandeis, the future U.S. Supreme Court Justice; Andrew Carnegie, the steel magnate; and Samuel Gompers, who founded the American Federation of Labor.

The activities and interests of the Wagstaff family, meanwhile, maintained its place in the upper tier of fin de siècle New York society. For example, David Wagstaff, Sam Jr.'s uncle, was an avid sportsman who raised pedigreed Labrador Retrievers and spaniels and collected first edition books about sports (this collection now resides at the Beinecke Library at Yale). He and his wife lived in Tuxedo Park, an exclusive enclave thirty miles north of New York City where blue bloods and Wall Street tycoons like J. P. Morgan lived in gilded-age Beaux Arts mansions. David Wagstaff made frequent appearances in the society columns in New York, as in this 1939 article in *The New York Times* about the National Horse Show: "The boxes and arena at the National Horse Show in Madison Square Garden were filled to capacity last night with a brilliant assemblage of society. . . . A prominent guest of the afternoon session was Mrs. Herbert Hoover, wife of the former President. . . . Mr. and Mrs. David Wagstaff entertained Colonel George Patton, Jr., U.S.A., and Mrs. Patton."[16]

The marriage between Sam Wagstaff Sr. and Olga Piorkowska Thomas was announced in the *Social Register*, and would produce two children, Sam Jr. and Judith. The family lived off Park Avenue, at 115 East 53rd Street, a prestigious residential address in the years before that stretch of Park became a corridor of modernist skyscrapers. In the late 1920s the Wagstaffs would move to 41 East 61st Street, between Park and Madison avenues.

Yet, by the time Sam Jr. was ten years old, that marriage, too, was ending. Divorce was an encumbered legal process in the early part of the twentieth century, requiring papers to be filed out of New York State and taking up brief residency outside the country, whether in Cuba, Mexico, or France. In 1931, a divorcée was still, in many respects, a scandalous figure.

Not yet divorced, and despite her tarnished status, Olga was being courted by two prominent men, both of whom offered proposals of marriage. Each was wealthy but neither sparked anything more than polite admiration. She decided to go to Europe—alone, without her children—to think about these offers, and it was during the crossing that she met Donald V. "Peter" Newhall. She knew nothing of his background except that he was an artist. In fact, Newhall was an Oxford graduate who had established himself as a professional painter in the social circles that required formal family portraits on the drawing room walls of country estates. Olga and Peter, as he was called, kept each other company aboard ship and then traveled together to see the bullfights in Spain—a rather scandalous excursion for a *married* woman in society to make without a chaperone. They were falling in love. According to her granddaughter Judy Jefferson, Sam's niece, only after Olga married Peter did she learn that the Newhall family, which hailed from San Francisco, was even wealthier than Wagstaff's, as well as those of the two suitors whose proposals she'd declined. Nevertheless, toward the end of her life, Olga imparted a bit of grandmotherly advice to Judy Jefferson: "Never marry for money," the wealthy Mrs. Donald V. Newhall told her. "*I* didn't."

Sam's mother, Olga, was that iconic high-society woman one might have glimpsed between the world wars draped in furs on her way to Elizabeth Arden for a facial and a manicure. It was the social milieu of women like Olga that Clare Boothe Luce, managing editor of *Vanity Fair* in the 1930s, turned into scathing farce in her Broadway hit *The Women*, a knowing indictment of those ladies of leisure with respectable names and fancy addresses who fashioned themselves pillars of society while ever so stylishly and deceitfully doing one another in.

Like her husband Peter, Olga considered herself an artist; and she, too, was not without talent. Her illustrations had appeared in *Harper's Bazaar* before she married Sam's father.[18] But as a result of her serial marriages to wealthy men, she became a "lady who lunched," a familiar figure in the Oval Room at the Ritz-Carlton Hotel or the more formal luncheons in the Iridium Room at the St. Regis. She and Peter hosted formal dinners in the Trianon Room at the Ambassador and attended balls at the Waldorf. There were parties given in their honor in Palm Beach and the Berkshires.

One such grand event, the annual Beaux Arts Ball in the Grand Ballroom of the Waldorf Astoria took place only weeks before the Newhalls were married. A tradition started in New York by the Society for Beaux Arts, the ball attracted much of New York society. The 1931 event, whose theme of which was "Fete Moderne—A Fantasy in Flame and Silver," was considered one of the last, great post–Jazz Age parties. The architects of New York's newest skyscrapers wore costumes of their own buildings: A. Stewart Walker came as the Fuller Building; Leonard Schultze as the Waldorf Astoria; Ely Jacques Kahn as the Squibb Building; and William Van Alen as the Chrysler Building.

The *New York Times* presented the Beaux Arts Ball of 1932 as an equally exciting party. The headline that January read, "City's Birth

Re-lived at Beaux-Arts Ball: Leaders in Drama, Letters and Art Crowd the Waldorf to Honor First President":

> Designated "A Pageant of Old New York and the First Inaugural Ball of the United States of America," it brought an attendance of several thousands prominent in society and the worlds of art, literature, and the drama, among whom were many descendants of persons famous in the early history of the city.[19]

The ball featured also a pageant loosely depicting the arrival in 1609 of Henry Hudson to the shores of 'Manhatta'; Donald V. Newhall was listed in the program as the Boatswain, enacting a gesture of friendship to the Native Americans.

Two weeks later, Olga and Peter's marriage was written up in the *Times*.[20] They had known each other at least a year, but the announcement might have shocked some people as it reported that the bride's "marriage had been terminated by divorce several weeks ago in Campeche, Mexico." The Newhalls had married in Elkton, Maryland, with Sam Jr. in attendance. A reception in their honor was held at the fashionable Surrey, a residential hotel just off Central Park, upon their return.

Sam's mother would from then on become known in New York society as Mrs. Donald V. Newhall. If it is true, as *Time* stated in 1969, that Noël Coward's greatest single gift was not "writing or composing, not acting or directing, but projecting a sense of personal style, a combination of cheek and chic, pose and poise,"[21] then something similar can be said of Olga Newhall. With her own combination of cheek and chic, Sam Wagstaff's mother was the type of woman epitomized in *Blithe Spirit* and *Private Lives*.

Soon after they were married, the Newhalls sailed to Europe for a two-year sojourn in St. Augustin, near Palma, on the Spanish island of Majorca. It was possible during the Depression to live well for little money in just such a European seaside paradise, and Majorca had become something of a destination for wealthy Americans concerned about their assets, as well as artists and British expats.

Ten-year-old Sam accompanied his mother and stepfather to Spain.

He was the favored child. His mother chose to leave Judy, then only seven, in the States in the custody of her father. By that time Sam Sr., too, had remarried, this time to Cornelia Scranton Swift, and they moved to Vergennes, Vermont. Soon to become a venerable New England figure, Sam's father would be elected a state attorney for three terms in the 1950s and '60s, and continued to practice law for the rest of his life.

The senior Wagstaff proceeded to enroll Sam's sister at Wykeham Rise, a girl's boarding school in Connecticut. It was an austere environment, and Sam Sr. barely paid attention to his daughter throughout her entire childhood. As far as he was concerned, he had fulfilled his obligation as a parent by providing her a worthy education and the supervision of the school authorities. Over the years, Sam Sr. would devote more time and attention to the children of his third wife than to either of his own children. When their father died in 1975 at the age of eighty-nine, Sam Jr. and Judith attended the funeral in Vermont, but more out of a sense of duty than from any semblance of feeling for the man.

And yet for all of her affection for Sam Jr., Olga never kept him too close. Olga and Peter set him up in the Ecole Internationale des Baleares, a boarding school in the Majorcan countryside, while they commenced their own stylish expat life.

Upon the Newhalls' return to New York in 1935, they took an apartment at 100 Central Park South and reestablished their social activities in Manhattan. But Olga and Peter left Sam in boarding school in Spain, where he was succeeding in his classical studies, improving his Spanish and French, swimming and playing with his schoolmates, and learning to play chess. Undoubtedly, the separation from his mother was a formative loss for the young Wagstaff, who was fascinated by the elements of self-invention and sublime decoration at play in his mother. It may be that her sense of style freed his imagination and made her more compelling, if not also more remote. His obsession with collecting may have been fueled by the sensory splendor of her things: the tactile sensation of her couture, its luxurious fabrics, the exotic feathers, the soft furs; the sculptural contour of her hats, the sparkle of cut stones; and the colors of her lipstick.

Olga was never a consistent, physical presence in Sam's daily life; her love for him was exciting but unpredictable. He had seen her leave his younger sister behind, as well as his father and, for a long time, the country they called home. No record exists of his response to all these ruptures, but surely he harbored doubts about whether he would be abandoned, too. His ambivalence about his origins and his own elusiveness and inscrutability suggest a fundamental psychological impact.

"Dear Mummy," Sam wrote to his mother in New York from Ecole Internationale des Baleares in Majorca, on April 29, 1936:

> I took a walk up to the house yesterday with some of the boys to see the kittens, but only Missie had kittens and both died, it certainly is a shame but Missie seemed very hapy [sic] and when she saw me she came up and rubbed my legs and purred. All the other cats seem alright [sic] and very friendly too except Tiger who seems to be very wild and meows all the time. Marina has five of the cutest little puppies you ever saw. They are mostly white with just a few little brown spots.
>
> I had lots of fun at the Lauries and Mrs. Laurie gave me two new kinds of cactus and I got a cactus that looks like an artichoke from Billy yesterday.
>
> Emilita has invited me to spend the day at her house next Saturday and then we will trade cactus.
>
> Although I hope Peter [his stepfather] gets lots of portraits to do, I hope I do not have to go back to America with the Newtons because I am having such a nice time here and we are swimming and all that sort of thing, which I would not be able to do in New York.
>
> I told Peter Ray what you said about New York and prosperity and he said you have nothing on Majorca because there are so many rich people with children. . . .
>
> I have learnt [sic] to play chess and I wish you would bring a chess board here if you see a nice one. Please tell me if I can have the medals in your next letter.
>
> With lots and lots of love,
> Sammy[22]

Evident in this letter is young Sammy's wish that his mother and stepfather return to live again in Majorca: New York and prosperity has "nothing on Majorca," he writes, asserting his will with a logical argument, yet ultimately testing whether he had the power to lure his mother back. With his good looks and charm, Sam adapted to Olga's idea of a "design for living," to her sense of who she was—not as a mother, but a woman in society. Just before his adolescence, she taught him how to smoke cigarettes to appear a more suitable chaperon for her at parties. Nothing, however, could change her essential approach to being a mother, which lacked the selfless regard that tends to engender a sense of comfort and security.

Nevertheless, his mother did not fail to set an elevated tone for him, and he never stopped adoring her for it. The Newhalls did not return to live in Spain; but, when they visited Sam in the summer of 1936, they stumbled into the midst of events that brought Sam's own European exile to a close. Tensions had been mounting in Spain between the socialist Left and the fascist Right, and that summer there were reports of violence among the Communist, syndicalist, and anarchist groups that were wreaking havoc on the public. Youths roamed the wealthier sections of Barcelona seizing automobiles, looting homes for guns, and making bonfires out of anything they could find. The lack of police enforcement or government control became an increasing threat as the public grew increasingly frightened.

Despite the fact that Americans enjoyed a certain level of privilege on European shores, the vacationing Newhalls recognized the growing danger of civil war and were anxious to return to New York. Coincidentally, the *Exeter*, a cruise ship, had just begun its journey from Mediterranean ports back to the United States when the captain, receiving word of the violence in Spain and hearing of Americans trapped there, detoured down along the coast of Spain to rescue them.

A *New York Times* article on August 5, 1936, was accompanied by three large pictures of passengers disembarking on American shores. "Bringing tales of terror," the story began, "twenty-six refugees from Spain, most of them Americans, arrived in Boston today aboard the

American Export liner *Exeter*." It listed among the refugees Mr. and Mrs. Donald Newhall and Sam Wagstaff. The article described the sacking of churches and convents, rampant street fighting, and wild-eyed youths running through the streets heavily armed and firing their guns randomly. Sam's mother and stepfather seemed to have made a harrowing escape before picking him up and boarding the ship: "Mr. Newhall, a portrait painter, said he and his wife, apparently mistaken for fleeing Fascists, had been held at rifle point by government troops in Palma after their car had been stopped," the article reported. "A sergeant, pistol in hand, finally forced the soldiers to release them, Mr. Newhall said."[23]

Not yet fifteen, Sam had experienced firsthand an event of historic proportion—the beginning of the Spanish Civil War—and for a teenage boy, it must have resonated with the adventure of stories like Robert Louis Stevenson's *Treasure Island*, Rudyard Kipling's *Captains Courageous*, or even Homer's *Odyssey*, a protagonist's return home fraught with looming violence, menacing villains, and an escape from a devastating war. In Sam's adventure, there were larger-than-life heroes, a rescue on the high seas, then his family's safe return announced in the papers.

Wagstaff returned to the United States a little worldlier, having been exposed to the rhythms of life in another culture and also to the menace of war. Olga enrolled him at the Hotchkiss School in Connecticut. The school's grounds had been conceived in the manner of a New England college campus and among the architects were Cass Gilbert, who designed the Woolworth Building in New York City and the distinguished firm of Delano and Aldrich, who designed several buildings at Yale. In this formal environment, where students wore jackets and ties, Sam took to his studies and performed well. He held office in a variety of the school's organizations, accordingly to the yearbook: president of the Dramat, the school's theater club, with which he appeared in a half dozen productions;[24] president of the Science Club; president of the photography club; and photographic editor of the school literary magazine. He was on the soccer team and in the glee club. They called him "Stoop."

———

ALTHOUGH SAM HAD RETURNED to the same continent as his mother, he saw her only on parceled-out weekends and she would remain an elusive figure in his daily life. Olga's inaccessibility and, to some extent, her own anxieties about being marginalized in society left him with an aspiration to be somewhat better than he was—as if his ascendance would lure her back to him. Perhaps it was that longing in some sublimated form that inspired Sam's teenage envy of the friends and acquaintances at school who were more socially prominent. These schoolmates returned to grand homes for their holidays and their surnames carried lapidary weight, as if gold-plated, like the van Rensselaers or the Rhinelanders. The young Sam would try on these names in his mind and imagine them as his own.[25]

Some of Olga's unconventional behavior—her three marriages, the risqué unchaperoned trip to the bullfights in Spain, her rather offhand attitude about motherhood—stood in stark contrast to her preoccupation with social status. While Sam felt the social pressure of his milieu, he would remain unaware of the silent strings his mother pulled on his behalf and of her private campaign to establish his position in society—and to reclaim her own. On October 2, 1936, two months after his return to native shores and his enrollment at Hotchkiss, Olga wrote a letter to the Social Register Association:

> *I am writing to request that you send me a listing blank for The Social Register of 1937. I was listed in the Social Register during the years in which I was married to Samuel J. Wagstaff. After my marriage to Donald V. Newhall we were away from New York for several years and I fear that any listing blanks sent to me were never forwarded.*
>
> *I have secured letters from a number of close friends who are listed in the Social Register and would like to know whether you wish them sent to the Governing Board. . . . My son, Samuel Wagstaff, Jr, makes his home with us, and I am particularly anxious for his sake to have his name enrolled in the Social Register.*

*As for my husband, Donald Newhall, I am enclosing some data
as to his family and antecedents so that you will know something
about his background....* [26]

Just as Olga represented an enchanted idea for Sam, her son was a
work in progress for Olga. Despite all of her social advantages, she worried that there was still something missing—that final notch of acceptance into New York society. She was determined that Sam would
acquire all the contours of a society gentleman. "I think his mother
really wanted to control him," Thomas L. Jefferson, Sam's nephew and
godson, said about his uncle. "She wanted him to go to the best schools,
have the best education, marry into the best family, and all that stuff." [27]
Sam was a sensitive child. It must have felt to him at times that he was
merely impersonating the young man he was expected to be. "He
wanted to please his mother," Jefferson said. "For a long period of time
he was, I'm sure, fighting against his homosexuality in its nature." If
nothing else, both Wagstaff and his sister would end up being listed in
the *Social Register*, but only under their father's name.

Soon after Sam entered Yale in 1940, his mother and stepfather
moved to a ten-room duplex at 130 East 67th Street, where they lived
well into the 1950s. By the time they moved again, to 39 East 79th Street,
Sam's sister, Judy, had become a mother herself, and Olga took to her
role as a grandmother with something less than enthusiasm. "Olga was
one of two women that I feared as a child," said Jefferson about his
grandmother. "She was very formal, very proper. I think she was probably from the school that children should be seen and not heard. I didn't
see her ever act particularly affectionately around us as kids." [28]

Newhall had an atelier in an apartment on a separate floor of the
same building, where he had set up his train sets and enjoyed tinkering
with the engines. For Tom Jefferson, playing in his stepgrandfather's
workshop was always the best part of a visit to his grandparents.
"Donald Newhall was different," he said. "I can remember running
up and him giving us a hug. He was more physically demonstrative
and accessible." The same held true for Tom's younger brother, Peter,
who never considered Olga a part of their lives. "We had a very

estranged relationship in that they—she—just didn't associate with children," Peter said. "She always had a charm bracelet that she wore, and she'd rattle it around, and that was how you knew she was in the house."[29]

Sam received this letter from his mother on the occasion of one birthday, when he was just a little older:

> *I'm sorry not to see you today and to give you the X numbers of kisses that I'd like to—however do take care of yourself and do please keep me informed about how you're feeling. I've done a lot today, out to lunch and everything. . . .*
>
> *Don't doubt that I love you more than I can ever tell you, and please be happy always. It's wonderful to be that way.*[30]

The letter, blithe yet perfunctory, is curiously absent the day-to-day concern of a mother for her son. The only motherly advice on Sam's birthday was the wish for him to be happy *always*. On one hand, it was a loving thing to say. On the other, Olga seemed to expect to play no particular role in helping her son arrive at a condition of happiness. Happiness might as well have been a state easily assumed or affected at will, as if the decision were as simple as making a choice about what to wear that day.

WAGSTAFF'S CONFIDENCE IN HIS early years derived largely from the entitlements of his class—the prep school regimen at Hotchkiss, followed by his membership while at Yale in the secret society Wolf's Head.[31] There was his military service in the United States Navy during World War II; as a lieutenant in the Bureau of Navy Personnel, he was on board a navy transit ship that reached Omaha Beach on D-Day, June 6, 1944. Once he returned from the war and accepted a job in advertising, he assumed what his family saw as his rightful place among the most desirable bachelors for a generation of New York debutantes. The writer Dominick Dunne, whom Sam had known in New York in the early 1950s, called him "the deb's delight," the escort in constant demand by young women from fine families.[32] In fact, a 1946 item in "Society Today," a column in the *New York World Telegram*, listed Sam Wagstaff as one of the ten most attractive bachelors in New York. In December 1950, the *Social Register* reported that "the Stork Club set is wagering that young Sam Wagstaff will walk to the altar with Julia Donahue, the dime-store heiress."

By that time, Sam had become expert at leading the double life of a homosexual, relying on his impeccable etiquette to shield his activities in the closet. He kept the expectations of young women from proper families at bay, squiring them to formal charity balls and Manhattan nightclubs, and leaving them with an all-too-polite peck on the cheek in front of the doorman. His dates would remain oblivious of the netherworld of gay life he would then venture off into afterward—the Bird Circuit, for example, a strip along Third Avenue in the East Fifties, where gay bars with names like the Blue Parrot and the Gold Pheasant were hiding in plain sight. There he could meet other men, with whom he would have clandestine affairs.

A residue of the high style of this period would, however, remain with Sam the rest of his life; in later years, while increasingly acknowledging his identity as a gay man, he could still straddle worlds. Barbara Jakobson, an art collector and a longtime trustee of the Museum of Modern Art, keeps a picture of herself dancing with Wagstaff in a small black frame on a shelf in the art-filled living room of her East Side town house. "Sam was the best date for anything," she said, remembering one benefit dinner dance she attended with him at the museum in the 1980s. "First of all, he was a great dancer; second, he knew the lyrics to every single Cole Porter song. There was a great forties vintage swing band at this party and we never sat down the entire evening."[33]

The closet was quite a well-populated place in the New York art world of the 1950s and '60s, habituated by Robert Rauschenberg, for example, who had romances with Cy Twombly and Jasper Johns. Ellsworth Kelly, Frank O'Hara, Henry Geldzahler, Allen Ginsberg, John Cage, Merce Cunningham, even Andy Warhol all were known by other inhabitants of the closet, even though being "gay" was not an identity that sat well with most of them.

In the 1930s and '40s, the photographer George Platt Lynes was also a notorious member of the tribe. His artfully conceived pictures of nude men, posed both individually and in groupings that approximated classical and mythical tableaux, were unapologetically homoerotic. Among the artists, poets, writers, and designers in his circle was Bernard Perlin, an artist and illustrator, with whom Lynes enjoyed a long, purely platonic friendship. In the introduction to David Leddick's *Intimate Companions: A Triography of George Platt Lynes, Paul Cadmus, Lincoln Kirstein and Their Circle*, Perlin's description of Lynes provides a glimpse of the aspirations and material accoutrements that defined a certain gay sensibility before the sexual revolution of the 1960s brought about the liberation of gay men:

> George Platt Lynes was the prototypical established gay man of the thirties, forties, and fifties. He personified everything most homosexual men strove for: to be extraordinarily handsome, successful in his work with universal recognition and status, living a princely life in excellent style, having a prodigious sex life plus love affairs that were serious and meaningful. He was the role model for us. He was the epitome of a stylish life, also an artist's life, successful and admired.[34]

Lynes found himself in the center of an artistic circle that included Monroe Wheeler, his lover of many years, who was the director of exhibitions and publications at the Museum of Modern Art; Glenway Wescott, a novelist and the third member of their ménage à trois; Lincoln Kirstein, who, with George Balanchine, founded the New York City Ballet; artists Paul Cadmus and Jared French; Cecil Beaton, the illustrious, at times even royal, portrait photographer; and Christopher Isherwood, the novelist.

The ease with which these gay men socialized in the mid-twentieth century was unique to the urbane denizens of haute bohemian New York. Yet the high gloss of Perlin's description of that world trivializes the more common experience of the majority of homosexuals in the United States in those years. Uncounted gay men and lesbians across the country were obsessively protective of their own secret, painfully isolated in their shame, and constantly fearful of being found out—a revelation almost certain to destroy their lives. The closet may have been a roomy place in the upper precincts of urban cultural chic, but it was a much more menacing hiding place for the majority of its inhabitants—even for privileged people like Wagstaff who had to maintain an appearance of heterosexual masculinity in the professional world of advertising in the 1950s and as a curator at the Wadsworth Atheneum in the '60s.

True to his time, Wagstaff came to straddle two eras in the evolution of gay identity in America. In his twenties and thirties, Sam was part of George Platt Lynes's rarefied strata of gay life in New York when he became romantically involved with Chuck Howard, a handsome former lover of Lynes who was also the model in some of Lynes's well-known images. All the while, Wagstaff maintained his role as a date for debutantes. Gerald Ayres, an aspiring playwright, dropped out of Yale his senior year and moved to New York in 1957. In college he knew a young actor named Ron Moore, who had also recently moved to the city. "Ron was living with a mysterious closeted gentleman on the Upper East Side and wasn't permitted to answer the phone in case it was the gentleman's family calling," Ayres said. "I had to ring twice, hang up and call again to reach Ron. I finally met the gentleman—it was Sam Wagstaff."[35] Ayres's initial impression of Wagstaff was that he looked as if he had been born on skis.

The secret language of the closet would later be given intellectual heft by Susan Sontag, no stranger to the closet herself, in her essay "Notes on Camp." Irony was the lingua franca of the gay world, the double meaning a necessary code whereby one homosexual could recognize another. Consider a musical number Wagstaff wrote while still an undergraduate for a production of *The Waterbury Tales*, a send-up of a scene in Chaucer's *Canterbury Tales*, by the Yale Dramatic Association in 1941. Wagstaff wrote the song perhaps in homage to *Stover at Yale*, a novel by Owen Johnson[36] that described undergraduate life in the early twentieth century and became something of an Ivy League "textbook for my generation," according to F. Scott Fitzgerald.[37]

DINK STOVER AT YALE

Let's be roommates,
Let's be friends,
Let's be roommates
Till the journey ends.

If we have stormy weather,
We'll throw aside all doubts,
We'll pitch our tents together,
Like Eagle Scouts.

Let's be roommates,
Let's be chums,
Let's be roommates
Till commencement comes.

Our lives will smell of heliotrope,
You use my towel, I'll use your soap,
Just roommates, I hope.

I'll help you if you're poor in Greek,
You'll help me when I public speak,
Just roommates
Not for a couple of days,

Not for a week,
Not for a year, but always.[38]

Same-sex desire naughtily rings out from every line of the song, and yet nothing about the 1941 production was hidden or furtive. In fact, *The New York Times* promoted the show as a social event: "Hundreds of relatives and friends of the members of the Yale Dramatic Association will throng the grand ballroom of the Waldorf Astoria tomorrow night for the New York production of the association's latest offering,

The Waterbury Tales. The show will be followed by supper and dancing." [39]

Like Wagstaff, Andy Warhol came of age in the 1940s and '50s, and he, too, cultivated a persona that would navigate in the most public and private of ways. According to Bob Colacello, editor of Warhol's *Interview* magazine throughout the 1970s: "If one topic was taboo at the Factory, it was Andy's sex life. He wanted—demanded—to know every detail of ours, but his was strictly off limits." [40] Warhol surrounded himself with an array of flamboyant personalities: beautiful women like Edie Sedgwick, Tinkerbelle, and Viva, one of his "superstars"; transvestites Candy Darling and Jackie Curtis; handsome masculine men such as Joe Dallesandro and Gerard Malanga; and gay men such as Billy Name and, yes, Sam Wagstaff. The range of characters in his entourage camouflaged his own homosexuality, allowing him to travel in a circle that cloaked him in an open secret. Jed Johnson, for several years Warhol's live-in boyfriend, once recounted that Andy "hid what he had. It was inconspicuous consumption. He'd wear a diamond necklace, but only under a black cotton turtleneck." [41]

When Wagstaff and Warhol met in the early 1960s, Sam was a curator at the Wadsworth Atheneum and still very much a proper gentleman; but he became, intermittently, one of the inscrutable regulars with whom Warhol surrounded himself. Warhol had come from humble origins, born of Slovak immigrant parents and raised in Pittsburgh; he was never comfortable with his own appearance, in particular his pallid skin and pockmarked face. As someone who felt like an outsider, Warhol fetishized the American WASP ideal, which Wagstaff—as if a representative specimen—embodied in looks, manner, and pedigree. [42] To Warhol, Wagstaff was a direct descendant of the society luminaries assembled by Mrs. Astor in "the 400," the quintessence of WASP refinement. Sam's façade was the perfect way to cloak his sexual proclivity. In the late 1960s, as he became less conventional, his homosexuality still was not so easily telegraphed within his newly adapted embrace of hippie style—long hair, love beads, Indian shirts, bellbottoms, and sandals.

Traces of Sam's early romantic and erotic life can in fact be found strewn throughout his personal papers, in the notes, postcards, snap-shots, and drawings that served as mementos of his longer affairs and his brief dalliances. Throughout this evidence a playful erotic charge emanates from the private language of assignations and intimacies—cloaked again in the semiotic language of the American mid-twentieth-century closet. The keepsakes from his liaison with Richard de Menocal illustrate this.

Once, in conversation with Steven M. L. Aronson, the writer and editor, Wagstaff claimed that the greatest love of his life had been Dickie de Menocal. Dickie's father, Daniel de Menocal, an international banker, was a close relation of a president of Cuba; his mother, Beatrice Wells Crosby, grew up on Washington Square in New York. "Dickie was reared in Beacon Hill and Newport, and he was an irresistible magnet for both sexes," said Aronson.[43] De Menocal's sister, Babs Simpson, was the legendary fashion editor at *Harper's Bazaar* and *Vogue* from the 1940s through the '60s. Because he had dark hair and refined features, the aristocratic Dickie was not typical of Sam's attractions. A graduate of the Boston Museum School, de Menocal did illustrations for Condé Nast publications, designed window displays for Lord & Taylor, and created costumes for Radio City Music Hall. In the early 1950s he began exhibiting his drawings and paintings. Among Wagstaff's papers is an announcement in 1953 for de Menocal's first serious exhibit of drawings at the Hugo Gallery on East 55th Street, "Fifteen Drawings Based on the Writings of Truman Capote."[44]

Dickie gave Sam several little sketches, among them a bugler boy, a seashell, a sensitively rendered nude male, and an intricate watercolor of a house, the last with a scrawled note below it: "Please write soon. Hope its shoulder is out of its cast by now. This is a sketch of an old house here in Bahia. Much love, Mouse." (Mouse was Sam's nickname for Dickie; Mouse called Sam "Moose.") There are also several slips of torn paper: On one is scrawled: "I love you, Sammy—M"; on another scrap is a note that says, "Dear Sam, I forgot tomorrow was a holiday. If you want to spend the night here, bring some breakfast. I'll be back from the the-ater not too late. M"; and on yet another, "Thursday—Sammy, Miss you very much, indeed. M."[45]

———

THROUGHOUT WAGSTAFF'S INVOLVEMENTS with Chuck Howard, Dickie De Menocal, and others, he kept his job in advertising. He'd begun working on Madison Avenue after graduating from Yale in 1944. He started at Benton & Bowles, which created ad campaigns for major clients that made their products immediately recognizable to national radio and television audiences, from Texaco's slogan, "You can trust your car to the man who wears the star," to Procter & Gamble's Crest toothpaste refrain, "Look, Ma, no cavities!" Wagstaff's major responsibility as an assistant account executive was the Palm Beach Company. Sam could have been a model for this prestigious apparel maker; his looks and his bearing represented precisely the kind of masculine, well-heeled image it wanted to project. But, while Wagstaff looked and acted the part of a gentleman in "the gentleman's profession," after ten years he found the atmosphere stultifying and the entire industry reprehensible. Had he not left when he did, he often said, he "would have killed himself from boredom and disgust."[46] His decision to leave was abetted by a case of hepatitis, possibly brought on by a sexual encounter, with which he was bedridden for several months. It was then that he appealed to his mother to cover the costs of going back to school. He wanted to study art history. Olga, who twenty years earlier had written on Sam's Hotchkiss application that her son was particularly "talented at decorating," agreed.[47] He was about to turn thirty-six.

Enrolling at the Institute of Fine Arts at New York University in 1957, he committed himself to a life in art. The institute was then, as it remains today, the venerable graduate school for art history in the country. Sam's first and most significant mentor there was Richard Offner, whose lifelong study of Italian painting of the thirteenth and fourteenth centuries established him as one of the towering art scholars of the twentieth century; his *Corpus of Florentine Painting*, first published in 1930, became a seminal text for generations. Offner, in turn, owed a great debt to Bernard Berenson, another giant in the field.

Wagstaff went with Offner on several expeditions in search of "gold ground" painting, trips across the hill towns of Tuscany through churches and villas in search of fourteenth- and fifteenth-century wood-paneled altarpieces with gold leaf backgrounds. Wagstaff learned from Offner to scrutinize works of art for details that distinguish one painting from another of the same period and also that distinguish works from one period to another. Offner made photographs of each section of a painting and kept a meticulous catalog of these "targos," as the photographs are called in art historical lingo, which he used as a teaching method in the comparative examination of one painting to another. From this tutelage Wagstaff was made aware of the hierarchies of refinement that can be drawn from such comparisons and that begin to form the basis of credible art historical judgment about the significance of any individual work of art. Furthermore, Offner trained Wagstaff's eyes in even more rigorous ways during their excursions to those Tuscan hill towns, where each church always had at least one altarpiece of interest. After examining the artworks, either immediately upon leaving the building or, later, over lunch or in the evening hours, Offner would ask Sam to recite for him the colors on all the robes of the saints and angels they had seen in that day's altarpiece painting. At a symposium at the Institute of Fine Arts in 2011, Laurence Kantor, a curator at the Yale University Art Gallery, repeated what the eminent art historian John Pope-Hennessy had recounted about these impromptu tests. The conversations between mentor and protégé were almost intellectually erotic as "Sam never hesitated, never faltered, and most surprisingly, never erred" in recounting the color schemes.[48]

Years later, while giving a public talk, Wagstaff recalled another of Offner's lessons: "If you study a painting very well, you know it very, very well—I mean hours of looking at it—and you suddenly look at a photograph of that same painting, often you will find one or two things in that painting that you know by now very well, one or two things in the photograph that obviously are not in the painting, and you take that photograph to the painting and can find that of course, the camera did not lie."[49]

Edgar Munhall, a curator emeritus at the Frick Collection in New York, had been Sam's classmate at the Institute of Fine Arts. For Munhall, too, Sam looked like a blond Gary Cooper, or, perhaps, Sam

Shepard. "Everyone was just in love with him. And he could not have been nicer. He was very, very friendly. He wore his fame very lightly," Munhall recalled, referring to his reputation within the institute. "He was just remarkable looking."[50]

Invariably, his handsome appearance was the first thing anyone who knew him would point out about Wagstaff. But while his looks may have been his most conspicuous attribute, they had a tendency to distract people from the other qualities that distinguished him—his intellectual curiosity, reservoir of factual information, and bold originality of thinking, not to mention the ambition, rigor, and discipline that would propel him to a life of consequence. By the time Sam graduated from the institute, not only had he acquired techniques of selling and convincing from his advertising years, but he now also possessed the knowledge, discernment, and vocabulary of the art historian. He would proceed with refined tastes, but equally with the acute sensitivity of an American homosexual living in the 1960s, to what was real and true within a social structure that condemned him to live a lie.

B E   H E R E   N O W

Money is like a sixth sense without which you cannot
make a complete use of the other five.

—W. SOMERSET MAUGHAM[1]

N 1959, WAGSTAFF WENT TO LIVE IN LONDON AND PARIS; HE'D
been given a David E. Finley fellowship through the National Gallery of Art to tour the museums of Europe and to familiarize himself
with their collections. In the course of his activities, he was introduced
to some titled society and cultivated sorts, among them Loelia (née
Posonby), Duchess of Westminster. Winston Churchill had been the
Duke's best man at Loelia's wedding. She had continued working as an
editor of *House & Garden*. Loelia soon introduced Sam to the art historian John Richardson, whose expansive circle of friends included
Picasso, Braque, Cocteau, Francis Bacon, Benjamin Britten, Peter
Peers, and W. H. Auden. Loelia would gallivant around the countryside, dragging Richardson and Wagstaff with her to some of Britain's
great houses. Drumlanrig was among them, a huge late-seventeenth-
century Baroque castle in Scotland owned by the Duke and Duchess of
Buccleuch, who had some very fine paintings. In fact, they often traveled with their Leonardo and Rembrandt from one house to the other.

Many years later, Richardson remembered the duchess leading them on a grand tour through Drumlanrig. There were entire rooms filled with linens. She would pull a set of towels off a shelf dated from the 1850s; the pillowcases were embroidered with the most intricate cross-stitching. "Those old-time grand ladies knew a hell of a lot about their things," Richardson recalled. "And they loved art historians, they loved good-looking museum people. And a nice, good-looking gay American who'd be lapping up the works of art on the walls . . . Sam fitted into that very well."[2] In fact, Wagstaff's pedigree was evident in the residual formality of his manner and in the starched structure of his diction. His "talent for decorating," as Olga had euphemistically described his aesthetic interests, further ingratiated him to such hostesses. He would end up as a weekend guest in any number of the manor houses of the British countryside, a throwback to a kind of elegant Jamesian figure, sipping his cocktail in black tie while studying the family portraits on the wall by Gainsborough.

In 1961—with formal art historical training, including a brief internship at the Metropolitan Museum, where he'd prepared a catalog for a Gauguin exhibition,[3] and his two-year immersion in the museums of Europe—Wagstaff was hired as curator of painting, prints, and drawings at the Wadsworth Atheneum in Hartford, the oldest public museum in the United States. Its impressive holdings, largely built on significant insurance money, include paintings from the Renaissance, the Italian baroque period, French and American impressionism, a celebrated Hudson River School collection, as well as American decorative arts and textiles.

Wagstaff's educational background made him something of a specialist in the pre-Renaissance period. However, he was vigilant early on about pursuing the young artists he knew in New York. Among these was Ray Johnson, whom he first met in 1959 through Gerry Ayres, the Yale dropout who would become a successful film producer. "I took Sam down to Ray's place," Ayres said, recalling the artist's apartment on Suffolk Street on the Lower East Side of Manhattan. "It was stripped bare except for painted gray floors, a solitary mattress—the only place to sit—and a bathtub in the kitchen. Ray went to a closet with double doors, said, 'My work,' and opened the doors. Out walked his scary, nutty friend Dorothy Podber—who owned a pet ocelot and a Great Dane named Yvonne—carrying a tea cup with a glove hanging from it, fingers down."[4] It was a live, walking Dada installation, hardly surprising since Johnson had gone to Black Mountain College with other artists, among them Robert Rauschenberg, and had studied with John Cage. In no time, Wagstaff soon began to champion Johnson's work and he had a number of his pieces in his apartment. "The best Ray Johnsons I've seen, ever," Richard Tuttle said about those pieces Sam owned.[5]

Tuttle, a postminimalist artist whose fiercely original work with common everyday materials has brought him international critical acclaim, was a student at Trinity College when he and Sam met in 1962. The Trinity radio station was broadcasting a panel discussion about art, and Wagstaff, a relatively new curator at the Wadsworth Athenuem, agreed to take part. Tuttle, a junior in the fine arts department, was the representative student on the panel. Wagstaff was asked by one of the two conservative professors on the panel how the paintings of Franz Kline, a contemporary artist, compared with those of Rembrandt, and the young Tuttle piped up with a contentious question: "How can anything be gained by the comparison?" As Tuttle described it, he and Wagstaff became instant friends. "Unpolitically, I had decided to do a paper on Franz Kline," Tuttle said. "Unpolitically because it of course would not be well received, but also I didn't like the actual painting, a late, color Kline. Sam invited me to visit the museum."[6] Wagstaff then gave Tuttle access to the resources at the Wadsworth Atheneum for his paper.

Wagstaff would become a mentor for as well as a friend to Tuttle. He began taking Tuttle with him on his weekend trips to New York, at a moment when pop art, which drew on images from popular culture and commercial products, was just emerging. Sam was religious about making the rounds to galleries and art events of a more alternative nature. According to Tuttle, there would be "landmark shows of refrigerators and temporary spaces cum galleries set up to break the images of their context that art would come to destroy. It was all very confusing, revolutionary, and stimulating. Then there would be the 'happenings' in the evenings, and the artists everywhere. Introductions. A whirlwind, before getting on the last train back to Hartford."[7]

In December 1961, Claes Oldenburg, one of the earliest pop artists known for his installations and oversize soft sculpture of everyday items, rented a storefront space on East 2nd Street. He opened a month-long exhibition of his sculpture, roughly in the form of consumer goods, calling it "The Store." There he would create some of the earliest "happenings," art events that doubled as mind-expanding parties. This was the kind of thing Sam would drag Tuttle to, but he also brought Tuttle to the galleries on West 57th Street and upper Madison Avenue: Sidney Janis, for example, to see Philip Guston; Martha Jackson to see Sam Francis; Jill Kornblee to see the early Dan Flavin.

Several years later Tom Wolfe published a satiric essay about the New York gallery scene called "The Saturday Route." Wolfe made a mockery of a then-new phenomenon, as gallery hopping became a fashionable trend that diminished, at least on the surface, the function of the galleries and the value of looking at art. "In New York there is the new religion, Art," Wolfe began, describing the route along Madison Avenue from 57th Street to 86th Street on which prominent New Yorkers and aspiring professionals alike would pass in and out of galleries as an excuse to be seen in the most fashionable light:

> Irresistibly, this promenade of socialites, stars, literati and culturati begins to attract a train of vergers, beadles, and hierophants of fashion. One whole set is called "Seventh Avenue"—as in "Her? That's Marilyn. She's Seventh Avenue"—designers, manufacturers, agents, who want to know what They are wearing on the Saturday Route.[8]

Wolfe described an afternoon parade that included serious museum curators as well as jewelry makers, furniture designers, and art journalists, but his procession devolves intentionally into a display of contempt for the "social climbers" and the "fashion plates" who seemed to be taking over the weekly ritual. For Sam, however, the thought of "being fashionable," of following a trend rather than, say, creating one, was as odious as it was for Wolfe, and it must have irked him that, as a curator with a discerning interest in contemporary art, he would have been lumped into this category. Wagstaff brought diligence and purpose to his weekend gallery walks, which had become his routine since long before Wolfe indicted the experience.

Beginning with Tuttle, Wagstaff kept up the tradition of the older patron and the younger artist. He would assume this role in various forms for the rest of his life. On more than a few occasions (as we have already seen with Jim Crawford and Gordon Newton), Sam would become enamored of a young artist of serious talent and draw him close, whether his romantic feelings were reciprocated or not. He would take the artist under his wing and introduce him to the art world of New York, and the artists of the moment; he would encourage the protégé in his work and provide financial support when needed. When Tuttle, for example, moved to New York in the mid-1960s and began his *La Boheme*–like existence as a young artist in a tiny cold-water garret, Sam arrived to visit him for the first time with a friend in tow—Andy Warhol.

From his platform at the Wadsworth Atheneum, Wagstaff slowly began to establish himself in the art world of New York, and he was vigilant about remaining current. He discovered new artists by talking to the artists themselves. Once, soon after meeting Ad Reinhardt in the early 1960s, he received this amusing note in beautiful calligraphic script: "Dear Sam Wagstaff, I guess you must have thought I was kidding when you asked me if I saw any interesting English painters and I answered 'Bridget Bardot and she's a nice girl too'? I meant to answer 'Bridget Riley and she's a nice girl too' —Ad."⁹

Sam began spending as much time as he could with younger artists. Aware, for example, that his Upper East Side apartment did not reflect the bohemian attitudes of the artists with whom he was now associating, he moved downtown in 1964, renting a loft on Bond Street at the corner of the Bowery. On the other side of the avenue long associated with drunks and bums was the portion of the Lower East Side currently being rechristened the East Village, home to the abstract expressionist painters and beat poets.

Sam's new loft made a great home base for his regular weekend trips to New York from Hartford, and, later, Detroit. In the early 1960s he also found his way to Mark di Suvero's studio in a commercial part of downtown Manhattan near the Fulton Fish Market. The space was so raw that the young sculptor had to set up lights on the floor in the hallway of his studio and go to a different floor to use the bathroom. Wagstaff liked di Suvero's work and he was particularly excited when di Suvero and several other artists—among them Forrest "Frosty" Meyers, Leo Valledor, and Robert Grosvenor—opened the Park Place Gallery in 1963, a cooperative studio where they set out to create public art. "It was a radical idea at the time," di Suvero said. "We shared everything. We shared our ideas, we showed the work of our friends, we worked on each other's work, shared all the income." [10] Park Place Gallery moved to LaGuardia Place in 1965, a pioneer in what was the heart of the Italian section of Greenwich Village, on the edge of what would become SoHo a decade later. The gallery would soon feature Carl Andre, Charles Ginnever, Eva Hesse, Sol LeWitt, and Joan Jonas, among many other artists who were to become prominent.

In the early 1960s, while working in construction, di Suvero had a serious accident that caused a crippling back injury, but not before he produced a piece called *For Giacometti* (1962), which Wagstaff wanted to purchase for the Wadsworth Atheneum. Di Suvero's attorneys counseled the artist not to accept any money since it would affect the outcome of his insurance claim, so di Suvero set up the Athena Foundation, and when Wagstaff purchased the sculpture, he made sure the museum paid the foundation.

Wagstaff's position at the Wadsworth Atheneum and his interest in the world of contemporary art greatly expanded his social and recreational opportunities. Ray Johnson would introduce him to John Cage, Merce Cunningham, and Robert Rauschenberg. Billy Name, a young artist, was working as a waiter at Serendipity III in the East Sixties, a trendy restaurant in 1959 when Andy Warhol, then a young illustrator, would come in to eat—and the two men would chat. Billy Name would soon become Ray Johnson's lover and when Name and Johnson parted, Name and Warhol tried to be lovers, although they would find better synergy as studio collaborators. In late 1963 Warhol found a studio on

East 47th Street that would become known as "the Factory," and Name was the one who "silverized" the studio, wallpapering the walls from floor to ceiling with aluminum foil. He worked with Warhol running the studio for the next seven years. Name also remembers Wagstaff spending time at the Factory from the very beginning, describing the day he first became aware of the handsome curator talking to Andy in the studio. "I was in the back, playing records. All of a sudden, Sam came running down through the loft to the back, just to ask what the piece of music was. It was Prokofiev's *Scythian Suite*."[11]

The Factory was always intended to be an artist's studio and, for the first year or so, Warhol used it primarily to paint. It had not yet transformed into the social phenomenon that it would become once Edie Sedgwick arrived in 1965, bringing with her the media and a steady stream of celebrity visitors. In the early days, friends would stop by informally, people like Henry Geldzahler, Barbara Rose, the art historian and critic, and Frank Stella, Name recalled. And Sam Wagstaff was among those who would come regularly to look at Andy's new work, talk to him about it, and then to sit, chat, and, maybe, have a drink. Sam was able to talk to them about art easily, on their level, Name explained, "with a straight mental plane of the aesthetics going on."[12]

One day soon after Wagstaff had put a stall shower in his new loft on Bond Street, he expressed to Warhol and Name his relief about how much easier it was to shower than to take a bath. After suggesting they install one at the Factory, as well, they dropped whatever they were doing and went—all three of them—downtown to Sam's loft to try out his shower. Wagstaff clearly was influential because, soon after, Andy had one installed at the Factory.

During this period Warhol made a series of silk screens of a single photograph repeated on ten linen panels in different colors. The picture, by Charles Moore, had recently appeared in *Life* magazine in a layout about the Birmingham race riot; it shows a police officer pulling at the leash of a German shepherd on hind legs as it attacks a black man trying to flee.[13] The Charles Moore layout in the May 17, 1963, issue of *Life* warranted a public comment from President Kennedy about the racial tensions in America, in which he observed the events of the civil rights movement to be "so much more eloquently reported by the news camera than by any number of explanatory words."[14] In 1964, Warhol gave Wagstaff two of these silk-screen canvases in red. In 1969, Sam would acquire from the Leo Castelli Gallery two more of the Warhol canvases from that series, one in blue and one in white. He paid $675 for those two canvases.[15] Sam then assembled the Warhol canvases as a four-panel grid of the same photograph in red, white, and blue, measuring six feet square. He would keep the work the rest of his life. Known as *Race Riot* (1964), it was sold several times after Sam's death, and today it is regarded as one of Warhol's uncharacteristically political statements.[16] In 2014, at a Christie's auction of postwar art, the gavel came down on *Race Riot* for $62.8 million.[17]

So keen was the friendship between Wagstaff and Warhol that Wagstaff had appeared in one of Warhol's earliest films, *Batman Dracula*, starring Jack Smith along with Baby Jane Holzer, Gerard Malanga, Billy Name, Ondine, and others. The two-hour film is shot in black and white and was first shown at one of Warhol's few gallery exhibits in 1964.

———

SAM'S SOCIAL LIFE WAS composed of many circles within the worlds of art, of fashion, and of culture in general. Throughout the 1960s, he maintained a close, if sometimes epistolary, relationship with Charles James, the fashion designer venerated beyond his field as an artist, whom he might have met through Cecil Beaton. The British James began as a hat designer, first setting up shop in the United States in 1939, but his clothing design was recognized almost immediately for its bold originality. His talent often exceeded his judgment, though, and his luminous career eventually deteriorated. While today he is considered "America's first couturier," and Christian Dior called him "the greatest talent of my generation," he was deified by the fashion world only after his death, in 1978.[18] A retrospective of his work inaugurated the new Anna Wintour Costume Institute at the Metropolitan Museum in 2014, and Roberta Smith, co-chief art critic at *The New York Times*, described the character of his oeuvre "as organic, forward-looking and self-evident as a Brancusi sculpture, an Eero Saarinen tulip chair or a Pollock drip painting."[19] James described fashion itself as that which "is rare, correctly proportioned and, though utterly discrete, libidinous," and referred to his own work as "a high form of eroticism."[20]

The letters between Sam and Charles James reveal a level of emotional honesty and intimacy often found between lovers, but there is no evidence that a romance existed. James would write Sam on Chelsea Hotel letterhead, where he lived. James would help Sam make the acquaintance of Jean and Dominique De Menil, known then as serious collectors of modern European art with homes in New York, Houston, and France; he also offered Sam a strategic tip in one letter, in which he cautioned that the De Menils were socially discerning beyond measure. Their interest in Sam would be contingent on Sam's curatorial interest in James's work—as long as Sam pretended not to know of their acquaintance with James.

In another letter, James bemoaned the fate of the artist in a field in which poseurs claimed to be making art, when artifice was as far as their vision could take them. He drew a distinction between what was and was not considered "camp," a locution circulating at the time before it was given intellectual definition in Susan Sontag's influential essay "Notes on Camp."

WAGSTAFF'S REPUTATION AS A curator grew during the 1960s as art making evolved from abstract expressionism to minimalism. In many ways, the avant-garde ideas that Wagstaff put on display in his landmark 1964 exhibition, "Black, White, and Gray," came out of his introduction to the community of artists in New York he was spending time with on his weekend visits to the city. That exhibition was the first museum survey to identify the evolving practice that came to be known as minimalism. Works on canvas, drawings, sculptural objects, and installation pieces, all made in shades of black, white, or gray, or incorporating any combination thereof, were chosen, in Wagstaff's words, to keep the viewer "from being distracted by the emotionalism of color."[21]

Although many of the artists in the show were not yet well known, many would become in time hugely significant. The artists in the show were George Brecht, James Lee Byers, Jim Dine, Dan Flavin, Jean Follett, Robert Indiana, Jasper Johns, Ellsworth Kelly, Alexander Liberman, Roy Lichtenstein, Agnes Martin, Robert Morris, Barnett Newman, Ray Parker, Robert Rauschenberg, Ad Reinhardt, Tony Smith, Frank Stella, Anne Truitt, Cy Twombly, and Andy Warhol. At the time all of them were making work—most with industrial materials—that expanded the definition of the art object. The pieces in the show aimed to distill expression to essential form.

In an essay outlining his ideas about the "Black, White, and Gray" exhibit, published in *ARTnews* in January 1964, Wagstaff wrote that for any number of contemporary artists of the day, "whose works tend away from Expressionism in a more austere direction, the composer John Cage has been an intellectual guide. Because Cage had studied Zen Buddhism at Columbia University in the late-1940s, the 'consciousness of being' would have a profound and lasting effect on his work. Whether his influence has been direct, as in the case of Johns, Rauschenberg, Warhol, etc., or whether it was just a parallel affinity, Cage seems to be a spiritual leader with an aggressive following."[22]

Wagstaff acknowledged that Marcel Duchamp, Barnett Newman, and Ad Reinhardt were of equal influence with many artists, but, as far as he was concerned, Cage's remarks about music—"There is too much there there" and "there is not enough of nothing in it"—represented a binding philosophy that many younger painters and sculptors in the show seemed to embrace.

In fact, so many of the artists in "Black, White, and Gray" were already exploring various ways of getting to nothing—or at least arriving at an economy of form that distilled the object to nothing but the thing itself. Materials were chosen for their matter-of-factness. Everything was stripped to the essential facts, a kind of plain-speaking emphasis on geometric form absent decorative detail, devoid of metaphor and pretense, in which the artist's own hand was conspicuously invisible.

There was an intentional lack of expressive technique coupled with an aggression of geometry and structure.

To arrange this minimalist show, Wagstaff sent letters to each artist requesting work, along with elaborate loan forms and instructions about the shipment of the work to the museum—administrative duties usually handled by lower-level museum staff.

Wagstaff's letter of invitation to Andy Warhol for the "Black, White, and Gray" show included loan forms for two of his "car crash" paintings: "I'm also enclosing a third set of forms in hopes that you will be able to make a sculpture of a pile of white boxes with silk screen sides as you talked about one day. How is that project coming?" Then he got carried away: "In addition, I would like a couple of drawings, really tough ones, as simple or as close to the original object as possible. I thought the big pencil drawing of a dollar bill, which I saw upstairs once was pretty frightening. How about it?" This was far more than he could have included from a single artist.[23]

To his friend Agnes Martin, Sam wrote, "I hope you survived the dance. I stayed to the bitter end and I must say had a wonderful time. Please think seriously about letting us have the white painting with nails for the show which runs from January 9th through February 9th."[24]

Wagstaff had gotten to know Jasper Johns by then, too, but Johns proved to be less forthcoming about lending work to the show than many of the other artists in those circles. "I remember once hearing you say something about not liking to lend to exhibitions yourself, but I wondered if you would do me a great favor of letting me have the drawing by Cy Twombly which you showed me one evening at your place," Sam wrote. "I will call you Saturday on the off chance that you might be free for dinner. I know this is awfully late notice."[25]

Clement Greenberg, the most revered art critic of the modernist era, was also a collector, and Sam wrote to him to secure his loan of a Barnett Newman: "Dear Clem, Many, many thanks for your kindness in lending Barney's painting for the show which is entitled Black, White, and Gray and will run from January 9th through February 9th. We will probably be making the pickup Friday, January 3rd. Our registrar will write you about this. I will be sure to have the trucker bring a sheet and four of the cardboard corners to protect the picture. I think we had better wrap it in corrugated on top of the sheet."[26]

Sam did not allow his role as an administrator to put any distance between him and the artists. He insisted on direct contact. In his letter to Warhol, for example, the "white boxes with silk screen sides" he refers to would only months later appear at the Stable Gallery as the now famous *Brillo Boxes*.[27] With the artists Wagstaff admired, the personal intermingled effortlessly with the professional.

He also knew how to engage the publicity machine. He wrote to Rosamond Constable and Charles P. Jackson at *Time*, Jack Kroll at *Newsweek*, Irving Sandler at the *New York Post*, Emily Genauer at the *New York Herald Tribune*, Dorothy Adlow at the *Christian Science Monitor*, and Barbara Rose at *Art International*, all saying ostensibly the same thing: "Here is a copy of the short blurb about the Black, White, and Gray show I told you of, which will appear in the January issue of *ART-news*. Do try to come up for the opening the evening of the 9th of January. I think there will be quite a few people coming."[28]

Indeed, more than a few people did make the two-and-a-half-hour journey in winter from Manhattan to Hartford for the opening, and for those adventurous and sophisticated New Yorkers, this first show of minimalist art was worth the trip. "I remember the opening for Black, White, and Gray," Wagstaff told Nicholas Fox Weber for an oral history of his role as a curator at the Wadsworth Atheneum. "A lot of people came from New York. Andy [Warhol] was there.... Tony Smith, it was the first time he had a piece of sculpture shown in public."[29]

Wagstaff's only lament was his inability to convince Larry Poons to lend a black-and-white painting he had seen on a visit to the artist's studio near South Street. Poons never responded to Wagstaff's several letters of request. He and his wife, Thalia, did come to the opening, though, traveling all the way up from New York on his motorcycle. At the opening, the Poonses told him it was a terrific show: "Next time we're going to have to answer your letters," Poons said.[30]

At the Wadsworth Atheneum, Wagstaff acquired some exceedingly helpful and beneficial friends. Mary Palmer, for example, was an urbane art collector in Hartford who volunteered at the museum. She became very close to Wagstaff during his years there, helping him navigate the not inconsiderable politics of the institution. She remained in awe of his sophistication, while parsing for him the conservatism of the Hartford city fathers, with their blue-blood roots and insurance industry money. Following the opening of "Black, White and Gray," the Palmers threw a party for the artists at their home. The evening made an indelible impression on Mary Palmer's eighteen-year-old son, John, an attractive blond-haired kid who would soon move to New York to work on films by Andy Warhol. "It was a wonderful time," John Palmer said about the party, mentioning the artists Jasper Johns, Andy Warhol, and Frank Stella—"these New York artists who were rather *in extremis* by Hartford standards [all] standing around in my living room in West Hartford kibitzing about the significance of what was going on in the show."[31]

Wagstaff, who by that time had become a good family friend of the Palmers, assumed the role of host at the party. John Palmer remembers him as "this patrician, oozing this phenotype, you know, his masculinity, his class, his beauty, his double-breasted suit and the cleft chin."[32]

Of course Palmer's clearest memory that night was standing in his own living room and talking to Andy Warhol: "It's the way the pixels feel, what Andy represented in the world, how his being and his Wittgenstein-ian lived performance with the body language and the whole fey thing, and everything he had created for himself was his own language, his signature."[33]

Not surprisingly, "Black, White, and Gray" generated controversy uncharacteristic of the Wadsworth Atheneum. Most of the culturally minded residents of Hartford just did not get it, anticipating the kind of problems Wagstaff would later have in Detroit. The show opened less than two months after the assassination of President John F. Kennedy. With a hard-edged austerity, the geometric objects made of industrial materials and the paintings with no color seemed to echo the deep black sorrow of the national mood. In a letter to Charles Cunningham, the director of the Atheneum, one prominent patron, John C. Parsons, expressed his regret that the museum even allowed such an exhibit: "While a function of a museum may be to show what contemporary painters and sculptors are doing, there should be some discrimination and selection based on quality rather than novelty."[34]

It is hardly without historical precedent that, when a museum exhibits work incomprehensible, or simply distasteful, to its viewers, hostile reactions are likely to follow. If viewers can't decode the visual or conceptual language, they feel duped. Several days after "Black, White, and Gray" opened, as if in an attempt to address the negative reactions of local art patrons, Wagstaff was quoted in an article in the *Hartford Times* defending the artistic and intellectual foundations of the show. His explanation, however, failed to include an explanation of the art itself. Instead, he suggested, not without a trace of curatorial arrogance, that the viewers' discomfort was evidence of the works' artistic significance. "The quality of the art in this exhibition is extremely high," Wagstaff said. "When you look at a Titian or a Rembrandt, you are on the bedrock of art. When you come to this exhibition, you are on thin ice."[35] By describing their discomfort, or dismay, as evidence of the power of an artwork—instead of, perhaps, offering a framework to assess its "artfulness," say, or to consider the artist's philosophy—Wagstaff had condescended, further alienating his audience.

A piece in "Black, White, and Gray" by George Brecht consisted of a table and two chairs; on the table were two place settings and a newspaper folded on one of the plates. According to Wagstaff, it was the most inscrutable piece in the show and drew perhaps the greatest number of hostile reactions. Sam was thrilled then to share a story about a woman who had returned to see the exhibit three times, citing the table and chairs in particular. "When I first saw the piece I realized I had never looked at any of the chairs really close in my house," the young woman told Wagstaff. "I went home and looked at every single chair in my house."[36] For Wagstaff, the Brecht piece had made this museumgoer aware of the visual world before her in her everyday life—the best illustration of what he had hoped to achieve with the show.

The influence of John Cage was evident in the works in "Black, White, and Gray" that aimed to achieve this 'consciousness of the natural state." While wit seemed merely a felicitous by-product in much of the show, it was a central feature of the work of his student Ray Johnson. Johnson's pieces had the simplicity of real-life actions, executed with deadpan humor that would leave the recipient in a tangle of perplexity. Frances Beatty, vice president of the Richard Feigen Gallery in New York, which represented Johnson for many years, recalled a phone conversation in which his idea for a show was to have nothing in the gallery. "Now, the thing is," she recounted in the documentary about the artist called *How to Draw Bunny*, "you never knew whether Ray was really going to do nothing or whether his nothing was one of his 'nothings,' because he did these performances and they were called 'nothings.' So, maybe he meant he was going to do a 'nothing.' Or did he mean he wasn't going to do anything? You didn't really know." In almost any conversation with Johnson, Beatty recalled, she felt like Alice falling down the rabbit hole. "You had had this great dialogue with Ray but you had nothing."[37]

The exhibit was a moment in Wagstaff's life when he felt the kind of personal achievement in which he recognized himself and found clear definition. While not a *succès de scandale* exactly, it stirred an intellectual controversy that riled the old guard and made him feel relevant. He was even more delighted by the two Merce Cunningham world premiere performances, *Winterbranch* and *Paired*, he had arranged to accompany the show. The exhibit challenged its audience, but the dance performances impressed them. Just as the January opening of "Black, White, and Gray" had attracted a Manhattan crowd willing to make the two-and-a-half hour journey to Hartford for the occasion, the Cunningham concerts drew a crowd from New York, too, including John Cage, the company's musical director, and Robert Rauschenberg, who designed the sets. The shows were sold out and Sam was elated, as was everyone at the Wadsworth Atheneum.

Jill Johnston, then the dance critic of *The Village Voice*, also made the pilgrimage to Hartford to attend the concerts. Her April 9, 1964 review of *Winterbranch* provides a stark and poignant image of the power in avant-garde dance of the period. She described the music by LaMonte Young as "the constant amplified abrasion, whining and screeching, of the sounds made by ashtrays pulled gently across the surfaces of mirrors." The sound was jarring in relation to the spare action on stage, with dancers she described as hunters quietly searching for prey in the animal kingdom of a jungle night: "Mostly I recall a beautiful tumble as they all clasp arms and make a slow, massive rise and fall of liquid branches following after a long stretch of flotsam burlap drifting across the bleak stage."[38]

Wagstaff's commission of these performances intentionally echoed the 1934 world premiere of *Four Saints in Three Acts*, an opera by Virgil Thomson with a libretto by Gertrude Stein, which had taken place in the same auditorium. Chick Austin, director of the Wadsworth Atheneum from 1927 to 1944, was considered in those years the most innovative museum director in America. It was Austin who first brought modern art to the previously staid Atheneum, and it was he who opened the institution's doors to not just art but theater, ballet, film, architecture, and this groundbreaking opera.

Austin was a colorful figure, often sparking controversy and shocking the museum trustees with his curatorial decisions and his personal behavior. He had studied art history at Harvard with Paul Sachs, whose legendary "museum course" would help place Austin and his classmates in positions of influence in the arts in the middle years of the twentieth century, among them Alfred H. Barr Jr., the first director of the Museum of Modern of Art; Henry-Russell Hitchcock, the eminent architectural historian; Philip Johnson, the first curator of architecture at the Museum of Modern Art; Beaumont Newhall, the first curator of photography at the Museum of Modern Art; Lincoln Kirstein, the co-founder of the New York City Ballet; and James Rorimer, who would later advise Wagstaff during his studies at the Institute of Fine Arts and who recommended him for the job at the Atheneum.

When Sam arrived at the Wadsworth Atheneum, Austin's legacy still loomed large over the institution, and comparisons were made. Both men had the kind of looks that drew immediate comment and attention. Both had impeccable academic credentials. Both were irreverent in similar ways. And both had vision, refined sensibilities, and élan. If ever there were someone to set a standard of excellence beyond the register of social respectability that Mrs. Donald V. Newhall had initially ordained for Samuel Jones Wagstaff Jr, it would be Chick Austin.

The premiere of *Four Saints in Three Acts* on February 7, 1934, was a cultural success of international proportion. The opera's opening coincided with of the first comprehensive show of Picasso's work in the United States, mounted by Austin at the Wadsworth Atheneum, confirming its cutting-edge status during the height of the Depression. For the formally dressed sophisticates in the audience, and there were many, including New Yorkers, its impact was on a par with two landmark 1913 events, the New York Armory show and the Paris premiere of Stravinsky's *Rite of Spring*.[39]

Chick Austin's reach was wide, and Wagstaff was also aware of the gay side of his personal life. Philip Johnson met his first lover, a black man named Jimmie Daniels, during one of his excursions to Harlem with Virgil Thomson in the 1930s. Jimmie Daniels would later come to be known among Johnson's friends, in campy parlance, as "the first Mrs. Johnson." Virgil Thomson was so impressed with Jimmie Daniels "impeccable enunciation" that he decided to write an opera "sung by Negroes." The result was *Four Saints in Three Acts*.[40]

ART IS ALWAYS AN attempt to give form to something essential of its own time even as it seeks the language of the future. The artist enters some inviolate preserve in which observation, contemplation, intuition, sensation, imagination, and craft lead to a fully realized expression of impulses and ideas—the artist in search of his own recipe for an evolution of consciousness. Sam Wagstaff was attuned to the frequency on which these artists were working independently and, also, simultaneously, and he was able to identify a common thread at that moment. "Sam liked real art," Michael Heizer later said about him. "He was smart enough to know what real art was. He was really up-to-date, being alive at the same time artists were producing. He was the guy who anticipated minimalism, and he was shortchanged."[41] In fact Sam was never officially recognized as the first art world professional to identify the movement.

Nevertheless, the work remained incomprehensible to the Hartford elite. Two years later, Kynaston McShine, a curator at the Jewish Museum in New York, mounted "Primary Structures: Younger American and British Sculptors."[42] This 1966 show of minimal art drew broader attention, including good reviews in *The New York Times, Time, and Newsweek*. Even today it is erroneously referred to as the first minimalist show. "Black, White, and Gray" was not mentioned in the reviews of "Primary Structures." While Wagstaff did not receive credit at the time for identifying the new movement in art, the mainstream acknowledgement of minimalism as a result of the McShine show proved a gratifying vindication to hold up to the old guard in Hartford.

Not all of Wagstaff's efforts were of a purely minimalist bent. While at the Wadsworth Atheneum, Wagstaff gave Richard Offner a 75th birthday present—an exhibition that paid tribute to his influence on the field. "An Exhibition of Italian Panels and Manuscripts from the Thirteenth and Fourteenth Centuries in Honor of Richard Offner" opened at the Atheneum on April 9, 1965.[43] Included were more than one hundred objects, mostly Italian panels, miniatures, textiles, and sculpture from the years 1250 to 1400. In what museum director Charles Cunningham called "a labor of love" from one student of Offner's, Sam was able to secure loans from the Metropolitan Museum of Art, the Morgan Library, the Cleveland Museum of Art, the Museum of Fine Arts in Boston, the De Young Museum in San Francisco, Yale University, and a host of individual collectors.

"It is somewhat presumptuous, I suspect, even to attempt an exhibition in honor of Dr. Offner, for, if it possibly met one's own standards, the chances of its meeting his would be slight," Wagstaff wrote in his introduction in the small exhibition catalog. "But then a man whose ideas of perfection are so integral with life must have met disappointment often before, and a token of esteem, imperfect, is still a token of esteem."[44]

Sam pointed out that the Renaissance ideal had ultimately cast a shadow on these pre-Renaissance works made in a period of intense religious fervor. "At first, all Madonnas from Siena painted in the first quarter of the fourteenth century, for instance, look alike," he wrote. "Then at the next stage of looking, each seems to be by a different hand; and, finally, one becomes aware of the character of the separate artists. The range in quality is as great as it has been in art ever since."

For Wagstaff, this tribute to Offner was a graduation, of sorts, in the form of a very public and official beau geste. In a letter Richard Offner sent to Wagstaff from his home in Florence, Italy, he expressed his awe at the scrupulous scholarship, the explanation of the art historical significance of each work, and the quality of the material exhibited. "But that this was done in my name is an honor I shall never forget," Offner wrote.[45]

AMONG STUDENTS, ARTISTS, AND intellectual pleasure seekers the use of marijuana, magic mushrooms, and LSD flourished in the mid-1960s. The drive to heighten sensate experience resulted in artwork that was increasingly performative and participatory. The term floating around art schools at the time was "phenomenological." Those who lived through the period might recognize the "stoned" humor in the work of that moment—antic, deadpan, absurdist, nose-thumbing, and, at times, even, silly. "Camp" humor, its offshoot, was imbued with irony and hyperbole and layers of coded references to the homosexual closet, not yet quite understood as a means of cultural oppression, but manifest in the work emerging from the margins.

The art world's major players were thinking at an even higher conceptual frequency. Tony Smith's stark and monumental geometric sculpture has had an abiding influence on subsequent generations of artists. As a curator at the Wadsworth Atheneum, Wagstaff organized Smith's first museum exhibition, in 1966, after which he and the artist would become very close friends. Smith was then fifty-four, almost a decade older than Wagstaff, and this show was what finally launched his important career, resulting in a cover story in *Time* the following year.[46] During the exhibit, Wagstaff conducted an interview with Smith for

Artforum magazine, in which the artist recounted an experience that gives insight into the kind of thinking and artistic inquiry at the foundation of minimalist art.[47]

Smith described a drive he had taken on the unfinished New Jersey Turnpike in the early 1950s, accompanied by three of his students from Cooper Union: "It was a dark night," he said. "There were no lights or shoulder markers, lines, railings, or anything at all except the dark pavement moving through the landscape to the flats, rimmed by hills in the distance, but punctuated by stacks, towers, fumes, and colored lights." In 1951, the experience of rolling through darkness with glimmers of industrial smoke and light in the periphery might have felt extraterrestrial. Smith pointed out that almost everything surrounding them in that landscape was artificial. And yet, while it couldn't be thought of as a work of art, the experience had done something for him that art had never done, he told Wagstaff: "At first I didn't know what it was, but its effect was to liberate me from many of the views I had had about art. It seemed that there had been a reality there that had not had any expression in art."[48] After that experience, Smith concluded that painting looked merely pictorial to him and that the art he was interested in creating from that point on could not be framed simply to hang on a wall. One would just have to experience it. That drive introduced Smith to the idea that art was no longer bound to a material form; he would begin to explore more experiential dimensions in the work he set out to make.

Not long after the Tony Smith show, Wagstaff learned that Charles Cunningham planned to step down as museum director. By that time he was a senior curator, and he believed that he was the natural candidate for the job. The job, however, went to James Elliott, a fellow curator, who had worked at a number of other museums. Wagstaff felt passed over. Despite Sam's very good standing as a curator, several unspoken details about his character weighted the choice against him—not least his euphemistic "unmarried" status. It would later be revealed that Jim Elliott was known among his friends to be gay, too, but he had married Judith Algar in 1966, and that marriage gave him an advantage. Wagstaff's homosexuality may have been an open secret, but it was never discussed. In 1967, Sam remained the Ivy League aristocrat with a European flair, dressing in tweed jackets, button-down shirts, and rep ties. Yet his temperament was not that of a diplomat. So, in late 1967, when the Detroit Institute of Arts discreetly inquired about his level of interest in a curatorial opening, he made the move.

John Richardson, who had moved to New York from London in the early 1960s, recalled Wagstaff during his years at the Wadsworth Atheneum: "Sam was exceedingly good-looking, very conventional, very WASP-looking, somewhat WASP in terms of thought," he said. Richardson considered Sam to be a charming, open-minded young curator initially grounded in the conventional art historical canon. "I, frankly, was surprised that Sam broke out into this other character."[49]

In fact, once he got to Detroit, Wagstaff, the Jamesian weekend guest in the ducal mansion tradition, rather dramatically assumed the look of a hippie, taking up marijuana and affecting an altogether looser attitude while retaining his ties to the people of influence he liked to characterize as "fancy pants." Still, glamour is the fairy dust of childhood sprinkled on our adult expectations, and, even the reconstituted Sam—long hair, jewelry, hippie lingo, and all—would not fail to leave an impression.

In 1968, at one of Mrs. William Rhinelander Stewart's dinner parties in her Park Avenue apartment, the writer Steven M. L. Aronson was first introduced to Sam. Janet Stewart was considered by many to be the most beautiful woman in New York, and, certainly, according to Aronson, the most fashionable "in every sense of the word,"[50] appearing regularly on the best-dressed list. Her husband's family had owned land in New York City since the eighteenth century and, among other distinctions, were responsible for erecting Washington Square Arch. When her husband died in 1945, his best friend, Vincent Astor, asked Janet to marry him. "Marry you?" Mrs. Stewart replied. "I don't even like you." When he explained that he was not in great health and that, when he died, she would inherit his vast fortune, Janet Stewart responded that she had enough money to live on. And "what if the doctors are wrong?"[51]

Sam had met Janet through his mother, Olga, and he had grown to adore her (he would later own a photograph of her taken by Irving Penn). The assortment of guests at her apartment that evening included the cabaret singer Blossom Dearie, the actor Ben Gazzara, and Jean and Alfred Gwynne Vanderbilt. Mrs. Stewart's favorite dessert to serve was the high-WASP classic, prune whip. "That night, no sooner had it been set down than the guy in the bespoke suit across from me gushed, 'Oh, this is yum-m-m-y!' " Aronson said. "It wasn't so much the infantile adjective that grabbed me as the giddy way he drew it out. As I would learn, pure Sam!"[52]

AS THE DECADE BECAME increasingly experiential in myriad ways, Wagstaff seemed, almost anachronistically, to be getting younger. His New York loft was located near the heart of the cultural ferment of the period. The Fillmore East, a few blocks away, would become the Carnegie Hall of rock 'n' roll, presenting concerts by the Grateful Dead, Jefferson Airplane, Janis Joplin, Ravi Shankar, Jim Morrison, the Mothers of Invention, Joe Cocker, Ike and Tina Turner. Nearby St. Marks Place was filled with head shops, the sidewalks lined with would-be hippie poets sitting on Indian blankets and selling vinyl records, tie-dyed T-shirts, macramé shawls, beads, and cloisonné jewelry. Would-be folksingers, and the Village seemed teeming with them, sat on stoops strumming guitars as the smells of incense, marijuana, patchouli oil, and noisome garbage infused the neighborhood. The spirit of the age was bubbling up from the streets of the East Village, merely blocks from the MacDougal Street/Washington Square scene, where, in the early 1960s, Bob Dylan, Joan Baez, and Richie Havens, among so many others, had been just street performers in the park.

In 1969, a little farther west of Washington Square and not a mile away from Wagstaff's loft, a routine police raid on a gay bar called the Stonewall Inn prompted the patrons, some of them transvestites, to retaliate and fight back in exasperation and indignation. Ironically, it was the night of Judy Garland's funeral, who had been lying as if in state uptown at Frank Campbell's funeral home, where thousands lined Madison Avenue to view a fallen camp goddess. Many historians believe that the timing of the Stonewall Inn raid on the night of Judy Garland's funeral—so tender a grieving moment for the bar's patrons—is what prompted these drag queens in wigs and heels, as well as those dressed in more ordinary clothing, to strike back at the offending officers with such unprecedented violence. Judy Garland, the chanteuse, had been a revered figure in the underground gay community. The uprising, which came to be known as the Stonewall Riot, is often cited as the symbolic beginning of the gay rights movement in America.

Less than two months later, the poster for the Woodstock music festival promised "an Aquarian Exposition: 3 Days of Peace & Music." Wagstaff, a middle-aged man with shoulder-length hair who had taken to wearing embroidered Indian shirts, beaded bracelets, and sandals, no doubt felt that the concert was an obligatory cultural event, and sat there on the ground amid hundreds of thousands of shirtless college-aged kids on a rain-soaked weekend afternoon. Around him reverberated the chords of the electric guitar, the metallic feedback from the speakers, the staccato beat of the drums. These seemingly revolutionary sounds drifted across the valley in Bethel, New York, as the sweet, pungent smell of marijuana lifted the entire crowd into a throbbing and hypnotic purple haze. Kinetic energy rippled across the hillside, all bobbing heads and swaying shoulders, as Jimi Hendrix, Creedence Clearwater Revival, The Who, John Sebastian, Country Joe and the Fish, Joan Baez, Blood, Sweat and Tears, and Ravi Shankar performed over the course of several days. Wagstaff—the man who knew the lyrics to every Cole Porter song—was getting stoned, too, listening to the scratch and metallic twang of rock 'n' roll music in the vast audience, the collective defiance of the status quo a logical evolution from Porter's "Anything Goes."

At the time, Sam was forty-seven, and his companion for the event was the twenty-six-year-old Richard Tuttle. On their trek up from Manhattan, Sam and Richard had pulled over at a convenience store. The two men wisely loaded up with bagsful of groceries, unsure of whether food would be available. They reached the field after much of the throng had arrived, and they saw no place to sit. "You had to park over the hill and you saw something, you couldn't imagine what it was, and as you got closer there were like a million people," Tuttle recalled.

"Sam wanted a good seat. So he took a whole bunch of bananas and just walked up to the very best spot and started throwing bananas and everybody leaped for them, and we got our seats. We did that twice."[53]

Wagstaff had the instinct to find his way to Woodstock, the most historic "happening" of all, and then the sense of entitlement to orchestrate a good seat. The gesture of his noblesse oblige—throwing bananas to the masses—was stylish, if not incidentally also intelligent, and far more in keeping with Colonel Wagstaff than Sam would have acknowledged. Once they were situated, Sam began smoking marijuana. "It was farmland and there was a little tree on the horizon. Sam found it very interesting, listening to the music and looking at that tree," Tuttle said. "It went on for about three hours and, finally, Sam said, 'Look at that tree.'"[54]

This might seem like an idle "stoned" utterance—but there, in its utter simplicity, resides something of the essence of Sam Wagstaff. Look at that tree. Listen to that beat. Smell that weed. Taste that banana. Touch that rainbow. *Be here now!* John Cage's guiding influence seemed to have spread to the masses, and Sam, too, was in tune with the Buddhist-influenced mantra of the moment: "Be here now." The then-popular book of the same name by Baba Ram Dass (Richard Alpert) offered a simplified explanation of Zen Buddhism for the masses. The idea captured a youth culture that pursued a hedonistic return to nature and the spirit, even if the excesses of the period may have been at odds with the tenets of Buddhist simplicity. For Wagstaff, though, as much as Woodstock served as a countercultural expedition in search of pleasure, it was also the cultural apotheosis of a more arcane art world evolution: the experiential in art as an idea, an approach, and a destination. The Zen Buddhist tenets manifest in the expression "Be here now" had been embraced in the 1950s by abstract expressionist artists such as Jackson Pollock and Willem de Kooning, and beat writers such as Jack Kerouac, William Burroughs, and Allen Ginsberg.[55] They aspired to represent in their work the spontaneous and improvisational process of creating it.

That entire set of ideas about art and art making in the 1950s and '60s was given definition by Allan Kaprow, an influential artist known to have coined the term "happening" for the performative and experiential art events that began popping up in the late 1950s. Of course, the original idea behind these gatherings can be traced to none other than John Cage, Kaprow's teacher, whose seminal piece *Untitled Event* at Black Mountain College in 1952 was arguably the first "happening" or "be-in." As Wagstaff said in his essay about "Black, White, and Gray" in *ARTnews*, Cage became the decisive influence for the artists of the late 1950s and '60s; nevertheless, Kaprow, who studied painting with Hans Hofmann and art history with Meyer Schapiro and eventually taught at Rutgers with Roy Lichtenstein and George Brecht, did his part to define the times in "The Legacy of Jackson Pollock," an essay published in *ARTnews* in 1958, not long after the artist's death.[56] Kaprow offered a manifesto of active, experiential, and participatory art making that first heralded the end of the inanimate art object.

Kaprow claimed that art would have to draw on other senses beyond sight, alone, to sound, movement, odors, touch, and more: "Objects of every sort are materials for the new art: paint, chairs, food, electric and neon lights, smoke, water, old socks, a dog, movies, a thousand other things that will be discovered by the present generation of artists," he declared, suggesting that daily events and experiential happenings, too, would emerge from a new approach to art making and add to "the alchemies of the 1960s."[57]

In fact, the alchemies in Kaprow's 1958 prophecy would lead Andy Warhol in the early 1960s to represent everyday objects like the soup can and the Brillo box; Roy Lichtenstein to paint Benday dot cartoon figures; Claes Oldenburg to make larger-than-life soft sculpture of food like hamburgers or, in a nod to Duchamp, a toilet; and Carolee Schneemann to produce her 1964 landmark performance orgy, "Meat Joy," at Judson Memorial Church in Greenwich Village, where people rolled around nearly naked and intertwined, rubbing one another with raw meat and raw chicken and red paint. Kaprow's prophesy would be realized in the entire fluxus movement, mail art, and the "snapshot aesthetic" that took hold in photography.[58] What was going on in the subterranean art world of the 1960s surfaced from a new approach to the everyday and the experiential. "Be here now" was given powerful meaning in the context of making—and experiencing—art.

In September 1969, one year after Wagstaff arrived in Michigan and one month after Woodstock, "Other Ideas," an exhibition he organized, opened at the Detroit Institute of Arts. It included work by Michael Heizer, Richard Tuttle, Fred Sandback, Will Wegman, Lynda Benglis, and Walter De Maria. In the introduction to the catalog, which had a cover made of cardboard, in keeping with the *objet trouvé* motif that embraced the use of everyday materials in art making, Sam wrote:

> Since Dada, there has been a movement, one might almost call it, away from "artness" toward "thingness," away from remove to immediacy, an attempt to position reality or pieces of reality within the esthetic. Even Abstract-Expressionism made us zero in on hand-writing (Pollock, de Kooning) or the lack of it (Newman, Reinhardt). Process has become important, more important than style or idealization, part of the attempt to embrace reality firmly.[59]

In 1966, Wagstaff received a postcard from Kaprow describing plans for a three-country "happening," which would fulfill the artist's intention to connect simultaneous "happenings" in Europe, South America, and the United States through Telstar, launched in the 1960s as the first communications satellite.[60] It never came to pass, but such an ambitious idea appealed to Wagstaff—"be here now" in several places at once.

Wagstaff was undoubtedly drawn to Woodstock by the event's complex social and philosophical underpinnings and by its place in a web of conceptual ideas surrounding art and art making, which first had been given voice in Kaprow's seminal manifesto, and even further brought home to Sam in the germination of ideas about art described in his *Artforum* interview with Tony Smith. In the end, though, the fact remains that Wagstaff, a sybaritic spirit if ever there were one, made the pilgrimage to Woodstock, got stoned, listened to the music, and stared at a tree.

Simply put, everything for Sam Wagstaff came down to looking. He was capable of looking at things for the straightforward act and the pleasurable sensation of "seeing" them. He understood what it meant to contemplate the world with his eyes. Imagine looking at that tree—the shape of its trunk, the stretch of its limbs, the suspension of its leaves, green in relief against an overcast sky. A tree is sculptural form, volume weighted and balanced in space; there is poetry in its generic simplicity; there is "itness" in its existence as an object. Sam was comprehending its very essence, grokking (as a popular term derived from Robert Heinlein's novel *Stranger in a Strange Land* would have had it) its very "treeness."

Wagstaff wasn't looking *for* anything in the tree; it was the act of looking itself that provided existential import, and also visual pleasure. Perhaps it was cause and effect that Wagstaff, himself so often looked at, would end up spending his life staring at things.

AND SO THERE HE was again in the summer of 1972 staring at nothing, so to speak, into an uncertain future, nine months after resigning a prestigious, frequently satisfying job. His good friend Agnes Martin, whose work he strongly supported and had bought and with whom he maintained a lively correspondence after her move to New Mexico in 1967, wrote in one letter during this period: "I do not worry about you. I have great confidence in you." Then, in the next paragraph, she reported matter-of-factly: "I am staying unsettled and trying not to talk for three years. I want to do it very much."[61] During the Michael Heizer debacle in Detroit, she had offered him a few words of wisdom: "You shouldn't worry—robs you of life. . . . It is written that you should do whatever it is you are going to do. Your Destiny you know. You cannot do otherwise."[62]

In addition, a substantial inheritance from his stepfather had made his decision to resign from the DIA just so much easier. When Donald Newhall died in early 1969, Sam had been given a position on the board of the Newhall Land and Farming Company, an enterprise that controlled a great deal of valuable land in California between Monterey and Los Angeles. In 1937, a parcel of its land called Newhall Ranch was leased to the Barnsdall Oil Company, which discovered substantial reserves on the vast property; forty-four oil wells were erected, which proved to be extremely lucrative. Then, in the 1960s, the company transformed their vast range of orange groves north of Los Angeles into a real estate venture that would become the planned town of Valencia (where, coincidentally, the influential California College of the Arts is now located).

Very little was required of Wagstaff to fulfill the role of a board member, other than a vote here and a signature there. So, in the summer of 1971, as he contemplated his greatly diminished standing among trustees at the DIA, he abruptly resigned from the board of Newhall Land and Farming, which allowed him to gain access to the attendant stock holdings of his board seat. His shares amounted to more than $500,000.[63] He had already received close to that amount in several disbursements soon after his stepfather's death, a portion of which he used to buy Pollock's *The Deep*. This new payment would give Wagstaff the kind of financial freedom that, even with all his privilege, he had never quite felt before.

"I left Detroit because I got some money and for the first time in my life I was free not to punch the other guy's time clock," Wagstaff would say ten years later. "I practically had to get myself fired to get out because I could not really resign somehow. After all, museums had been my life for eleven years, and it was like wanting to stay in the womb. It was very tough for me to leave. But I knew I had to and I didn't want to."[64]

By the time Wagstaff returned to New York from Detroit, the political provocations of the 1960s antiwar movement and the psychedelic rock 'n' roll drug culture had attracted an influx of younger artists and musicians to his neighborhood. John Lennon, who was living in Greenwich Village with Yoko Ono in the spring of 1972, released an album, *Some Time in New York City*, which included "John Sinclair," the song Sam had been present to watch him sing only six months before in Ann Arbor.

The Hare Krishna had become by 1972 a visible—if incongruent—presence on the streets of New York, their shaved heads, long saffron-colored robes, and harmonic chanting accompanied by the expectant rattle of tambourines. Wagstaff, too, had become interested in Eastern mysticism, although he sought a less conspicuous method of practice than Krishna consciousness. He had recently taken up the teachings of the Arica Institute, an association built on the spiritual ideas of George Ivanovich Gurdjieff and P. D. Ouspensky. Gurdjieff was an early-twentieth-century Russian philosopher whose beliefs were formed during his travels through central Asia, India, and Tibet; he posited that in order to reach a higher consciousness of being we need to transcend the numbed state induced by the habits of daily life. To do this, he believed, one "has to make a new beginning." Ouspensky, an esotericist who made a lifelong study of religious beliefs, was a student of Gurdjieff's who broke from his teacher's hegemony, forming a system of practice in which higher consciousness could be achieved in continuity with the ordinary habits of daily life. At the time, the books of both philosophers were finding their way to college campuses across the country. From the Arica Institute, Wagstaff learned a series of exercises that drew on the breathing techniques of transcendental meditation and yogalike stretching. He conducted these exercises at home every morning in an attempt to clear his mind, balance his *chi*, and open himself to new possibilities.

He began to commission elaborate annual readings of his astrological chart; he went to psychics and notable palm readers. He had an analysis done of his handwriting from a specialist. He would consult the *I Ching* with friends. His interest in the occult may have fallen somewhere between sincere curiosity and idle entertainment, but he was searching for something, aware that cold, hard reason was going to take him only so far.

So he walked around in the oppressive New York heat with an imperative to arrive at some conclusion about his life. He looked at a lot of art, of course, and the photorealist paintings that hung on art gallery walls in Manhattan that summer of 1972 unsettled him. Paintings that attempt the same optical precision of a photograph did not seem to him a step in the right direction. He didn't even like photography. While Andy Warhol and Robert Rauschenberg used the photographic image in service of new methods of representation on canvas, Wagstaff had long believed in a hierarchy that privileged the fine art of painting over the applied art of photography. Photorealism seemed to him like nothing more than a cheap joke.

All around him, too, were harbingers of change. In fact, David Bowie's hit single, "Changes," played endlessly on the radio in candy stores and diners. While glam rock was emerging as something new and strange, it was recognizable to Wagstaff as an interesting confluence of Andy Warhol superstar theatrics, the nascent androgyny surfacing from the gay world, and old-fashioned rock 'n' roll. Not coincidentally the flip side of "Changes" was Bowie's "Andy Warhol."

Contemporary art, rock 'n' roll, and a more androgynous sexuality all converged at Max's Kansas City on Park Avenue South, just north of Union Square. Warhol and members of his entourage from the Factory often spent their evenings in the rarefied back room. The nightclub had "nothing fancy" about it, in the words of the cultural historian Steven Watson, but "the décor immediately announced that Max's was a place for art and artists. On view were a John Chamberlain smashed-car sculpture, a Donald Judd box, an Andy Warhol soup can, a Dan Flavin light sculpture, and a plate glass window sand-blasted by Michael Heizer."[65]

Upstair's at Max's, the serious music scene provided a small venue for rock stars, but it was equally a launching site for new groups. On any given night one could hear the Velvet Underground, David Bowie, Iggy Pop, or Alice Cooper. On John Lennon's album *Some Time in New York City*, in a song titled "New York City," Lennon sings about Max's Kansas City, "got down the nitty gritty," and about playing there with the Plastic Ono Elephant's Memory Band. In the summer of 1972, a young unknown named Bruce Springsteen performed there for the first time.

Wagstaff would on occasion go to Max's and loll in the back room with Warhol, Ray Johnson, Robert Smithson, or any of the other artists he knew well. It was as much a place of comfort and conviviality for him as the Knickerbocker Club had been for his father. In this environment his in-the-know friends kept raving about a campy little act at the Continental Baths, a gay bathhouse on the Upper West Side where men would walk the hallways wearing nothing but white towels wrapped around their waists and cruise for sex; intermittently, they would gather around a piano to watch a young, campy, foul-mouthed singer named Bette Midler performing her cabaret covers to 1940s songs like "In the

Mood." Hardly wedded, though, to a nostalgic repertoire, she released that year a sultry ballad, "Do you Want to Dance?" a cover of a tune first popularized by the Beach Boys. Midler's version was slow and seductive, tropical, erotically charged—a more specific harbinger of the meeting soon to take place between Sam and Robert Mapplethorpe, a young man in his midst, which would provide a clear direction.

J A R D I N   D E S   N A B I

What a wonderful phenomenon it is, carefully considered,
when the human eye, that jewel of organic structures, con-
centrates its moist brilliance on another human creature!"

—THOMAS MANN[1]

RAINFALL IN NEW YORK WAS AT A RECORD HIGH IN JUNE
1972. Tropical storm Agnes had caused serious damage along
the eastern coastline before it hit Manhattan on June 22, churning up
the air, flooding the streets, and leaving the atmosphere charged in its
aftermath. That weekend, Wagstaff sought refuge from the city at an
isolated cottage on Fire Island owned by Sam Green, an art world
acquaintance. It was a little bungalow in the small hamlet of Oakleyville, a scruffy, although quietly fashionable, warren of ramshackle
beach cottages. When the sun is out, the reflections on the ocean to the
south and the glassy waters of the Great South Bay to the north create a
unique and astonishing kind of light.

Cars are not allowed throughout the residential communities of this
slender barrier island. The only way to get to Oakleyville, a particularly
isolated enclave, is by private ferry from Long Island to the more exclusive, if more conventional, neighboring town of Point of Woods, then

known to be a "restricted community," a not so subtle euphemism for the bigotry that through the decades denied Jews (and Catholics, too) the right to rent or own property. Oakleyville, by contrast, was a beach community with footpaths snaking from one house to another through a dense, leafy scrub of beach forest. Because it attracted art world denizens from downtown Manhattan, among them the photographer Peter Hujar and the artist Paul Thek, it had the kind of bohemian profile that appealed to Wagstaff, offering greater distance and freedom from the starchy prejudices and straitened minds of old money.

The two Sams had known each other well through the museum world for a decade, and Green, who was often traveling that summer, let Wagstaff stay at his Fire Island house when he was away. Privately, though, Green was said to be not entirely fond of Wagstaff. At least one source of Green's antipathy can be traced to the 1966 Tony Smith show Wagstaff had organized at the Wadsworth Atheneum. Green was then a curator at the Institute of Contemporary Art in Philadelphia, where, in an unusual collaboration, he mounted a concurrent Tony Smith show. Both museums shared the cost of the exhibition catalog, but, according to Green, Wagstaff hoarded the bulk of the credit.

"Sam had already stabbed me in the back by claiming that he had discovered Tony Smith. I discovered Tony Smith at the ICA," Green asserted only three years before he died.[2] (However, in 1964, two years before the concurrent shows, Wagstaff included Smith's work in his "Black, White, and Gray" exhibit at the Wadsworth Atheneum.) When Green received an early copy of the Tony Smith exhibition catalog, printed by the Wadsworth Atheneum, his name was nowhere to be found. He maintained that he had to persuade the Wadsworth Atheneum to reprint the catalog. Regardless, the catalog is titled *Tony Smith: Two Exhibitions of Sculpture*, and the preface includes signatures from the directors of both institutions.[3] The *Time* cover story about Tony Smith, which came out a year later, cited the simultaneous one-man shows at both institutions as the reason for Smith's rapid rise from "a cool minimalist to the hottest thing in sculpture."[4]

Green's resentment of Wagstaff seems to have only intensified during the latter's Detroit years. Green, who strove unabashedly to be included in the upper tiers of New York society, was irritated by Wagstaff's class-based, weary disregard for that "fancy pants" world. After once visiting Wagstaff in Detroit, Green was appalled at his indifference to social conventions, even as his job required him to move in the deeply proper orbit of the DIA trustees. "If I were a museum trustee, I would have thrown Sam out," Green later said. "His life in Detroit was so stylized. Not in terms of grandeur. On the contrary, he couldn't even give a fund-raising cocktail party in that apartment."[5] Green scoffed at the absence of furniture, dismissed the art leaning against the walls as too self-consciously chic, and concluded that such a posture of hipness "didn't sit well with what was expected in Grosse Pointe."

Green himself had constructed his entire identity around what he thought might be expected in places such as Grosse Pointe, or, say, Greenwich, Connecticut. His elocution was overdetermined, his language too grand, his associations with famous people designed to impress. Of course, he was hardly an arbiter of the kind of restraint and circumspection that trustees of great museums preferred. When he died in 2011, Guy Trebay described him in *The New York Times* with the kind of wit that would have summoned a chuckle from Wagstaff:

> Over five decades, [Sam] Green played pivotal roles, first as a curator, then as an art dealer, a municipal adviser and, finally, as a society gadabout and preservationist whose scope took in the more remote corners of the planet. . . . At the very least, Sam Green was a fabulist, an unabashed poseur blessed with good looks, a natural flair for storytelling, a knack for self-promotion and a markedly elastic relationship to the truth.[6]

One example of his "fabulist" tendencies can be found in his claim to a pedigreed ancestry. Born Samuel McGee Green in Boston in 1940, he would change his name to Samuel Adams Green, claiming to be a descendent of two American presidents. Still, his friendships were the stuff of legend. Andy Warhol was a close chum, as were Greta Garbo (who was rumored to meander along the sandy footpaths in Oakleyville during her visits to Green's cottage), Candy Darling, Cecil Beaton, and

Yoko Ono. Peter Allen, the singer and first husband of Liza Minnelli, was a regular guest at his beach house, and John Lennon was said to use it occasionally as a hideaway. "There are endless, endless social climbers in New York," John Richardson observed, "but Sam Green seemed to me unlike any other."[7]

Sam Wagstaff, the guest, either unaware of his host's true feelings about him or, more likely, unfazed by them, spent blithe and languorous stretches of time that summer at Sam Green's beach cottage, weekends that often spilled seamlessly into the following week. There were no grocery stores, restaurants, or bars—one had to walk to Point of Woods—and Wagstaff could putter about barefoot and in a bathing suit all day long. Sometimes he would lie nude on the beach, taking in the soothing ease of the ocean breeze and the rhythmic lulling of the waves. At sunset, gold reflections undulated on the bay and as the light faded, the birds began their nightly serenade. The evenings were dreamlike on the deck with candlelight, cocktails, and marijuana: *dolce far niente.*

Wagstaff had bought a camera that summer, and he was experimenting with it on Fire Island. Another friend of Green, Richard Turley, who was about to start a job in a law firm on Wall Street and who later represented artists such as Nan Goldin and Cookie Mueller, was also a frequent visitor to the cottage in Oakleyville. Turley described one weekday when his visit happened to coincide with Wagstaff's. The two men spent the afternoon on the beach, and Turley remembered Wagstaff's making a fuss about how difficult it was to get the right camera settings in the sun. Every once in a while, Turley got up, ran into the water, and rolled with the waves. They were the only two people on the beach and seemed to languish luxuriously in the midweek summer isolation.

"At one point I was coming out of the water and Sam was sitting there on the blanket pointing his camera at me," Turley said. "As I got closer, he lowered the camera and said that I looked so good in my bathing suit, so handsome and attractive, would I mind taking it off so he could take some pictures of me, naked." Turley had always been quite modest about his body, but the way Sam asked him in such a matter-of-fact manner made it seem almost ridiculous not to simply oblige him. So he shed his suit and stood with the ocean behind him as Sam took some pictures. "And that was that."[8]

Turley was heterosexual, but sexual currents were stirring in Sam nonetheless. Whether he was attracted to Turley specifically or by proximity, at that moment the more manipulative aspects of Sam's character were in evidence. For years to come, whenever Turley ran into Sam, he asked about those pictures. Sam was ever so apologetic, claiming that he had not yet had them developed. Then one day a mutual friend told Turley that he was at Wagstaff's apartment for a small gathering and some nude photos of Turley were passed around. "It still annoys me when I think about it," Turley said.[9]

Upon Sam Green's return from Europe, he invited Turley out for the weekend, indicating that Wagstaff would be making a ceremonial visit in which he planned to offer compensation for the extended use of the house over the season. Everyone was curious about how he was going to repay Green.

"We were having cocktails when Sam Wagstaff arrived," Turley said. Wagstaff carried a small shopping bag and presented it to his host, thanking Green for his kindness with a bottle of Château d'Yquem, Wagstaff's favorite wine, and a hand-wrapped package of foie gras, with truffles, from William Poll, a Manhattan gourmet shop. Green opened the wine and put out the foie gras for his guests. According to Turley, Sam Wagstaff then sat down and proceeded to devour the entire plate of foie gras and drink most of the wine himself, oblivious of the exchange of appalled glances around him. In Turley's view, the incident spoke to some essential selfishness in Sam: "Sam Wagstaff was aware of the finer things in life but never extended the generosity to anyone— anyone other than Robert Mapplethorpe."[10]

THERE ARE TWO COMPETING stories about who would introduce Sam Wagstaff to Robert Mapplethorpe during that bygone summer of 1972. Sam Green claimed, as he was wont to take credit for so many things, to have been the official matchmaker—out of spite. "Robert was the most ambitious and insistent person that I knew," Green said. "He continuously harangued me to see his mediocre art. After my first visit to Robert's studio, he made it clear he was looking for a male patron. I had an ax to grind with Sam Wagstaff, so I had intended to put them together in Oakleyville." Still, years later, Green claimed to have been pleased that the introduction was successful. "Sam and Robert were one of the great unions of the twentieth century," he said. "It worked for everyone. Robert was a master manipulator and he would do anything. When I introduced the two of them, I knew how much they needed each other."[11]

But the actual introduction came from another visitor to Sam Green's beach cottage. David Croland, a tall, slender young artist and model with fine features and dark hair, was a fixture of Andy Warhol's Factory (by this point the Factory had come to refer to more than the physical studio, at times encompassing the people circulating around Andy, including his "superstars"). Croland had modeled for David Bailey and others in London in the late 1960s before being discovered by the Warhol superstar International Velvet (Susan Bottomly) while shopping at Fiorucci in New York. Croland, like so many gay men who came out gradually in that era, was still in his "bisexual phase" and was romantically involved with Bottomly for a while.

Croland had met Robert Mapplethorpe in 1970 through his friend Tinkerbelle, a contributor to *Interview*, who knew Mapplethorpe from the back room at Max's Kansas City. One day Tinkerbelle brought Croland to Mapplethorpe's loft on West 23rd St, several doors away from the Chelsea Hotel. Robert was living there with Patti Smith, his girlfriend while in art school, whose fame as a poet and rock star would come later. Although Mapplethorpe and Smith had been together for several years, by that point they were more like psychic twins than lovers. Croland and Mapplethorpe soon became lovers, keeping their romance a secret from Smith for almost six months.[12]

In *Just Kids*, Smith's memoir about her relationship with Mapplethorpe and their coming-of-age as artists, she evocatively describes a gradual shift in the nature of their bond during the period when they lived near Pratt Institute in Brooklyn, contrasting her need for artistic exploration in the world outside of herself with Robert's mode of discovery, which was turning increasingly inward. That was when Robert had begun his first homosexual romance, with a young man named Terry, whom he met through a fellow student at Pratt. Robert and Terry were open about their sexuality with Patti, but it was not an easy emotional transition for her. "He had never given me any indication in his behavior that I would have interpreted as homosexual," Smith writes.[13]

It was Croland who would finally guide Mapplethorpe to the stratum of the art world he had been eager to penetrate. Croland introduced him to Henry Geldzahler, the curator of twentieth-century art at the Metropolitan Museum and a close friend and supporter of Warhol; to John McKendry, curator of prints and photographs at the Metropolitan; and, of course, to Warhol himself, whom Mapplethorpe worshipped from afar and whose cultural status had already eclipsed any other artist of that time. By 1972, Croland and Mapplethorpe had ceased being lovers, but they would remain close friends.

On Sam Green's deck in Oakleyville one weekend afternoon that summer of 1972, Wagstaff took a flirtatious interest in Croland. The young man might have fit his type in certain ways—young, gaunt, and artistic—but Croland had Semitic features, and he was far too socially charming, animated, and garrulous to conform to the template of Wagstaff's basic attractions. Still, Sam asked to see Croland again in the city and made a date to look at his drawings the following week.

Croland already knew about Wagstaff by reputation and, of course, about his long friendship with Andy. He was happy to have such an aficionado coming over to see his work. During Sam's visit to his small apartment on Irving Place in Manhattan, Croland showed him some drawings he had been making as textile designs for Halston and other fashion designers. "These are like paintings," Wagstaff said, and he ended up buying ten of them. "I'm going to keep some and give some to my sister." Then, as Wagstaff was leaving the apartment, he spotted on the drafting table a small, framed photo-booth portrait of a young man in a sailor cap. He leaned over to look at the portrait more carefully. "Who is that?" Sam asked, an unmistakable lilt in his voice. "I want to meet him."[14]

Robert Mapplethorpe was precisely Wagstaff's physical type—lanky, with taut features, a light complexion, and an unpolished physicality. Ellen Phelan made the astute observation that if Gordon Newton, Richard Tuttle, Michael Heizer, and Robert Mapplethorpe were all assembled in the same room, one would think they were related.[15] All had the same chiseled features and coloring; all of them were young artists when Sam first met them; each one was original, inventive, and fierce in the exploration of his own ideas.

Seeing Wagstaff's response to the portrait, Croland knew he was about to facilitate yet another advantageous introduction for Robert Mapplethorpe. He duly wrote down Robert's number for Sam. Then, overriding his resentment at Robert for exploiting his connections yet again, Croland called his friend to announce that, this time, a patron unlike any other was about to give him a call.

Aside from an attraction that so far existed in miniature and only on photographic paper, Wagstaff had few other clues about Mapplethorpe. There was his association with David Croland and the proximity it gave him to Warhol's Factory. Then each phrase David Croland used to describe Mapplethorpe's work could be repeated over and over: he had described the assemblages as "pornographic constructions with Catholic iconography" that included "naked self-portraits draped with studs and jewelry."[16] In the context of the important artwork of the period, whether minimal geometric abstraction, pop iconographic imagery, or the conceptual possibilities in earth art, what Croland told Sam about Mapplethorpe's subject matter resonated as something distinctly new.

The juxtaposition of sex and Catholicism—the height of Western religious tradition, which stood in stark contrast to Wagstaff's embrace of Eastern mysticism—was enough to pique his curatorial interest. Sam's imagination roamed more broadly as he thought about the stranger in the sailor cap so that, by the time he picked up the phone to call Robert, he was already a little bit in love with the idea of the louche young man with a name that, like his own, might have sprung from the underworld of Charles Dickens: David Copperfield, Luke Honeythunder, Paul Sweedlepipe, Robert Mapplethorpe. His mood was playful and his voice flirtatious when Robert answered the phone. "Is this the shy pornographer?" Sam asked.[17]

Mapplethorpe may have been hungry for attention, money, and artistic acknowledgment, and he was nervously eager for a patron who could give him the kind of financial support that would free him to make his art. But, when he heard the clever question delivered in that baritone drawl, he laughed a genuine, happy laugh.

THE TWENTY-FIVE-YEAR-OLD ROBERT MAPPLETHORPE was stylish, appealingly soft-spoken, but decidedly still rough around the edges. His obvious talent came with an underlying arrogance—not unfamiliar to Wagstaff—that often propels such artistic ambition. Mapplethorpe's beginnings were uninspired: he was the third of six children in a middle-class Catholic family; his adoring mother suffered from manic depression and his withholding father was missing the parental gene for encouragement. Nevertheless, he had made it to art school, where he developed an imperturbable confidence and an unyielding belief in himself as an artist. "I came from suburban America," Robert said of his hometown, Floral Park, New York. "It was a safe environment. And it was a good place to come from in that it was a good place to leave."[18]

Mapplethorpe enrolled at Pratt Institute, one of the preeminent art schools in the country, in 1963. The social upheavals that would come to define the 1960s were barely rumblings at that point, but evident at Pratt and other urban art schools was a visible bohemian repudiation of bourgeois conformity. While the environment there encouraged serious artistic exploration and the course of instruction centered on the high-minded fine art disciplines, the faculty promoted an almost religious belief in painting. Despite the school's reputation, it failed to provide the rigorous instruction one might have expected. Pratt students, meanwhile, cultivated theatrically personal styles, often aided by recreational drug use and copious sexual experimentation. When Robert arrived, the atmosphere on the Brooklyn campus had not quite yet assumed the quality of a mannered, antic, if not hedonistic, drama; during his years there, it would acquire the sensibility of the Fellini film *Satyricon* as students went to class in outlandish costumes. Increasingly, the anarchic posture of rock 'n' roll and the influence of hippie drug culture became evident as the students grew long hair and wore tie-dyed T-shirts and paint-splattered jeans. At the same time, noncon-formity was prized as much as creativity, and students could be seen perched by themselves in the corner of the cafeteria or on the front steps of the main building drawing with their Rapidograph pens on large Strathmore pads or blocking out ideas in their journals.

Mapplethorpe, however, entered Pratt intending to fulfill his father's expectation that he learn a trade that could earn him a living—either in Pratt's more conservative engineering program, with graphic arts training in the design school, or through courses in the school of library sciences. As a member of Pershing Rifles, an elite military fra-ternity related to the Reserve Officer's Training Corps, the teenaged Mapplethorpe cut a surprisingly conventional profile in his first years in art school.

Within two years, though, as the school was becoming more radi-calized in the wake of the Vietnam war, Mapplethorpe gravitated to the fine art program. He had been making elaborate drawings from an early age, and art is what he wanted to study. Among Robert's school-mates was Robert Wilson, the artist who went on to create with Philip Glass the operatic masterpiece *Einstein on the Beach*. Sylvia Plachy, Jan Groover, Judy Linn, and Betsey Johnson, each of whom would become prominent in the world of photography or fashion, were also studying at Pratt.

It was here that Mapplethorpe met Patti Smith. In the summer of 1967 she had found her way to Brooklyn not as a student but because she was staying with a friend of a friend after moving to New York from her working-class hometown in southern New Jersey. Smith's first encoun-ter with Mapplethorpe near the Pratt campus was brief. But, a short time later, purely by coincidence, Robert was standing in Tompkins Square, a junkie-haunted, garbage-strewn park in the East Village where hip-sters often congregated in what felt like a perpetual streetwise "happen-ing." The atmosphere was always at once festive and ominous, street musicians playing their guitars on benches, students looking to buy marijuana, and innocent people getting robbed at knifepoint. Smith, barely twenty years old, sitting early one evening with a first date in the park, had become increasingly uncomfortable in the older man's company. She recognized Mapplethorpe not only from that chance meeting at Pratt, but also from a more recent encounter, when he had come into Scribner's, where she worked, and they had briefly chatted. Now, as something of a damsel in distress, she ran up to him to ask if he would rescue her by pretending to be her boyfriend. He agreed and they ran away from her date, to the other side of the park. Indeed, they became a couple that night.[19]

It was an auspicious—and in the end historic—meeting. That night, Robert Mapplethorpe and Patti Smith discovered in each other something profoundly sympathetic. Soon after, they moved in together, sharing a small apartment on Hall Street in Clinton Hill along the southern border of the Pratt campus. Smith would come home from her job as a clerk at Scribner's, the renowned bookstore on Fifth Avenue in Manhattan, and read or draw while Robert fulfilled his assignments for school, developing a style of collage and assemblage out of his own drawings, found photographs, cutouts of artwork from the ancient world, and other found objects. During that period Robert's style of dress reflected his art school evolution and growing self-consciousness, from sheepskin vests to the more mannered, and fateful, sailor outfit. Smith described it in her memoir: "In his sailor dress and cap, he resonated a Cocteau drawing or the world of Genet's Robert Querelle."[20]

Mapplethorpe short-circuited his graduation from Pratt in 1969 by skipping one final course. He and Smith crossed the river into Manhattan and, with a combination of characteristic luck and ambition, found their way to the Chelsea Hotel. The hotel had already been immortalized for them in the 1966 Warhol film *Chelsea Girls*. They had been told that Stanley Bard, the hotel's proprietor, would accept a barter of artwork for a room in lieu of cash, and, indeed, the lobby was decorated with the residents' drawings and paintings, large and small, hanging on the walls in ersatz salon style. Still, when Robert and Patti approached

Bard, it was Patti's employment at Scribner's that persuaded him to give them one of the smallest rooms in the hotel. The bathroom was in the hallway. He charged them fifty-five dollars per week. Patti's weekly salary was sixty-four dollars, so they could barely afford it.[21] Robert continued to make artwork and beaded jewelry, but it failed to bring in additional income.

That year, the breakthrough movie *Midnight Cowboy* was released. The story of a petty thief and a male prostitute scraping by in Times Square, it was shocking in some quarters, but the movie instantly became a classic and was said to give Mapplethorpe the idea of turning sexual favors on 42nd Street to supplement their meager income. It started out as something of a romanticized adventure, but the novelty gave way to the reality of having sex with people who didn't interest him, and he gave it up.

At the Chelsea Hotel, Robert and Patti as a matter of course came in contact with Bob Dylan, Allen Ginsberg, Gregory Corso, Charles Bukowski, William Burroughs, Janis Joplin, Milos Forman, and Virgil Thomson—whose extended stays or residences there provided a respite from the demands of the public. Most of the hotel patrons were eccentric; they also tended to know about all sorts of interesting or arcane events in the city, sometimes dragging Mapplethorpe and Smith out with them at night on cultural odysseys, exposing them to poetry readings at St. Mark's Church in-the-Bowery or experimental theater performances. One night it might be a concert at the Fillmore East and a backstage visit with the musicians, another a wild, avant-garde production of *Orlando Furioso*, by Teatro Libero di Roma, in an enormous tent in Bryant Park, where life-sized wooden puppets on tin horses performed as the audience roamed through a labyrinth where many scenes took place simultaneously.

Soon after settling in at the Chelsea Hotel, Mapplethorpe and Smith found their way to Max's Kansas City. They may, as young artists, have been poor but it must have felt as if they had arrived in the right place. Just as Montparnasse had replaced Montmartre as the center of the art world in Paris in the 1920s, the art world axis in New York had recently shifted its psychic temperament. In the 1950s, Cedar Tavern on Univer-

sity Place was known for the masculine bravado and philosophical pos-
turing of its patrons—Jackson Pollock, Willem de Kooning, Mark
Rothko and Franz Kline—who would argue through many a drunken
evening. A little farther south, the San Remo on Bleecker Street attracted
an equally intellectually charged but less rowdy group of writers like
Jack Kerouac, Allen Ginsberg, Frank O'Hara, and Delmore Schwartz.
Eventually both gave way to the theatrical androgyny and urban-
cowboy swagger of the Chelsea Hotel and Max's Kansas City.

The shift from Cedar Tavern to Max's might well represent the evolution in art itself from one decade to another. Abstract expressionism
was a Buddhist-influenced process of expressing interior reality at the
actual moment of experience, and, at night, the conversation at Cedar
Tavern was an ongoing existential argument. Pop art was focused on
the iconography of popular culture, so, of course, nightlife at Max's was
a heightened display, in homeage to but equally in mockery of the full
range of Hollywood tropes.

In Max's more outré back room, Robert and Patti inched their way
into the ethos of Andy Warhol and his superstars, whose nightly soirees
proved to be the Algonquin Round Table of the 1970s. Mapplethorpe
on occasion would wear his sailor suit, while Smith was not compelled
to dress up at all, preferring the uniform of comfort and anonymity—
T-shirts and jeans. "They were this couple and they would sit away
from everybody, as if they were shy," said Gerard Malanga, the Factory
mainstay who is also a poet.[22]

Among the regulars at Max's was Robert Smithson, at the time gaining prominence as one of the land artists with his just completed *Spiral
Jetty* in Great Salt Lake, Utah. Smithson would dominate the conversation at one table, often inviting another artist like Richard Serra or John
Chamberlain to join him, and everyone would talk about his work.
Mapplethorpe met Brice Marden and Robert Indiana there. During that
period Marden went to Robert's studio to look at his work—the assemblages, collages, and framed pieces—and he said he would mention
them to Klaus Kertess, his own dealer, at Bykert Gallery.[23] It was in just
this way that artists at the time would slowly become known.

Between Max's Kansas City and the Chelsea Hotel, Mapplethorpe and Smith found themselves at the epicenter of cultural ferment in the art world, two young impoverished artists in waiting, cutting their teeth on what was becoming the very essence of urban cool. Perhaps in homage to Warhol's *Chelsea Girls*, Robert agreed to star in a movie filmed at the hotel by fellow resident Sandy Daley. The film bore a self-explanatory title, *Robert Having His Nipple Pierced*, and was narrated by Patti Smith.[24]

Mapplethorpe's sexuality had already begun to evolve in those years. He was getting to know Candy Darling, Holly Woodlawn, and Joe Dallesandro—those inhabitants of the back room at Max's whose gender-obfuscating antics were as much a kind of nose-thumbing challenge to convention as a sincere display of personal desire. Their life-as-art gestures turned out to be of revolutionary significance, paving the way—at least in the media—for a social movement that eventually became known to the mainstream as the gay, lesbian, bisexual, and, much later, transgender community. Lou Reed wrote "A Walk on the Wild Side," about this group in the back room at Max's, and the song's seductive and mysterious tone heralded the persona Mapplethorpe was cultivating there, too.

And so, by the time Robert answered the phone and laughed at Wagstaff's wry opening gambit, he had already received a sterling introduction to the art world demimonde. His ambition had already been fueled and encouraged by his new connections. At the uptown dinner table of John McKendry and his socially prominent wife, Maxime de la Falaise, who had been a fashion model in London in the 1950s, Robert was introduced to an assortment of titled Brits, chic Parisians, and well-placed New Yorkers for whom this attractive, poetic waif from the downtown netherworld was a precious novelty.

Steven Aronson said that Mapplethorpe "was the one you wanted to talk to" at the McKendrys' table. "He was marvelous looking, absolutely. He had the besmirched beauty of an urchin, and of course that wonderful whiny voice. He was positively languid, but then he began to talk about his work, and he became adrenalized—really, it was the only time he ever came alive. He made you feel as if a visit to his loft was an urgent matter. So you went, and you weren't sorry."[25]

Robert had a mischievous sensuality that the art-rock fashions of that period seemed to intensify. With his Mick Jagger–like androgyny, he made himself an object of desire. Still, he had grown weary of the expectations of super-daddy love; the older men whose favors he accepted were not generally attractive to him. Often, as is typical of young artists, Mapplethorpe had to balance a polite regard for his patrons even as he struggled to avoid their affections. It was tantamount to singing in an extended falsetto, and it strained his taste as much as his stamina. "Robert was highly sought after by both men and women," Smith wrote in *Just Kids*.[26] A string of secret admirers would come to the Chelsea Hotel, soliciting her permission to pursue Mapplethorpe romantically and even cheekily asking her advice about how to secure his affections. "Love his work," Smith would tell them, but they ignored her. Sam Wagstaff, she wrote, was "the only one who truly grasped this."[27]

Losing no time, Wagstaff visited Mapplethorpe's studio within a day of making the call. The second-floor loft had northern light from the floor-to-ceiling windows that faced a big YMCA sign across the street. There was no running water, but even so Robert and Patti were living there now; they snuck back into the Chelsea Hotel several doors away as often as they could to shower. The loft was divided in half by several black sheets that hung from a clothesline, separating Robert's workspace from Patti's. The rent was one hundred dollars a month, still beyond their means.

The afternoon visit set off a profound upheaval for Wagstaff. A leather motorcycle jacket was hanging on a coatrack near the entrance. Below the jacket hung a pair of jeans. Together they composed a kind of urban scarecrow. Sam could hear muffled murmurs, as if people were having sex somewhere else in the loft. Robert smiled, reached into the pocket of the jacket, and pulled out a tape recorder. The murmurs had been recorded. Sam's eyes then dropped to what appeared to be an unusual bulge at the crotch in the jeans hanging on the coatrack. Again Robert smiled. "It's a baguette," he said.[28]

Wagstaff had encountered impromptu installations by artists in the past, as in the live, walking Dada piece he encountered at Ray Johnson's apartment in 1959, when Dorothy Podber emerged from the closet with a tea cup and glove. This coatrack tableau was just the kind of thing that Sam would find appealing, an erotic provocation with a diabolical charge. It was sexy, arresting, and thoughtfully conceived, even as there was a strong whiff of adolescent hijinks about it that led Sam's attention beyond the aesthetic. Sam had his own juvenile streak, which would now and again push through the patina of maturity and accomplishment. Observing the way Sam shed some of his controlled, patrician bearing while he was in Detroit, Susanne Hilberry, his assistant at the DIA, had concluded that the recreational drug use and the sexual freedom of the late 1960s "gave Sam permission to explore the adolescence he never had at Hotchkiss."[29]

Mapplethorpe suggestively showed Wagstaff a naked self-portrait, an assemblage with three small Polaroid images stacked as a vertical triptych to create a single figure. Over the Polaroids lay wire mesh he had cut out of a brown-paper potato sack and spray-painted purple. It gave the impression that the male nude was standing in a doorway, behind the window of a confessional, or, even, locked behind bars. The viewer had to peer through the mesh to see Robert's entire naked body. The spectacle of his bare flesh, his nipples and navel, his pubic hair and penis, and the defiant but seductive expression on his face amounted to further provocation for Wagstaff. Mapplethorpe could not have been more overtly seductive; by the end of the visit he had won the patron's approval.

Wagstaff had turned out to be nothing like the other older men seeking Robert's affections. His informed interest in Robert's work was as much a seduction for Robert as the variety of sexual decoys had been for Sam. Klaus Kertess, who was also an art critic, knew Sam Wagstaff quite well, not only from Sam's visits to his uptown gallery but also as his longtime neighbor in the building at 54 Bond Street. He described Sam's appeal to any artist: "His eyes would light up when he'd describe something he'd seen. He just took joy in seeing work and being around it," Kertess said. "That openness, I think, is what drew so many artists to Sam."[30]

When Wagstaff became the earliest champion of minimal art, it was because he saw something completely new. The same was true when conceptual artists began employing everyday materials, and he saw it as a way into the future for art. He got excited by conceptualism's off-shoots, like fluxus-based mail art, in which he became a participant, receiving Dadaesque letters and odd correspondences through the mail from Ray Johnson and George Brecht. Next, he embraced the highly conceptual and limitless possibilities of earth art. Now, once again, he was confronted with a young artist whose collages and assemblages were both formally rigorous and overtly homoerotic. While the form referred to pop art, Mapplethorpe was doing something Sam had never seen before—addressing his own homosexuality with matter-of-fact ease. It was time for a movement that went beyond painting, and in the ineffable allure of Robert's experimentation with assemblage and homo-erotic imagery, Sam saw a new direction.

Robert sensed he was in a situation fundamentally different from his usual interactions with wealthy men. First of all, Sam's striking appearance drew repeated comment from virtually everyone who knew him, to the point that it can become tiresome. "You didn't have to search very far to think why somebody might want to go out with him," Edmund White, the distinguished novelist, literary essayist, and biographer of Jean Genet, said. "Then he was also very rich, and then he was also very powerful in the art world. Those three things made him quite a catch."[31]

For Wagstaff, meanwhile, despite all the natural confidence he brought to the moment, the Detroit debacle continued to lurk and he felt something less than his best self; he was uncertain of his future and still somewhat attached to Gordon Newton. According to Patricia Morrisroe, Mapplethorpe's biographer, it was no secret among Sam's friends and acquaintances at the time that he was "looking for someone to spoil."[32]

Robert was natural and at ease in his body, ever so polite and gentle in his solicitation of Sam's opinions and observations. "If you read books of etiquette in the eighteenth century in France," said Ed White, "what they all talk about is the importance of naturalness. They say only the greatest aristocrats can respond in a totally quiet, easygoing, natural way. That's the one quality they all prize, and I think Robert had that."[33]

Sam and Robert continued on to dinner that night. Falling in love over dinner is not an experience to be missed—even if dinner consisted of scrambled eggs, a Coke, and a Kool cigarette, Mapplethorpe's standard fare throughout his twenties. Every sip of your drink and every bite of your meal merely restrains the urgency of desire. Robert's sweetness of manner clashed powerfully with the sharp-edged menace of his sexual candor; he flaunted his carnality in a way that was perhaps too flamboyant even for Sam, but tempered it with a boyishness and physical grace. Sam had a saying "All artists are aristocrats," but Robert appeared to be something of a sorcerer, too.[34]

Sam, who was never shy about staring at anyone—and was often enough unconscious of the discomfort his penetrating scrutiny induced—stared at Robert now and then throughout the evening. The presence of Robert's sexual mystique emerging from the freshness of his youth conjured the same feeling of giddy sacrilege that defined his artwork. To Sam, a curator and art historian, Robert's presence resonated in line with a long tradition of homoeroticism in arts and letters, that of a sexual and artistic partnership between an established older man and a younger one. Like Sergei Diaghilev and Vaclav Nijinsky in the ballet world and the writers Paul Verlaine and Arthur Rimbaud, the older man sees a kind of talent or genius in his young inamorato. He nurtures it, even if his judgment is clouded by his love (as Ed White has observed, Oscar Wilde thought his young lover Sir Alfred Douglas "was very talented"). Even while Sam and Robert were growing to know each other, there was a contemporary West Coast version of this sort of relationship: the British writer Christopher Isherwood and his Los Angeles–born lover, the painter Don Bachardy, who was three decades his junior. After all, White explained, "Robert was charming in a quiet way. He was an interesting person without being predictably intellectual or pedantic or anything like that. He was an original. Plus he was sexy."[35]

At dinner that night the two men discovered an extraordinary coincidence, an omen that their meeting was not only inevitable, but, to them, ordained in the mystical realm of astrology: they shared the same Scorpio birthday, November 4. By the end of that first meal, Sam and Robert both felt so enlivened that they went around the corner to David Croland's apartment, and invited their mutual friend out for a drink. "Robert was seriously smitten," Croland said, recalling his impression of the two of them that night. "You could see it. It was really very sweet. They were very happy. You could tell that they were together. I noticed that instantly."[36]

When Wagstaff brought Mapplethorpe home that night, his residence was not what the young artist would have expected. There was no sign of wealth in this long, mostly empty loft with only a few scattered pieces of secondhand furniture. Everywhere was a pack rat's abundance of paper bags or boxes filled with prints and postcards. The black Tony Smith sculpture *Throne* dominated the space. Toward the back of the loft was Sam's unmade bed, which was actually just a mattress on the floor—no better than Robert's own, and laid out in a tableau much like his own postadolescent disarray. Still, it had the "privileged bohemian" appearance of studied destitution as much as cavalier disregard. It had been only recently, when Wagstaff had reached his late forties, that his stepfather's inheritance gave him financial freedom, even though the penniless prince, who had first moved in almost a decade before while living on his meager curator's salary at the Wadsworth Atheneum, had been a prince.

Being perceptive, as he was, Sam was likely attuned to the appraisal going on in Robert's own mind. For all of Robert's insouciant charm at dinner, the absence of visible wealth in Sam's loft and his undergraduate-like living conditions would no doubt have soured the struggling young artist's mood. In order to rescue the moment, it is possible to imagine that, with characteristic sangfroid, Sam allowed a knowing, mischievous smile, assuring his guest that the state of the loft was by no means representative of his circumstances. It would be just like Sam to then ask Robert if he would like to see a small painting. He would find a package among the pile of papers on the table with a letter on top, indicating it had been shipped from the Art Institute of Chicago, where it had been on loan. He would unwrap the small oil painting on cardboard, small enough to hold in his hands, and they would look at it under a bare lightbulb. Sam would offer the name, *Le Jardin Nabi*,[37] mentioning that it was a postimpressionist work from one of the Nabi artists, a rebellious group who followed the example of Gauguin at the end of the nineteenth century in France. That might have piqued Robert's interest enough to ask who painted it. "Oh, Vuillard," Sam would say casually, prompting Robert to ask whether Sam owned it. It would be just like Wagstaff, ever the understated gentleman, to merely nod, offering just the flicker of reassurance, as well as the dash of glamour, that the young artist needed to understand that things were not exactly as they seemed.

THE IMMEDIATE ACKNOWLEDGMENT OF sexuality, if not romance, between Wagstaff and Mapplethorpe was refreshing and liberating—a contrast to Sam's feelings for the young heterosexual artists Heizer, Newton, and Tuttle, all in one way or another necessarily partitioned from the realm of his erotic desire. While his relationship with Jim Crawford had been romantic, Wagstaff in the end had lost interest in the young artist because he lost interest in his work. With Robert, the intellectual and the artistic, the romantic and the sexual forces all came together almost as naturally as breathing—and all at once.

With little forethought or caution, Sam and Robert became immediately inseparable, spending days at a time in Oakleyville, on Fire Island. The photographs they took of each other invoke all the intensity of a transformational summer romance: two bodies lying together in the dunes, an overwhelming magnetism between them, a longing stoked, it would seem, by the sun's reflections on their coconut-oiled skin.

They spent their time walking on the beach, chasing each other in and out of the water as nymphlike playmates, frolicking that carried with it a sense of expectation. Then, lying naked on the towels in the dunes, getting stoned, laughing hysterically, photographing each other with a genuine intimacy that comes across in the pictures as magical.

Over the course of these months, Sam photographed Robert with his Leica from his favored angles. In one, which could be characterized as a crotch shot, Robert is lying naked on the beach, his legs spread, his smiling face behind the display of his genitalia. Those early pictures capture some essence of Mapplethorpe, purer and more innocent than the simmering urban persona that became his public image.

At fifty, Sam was still in great physical shape, his slender swimmer's body muscled and taut. That summer he began to take nude self-portraits, as if perhaps this new love for Robert bursting inside his body could be documented, captured on film and, therefore, based in fact. The camera proved a safe artistic outlet for Sam, and his experimentation would evolve soon enough into deeper exploration of photography—not as art appreciation but as a means of art making.

As Robert, who had been using a Polaroid camera for almost a year, started a series of pictures chronicling the intimacy of their new romance, Sam watched closely. He seemed to love talking about his new lover's work, even though neither of them considered the Polaroids finished works of art. Still, Robert was methodical in terms of craft, taking great care to position his subjects just so. Sam pointed out the classical gestures of his subjects in the frame even before Robert understood what he had done. Robert liked having the ability to take candid pictures, and that summer he photographed Sam in many ordinary situations— shaving, taking a shower, even standing at the toilet urinating.

Sometimes Robert photographed himself and Sam in the middle of having sex, pursuing the authentic moment even as he composed the scene. In one pair of Polaroid images, pasted as a diptych to a page of an album, both appear naked.[38] In the first, Sam is seen from above kneeling over Robert in a caninelike squat, only his back visible to the camera; Robert is lying underneath, his legs spread and resting on Sam's shoulders. In the second, Sam's hands support Robert's legs in the air, his head lowered between them. Both images border on the animalistic: Sam, the older man, sniffing out and licking Robert's young flesh. The diptych captures Sam's romantic intoxication, a man on his knees appearing totally free of constraint.

Perhaps more than any other document, the Mapplethorpe diptych is persuasive evidence of Sam's submission to desire, to his worship of his new partner. It provides something of an explanation for Sam's decision, after knowing his "shy pornographer" not even three months, to give Robert $15,000 to buy a loft.

Do you come from on high or out of the abyss,

O Beauty? Godless yet divine, your gaze

indifferently showers favor and shame,

and therefore some have likened you to wine.

—CHARLES BAUDELAIRE
(RICHARD HOWARD, TRANS.)[1]

PART TWO

APOLLO AND DIONYSUS IN MANHATTAN

FIVE

KAMA SUTRA, BABY

WAGSTAFF'S PENURIOUSNESS—MORE COLLOQUIALLY called stinginess—was a running joke among his friends. If he shared a taxi with an acquaintance, it never occurred to him to pay his portion of the fare. When he dined out with friends, it was rare that he picked up the tab. Often he preferred to take the subway and eat in cheap restaurants. Perhaps this was a holdover from a time when he was less flush. For years Wagstaff supported himself on modest museum wages, perhaps with a stiff upper lip, though certainly with the entitlement of the penniless prince.

Imagine the astonishment of Wagstaff's friends, then, when they found out he had bought a loft for a young artist he'd just met. Some saw this *grande geste* as the impetuous display of an older lover's misguided obsession. Those close to the couple knew that the affair was not one-sided, but the extravagance of Sam's gesture was still astounding. "Sam was besotted with Robert—he was mad about the boy, *nuts* about him," said Steven Aronson, summing up the general view of the situation.

"Sam never picked up a bill—'old cement pockets,' some of us called him—but for Robert he couldn't do enough. I think Robert loved Sam, too. And not only because Sam was such a prize—educated, cultivated, well connected, well favored, well heeled."[2]

Whether or not it was evident to those who knew Sam, the timing of the gift was dictated to some degree by circumstance. Mapplethorpe needed to move out of the West 23rd Street loft near the Chelsea Hotel. Smith had just taken an apartment with her new boyfriend, rock musician Allen Lanier, and he simply couldn't afford to pay the rent on his own. Sam of course wanted to bring his new lover closer to home. Robert's new loft, at 24 Bond Street, was just down the block from Sam's.

Although no one questioned the act of pure—if unprecedented—generosity from Sam, Robert was viewed by many to be an unscrupulous hustler. "I think Robert was a very clever, genteel, long-range opportunist," Edmund White said, "in the way that millions of women have been since the beginning of time—you marry a rich husband."[3] In the case of Wagstaff and Mapplethorpe, judgment seemed to fall harshly on Robert. But Sam was not innocent. While there was genuine love and regard between them, the question of exploitation persisted throughout their relationship.

"There's nothing sinister about it," White said about Mapplethorpe accepting the money for the loft. "I think it's perfectly normal for a poor Catholic boy from Long Island, who's eaten up by ambition, to hook his wagon to that particular star."[4] Mapplethorpe would tell Patricia Morrisroe, his biographer, that Wagstaff "swept me off my feet. It was love at first sight. After that, everything turned around for me." Still, Mapplethorpe was not circumspect about his motivations. "If Sam hadn't had the money," he explained, "I might not have been involved with him. He was a package, so to speak."[5] Paul F. Walter, an art collector and a trustee at the Museum of Modern Art, got to know Sam and Robert not long after they met. "They were just very much in love, so that's the fundamental part. And Sam loved protégés and he loved to proselytize. He found somebody who he was very much in love with but also whose work he believed in. All that fueled Sam's interests."[6]

Mapplethorpe, whose focus on his own art making never wavered, spent a great deal of time working on his collages and assemblages. He was accustomed to sacrificing for his artwork—not only creature comforts but also decorum. His artwork anchored his priorities. Nothing was more sacred.

Robert's stint as a street hustler had supported him only at a subsistence level. He was never ashamed of it; it just wasn't satisfying and didn't pay well enough. Wagstaff, too, might have been drawn in by the lore of Mapplethorpe's recent past, which flew in the face of social acceptability, only adding to its allure. Wagstaff had spent his life trying to unshackle himself from old-world conventions, while Mapplethorpe had grown up oblivious, if not contemptuous, of them.

"Sam had a leg up at every single turn in his life," John Egner said. "He knew how to finesse anything easily in our culture. And when he met somebody like Gordon or Robert, they were the opposite. They were almost a kind of purer being that was not inculcated with the layers and layers of propriety and decorum—things that I think Sam spent a lot of time in his life trying to get rid of."[7]

Robert was already working very consciously before he met Sam to fraternize with socially prominent people, those who could provide financial support, of course, by buying his work. In the process, he had studied their manners and habits and begun to adapt some of their more refined aspects to his own evolving persona. In this regard, Wagstaff was able to provide further instruction. Mapplethorpe's goal was not merely to be a celebrity; he wanted to be known for his work and wanted the work to reside in a meaningful way in the world around him. "Maybe the misconception is that he was sometimes calculating," David Croland noted. "But Robert didn't calculate. He was very pure in his quest to have his art seen at the proper places. He was very good at meeting the people who were inspiring to him, [and] those who could help him present his work in the proper setting."[8]

Lynn Davis, a photographer who met Mapplethorpe early in their careers and would become his good friend and gallery-hopping companion, said that Robert was not "that cutthroat kind of ambitious. He was always looking at art. We would go to exhibits and then we would come back afterward and we would always tell each other which one was our favorite. He was fun. He was naughty. He liked to have a good time."[9]

BEFORE HE MET WAGSTAFF, Mapplethorpe's work consisted primarily of a mode of collage that incorporated photographic images he had been cutting out of popular and pornographic magazines. The elaborate frames he built for the collages became integral elements of the work. When Robert first started to make the collages, he asked Judy Linn, a fellow student at Pratt, to take pictures of him and of Patti, which he incorporated into his collages. Then, in newsstands in Times Square and Greenwich Village, he discovered beefcake magazines often sold in plastic covers or brown paper wrappers that conformed to decency laws. Titles like *Young Physique*, *Physique Pictorial*, and *Drum* featured male nude studies in ersatz classical poses.

Mapplethorpe was frustrated, however, by having to rely on other people's pictures; he wanted the raw material in his collages to be his own. "That was why I went into photography," he later said. "It wasn't to take a pure photographic image, it was just to be able to work with more images."[10]

In 1971, the year before he met Wagstaff, Mapplethorpe was given a lofty introduction to photography by John McKendry of the Metropolitan Museum of Art, whom he had met through Croland. The situation was complicated, or what was termed in those days "sophisticated": McKendry, in his forties and married to Maxime de la Falaise, fell in love with Mapplethorpe. He continued to make a spectacle of himself with his ardor long after the young Mapplethorpe insisted that a romance was out of the question. A *chic* cinematic parallel to McKendry's situation was playing in theaters that fall. *Sunday, Bloody Sunday* told the story of an accomplished middle-aged doctor who falls in love with a much younger, emotionally uncommitted bisexual sculptor. The first mainstream movie to address bisexuality with frank intelligence, the film dramatized how the doctor's pursuit of the younger man becomes increasingly abject and futile.

Despite the awkwardness of the situation, McKendry shared with

Robert his curatorial knowledge about photography. On several occasions, McKendry invited Robert, and Patti, too, to visit the study room at the museum; they were given private viewings of vintage photographs from the collection. There, his tutelage provided Mapplethorpe privileged access to these rare specimens. In fact, Robert was able to hold these historic prints in his hand. His exposure to beautifully printed images by Nadar (Gaspard-Felix Tournachon), Frank Meadow Sutcliffe, and others led him to conclude that photography was a form of art in itself.

McKendry also taught Mapplethorpe about the evolution of photographic techniques and printing processes. Recognizing Mapplethorpe's keen response to the medium, he gave him his first Polaroid camera and arranged through his contacts at the Polaroid Corporation for the young artist to have an ongoing supply of film. Mapplethorpe eventually began to rely on that camera, setting up pictures of his friends, flowers, and everyday objects that he would incorporate into his collages and assemblages.

The square-format Polaroid SX70 was a marvel in the early 1970s, when common photographic practice required film to be developed in a darkroom, the negative printed in an enlarger, the image to emerge on paper bathed in liquid developer, followed by the fixer, and, finally, the print placed in a dryer so it would be stable enough to hold in one's hand. By contrast, the Polaroid print materialized directly from the camera in less than a minute after exposure.

As a result of owning a Polaroid, Mapplethorpe made a great many self-portraits, using the camera as a mirror with which to explore the actuality of his own body and to experiment with the visual expression of his erotic desires. Because of the informality of the Polaroid, it felt more like play and less like serious photography—indeed, more like Robert himself. While photographing himself naked, he was able to shed his persona; these self-portraits reveal the curiosity of an artist exploring the medium even as he was searching for something true about himself—emotionally, sexually, existentially.

Although photography had long been ubiquitous—in newspapers and magazines, on billboards, in family snapshots, driver's licenses and passports—it was only in the early 1970s that attitudes about photography evolved beyond its applications as a journalistic medium and a utilitarian tool. Art schools were setting up autonomous photography programs within their fine arts curricula. In Boston, Minor White, founder of *Aperture*, who was teaching at the Massachusetts Institute of Technology, had opened Cameraworks, an independent school of photography. In New Haven, Walker Evans was the presiding dean at the School of Art at Yale, which had just established its own MFA program in photography. In Providence, photographers Harry Callahan and Aaron Siskind held court at the Rhode Island School of Design. In Rochester, Nathan Lyons's Visual Studies Workshop was attracting consistent attention. In San Francisco, Linda Connor and Henry Wessel were on the photography faculty at the San Francisco Art Institute, while in Los Angeles John Baldessari and Robert Heinecken were teaching at California College of the Arts and UCLA.

In 1972, aside from the Museum of Modern Art—the presiding institutional showcase for photography—only a handful of galleries in New York were showing photography exclusively, among them the Witkin and Light galleries. Their presence, though, gave legitimacy to the idea that photography was a viable art form.

In fact, throughout the 1960s, a logical evolution in art making had been taking place as artists began to incorporate the photographic image into their work—in particular, Andy Warhol and Robert Rauschenberg. These trailblazers, however, had to withstand the prejudices of curators, such as Sam, and critics alike, who continued to uphold the aesthetic hierarchies that relegated the photograph to second-class status—merely another material, like steel or plywood, in service of the larger art object, or idea, into which it was being incorporated.

Warhol was ahead of his time, since photographs were the basis of his grids of repeated images. In 1963, he took a young art collector named Ethel Scull to a photo booth in a Times Square pinball arcade. He directed her to talk, smile, and take her sunglasses on and off as he fed one coin after another into the automatic machine. Warhol then took the small cache of photo-booth portraits back to his studio, enlarged them, silk-screened them in different colors, and rearranged them in panels on canvas. *Ethel Scull Thirty Six Times*, today owned jointly by the Metropolitan Museum of Art and the Whitney Museum of American Art, is a grid of these portraits, and one of Warhol's earliest pop multiple-image pieces, a work in which he employed a matter-of-fact trinket of photographic technology as the basis of his representational work.

That same year Warhol made *Let Us Now Praise Famous Men*, a silkscreen painting in which he used photographs of his friend Robert Rauschenberg as well as pictures taken of Rauschenberg's family. The title plays off the classic 1941 book of the same name by James Agee and Walker Evans, with its righteous scorn for "famous men," those in power who stand in stark contrast to the abject poverty left in their wake, captured in Evans's well-known photographs of sharecroppers during the Depression. Warhol's repetitive use of the Rauschenberg photographic portrait and family pictures reflects the mechanical reproducibility and the everyday, all-purpose ubiquity of the photograph, summoning both Rauschenberg's humble Southern beginnings and his growing celebrity. Warhol set the stage for the photograph to come into its own by the end of the decade.

Wagstaff was hardly inured to the work Warhol was doing with photographic imagery. After all, he owned *Race Riot* and put it on his wall. The pictures document a scene in which police with guard dogs on leashes are breaking up a protest by black people in Montgomery, Alabama. It was the first work of art Wagstaff acquired with photographic imagery as the dominant visual language. The photographs were mediated by acrylic silk screen on canvas, subordinating the significance of photography with a pattern of repetition, thus making it palatable to Sam in the larger context of painting and in the realm of conceptual art.

Robert Rauschenberg had been making photographs quietly since his Black Mountain College days in the late 1940s and early '50s, often casual but observant pictures of his friends and intimates—Cage and Merce Cunningham, Jasper Johns and Cy Twombly—in their studios or at the beach. The ordinary, spontaneous moments in Rauschenberg's pictures are observed with a focused eye and lyric purity that one also sees in the photographs by Allen Ginsberg made around the same period, or Alfred Stieglitz several generations before. In 1962 Rauschenberg made a photographic self-portrait of his own reflection with a camera in a mirror and placed it at the center of one of his combines. "I've never stopped being a photographer," he told an interview as late as 1981.[12] Throughout the 1960s, Californian artists, too, such as John Baldessari and Ed Ruscha, explored the photographic image consistently in service of larger conceptual—and perceptual—ideas about art making. Ruscha's artists' books were based almost entirely on the "photograph" as a forensic individual object and, also, as a medium for serial observation. Baldessari used the photograph in his conceptual work to make specific comment about mediated perception. Robert Heinecken addressed the medium directly by challenging popular media applications of the photographic image and the way those images were interpreted. Still, the artwork that defined pop art or conceptual art was not considered photographic, yet the photographic image composed the visual language that redefined contemporary art. In fact, throughout the decade the photograph could be seen on museum walls and in collectors' homes conditioning the eye to its singular vocabulary while masquerading in the conceptual language of other mediums.

By the early 1970s art students were attracted by how accessible, spontaneous, mutable, and "cool" photography was. At the same time, museum curators, such as the eloquent, if stentorian, John Szarkowski at the Museum of Modern Art, as well as art scholars continued to identify a canon within the history of photography. Young artists were trying to emulate those visual precedents found in the photographs of Edward Weston, Ansel Adams, Alfred Stieglitz, André Kertész, Walker Evans, and others. Experimenting with the Polaroid and recognizing the expressive possibilities of the medium from his tutelage with John McKendry, Mapplethorpe himself urged the curator to use his position at the Met to bring greater attention and respect to fine art photography, which some scholars referred to as "lens-based art."

For photography students in the early 1970s, "street photography" marked the contemporary moment.[13] They either worshipped the work of Robert Frank, Bruce Davidson, Diane Arbus, Lee Friedlander, and

Garry Winogrand or actively rejected the documentary conventions of the medium that were just then finding definition in art world terms.

As if the tail were wagging the dog, even painting showed the influence of the photographic image with the emergence of the photorealist school. Recognizing that photography was changing the way people saw the world, artists such as Robert Bechtle, Chuck Close, Robert Cottingham, Richard Estes, Audrey Flack, Ralph Goings, and Philip Pearlstein began to render a 35 millimeter universe on canvas. They painted ordinary scenes from daily life with the kind of optical precision that defined the photographic image. Their bravura paintings had a technically daunting resemblance to photographs, with lens-sharp clarity and a viewfinder-like cropping of scenes that looked like happened-upon moments. The use of an airbrush in these paintings created a seamless surface that added to a simulated photographic look. The unspoken dialogue that took place between the photorealist painters and photographers of the late 1960s and early '70s, from Friedlander and Winogrand to William Eggleston and Stephen Shore, can be viewed as a tug of war between the brush and the camera, a dialogue between the created image and the captured one. But there is no question that the ubiquity of the captured image in the Western world of the mid-twentieth century was changing the foundations of painting and conceptual art, too.

By that time, the ubiquity of the photographic image had come to alter the way people saw—and framed—the world. Photojournalism in magazines such as *Life, Look,* and *Esquire* had become the recognizable and respected style for the photographic image. The artificial staginess of the advertising image was a commercial counterpoint, but in both journalism and advertising the photographic image had become pervasive. It presented visual information with such a fidelity to the way things actually look that initially critics, art historians, and an art-viewing public found it difficult to understand how photography could be a medium of high-minded aesthetic consideration.

Despite such resistance, serious photographers were taking life's most ordinary, incidental moments, both domestic and public, as their subject matter. The term "snapshot aesthetic" was coined to identify this formal attempt to make photographs of daily life that possessed the actuality of a happened-upon moment. The snapshot aesthetic combined the un-self-conscious informality of family snapshots, the authenticity of documentary photography, and the active style of news pictures. The legendary photographer Lisette Model wrote, "Innocence is the quintessence of the snapshot. I wish to distinguish between innocence and ignorance. Innocence is one of the highest forms of being and ignorance one of the lowest."[14] The candid photos that Mapplethorpe took of Wagstaff in 1972, while documenting a new love affair, also exemplified the snapshot aesthetic.

The artist most responsible for this approach to photographic art making was Robert Frank, whose book *The Americans* had been published in 1959. The Swiss-born Frank was brought up in a tradition of European photography between the world wars, in which bold geometry was the underpinning of photographic composition. Immigrating at the age of twenty-three to the United States in 1947, Frank studied briefly with Alexey Brodovitch, the visual maestro of *Harper's Bazaar*, for whom bold geometry was less important than pure visual expression. In the early 1950s, Frank cultivated friendships with Walker Evans, then the picture editor of *Fortune*, and Edward Steichen, director of the Museum of Modern Art's photo department.

In the few publications that deigned to cover photography in the 1950s, such as *Popular Photography* and *Modern Photography*, Frank's photographs were dismissed for their raw, informal look. Although at first glance they might have seemed amateurish, they possessed the same spontaneity and modesty that characterized the work of the beat poets and writers with whom Frank associated. The similarities between the work of the photorealist painters and that of the photographers working with the snapshot aesthetic may not have been deliberate, but in retrospect the two groups seem inextricably connected. Photorealist artists had captured the immediacy of a 35 millimeter universe in paint on canvas and, while critics rejected the movement as an abomination, in fact it was a visionary observation that identified the way the photograph, which was everywhere in popular culture, had changed the way human beings looked at the world. No painting of the period better exemplifies the exploration of a photographic vocabulary on canvas than David Hockney's *A Bigger Splash* (1967). The British artist, by then living in Los Angeles, painted a contemporary residence, still and precise in the Southern California light. The only active movement is in the splash of water in the backyard swimming pool. The fact of the movement, however, in brushstroke underscored the reference to the camera's ability to stop time in visual terms.

And yet, photorealism was dismissed by critics and other artists for trompe l'oeil bravado, an example of style trumping substance. Just as painters in the nineteenth century regarded the camera as a mere tool absent the potential for creative expression, many artists in the early 1970s still believed that the photographic image—or a painting that seemed to mimic it—lacked the ideological grandeur and artistic validity of "pure" painting.

The growing respect accorded photography as a fine art was certified by the 1972 Diane Arbus retrospective mounted by Szarkowski at the Museum of Modern Art, only one year after her suicide. Arbus had made intimate portraits of strangers and acquaintances in their homes or on the street. Viewers were appalled by the unflattering aspects of her portraits, and, yet, fascinated by their powerful emotional resonance. A debate lingers still about whether she sought to find the grotesque in her subjects; certainly her pictures reflect her own psychological experience of the people she photographed. Still, that landmark show established Arbus as one of the most consequential twentieth-century artists.

Hilton Kramer, the art critic of *The New York Times*, who was hostile to the idea of photography in the realm of the fine arts, acknowledged that few contemporary photographers had had as strong an impact on the practice as Diane Arbus. The retrospective "brings us a body of work that is at once a classic and a matter of controversy," Kramer wrote in his review of the MoMA show. "For many connoisseurs of photographic art, especially for the younger generation of photographers on whom Mrs. Arbus has been a decisive influence, the exhibition is a summary— and vindication—of a new aesthetic attitude. For others, less familiar with the imperatives of her style and less prepared for the shocks it contains, the exhibition is likely to be, at the least, a revelation."[15]

It was in this period of this intense artistic fermentation that Robert Mapplethorpe made the transition from collage and assemblage to photography. Robert had never wanted to be a photographer—he hadn't thought of photography as a high enough art form. He told an interviewer: "But then I realized that all kinds of things can be done within the context of photography, and it was also the perfect medium, or so it seemed, for the seventies and eighties, when everything was fast." Mapplethorpe liked the immediacy of the photographic process, the fact that he could set up his pictures, make the exposures, and see the contact sheets within a day. "If I were to make something that took weeks to do, I'd lose my enthusiasm. It would become an act of labor and the love would be gone."[14]

If Mapplethorpe's intention was to explore the medium of photography with integrity of method and practice as well as serious professional aspiration, he needed to set up shop properly. He needed a studio in which to make photographs and to experiment with form, and he also needed the right kind of equipment and the lights and the necessary materials. As a result, Wagstaff bought Mapplethorpe a Hasselblad, the square-format camera made famous with its use by the Apollo astronauts during the 1969 landing on the moon. The Hasselblad, then as now the Rolls-Royce of cameras, was ideal for studio photography because of the precise lenses, its compact size, and its versatility. It is the camera that launched Mapplethorpe's studio work in the loft Wagstaff had bought him on Bond Street.

THIS WAS THE BEGINNING of an enterprise in which Mapplethorpe's career would become Wagstaff's lifetime curatorial project. Edmund White surmised that one reason Sam found Robert so attractive was "partly because he had already decided he was an important artist."[17] Equally, however, the honest acknowledgment of their physical intimacy was in itself liberating for Sam, the openness of this love affair bewitching.

Such forthrightness was so different from the closeted liaisons he'd had in the past. The discretion that Sam and other homosexuals of his generation felt compelled to use resulted in coded correspondence, as we saw with Dickie de Menocal. Even the mementos of love were playfully indirect in any expression of intimacy. One picture in Sam's papers, showing a handsome but bony-faced young man, has the seductive inscription "To Uncle Moose, from a fat, ugly Russian Wolfhound . . . July 31, 1964." It is signed Hutch, presumably short for Hutchinson.[18] A slide of a beautiful naked young man lying on his stomach on a couch, his calves up in the air and ankles crossed, might also be Hutchinson. Yet another letter from Hutch was written on International Red Cross stationery: "Dear Moose, Just bumped off only flight of the day to Spain (via Germany). Next is Tuesday at 7. . . . We've set Wednesday as the limit. Miss it, Hutch." The use of ungendered third-person pronouns for the object of affection—Hutch misses "it," not "you"—also appears in several notes from Dickie de Menocal. When he writes Sam, "I hope its shoulder is out of its cast by now," the "it" refers to Sam as an object, not a person.[19] Sam himself would use this very locution often in letters to Mapplethorpe. It may have been a holdover from years of speaking in code from inside the closet, but more likely, it was an inhibition established in Wagstaff's childhood about expressing emotions openly.

In 1962, while Wagstaff was a curator in Hartford, he bestowed a local award on an art student named Dan Basen. Several years later, Basen would create his own versions of "happenings." One consisted of his calling pay phones on the main street of his hometown in Connecticut. If a male passerby picked up the phone, Basen would try to engage him, sometimes successfully, in explicitly erotic conversation.[20]

Wagstaff was very supportive of Basen's work throughout the 1960s, occasionally buying drawings and introducing him to artists and art dealers, as was his wont. There is a great deal of correspondence between Wagstaff and Basen, but two letters reveal an erotic component to their relationship that borders on emotionally dangerous ground. In November 1967, Basen writes, "Dear Sam, Remember when we met? When I walked you home and told you how I'd like to do it to you? And I did. And it was good—Remember? Oh Sam, I need it again. Pink tits between my cock there. . . . Basen."[21]

Three years later, soon before Basen committed suicide, he wrote a letter that reveals his increasingly psychotic behavior. It's full of errors, rather disconcerting, but evocatively sinister: "Sam, I still remember what you look like: tall, longish light-colored hair. Identical blue eyes. Parallel cheeks. Full mouth. Wide shoulders. Good pecks. Unharried chest. Tapered trunk. Narrow hips. Uncircumsized staff. Boyish ass and legs. Slip-ons. And a glorious red radiation. Some night, when you're sound asleep, I'm having you carried off by plane to the center of Asia. You won't wake too soon, needle will see to that. But you'll wake wide open when you do—alone—in a stand of maples. And wearing that maroon silk burst, so please have it laundered. Shaft of sun through the sleeve of your colorful tent cooks two eggs. . . ."²²

Once Wagstaff was ensconced in Detroit, he was less concerned about how his sexual activities and romantic liaisons would affect his reputation. There, he was acquainted with a world of closeted gay men, enough of whom held well-respected positions, some of them colleagues at the Detroit Institute of Arts. By then, he did not feel compelled to hide his relationship with Jim Crawford or other brief romances. Nevertheless, there was a vigilance that came with his position with which he continually had to measure how much to reveal to whom about his homosexuality.

Stepping out of the closet at that time was subject to risks beyond the simple acknowledgment of one's homosexuality—in itself, enough of a taboo to be shocking. It brought with it the potential for associating with a world on the fringe, such as psychotics like Basen, as well as the many troubled individuals less successful at navigating the societal contempt thrown at "their kind."

However, by the time Sam met Robert, there were openly gay men strolling the streets of post-Stonewall Manhattan, reveling in a freedom he could not have imagined as "the deb's delight" in a swank leather booth at the Stork Club in the 1940s. The parallel universes he had traversed for so many years were finally converging. Wagstaff had abandoned the pretense of heterosexuality, but his dalliances and romances in the late 1960s still transpired through a scrim of discretion. Now, with Robert, the veil not only lifted but it dropped away and shredded into pieces. Sam could finally integrate his private desires with his public identity, and he began to reside more completely in his body, exhibiting at this juncture at least a tentative sexual openness that was astonishing for a man of his social background.

Mapplethorpe was very aware of the double life Wagstaff had been obligated to lead up to that point. Even when Olga, his mother, or her friends suspected Sam's attraction to men, Sam never felt comfortable divulging the truth. "Sam really respected the way I was honest about being gay," Mapplethorpe said. "I helped Sam to be more open about his sexuality."[33]

Not only did Mapplethorpe fit the very template of Sam's primal romantic attraction and help Sam integrate his sexuality into his public identity, he also had the more essential attribute of being a gifted artist. While Mapplethorpe was something of a tabula rasa on whom Sam could project a sum of unrealized ambitions of his own, in the astringent appraisal of more than a few friends, Sam harbored the wish to be an artist himself.[24]

FROM MINIMALISM
TO MAPPLETHORPE

The only true voyage, the only bath in the fountain of youth,
would be not to visit strange lands but to possess other
eyes, to see the universe through the eyes of another, of a
hundred of others, to see the hundred universes that each
of them sees.

—MARCEL PROUST[1]

PERHAPS IT WAS THE NAME OF THE EXHIBITION, "THE PAINT-
erly Photograph," and the setting where it was mounted, the Metropolitan Museum of Art, that allowed Wagstaff to shed the residual
traces of his prejudices about photography.[2] Attending the show in January 1973 with Mapplethorpe, he paused before a pair of framed Edward
Steichen prints of the Flatiron Building, the same image of the New
York City architectural landmark repeated on the wall. It was quite a
modern idea to exhibit these two prints of the same historic photograph
side by side, inviting comparison of the blue and green tints that distinguished one from the other. As Wagstaff looked at the singular image

intently and studied the subtle differences between the prints, he had something of an epiphany.

The Flatiron Building was considered radical at the time of its construction in 1902 because of its shape, its broad Beaux Arts facades narrowing to a fine triangular point at the intersection of two thoroughfares, Fifth Avenue and Broadway. Steichen's photograph, *The Flatiron* (1904) might be considered an equally bold piece of work—a stark and beautiful urban study in lusty shades of black and gray, the branches of the trees in the foreground fashioning a delicate calligraphy against the solid, monumental geometry of the building behind. It's one of the finest examples of pictorialism, a movement at the turn of the twentieth century in which photographic art making drifted from the optical precision that rendered objects true to life toward a more painterly, interpretive resolution.

Pictorialism evolved in reaction to the chauvinistic art world attitude that considered photography a craft, and the camera merely a tool, unable to compete artistically with the expressive purity of painting. Photography's invention was concurrent with a shift toward realism in painting, but artists were not predisposed to exploring the new medium that provided a true-to-life image of the actual world; in fact, they grew indignant at the idea that a mechanical method of representation could be elevated to the stature of art. In 1862, Ingres was among the artists of his day who denounced photography, signing an official petition in Paris: "Let it keep its place," he said in a denunciation of any "industrial" techniques in the realm of high art.[3]

A single exposure of light on glass could produce a scene with the same descriptive clarity of a meticulously detailed painting. It is not hard to imagine that Ingres—so deft in his true-to-life rendering of the human figure, the texture of skin, the sheen of satin, the patterns of marble—felt threatened by a cold mechanical device usurping his mystique. In a gesture of repudiation of photography, François Bouvin, another nineteenth-century realist painter and a friend of Gustave Courbet, refused to have his portrait made by the eminent photographer Nadar. Aaron Scharf, the British historian of photography, cited one English artist who characterized art and photography as rivals that "stand opposite to each other like two armies in battle array."[4] Toward the end of the nineteenth century, painting itself would veer toward greater perceptual abstraction, partly in reaction to the optical precision made possible with the camera. Not to be outsmarted or left out of a dialogue with history, the pictorialists followed the painters.

When Wagstaff began his career as a curator, his prejudices about photography were grounded in this ideological divide. "Tell me what a Brahms concerto means and I will tell you what a painting means," he told the *Hartford Times* in 1961, implying that you cannot verbalize what is essentially a sensory experience. "People confuse painting and photography," he said, implying that a photograph is full of facts and a painting is a more inspired thing. Painting, he asserted, is art while photography is not art 99 percent of the time. "The beautiful photograph is almost invariably beautiful because of the subject matter. A painting is beautiful because of its form, its texture, its color."[5]

The Flatiron was the first photograph in which Wagstaff recognized and acknowledged the "subject" and the "image" to be inextricable and of equal weight. For him, it was a visual construction in which shape, tone, light, space, and juxtaposition all danced on the surface of a single piece of paper—nothing less than a perfect alchemy of emotion, perception, and (significant) form. For Wagstaff, *The Flatiron* looked neither like a photograph nor a drawing, floating in the visual ether as an invention all its own.

Its beauty was sublime, timeless—and yet *The Flatiron* was rooted in its moment, just as the twentieth century was being born. The image perfectly captured the dualities of a transitional era: its genesis was both mechanical and handmade, its form both representational and abstract. Five years after Wagstaff saw *The Flatiron*, while showing slides of pictures from his collection of photographs to students at Pratt Institute, he described the moment he first stood before it: "In the face of such a picture," Wagstaff said, "I kept looking back on that period in American painting and sculpture and trying to find something that was of equal stature and I don't think there is, probably for five years on either side of that picture. . . . It seemed to me like a stupendous milestone in the advancement of the human mind in America."[6]

Looking at the catalog for "The Painterly Photograph," Wagstaff saw that someone he knew had organized the show. Weston Naef had been a graduate student at Brown University in the mid-1960s. His doctoral study in art history required him to mount an exhibition, the subject of which was French lithography of the nineteenth century. A professor had directed Naef to Wagstaff, who had been collecting French lithographs. Wagstaff agreed to lend works to Naef's exhibition.

Naef was now assistant curator of prints and photographs at the Met, under John McKendry. Soon after that first viewing of *The Flatiron*, Wagstaff contacted him and the two of them walked through the entire exhibition together. Sam was less enamored of other pictorialist works in the show but, standing in front of the two Steichen prints, he talked about seeing this image of a building—just a mile from where he lived, one that he had passed innumerable times in his life—as if seeing the structure for the first time.

"He may have seen a reproduction of it," Naef recalled, "but this is a case where a reproduction does no justice to the beauty and size and the scale of the original. So he was mesmerized by these particular pieces, I think, because they represented the kinds of permutations and combinations that he so admired in the work of people like Tony Smith, Robert Morris, and Frank Stella, but they also had this other foot in a historic, romantic past."[7]

Nevertheless, in Wagstaff's mind, Edward Steichen began with a strike against him. In 1955, decades after making *The Flatiron*, Steichen, as director of photography at the Museum of Modern Art, had organized "The Family of Man," a show that included more than five hundred pictures from photographers all around the world, professional and amateur alike.[8] Wagstaff was not alone in judging the exhibition something of a sentimental hodgepodge.

Now, for the first time Sam could see the significance of the work Steichen had done earlier in his life, when he was Alfred Stieglitz's protégé and collaborator in the Little Galleries of the Photo-Secession, later to be known as 291 Gallery. Together, Steichen and Stieglitz were founders of the Photo-Secession movement, a determined mission to "secede" from the kind of picture making that the then-current camera club phenomenon bred, which encouraged hobbyists and, as Stieglitz asserted, fostered photographic "mediocrity." The pair's images assumed the ambiguities of paint on canvas before their eventual embrace of the optical precision characteristic of the straightforward photograph. Perhaps this presaged their later interest in Picasso and Braque, Matisse, Rousseau, Cézanne, Brancusi, and Duchamp—the avant-garde artists they were first to show in the United States, at 291 Gallery.

In his catalog essay for "The Painterly Photograph," Naef compared the Photo-Secession with other secession movements in Europe, such as the Fauves and the Nabis.[9] The Photo-Secessionists saw their work as part of the international avant-garde. This, no doubt, further caught Wagstaff's interest. He, too, felt most at home assuming a posture of "secession," whether from the strictures of his own upbringing or from the bourgeois conventions that had constrained him in Detroit—those forces that conspired to tamp down his originality and almost feral independence of spirit.

In *The Flatiron*—originally a series of three prints all made from the same negative, though only two were in the show—Steichen was trying to convey the chromatic progression of twilight, as Whistler had done a generation earlier in his *Nocturne* paintings. Steichen brushed layers of pigment suspended in light-sensitive gum solution onto a platinum print. For each one, he varied the coloring slightly to create the effect of the sun going down at the end of the day.

It is worth noting that Wagstaff's earlier vehement dismissals of photography had curiously coexisted with an appetite for collecting picture postcards. Likewise, he had already been experimenting with the camera himself before meeting Mapplethorpe. While in Detroit he had become acquainted with Enrico Natali, a young photographer who had lived in New York and Chicago but was at the time making simple, straightforward black-and-white portraits of the members of Detroit society. In 1969, Natali saw an exhibition at the Detroit Institute of Arts of photographs by J. Edward Bailey, a local photojournalist. Surprised that photographs were even being shown at the museum, Natali contacted Fred Cummings, then the executive director of the DIA, to show him his portraits.

After looking at Natali's pictures, Cummings called Wagstaff over. "These are the people I have been trying to avoid my whole life," Sam told Natali as he examined the portraits.[10] Nevertheless, Wagstaff seemed to take the pictures seriously. He liked them enough to follow up with a call to Natali, whom he commissioned to make a series of portraits of the members of the Friends of Modern Art, the DIA patron group, offering a five-hundred-dollar fee. Wagstaff's idea was that once the portraits were taken, Natali could sell them to each of the subjects. Natali, whose work ethic made it difficult for him to accept the money outright, gave Wagstaff a Leica as a form of leverage. Then the young photographer proceeded to teach the curator of contemporary art how to use it.

In a 1982 interview, Wagstaff recounted his early meetings with Natali and the importance of seeing his work. Natali's photographs were, Sam said, "the first photographs that I looked at with any kind of critical thinking in mind." Natali presented him with his first conscious recognition of photography's potential. "It was like a first taste of caviar or a first oyster. . . . Strangely enough, it was Detroit and Enrico which began my interest in photography. And I realized if someone could delineate their eccentricity of vision so successfully, that photography was way beyond what I thought about it."[11]

Natali worked simply, using one camera, a 35 millimeter lens, and Tri-x film. By limiting the equipment, he could forget about the mechanics and let his eye lead the way. His pictures fall into a documentary tradition of simplicity and clarity that includes August Sander and Robert Frank. He owed his own photographic education to Hugh Edwards of the Art Institute of Chicago, an unsung hero in the world of photography with whom Natali spent a great deal of time before he moved to Detroit. In the 1960s, Edwards had given the first one-man show at the Art Institute to each of several important photographers, including Robert Frank, Danny Lyon, Duane Michals, and Natali himself.

In 1970, Natali showed his small 5-×-7 prints to John Szarkowski, the director of the photography department at the Museum of Modern Art, who registered interest in the work but told Natali that he would have to make larger prints. Natali refused, a decision that perhaps

explains why his name is not known today among the canonized photographers of his generation.

Two years after they met, Natali asked Wagstaff to write him a recommendation for a Guggenheim Fellowship. Sam's letter reflects the
full range of his ambivalence about photography before viewing *The
Flatiron*. His opening lines assume a posture of utter disdain for photography: "Natali takes his life in his hands asking me to recommend him
for a grant," Wagstaff wrote to the Guggenheim Foundation. "As a
loather of photography, sui generis, I give brick-bats there, not praise."
He then softens his position a bit, but not without some attendant crank-
iness. He highlights the singularity of Natali's work even as he justifies
the puzzling choice of an artist to wield a camera instead of a paintbrush
or chisel: "He knocks over my innate prejudice in 1/60th of a second
and shows me what could happen if more photographers had a brain or
an eye. It isn't that the medium is lousy, it's the dim wits who practice it,
evidently." He offers what amounts to praise by noting that Natali's
photographs are astringent as opposed to sentimental, ruthless in their
straightforward observation. The last lines of the recommendation,
however, suggest the criteria by which Wagstaff would come to endorse
photography as a collector: "At last an artist-photographer who isn't
'discovering' motherhood, irony, old Jews, the downtrodden or the
'folly of it all,' or some other old hat. 'No point of view takes a great
picture.' At last!"[12] Despite Wagstaff's repudiating the medium, the letter in support of Natali's application was persuasive and he received the
Guggenheim grant.

When Wagstaff stood before *The Flatiron* in January 1973, it was not
only the photograph that resonated. He was at the show, of course, with
Robert Mapplethorpe, who was not shy about expressing the importance of photography, and who had absorbed an orientation to the
medium from John McKendry. And Enrico Natali, who taught Sam
how to use a camera, had had as a mentor Hugh Edwards. Without quite
realizing it, Wagstaff was hearing the echoes of these two curators with
significant knowledge of the underappreciated medium. The institutional weight of such tutors must have held sway.

VERY SOON AFTER ATTENDING "The Painterly Photograph," Wagstaff set out on a single-minded mission to acquire photographs. Yet he heeded a suggestion by Mapplethorpe to wait, briefly, until he consulted Patti Smith. "Robert asked Patti to get a tarot card reading on the subject of whether I should collect photography or not," Sam would tell an interviewer for Spanish television in the late 1970s. "She did the reading and she said 'it's very, very favorable. Tell Sam to go ahead.' So, I began to collect with Patti Smith's approval. I began to collect photography."[13]

While his curatorial background led him on a pursuit of the best of the medium, his obsessive approach to collecting attuned him to workaday examples as well. He was especially drawn to *cartes de visites*—studio portraits that served as calling cards in the nineteenth century and were often exchanged among friends and relatives as keepsakes; cartographic survey photographs that documented the vast open landscapes of America and Europe; and, of course, postcards that represented a specific geographic locale. These purchases in his collection were both idiosyncratic and prototypical of their genres.

Following Wagstaff's *Flatiron* "revelation," Weston Naef introduced him to George Rinhart, a photography collector and dealer. "He told Sam that if he wants to collect photographs he should come and see me," Rinhart said. On a winter afternoon in January 1973, Wagstaff appeared in the front room of Rinhart's New York town house. "Heavens," Rinhart said. "Good-looking hippie, but he was wearing *beads*."[14]

With his long hair and wearing an embroidered Indian shirt and jeans, Wagstaff looked around for a minute or two before his eyes fell on a set of prints by Frederick H. Evans, which would become Sam's first significant acquisition in the field of photography. They were a group of platinum prints of Kelmscott Manor, an early seventeenth-century farmhouse on the banks of the Thames, eighty miles or so from London. Kelmscott was the country home of William Morris, who was considered the leader of the Arts and Crafts movement in England. Morris had commissioned Evans to photograph the house in 1896. The album of twelve prints Sam acquired documents the rooms of Kelmscott Manor and its grounds as if the photographer were taking the viewer on an intimate walking tour. The platinum process gave a silvery tone to the walls, columns, wood beams that echo on the paper the beautiful ambiguities of graphite. One might say that Wagstaff did not at first travel far afield from the interpretive Photo-Secession prints of *The Flatiron* to the romantic, if very precise, Pre-Raphaelite atmosphere of Kelmscott Manor. Both were movements in rebellion against presiding artistic beliefs.

Sam didn't blink when Rinhart quoted him $3000 for the set. "I'll take them," Wagstaff said, writing out a check on the spot to a slightly nervous Rinhart—it was too late in the day to call the bank to see whether the check was good—and leaving with the prints under his arm. The next day, the bank assured Rinhart that Sam's account was "good as gold," and Wagstaff's photography collecting career was underway.[15]

It remains suprising that only forty years ago so few people looked at a "photograph" with any serious regard for composition, tonal detail, and precise resolution. Even fewer people took special care in handling the fragile print, and almost no one could proclaim the monetary value of these little gray pieces of paper based on their vintage, the historic relevance of their subject matter, and their significance as art objects. Nevertheless, Wagstaff agreed to pay $3000 for twelve 5-×-7 prints mounted on 11-×-14 boards. At the time, surely, that seemed a lot of money for so small a pleasure.

Simultaneously, Mapplethorpe also became interested in collecting photographs. The two men—at times with Patti Smith in tow—embarked on informal shopping expeditions, scouring flea markets, rare bookstores, and New England farmhouses. More methodically, they investigated galleries and visited the homes of private dealers. Soon enough Sam and Robert began to frequent auction houses in New York, London, and Paris. One day they traveled together to the home of a pornography dealer in Staten Island, where Mapplethorpe was hoping to purchase some homoerotic drawings by Tom of Finland. It turned out that the dealer had only photocopies of the originals. Then he brought out several books of original photographs, and Robert asked him if he knew of a German baron who had photographed adolescent boys in Italy at the turn of the century. The dealer pulled out a set of original photographs by Baron Wilhelm von Gloeden. Mapplethorpe later told an interviewer that "this was really the first acquisition Sam or myself made in photography. . . . [It] started the whole thing going."[16] Mapplethorpe was referring to the von Gloedens but, for Wagstaff, the Kelmscott Manor album was the very first group of pictures in his collection.

Wagstaff's turn to photography seemed improbable or even quixotic to his friends, but he was thrilled to have the field to himself. "He was buying things like a madman," Robert recalled. "He saw beauty on every level, from the amateur all the way up—in postcards and everything. We were both living on Bond Street. On his way home, he'd stop by with shopping bags full of great photographs, and some not so great. He'd come over and want me to be his audience, and I was for a while, until I finally said, 'Sam, I'm taking my own pictures. I'll never take another picture if I look at these things.'"[17]

The art critic Jed Perl became acquainted with Wagstaff not long after his turn to photography. At the time Perl was in his early twenties and dabbled in buying and selling illustrated books. He sold Sam a few books, one a children's book from the 1930s, another an album of albumen prints of Venetian scenes from the 1880s. On a visit to the loft on Bond Street, Wagstaff brought out the von Gloedens. "He showed them to me, one by one, for half an hour," Perl said, describing the scrutiny with which Sam studied these pictures, featuring young, often preadolescent Sicilian boys in languid, homoerotic poses (today von Gloeden portraits have camp appeal because of their overly theatrical references to Greek mythology). "He was interested in the fact that they were sort of done for the trade [as under-the-counter pornography], that the prints were imperfect."[18]

For Wagstaff, the freedom to stare at the photographs carried a distinct erotic component. Even in 1973, his eye was not allowed to roam freely on the street or in most of the rooms he occupied, or to gaze at a stranger he might have been attracted to. The eye of the homosexual was trained in a code of furtiveness; it could not exercise an almost inalienable right to look openly at what—or at whom—it wanted to see. Now, holding a photograph by von Gloeden in his hand, Sam would feel a new kind of power: the license to stare—and baldly so.

For Perl, Wagstaff's incarnation as a collector called to mind Leo Stein and Peggy Guggenheim, who collected according to their own essential sensibilities, ever mindful of the historical importance of their acquisitions. Collectors in that realm leave nothing behind. They have to survey and acquire as much as they can before distilling their choices to the ultimate simplicity of a vision. In the right hands, Sam would later tell a group of art students, collecting works of art not only shaped an aesthetic but also identified and preserved the best of a man-made form. Scholars, he pointed out, do not have to possess whatever it is they are extending their scholarship over. But collectors "have to have the proprietary interest."[19] As if the collection, like a child, had to be nurtured to absorb the values and the sensibilities of the collector. That way, eventually, it can assume a life in the world on its own. As Wagstaff transformed himself into a collector of photographs, he would also, like Leo Stein or Peggy Guggenheim before him, assume the role of something rarer: a tastemaker of historic consequence, and a trendsetter.

SAM WAGSTAFF'S SUDDEN AND obsessive turn to the "inferior" medium of photography in early 1973 was of a piece with his decision to buy the loft for Mapplethorpe only three months into their romance. "He made an overnight switch to photography as far as all of us could tell," Klaus Kertess recalled. Implicit in the shock was a feeling of betrayal. "Agnes Martin said, 'Sam's not a collector, he's a friend of "art,"' and there are not many." Martin was referring to the fact that when Wagstaff bought contemporary paintings or sculpture, it was often an extension of his relationship with the artists. "Art," as Martin used the word, emphatically excluded photography.[20]

For Wagstaff, this sudden new interest stood in stark contrast to his earlier public proclamations against the medium as an art form. As we have seen, Wagstaff became absorbed in the lives of the young artists he supported, even those who had not captured his romantic interest. He would regularly correspond with them about their work and help them out financially now and then, which meant that when they were strapped for cash, he would buy one of their pieces. Many of the artists were men—Dan Basen, George Brecht, Walter De Maria, Mark di Suvero, Neil Jenney, Ray Johnson, for example. He was also in the habit of introducing young artists he believed in to anyone who might be able to help get their work seen, such as Richard Tuttle to Andy Warhol, or Gordon Newton to Tony Smith.

By the mid-1960s Wagstaff's reputation in the art world had been firmly secured. He was known as a reliable champion of contemporary art, and several exhibits he mounted at the Wadsworth Atheneum had broken new ground. Wagstaff walked a fine line between the very conservative city fathers of Hartford, who sat on the museum's board and to whom he ultimately had to answer, and the avant-garde artists in New York whose work excited him and whose company he much preferred. When it came to the art movements of the era—minimalism and pop art, in particular—he became an emissary between Hartford and New York, a translator of an entirely new visual language. He relished the role of provocateur and, as an advocate of artwork that most people found incomprehensible, he seemed to find his calling. Until 1973, as far as he was concerned, the language of ideas he was channeling from the art world existed in a different universe from the lingua franca of the pedestrian photographic image.

Agnes Gund, a philanthropist and collector who for years served as president of the board of trustees at the Museum of Modern Art, first met Wagstaff when he was still in Hartford. His conversion to photography took her by surprise. "I was sort of stunned," Gund recalled. She knew of Wagstaff's academic background at the Institute of Fine Arts. It was one thing for him to make the bold transition from the Renaissance to the minimal and conceptual ideas of the modern era. But in order to know how to collect photographs, Gund maintained, one had to be versed in the history of that medium; a breadth of knowledge was required about who the photographers were, how the mechanical processes evolved, and what materials had been available in each era. Yet at the same time she admired him for it. "Sam wasn't affected by the opinion of the group, and I always thought that it was why he was able to go off and learn about photography."[21]

Photography may have maintained a subordinate position in the realm of art making throughout the 1960s, but ironically the supposedly lowly photograph was rapidly being absorbed into artwork of the highest visibility. In fact, the march of the photographic image through the studios of the most prominent artists during that decade becomes ever more notable today as, increasingly, we understand the effect of photography on the way we see the world. Wagstaff's eye was being conditioned to the language of photography long before his interest in the medium surfaced. In order to understand his revelation in front of Steichen's *The Flatiron* in 1973 then, it is important to go back to the essential ideas of his 1964 exhibit, "Black, White, and Gray," and beyond to the work of John Cage and Andy Warhol.

Cage did not compose in accordance with the traditions and structure of musical form, nor as a way of applying his own sense of order on the conventions of rhythm, melody, and harmony. Rather, he conceived a set of circumstances in which art could adapt itself to its surroundings. The natural flow of sound in the environment was essential: "Much of this art seems strongly anti-tradition, even recent tradition," Wagstaff wrote in his essay on "Black, White, and Gray" in the January 1964 issue of *ARTnews*. "Much of it seems sparse, pared down to a minimum; much of it is conceptual, idea art, as opposed to the retinal or visceral. In this respect one thinks of Cage's 'music to be seen.' "[22]

Cage's best-known piece, *4′ 33″*, calls for a performer to stand silently on stage with a musical instrument, whether a piano, flute, or cello, and do nothing for four minutes and thirty-three seconds. The audience is forced to listen to the sounds that surround them. At its premiere in Woodstock, New York, in 1952, people in the audience were intermittently baffled and offended. "They missed the point," John Cage said. "There's no such thing as silence. What they thought was silence, because they didn't know how to listen, was full of accidental sounds. You could hear the wind stirring outside during the first movement; during the second, raindrops began pattering the roof; and during the third, people themselves made all kinds of interesting sounds as they talked . . . or walked out." [23]

Just as with sound, we take our sight for granted. Most of what passes through our line of vision in the course of a day is grasped automatically, unconsciously, until we stop to consider not only what we are looking at, but *that* we are looking at it. The work in "Black, White, and Gray" was presented to allow the viewer to be conscious of the act of seeing. To know sight as a sensory experience can bring us to an awareness of our own being: "Look at that tree."

"Sam really was one of the most influential curators in advancing the cause of minimalist art," Barbara Jakobson said. "He knew an important movement when he saw one. And it's interesting how later he transferred all of that to photography." [24]

WHILE WORKING AT THE Wadsworth Atheneum, Wagstaff was a frequent dinner guest at his friend Mary Palmer's. In the months before the "Black, White, and Gray" show, he had sparred with her teenage son, John, over the aesthetic value of photography, often arguing late into the evening. John asserted that photography was an art form as significant as the brush. Little did Wagstaff anticipate that his own hardened attitudes—his belief in the supremacy of the created image over the captured one—would only fuel John Palmer's resolve to prove him wrong.

In the spring of 1964, a few months after the exhibit opened, John Palmer moved to New York to work for Jonas Mekas, the experimental filmmaker, founder of Anthology Film Archives and editor of *Film Culture* magazine. One day while delivering a package of magazines to the Empire State Building, Palmer, an aspiring filmmaker himself, looked up. Having met Warhol in his own living room on the opening night of Sam's show, he said to Mekas, "This would be a perfect film for Andy Warhol." Mekas suggested that he tell Andy, and several months after John did so, Warhol would make *Empire*. [25]

The Empire State Building was then the tallest building in the world, dominating the very center of the Manhattan skyline. New York itself was the international cultural capital and the bedrock of what would later become known as the global economy. Broadway set the standard for theater; the Museum of Modern Art was the presiding international contemporary art museum; the new buildings of Lincoln Center had just been erected as monuments to classical music and the ballet. The Empire State Building, then, stood as not just a symbol of New York, but as a beacon of hope, of industry, a reach toward the future—not only the tallest but also, perhaps, one of the most elegant buildings in the world. In other words, it was exactly the kind of immediately recognizable symbol that would attract Warhol. According to Gerard Malanga, John Palmer gets full credit for coming up with the idea for *Empire*.

In fact, Wagstaff had an unwitting role in bringing the film about: "It meant a lot to me relative to the importance that Sam had in my own life to show him the truth about photography with the *Empire* thing," Palmer, who went on to direct the 1972 Edie Sedgwick film *Ciao! Manhattan*, would later say. "It's as if *Empire* was proving my point to Sam and using Andy as a vehicle."[26]

Palmer arranged for use of an office at the Rockefeller Foundation on the forty-first floor of the Time-Life Building, which had an unobstructed view of the Empire State Building. The crew consisted of Warhol, Mekas, Malanga, and Palmer. Mekas was the cinematographer and used a 16 mm Auricon camera. They filmed the Empire State Building for 6½ hours straight, from 8:06 p.m. to 2:42 a.m. "John Palmer, Jonas Mekas, and I changed the reels for Andy," Malanga said. "Andy barely touched the camera during the whole time it was being made. He wanted the machine to make the art for him."[27]

Warhol thought of the Empire State Building as the towering erection of the Manhattan skyline and, while shooting, they joked about the length of the film in penile equivalents: 6½ hours of real-time footage equaled 6½ inches; the length of the film projected in a theater is just over 8 hours—or an endowment of 8 inches. "The Empire State Building is a star," Warhol announced when the filming was over. "It's an eight hour hard-on. It's so beautiful. The lights come on and the stars come out and it sways."[28]

Wagstaff's turn to photography with such obsessive fervor almost a decade later becomes more understandable when seen as an evolution from minimalism to photography. In particular, consider Andy Warhol's *Empire* as an eight-hour film about an inanimate object shot with a stationary camera. It exemplifies a kind of John Cage–infused minimalist gesture of photographic exploration, drawing parallel to the stillness of a photograph even as the passing of time is captured in the moving image. The viewer gazes at the screen in the same way that one looks at a photograph. There is no action. Nothing is happening. The Empire State Building is a focus for the eye in the same way that, in meditation, the mantra is a focus for consciousness. Cage's influence is obvious: the "nothing" that happens in his own *4'33"* is essentially the same "nothing" that happens in *Empire*.

For years people did not understand what made Warhol's work anything more than the ordinary object it depicted, whether a constructed Brillo box, a painted Campbell's soup can, or the filmed Empire State Building. But, equal to Warhol's choice of objects—emblems of cultural identity at the height of twentieth-century American optimism and mass-market capitalism—is his examination of the means of presentation itself, whether it is film, canvas, or print.

Perhaps there is no better example of the intersection of minimalism and photography than *Photopath, 1967–69* by Victor Burgin. A floor piece that measured sixty feet long, it resembled a flattened version of the long planks made of wood or brick or metal by Carl Andre or Robert Morris. Burgin's installation consisted of photographs of a gallery's hardwood floor, all printed to scale and laid out in a diagonal stretch on top of the precise floorboards in each photograph. *Photopath* is at once more and less literal than any minimalist object. This work comes closest to the idea of "nothing" than almost any minimalist object of the period—the photograph and the photographed object become one and the same.[29]

As these explorations with the photographic image were taking place on the conceptual side of contemporary art, the photograph itself began to receive more official acknowledgment as an object of creative expression. "New Documents," a landmark 1967 show at the Museum of Modern Art, first conferred importance on the work of Diane Arbus, Lee Friedlander, and Garry Winogrand. The exhibition, considered radical at the time, identified a new direction in photography: pictures with a casual look, and subject matter that was difficult for any critic to identify and categorize—the snapshot aesthetic pioneered by Robert Frank, or the "nothing" that the artists in "Black, White, and Gray" had been trying to get to—whether in the existential or the spiritual realm. In the wall text for the exhibit, John Szarkowski, the curator, suggested that until then the aim of documentary photography had been to show what was wrong with the world as a way to generate interest in changing it. But the artists in this show signaled a change: "Their aim has been not to reform life, but to know it." [30]

The ill-fated 1971 Michael Heizer show for which Wagstaff had commissioned *Dragged Mass Displacement* at the Detroit Institute of Arts was called "Michael Heizer: Photographic and Actual Work"; it was a survey of the artist's land art projects consisting of wall-sized photographs that documented his earthworks. In Sam's mind, however, the art consisted of the earthworks in the documentation, and not the photographic images themselves.

By the time Wagstaff met Mapplethorpe in 1972, his curatorial prejudices against photography had been chipped at considerably. Yet Mapplethorpe had not declared photography as his medium. His framed collages and assemblages were more conceptual than photographic—not unlike what the artists of the 1960s were doing with their mixed-media work. Wagstaff's belief in Mapplethorpe as an artist derived from these assemblages. It was only when Robert took possession of the Bond Street loft and started using the Hasselblad Sam had bought him that photography became his medium exclusively. When it did, his presentation acknowledged a minimalist aesthetic in stark, cool, posed subjects, clean lines, fine detail, distilled lighting, and crisp framing. "Mapplethorpe was interesting historically because he didn't totally reject the idea of conceptual art or minimalist art, he just incorporated it into photography," said Richard Marshall, an art historian who organized the Mapplethorpe retrospective at the Whitney Museum in 1988.[31] His subject matter—whether male genitalia or the petals of a flower—was presented at the same cool objective remove.

In January 1973, six months after Wagstaff and Mapplethorpe met and only days before the two went to see "The Painterly Photograph" exhibit at the Metropolitan Museum, Mapplethorpe had his first show of photographs. The Light Gallery mounted a small show of his Polaroids in its experimental second room.[32] The opening of Robert Mapplethorpe's show at a proper Madison Avenue gallery drew a stylish and overflowing menagerie of drag queens, men in leather, well-known artists, and uptown society people. This experience—a diverse and lively reception for a show of photographs—was still in Sam's mind when a few days later they went to the Met and he responded so passionately to Steichen's *The Flatiron*. That, and the music of photography trumpeted by two young Gabriels—Enrico Natali and Robert Mapplethorpe—from their tutors—Edwards at the Art Institute of Chicago and McKendry at the Met—must have given Sam the feeling that he was on solid curatorial ground.

Then, too, Warhol's *Empire* and Steichen's *The Flatiron* each present a New York City architectural landmark as symbol, and, while they cannot be equated in formal terms, both blur the boundaries between one form and another, between the handmade and the mechanical, between the created image and the captured one. Whether Wagstaff made a connection between the two while standing in front of *The Flatiron* that day, the march of the photographic image through the studios of the artists he knew and admired and exhibited throughout the 1960s had finally taken effect.

SEVEN

TRANSFORMATION

What we think is less than what we know. What we know is
less than what we love. What we love is so much less than
what there is. And to that precise extent we are so much less
than what we are.

—R. D. LAING[1]

S AM WAGSTAFF SAT AT HIS MOTHER'S BEDSIDE FOR WEEKS
during the spring of 1973 as she lay dying. It was less than a
year after he had met Robert Mapplethorpe, who was currently in Britain, and only months since he had begun to collect photographs. Olga
Newhall had been quick to detect her son's new romance, observing
during one of Sam's visits early into his relationship that he was wearing
an uncharacteristically stylish new shirt by Yves Saint Laurent. "You
must have met someone," she commented.[2] It was a disappointment to
her that the "someones" in Sam's life were always men, and a disappointment to him as well that she was never able to accept that.

Sam was now experimenting with taking pictures of his own. In the
days before Olga died he turned his Leica toward her, and he also photographed her moments after her death on May 13, at the age of seventy-
nine. The photographs he made of his mother's corpse are in keeping

with the practice of postmortem photography, a Victorian custom when photographs of the dead served not only as *memento mori* but also proof to distant relatives that an individual had in fact died. Of course, the camera functioned as something of a shield, too, distancing the photographer from the bald reality of his mother's death. Still, Sam was not afraid to stare bald reality in the face: the pictures of his mother's corpse are straightforward and unadorned. After photographing her body, Sam walked around documenting the rooms of the apartment. The pictures reveal the white curtains billowing like ghosts in the bedroom windows and the many bouquets of flowers in vases situated throughout the apartment, an homage to the memory of Olga in full bloom. Later he would label the envelope for the group of pictures, which were commercially developed, "Ma's funeral."[3]

The following year Wagstaff would walk into the Robert Schoelkopf Gallery on Madison Avenue and buy a small album of unusual *cartes de visites* from the 1860s with the signature of William H. Mumler (1832–1884). Scattered throughout the portraits on these cards were evanescent impressions—almost imperceptible figures—floating around the sitters. Today, Mumler is regarded both by historians of photography and occultism "as the first photographer to claim to capture a client's likeness in the company of a deceased person's ghost, called up for the occasion."[4] These portrait cards are considered outstanding examples of the minor genre of spirit photography.

The mingling of the apocryphal with the actual in the Mumler photographs might have had the resonance of Wagstaff's own memories of his mother throughout his intermittently enchanted and yet emotionally deprived childhood. His mother set a stylish tone for him, and he never did stop adoring her for it. When she died, he kept a few of her possessions and they would become talismans of loss, love, and her ineffable style.

In the weeks following Olga's death, Sam also photographed Patti Smith, who by that time had become a good friend. The portraits show her wrapped theatrically in one of Olga's long feather boas, one of the few mementos he kept from his mother. "Took a lot of pictures of Patti," Sam wrote to Mapplethorpe in London, "crazy but not so crazy as I'd have liked. Think some of them will be good even if rotten in the glamour vein of 1930s *Vogue*. I think it was the 4th time she'd posed in as many days or something."[5]

Wagstaff had insisted that Mapplethorpe go to London for the photography auctions while he remained in New York at Olga's bedside. When she died, Sam assured Robert that he should stay in London to buy the photographs they had agreed upon while perusing the auction catalogs. In the years before the invention of electronic communication, people corresponded through letter writing, and, during those difficult weeks, Sam and Robert sent handwritten letters to each other on the onionskin used for international airmail almost daily. "I feel a little bad about not being with you for your mother's funeral," Robert wrote to Sam, "but those things depress me so."[6] Whether Mapplethorpe, in his midtwenties, felt unable to comfort a man of Wagstaff's age over the death of a parent or he was simply oblivious of the need to do so, it was a callow excuse. Still, Sam's letters to Robert remained alternately melancholy and chatty, filled with the details of Olga's illness and her death alongside pointed reminders of everything Robert was missing while he was gone: "Night before Patti did my cards and pretty much corroborated what the astrologer had said. She's such fun. We ate at Spring Street and had a ball. She says to tell you how much she misses you, even to the extent of calling your name in her sleep, which didn't annoy Alan [Allen Lanier] too much!"[7]

During Olga's final week or two, Sam reported to Robert on his evening activities, whether a movie he had seen, a dance concert he attended, or a party he was dragged to by Tony and Jane Smith, who also brought along Tennessee Williams. He'd ask about Mapplethorpe's work while weaving in avowals of love: "Was amused to hear you've been doing flowers (because I have, too)," Sam wrote in one letter, only hinting at his own forays into photography, then deftly turning the subject back to his passion for Robert and Robert's work: "I'm looking forward to seeing them because anything you do has for me a very exquisite precision and a rare point of view of love from an unusual angle."[8]

Nevertheless, Sam was desolate in Robert's absence, deprived of the physical comfort and emotional warmth of a lover's proximity at such a primal moment. Still, Sam refused to make any request for Robert's return. In a letter to Robert following the funeral, he wrote that "the memorial service went well—about 20 people came and I think it was the sort of party my Ma would have approved of. There's lots of caviar left over, might bring you some."[9]

Sam was the executor of Olga's estate and his plan was to meet Robert in London after he took care of the initial paperwork. The truth was that tensions had been brewing between them even before Olga's death. For Wagstaff, there was no easy resolution to the fact of Mapplethorpe's sexual promiscuity, which was not unusual for a young gay man at the dawn of the gay liberation movement. Despite the level of tolerance Sam tried to maintain, it continued to feel like an emotional betrayal. Yet for Mapplethorpe, Wagstaff's photographic experimentation was a nuisance and a distraction, even a threatening one. Soon enough Sam was accusing Robert of trying to "inhibit" his creative energies. Perhaps it was out of self-protection as much as umbrage and frustration that Sam suggested on one transatlantic call that they should think about spending some time apart.[10] Still, a week after Olga died, Wagstaff wrote to Mapplethorpe as if with the cool reserve of a first cousin talking about the will after a death in the family:

> Had a meeting (reading of the will!) with lawyer and my sister yesterday. It looks to me as if I might be able to fly over on Wednesday. I'm shooting for that anyway. . . . I get about a million and my sister slightly less, but that's only a fourth or so of the value of the stock [from Newhall Land and Farming]. At any rate, there's lots of potential and I'd certainly like to make the most of it.[11]

WAGSTAFF HAD ALWAYS BEEN proud of Olga's brief career as a fashion illustrator for *Harper's Bazaar*. He would often say that he learned about "line" from his mother's drawings. When Olga married Donald V. Newhall, they had in common, among other things, their trained "eye." For his part, Newhall turned out to be a warm and supportive stepfather to the young Wagstaff, as well as an early example for him of a working artist. During a slide presentation about photography in the late 1970s, Wagstaff recounted a lesson he had learned: "I had a stepfather who was a portrait painter and he told me a very interesting story once. When he first started painting he would paint a portrait and the sitter or the sitter's family would have a party, and they would invite all of the family and dear friends for the unveiling of the portrait. And my stepfather used to get very depressed because invariably the close relatives would come and say, 'Oh, you're Mr. Newhall, the portrait painter, it's too bad that you made cousin Willy, or Uncle Harry, or whoever, look so old, because of course they don't look nearly as old as you've made them look in your picture.'" In the minds of relatives, Wagstaff explained, time had stood still. They were not able to see the subject of the portrait as they existed in the present. "Photography," Sam went on, "trumps painting in this regard. It can't help but freeze moments in time, regardless of how people remember the present or the past."[12]

In Sam's deathbed photographs of his mother, an old woman with white hair appears withered and diminished, lying beneath the sturdy upholstered headboard amid layers of bed linens and the pillows that seem to keep her comfortable. But in Sam's memory Mrs. Donald V. Newhall would always be a symbol of vigor and glamour, a force of nature, an anchor that kept Sam tethered to an exclusive world he claimed not to care "brickbats" about.

Wagstaff dutifully as well as genuinely loved his mother. He appreciated the elegance and worldliness and even the affected drama of her way of being. Over time, though, he recognized the intellectual limitations and prejudices masked by her refinement and the idle rituals of her set. He would not allow himself to be constrained in the same way. "Art was more important to him than playing all these social-status games that his mother was playing," Richard Tuttle said. "That was a dimension of nobility about Sam that was extraordinary."[13]

The fact remained that Wagstaff had long ago abandoned his own childhood aspiration to be a van Rensselaer or a Rhinelander. The possibility of accomplishing something on his own terms may have come a little later in his life, when he was in his thirties, but he became determined to eclipse the standard of cultivation set for him by his socially discerning and at times comically calculating mother.

By then Sam had firmly established himself in a rather lofty circle of like-minded friends and collaborators—Andy Warhol, Merce Cunningham, John Cage, and Robert Rauschenberg—not only within the art world but also in the roomy closet of midcentury Manhattan. Wagstaff's short legacy as a curator, with the landmark exhibition "Black, White, & Gray," and his commission of the two Merce Cunningham premieres at the Atheneum that drew on the same high-minded cultural impulses as Chick Austin's commission of *Four Saints in Three Acts*, were both grand gestures that eclipsed all class distinction, aspiring toward intellectual enlightenment in the language of the senses. No entry in the *Social Register*, no family pedigree, could come close to the honorable reach toward true excellence that, from that point on, redefined Wagstaff's standard.

THAT SUMMER, SAM RENTED his own house on Fire Island, next door to Sam Green's. There, he began to make a series of informal self-portraits, turning the camera on his own body, in the house and outside. In some, his fifty-one-year-old face is distorted into grotesque expressions; in others he stands at the ocean with water swirling around his feet; then he kneels in the water as droplets splash against the lens; and, finally, he lies in the water and photographs his feet bobbing on the surface. He photographs himself looking down at his lean torso, at his genitals, and at his feet; he urinates into various pots on the deck of the house; his erection juts straight out toward the edge of the picture frame. In a different set, he stands before the mirror photographing himself in a bathing suit and, then, in the various stages of its removal until he is naked. In another series, he is lying down on the deck outside, looking out at his body again, photographing himself in three different swimsuits of the same type, first in red, then in blue, and then in white. Sam assembled them as a grid.[14]

While Wagstaff continued to take photographs for several years, these sets of pictures in particular express the rapid transformation he was undergoing immediately following Olga's death. There is a saying that your mother gives birth to you twice: once when you're born and again when she dies. Sam's pictures compose a visual exploration of his most natural self. His nakedness and facial distortions and the swirling sea conjure nothing so much as a reenactment of birth in the period following his mother's death.

Undeniably, Sam was entering a new existential phase: financial security, sexual liberation now that Olga's disapproval no longer hovered over his relationships, and emotional expression in openly loving Robert. For the first time in his life, Wagstaff felt free to explore himself in the role of the artist, to express himself visually without the weight and the vast implications of his art historical training. Olga, too, like Robert, had conveyed to Sam that his proper role was not to make art but to support the creativity of others. She, who abandoned her career in illustration for the sake of her marriages, had been obligated to stand in the background. With her death Sam was free to assert himself as an artist—if he so chose—without her judgment.

And yet the more enthralled Wagstaff became with taking pictures, the more impudent Mapplethorpe became. Whenever Sam picked up a camera, Robert threw a childish temper tantrum: "You're the collector," he reminded him. "*I'm* the artist."[15] In one letter Sam wrote during this period, he tried to navigate Robert's feelings about the issue with delicacy even as he drew his own clear line in the sand:

> *I didn't mean that you stifle my creative thing—small though it be—I really meant that to be alone provided the opportunity to go out—do something on my own—almost the necessity to do so. . . . Taking pictures is a good way of getting rid of shitty ideas and of searching for new ones. I can see that it's a strong kind of psychoanalysis. There's no point in my pretending to myself that I have an eye if I can't go out and prove it.*[16]

Wagstaff's picture making remained an area of contention between them, but it did not prevent Sam from having his way with the camera. He found plenty of time by himself to make photographs, either in Oakleyville on Fire Island or in the city when Robert was in London—to try to "go out and prove" that he had an eye. At the same time, there is ample evidence from Sam's negatives that he used the camera as a way to get many young men to strip for him. The intimacy of the sittings and the evident playfulness between photographer and subject suggest that Sam knew some of the men he photographed fairly well. He would photograph them over the course of an hour or an afternoon, documenting the slow unveiling of the male body from the immediate circumstance for which his models were initially dressed—whether a social visit in Oakleyville, a walk in the woods, or sunbathing on the beach—until they were naked, sometimes aroused, and occasionally laughing during an intentional pose or a spontaneous gesture before the camera. His pictures manifest serious visual examination of his subject matter, but they are most striking as evidence of the new freedom with which he was expressing his desire.

"I must tell you that we artists cannot tread the path of Beauty without Eros keeping company with us and appointing himself as our guide," writes Thomas Mann in *Death in Venice*.[19] Wagstaff and Mapplethorpe both chose photographic subject matter and a way to represent it that today epitomizes the gay sensibility—the line of beauty in the male body, an erotic charge to aestheticized objects, significant form. In the early 1970s, as homosexuality and photography both were surfacing from the margins of legitimacy, Eros seemed to be guiding Robert and Sam from the outside as well as from within.

The visual dialogue evident in the photographs by these two men is striking, whether Robert ever chose to acknowledge it or not. There is a shared sensibility between patron and artist, as well as a kind of lovers' discourse played out in a photographic language. Whether Sam showed Robert his pictures or made the pictures surreptitiously to inform himself about Robert's work, one thing is clear: Wagstaff's photographs contain many of the signatures that were to become hallmarks of Robert Mapplethorpe's work.

Perhaps aware of Robert's feelings, Wagstaff never put forward his own pictures. He never had them printed in the formal manner of art objects. But within the entire cache of the photographs he made is a scrupulous visual examination of the male nude, found objects, and flowers, all influenced as much by the photographs throughout the history of photography he was collecting at the time as by the historic moment in which he and Robert both were making pictures—the rise of the gay rights movement.

During that summer of 1973, even as the constricting expectations of his mother lifted permanently following her death, the sting of her disapprovals lingered. Olga always had dangled her affection from a distance, and Robert's resistance about returning to New York for Olga's funeral elicited that familiar state of longing; his censure of Sam's creative exploration, too, echoed hers; and Robert's promiscuity interfered with the purer emotional connection that Sam had longed for. The withholding of affection and the challenge to his sense of emotional security resonated with the deprivations of his early life. According to Sam's nephew Tom Jefferson, his uncle once told him there were only a couple of people in his life whom he genuinely loved: "One of them was his mother and the other was Robert Mapplethorpe."[20]

EIGHT

CIRCLES OF INFLUENCE

It is only the shallow people who do not judge by appearances. The true mystery of the world is the visible, not the invisible.

—OSCAR WILDE[1]

WAGSTAFF AND MAPPLETHORPE MADE A PILGRIMAGE to Ridgefield, Connecticut, in late 1973 to visit Bernard Perlin, who had been a close friend of George Platt Lynes. When Lynes died of lung cancer in 1955, Perlin inherited all the photographer's negatives and prints, which he stored in files in the barn behind his studio. Sam and Robert's visit proved disagreeable to Perlin. First, they made him pick them up at the nearest train station, in Brewster, New York, even though Sam could well have afforded a taxi. When their train arrived, they announced they were hungry and insisted on a late impromptu breakfast in the station café, which put Perlin out further as he sat there and watched them eat.

Perlin, then fifty-five, often spoke of his years in the George Platt Lynes circle in New York in the 1940s, describing artists and writers and dancers who spent their days in diligent pursuit of their craft, their evenings filled with rich cultural activity and stylish festivity that served as their just rewards. Lynes's circle included Pavel Tchelitchev, Lincoln Kirstein, the illustrious Russian émigré choreographer George Balanchine, and with friends like Gertrude Stein and Jean Cocteau, his reach clearly extended to Europe as well. As Lincoln Kirstein described Lynes, he was "a dandy devoted to the program that every dandy since Beau Brummel has slavishly pursued: the rehabilitation of the commonplace, the elevation of contemporary behavior into myth."[2]

Lynes photographed many accomplished people in the arts, not only on assignment for *Vogue* or *Harper's Bazaar* but also for his own artistic purposes. He created a pantheon of luminaries in arts and letters that stands as a piece of the historical record as much as serious portraiture, in a tradition that includes Julia Margaret Cameron in nineteenth-century Britain or Nadar (Gaspard-Felix Tournachon) in nineteenth-century France, as well as his contemporaries Cecil Beaton and, to a lesser extent, Carl Van Vechten. His successors at *Vogue*—Richard Avedon and Irving Penn—also owed something of a debt to him.

In addition, Lynes often photographed the male nude in individual figure studies or in staged narrative scenes, pictures imbued with theatrical lighting and mythological symbol. The nudes are original, stylish, graphically articulate, visually accomplished, and driven by erotic passion that reaches for aesthetic idealization. George Balanchine wrote that Lynes's "secret was plasticity . . . the bodies seemed to exist in an actual aery ambience, akin to the three-dimensional vitality in sculpture."[3]

While Wagstaff had known Perlin peripherally in the early 1950s, it was, of course, as a result of Sam's affair with Chuck Howard, who had been Perlin's casual lover before becoming Lynes's live-in lover and occasional model for three years, until 1951. It is relevant to reiterate that the thirty-year-old Wagstaff met Chuck Howard soon after his relationship with Lynes had ended. Howard was the "boy next door" with dirty blond hair; he was slender, witty, and a great deal of fun to be with. "Chuck was absolutely lovable. He had a thousand best friends," Perlin said. "Sam was smitten with Chuck and wanted to marry him."[4]

According to Perlin, Wagstaff's relationship with Howard lasted less than a year. On the rebound from Lynes, Chuck wanted something less intense with Sam. Perhaps Lynes was something of a rival in Sam's eyes.

At Perlin's house, decades after that affair had created for Sam a lingering semblance of disappointment, he and Robert spent several hours going through the Lynes photographs. In the eighteen years since his death in 1955, Lynes's reputation had receded into obscurity. Sam thumbed through the pictures as Robert quietly looked on. Eventually Sam selected about a dozen for Perlin to put aside for him. But then Sam never contacted Perlin about the pictures again. Perlin couldn't figure out what they were looking for. The whole episode left him feeling polluted and exploited.[5]

There was plenty for Wagstaff to like about the Lynes images, so it is conspicuous that he didn't bother to take any with him. Clearly, he made the trip with a mission. Of any photographer in the history of the medium, Lynes came closest to providing a template for what would later be the hallmarks of Mapplethorpe's work, both in his photographs of the male nude and in his portraiture—in particular, homoerotic imagery at once classical and experimental. Sam and Robert no doubt studied Lynes's style. While Mapplethorpe may have been working out some ideas by studying Lynes's pictures, it would have been a strategic choice on Sam's part not to create any evidence of the connection by buying any of them.

Of course, there was also Sam's personal curiosity. Undoubtedly he knew he would find pictures of Chuck Howard among Lynes's prints—some nude, some not. Maybe he was showing Robert what a former lover looked like. Maybe he was trying to identify his own primal habits of attraction, drawing private comparisons between Chuck Howard and Mapplethorpe—who, aside from the differences in style from one era to the next were, not surprisingly, similar physical types.

Perlin saw Wagstaff only one more time—at an exhibition of George Platt Lynes photographs at Sonnabend Gallery several years later. According to Perlin, Sam tore through the show, disparaging the work and muttering that the photographs were too expensive.[6]

———

EARLY IN 1974 SAM used the U.S. mail to send a letter from one end of Bond Street to the other. It was a *cri de coeur* from the older man to Robert:

Dear Muffin,

Just a little note to wake you up by some morning and to tell you how much I love you and need you. All the things (nice things) I want to say to you and never seem to have a chance to—they pass by unsaid too often, but I am very proud of you—just in general—and especially as a loyal and beautiful lover. I know I disappoint you often. I wish I didn't and it doesn't mean I don't feel that you're a tremendously important part of me and of my life. Sometimes, like now and in the last few months, I get into low spots and I suppose I drag anyone close to me down with me, but this period will pass if you'll hold on a little bit.[7]

The combination of Sam's mother's death, his insecurity about Robert's feelings for him—given Robert's acknowledged promiscuity, never mind his youth—might have brought Sam to an uncharacteristic vulnerability. His own unrealized artistic aspirations seemed to underlie his tone as he went on:

Don't' ever think that I'm not completely for you, or don't listen, or believe what you have to say. I'm just slow and maybe too proud to show you that I understand your (usually, I have to admit) sensible point of view. There's so much we can help each other with. Any relationship that lasts is difficult and at times tedious and the daily thing whittles down too many points that seemed higher before; only the increased friendship and deeper love and understanding can replace those former highs. I hope we can keep finding new ways to be closer. There must be lots of joys of being closer that we haven't found yet. I hope you're hopeful and not discouraged about us. I know I don't always feel sympathetic about your moods and depressions as my easy way out is to try to hide from thinking that I'm responsible for them. Mine aren't any less easy to cope with I know. Maybe we should talk more about us or maybe it is better to take it for granted. Often I feel I don't know you as well as I should and that allows me to fill in the missing parts all wrong.[8]

In the next passage, Sam the patron and Sam the lover are entwined, sincerely, with humility, his self-evaluation in service of a philosophical appeal to try to make the relationship work and put them both on equal footing:

Don't worry about the money thing. I will [??] down and get it more under control. It's silly not to spend much more on ourselves and our lives. It's always been my thing to deny myself and the people around me for collecting something as if I were driven to not enjoy—some dumb self-hate or something which I drag you into. You do help me there as in so many other ways. You just have to keep after me it's so ingrained.

Muffin, I love you and wish I could make you much happier than I do, but you have to help me there, too. I know how hard it is to be dependent on someone else, how unfair and tricky for a relationship especially for one's pride and I congratulate you on how beautifully and lovingly you handle it. That's only one of the many good things you bring to us. Be happy and work hard. I love you and kiss you.[9]

Sam was fifty-two, a man whose aspirations for romantic love had evolved over the years. He was ready for something grander and more substantial than he'd ever allowed himself. But Robert, barely half Sam's age, could not fully appreciate the subtleties, much less the monogamous impulse, of his lover's plea. Nor could he handle the enormity and purity and even the responsibility of the love being expressed and offered—not at that point in his life, not with his own self-absorption as an artist, and not in the midst of the sexual carnival of New York City, where he was finding the essential matter for his work.

Strangely, the letter reads as if it were the kind of message Sam would like to have gotten from Robert—some newly penitent, appreciative, and surprisingly virtuous Robert. Perhaps Sam wrote the letter as a projection of the kind of acknowledgment of love, attachment, commitment, and respect he'd been hoping one day to receive from his lover. That never came. Occasionally, however, Robert would throw Sam a bone, as in a letter he sent at the time of Olga's death with a back-handed apology for giving Sam a hard time about taking pictures himself: "I am selfish but then that's an atribute [sic] that all artists possess." [10]

Love between two men can manifest itself in ways that seem foreign to the committed heterosexual couple. On a purely physical level, the fundamental composition of two male bodies together determines the manner, purpose, and freedom of the sex act. First, the sex drive is incontrovertibly dislodged from the underlying possibility of procreation; secondly, the varying levels of testosterone in the body propel sex between two men to be less a form of emotional connection than an animal act of physical gratification; finally, lust itself is the desired feeling and the destination, and not affection, which, of course, may or may not follow sexual congress. Men have a tendency to withdraw into themselves after orgasm—and although this is an eternal cause of consternation between the sexes, two men together implicitly understand this impulse and are less prone to make an issue of it. So often, sex for a man is less about lovemaking than about carnal desire and sensate pleasure brought about by physical worship—of the object of desire or even of the self. There might be a mutual regard for bringing each other to orgasm and it may be in the spirit of camaraderie or good sportsmanship, but the desire for one's own pleasure is always competing. There is no doubt that love and companionship long outlast the lust that might first have brought two men together. True enough, by 1974, Sam and Robert's relationship began moving toward a spiritual ideal, even a platonic love that long outlasted their carnal interest in each other. But that doesn't mean that for Sam there weren't some profound emotional adjustments along the way.

Only a month before Sam wrote this love letter to Robert, declaring his hope that they would find "new ways to be closer," the gay rights movement marked an important milestone. On December 15, 1973, the American Psychiatric Association voted to remove homosexuality from its list of psychiatric disorders. This shift in policy was reported on the front pages of newspapers across the country. On the streets, in bars, at restaurants, movie houses, Broadway theaters, and on the subway, the gay male gaze, now no longer psychiatrically pathologized, roamed ever more freely. The veil of fear about being discovered, much less arrested, was beginning to lift, the double life of the closet increasingly a vestige of the not so distant past. Nonetheless, for many gay men who had for so long internalized the fear of discovery, New York City continued to serve as a kind of big open closet in which they proceeded to live out their fantasies while at the same time hiding in plain sight from parents, friends, and employers. Mapplethorpe exemplified this paradox: one of the most visible gay men in Manhattan, he kept his sexuality a secret from his parents a mere borough away in Queens—to such an extent that he maintained a charade, for their benefit alone, that he was married to Patti Smith.

For that young generation of gay men in Manhattan, it became a game and a thrill just to walk out the door and into the streets—a riotous carnival of titillation and sexual opportunity, supported by an intricate code of signals that formed a semiotic language of gay communication.

In that sexualized atmosphere, Sam and Robert walked streets that crackled with an erotic charge. Searching eyes scanned the sidewalks in broad daylight; for a while the heterosexual world was oblivious of those cruising eyes all over town, eyes that locked in passing like fish tugging on the line, a new sexual conquest reeled in with a furtive glance over the shoulder, followed by a smile of recognition between strangers, a pause, a brief conversation, and then, and then. Such was the era before AIDS, when two gay men meeting had little emotional investment other than to simply fuck first and get to know each other later—or, more likely, not.

Sam and Robert were monogamous in the first months of their relationship and they spent almost all their time together. Especially once Robert moved to Bond Street, they were so close that they regularly dropped by each other's places unannounced. But not long after Mapplethorpe moved into the loft, Wagstaff walked in one day to find him in bed with someone else. Sam was furious and lost his temper, but Robert, anything but penitent, asserted that this is who he was and he wasn't about to change. For Robert, it required skill to maintain that delicate balance between his need—artistic and personal—to experience his own sexuality as broadly as possible and his wish to keep Sam close.

A month or so after Sam's *cri de coeur* to Robert, he received a letter from his young lover written in the baby-talk patois typical of their relationship: "I promise to work real hard this year. Maybe by next year muffin will be bringing home some of the monies. You've been really good to me. I love you Sammi."[11] But not long after that, Robert wrote another letter that reflected a degree of circumspection and remorse: "I don't want our relationship to fall apart. I know it's hard with me all sexed up 24 hours. I've got to control myself as it seems to be too much for you. Or maybe you're just tired of me. I don't understand it—but somehow it's gotta work. I don't really want to be with anyone else. I really do love you." But he didn't stop his habit of cruising the gay bars every night.[12]

Meanwhile, Sam was not one to wallow in emotional victimhood. He could play Robert at his own game. Now that it was clear that monogamy was not a realistic option, Sam—an avatar of cultural change and a hedonist in his own right—wasted no time. One day in early March, he picked up a young man in what was affectionately referred to in those years as a subway *tearoom*—a subway bathroom— where gay men were known to cruise each other. Mark Kaminsky, a twenty-one-year-old student at Pratt Institute studying drawing and architectural design, was blond, very handsome, and well spoken. Sam took him home and, almost immediately, set him up as a second lover.

Perhaps a week after Sam met Mark, he and Robert went to London for more photography auctions. Sam dangled the new arrival of Mark before Robert just enough to get the desired result. That Mark was attractive and an art student at Pratt was enough to summon Robert's insecurity. Sam, himself increasingly infatuated, wrote several letters to Mark during his week in London; the first written the day he arrived, thanks Mark for the night they spent together and for waking him in time to catch his flight. He also let Mark know he had told Robert about him: "Things a little edgy with Robert but he's really terrific and I hope that whatever happens we will be friends and do things together," Sam wrote. "He's taken some weird and sexy pictures here, beautiful as always. . . ." [13]

In Sam's next letter, he confesses his attraction to Mark and suggests that Robert has become suddenly more affectionate:

MARCH 11, 1974

Dear Mark,

A quick note to say hello and to tell you that I think of you a lot—too much, as a matter of fact, especially how beautiful you were the last evening we had dinner. Incredible to fall for someone's blond hair! How crazy—and with a no-good hiding inside. I should be ashamed, but magic (black magic or otherwise) is magic and there's no denying it. How are you? Things are going much better with Robert since I've told him a little about you (isn't that crazy, too!). He's been so nice and attentive and really great to be with for the 1st time in a long time. . . . [14]

Sam wrote again the following day, his infatuation leading him into a kind of stream-of-consciousness poetry. He had met Mark only two weeks before:

Seem to have developed a compulsive writing jag directed at all that sun drenched-ness of yours and that I think of constantly and that warms me here in moments of all kinds. . . .

You really shine, Baby, like some yellow beacon just getting kindled sleepy dreaming out of range outrageous stereotype of everything I like to look at Cheshire cat stretching in the sun show off even when you don't know you are or who you are. I do see you as that ideal I want you to be and you are. . . .

If you're a passing fancy then life is full of flowers that one picks

or can't or leaves untouched or lives in a greenhouse with or rolls in
the fields for. Words are such shit, they come out wrong or not enough
not like touching or being naked or kissing you all over when you're
brown in the sun and laughing. . . . A hug, you no-good green-eyed
monster and an extra kiss on your balls.[15]

JUDY LINN HAD FIRST glimpsed Wagstaff in the late 1960s. She was
in a restaurant on a visit home to Detroit from Pratt, where her friendships with Mapplethorpe and Smith had begun. Sam was the "movie-
star gorgeous" man presiding at the table next to the Linns after an
opening at the DIA, but it was not until 1972 that Judy would officially
meet Sam, in the first months of his new relationship with Robert. Once
Sam started to collect photographs, the two of them established a genuine rapport. The first time she went to Sam's loft on Bond Street, he
mentioned his interest in Stieglitz. She lent him her Stieglitz books and
soon enough Sam was calling her up spontaneously to ask whether she
wanted to go out to dinner or come over to see some new pictures.[16]

"I think Robert was bored with it all and couldn't take sitting
around and looking at these photographs so much," Linn said. "But I
would go over there and get to look at photographs and it was great
fun." Sam would get so excited about showing her his newest acquisitions, lamenting the amount of money he spent but always justifying it
at the same time "because they're so beautiful." He once showed her
fifteen Adam Clark Vroman prints he had just bought. "Perfect, perfect, perfect platinum prints," Judy said. "You could see the tonalities
of everything in the photograph—it was a Navajo Indian in his home
and Sam pointed out that everything Indian-made was one tonality,
and everything Western-made, such as an umbrella, was a completely
different tonality."[17]

Sam folded Linn, a photographer, into the new and developing circle
of colleagues and acquaintances who shared his interest in photography.
Marge Neikrug was another person Sam was getting to know. She was
a cultivated woman, well turned out in Chanel suits, perfectly coiffed in
a modern and unpretentious style. Her eponymous gallery, one of the

first in Manhattan to show photographs exclusively, took up the ground floor of her town house on East 68th Street, and Neikrug enjoyed Sam's company for his genuine curiosity and the reach of his knowledge. When Sam started to buy photographs, he would walk into her gallery and spend an hour at a time looking at a single picture. He would pick it up and study it, then put it down and cross the room to look at it from a different angle; he'd hold a picture up to the wall and then stare at it again in his hand. The pictures were not expensive at that point, but eventually, Neikrug got annoyed at all the time she'd spend watching him shop. "A cheap bastard," she called him affectionately, recalling those afternoons.[18]

Marge looked forward to the occasional evenings when she would go out to dinner with Sam and Robert. Sam had his own motives, of course, and he succeeded in arranging for her to show one of Mapplethorpe's early photographs in her gallery, in April 1973. It was an uncharacteristic picture of a boy on the street mounted on an asymmetrical piece of varnished wood. When the piece didn't sell, Sam bought it himself for two hundred dollars.[19]

In those early years, when photography had yet to establish itself in the fine arts, it was easy for Sam to figure out where to search for photographs. By 1974, Robert Schoelkopf Gallery had begun to introduce occasional photography exhibits among the painting shows they were known for, and other galleries would soon follow. The flea markets and antique bookstores continued to provide great satisfaction when he discovered an unexpected gem. In addition, curators at the Museum of Modern Art and the Metropolitan Museum directed him to private dealers, some of whom were in possession of the finest rare albums and prints. While Sam's exploration of the field was methodical and at the same time maniacal, he went in as much for the pleasure of the hunt as for the moment he could share a new discovery with Robert. This was a language they shared. The act of looking at pictures together had become a version of lovemaking and provided some of the intimacy that sex had given them at the beginning but, increasingly, Robert took less interest in the nineteenth-century works Sam was collecting.

Wagstaff received a call in early 1974 from George Rinhart regarding a set of albums of calotypes by David Octavius Hill and Robert Adamson, 268 images in five separate volumes, dating from 1845. Seen the previous year by Weston Naef of the Met while visiting the Royal Scottish Academy, the albums were thought to be from the collection of Heinrich Schwarz, an authority on Hill and Adamson, whose study of their calotypes had been published to accompany an exhibition at the Museum of Modern Art in 1941.[20]

David Octavius Hill painted scenes of Scottish life in the 1820s and '30s. His work was taken seriously enough that he was eventually made a member of the Royal Scottish Academy.[21] In 1843, 470 ministers resigned from their Church of Scotland parishes for reasons of conscience, stood up in an assembly hall, and walked out en masse. Hill, a witness to the spectacle, attempted to preserve the historic incident on canvas, but realized soon enough that making a painting that would contain almost 500 portraits was not feasible. Meanwhile, he had heard of experimentation with a new process by which impressions of the camera obscura could be fixed on paper. This led him to a young chemist named Robert Adamson, who was versed in the new calotype process, developed by his older brother, John. "Thus the partnership began which was to produce the noble and extensive series of portraits which for powerful characterization and artistic quality of uniformly high excellence have certainly never been surpassed and possibly not even rivaled by any other photographer," wrote J. Craig Annan in *Camerawork*, Alfred Stieglitz's magazine, in 1905. "This may seem an extravagant appreciation of Hill's work, but it has been arrived at after mature deliberation."[22]

Rinhart told Wagstaff that the Hill and Adamson albums were about to land on his doorstep. The Scottish gentleman who had shown the volumes to Naef had just crossed the Atlantic, and he was arriving that afternoon to show them to Rinhart for possible acquisition. Rinhart suggested that Sam drop everything to come see them. At the scheduled hour, Rinhart greeted the fellow, a headmaster at a private school in Scotland, and took him into his office in the back of the house. When Sam arrived soon after, Rinhart asked him to wait in the front parlor.

Rinhart looked over the bound volumes in his office and negotiated the price he wanted to pay for them: $150,000.

Then he brought the volumes into the front parlor, where, according to Rinhart, Sam looked through each one carefully, turning the pages while periodically making a sound he made whenever his eyes fell on something he liked—a kind of *fwooh*, his lower lip flipping out from under his upper teeth, followed by a quick rise and fall of his bushy eyebrows. While looking through the last volume, Sam asked Rinhart how much he was asking for the entire set. Blithely, Rinhart floated a $225,000 price tag. Sam asked Rinhart how much he was paying the Scot in the other room and Rinhart told him. When Sam balked at the difference, Rinhart shrugged. "If not you, I will sell it to someone else for my asking price." Sam bought the five volumes on the spot, agreeing to pay a total of $215,000.[23]

If ever there were a conquest to bring back to Robert, this was it. The Hill and Adamson pictures were made in the first decade following the invention of photography, and the albums Sam purchased were comprehensive. They documented not only this population of ministers, but the buildings and streets of Edinburgh, a fishermen's village, and many other details of daily Scottish life. The facsimile representation of the world was pure magic in the 1840s. So many elements factor into the aesthetic and historic significance of this set of volumes today, not least the methodology of the two photographers. In the pictures taken on the streets of Edinburgh, little ghostly wisps appear where people passed through the frame too quickly for the camera to capture. But in 1974, there was scant scholarship and literature about Hill and Adamson. In buying the five albums, Wagstaff was operating at a level of instinct and intuition.

Photographs, particularly those from the nineteenth century, could be handmade rarities. When the subject was well observed, the technique exemplary, the quality of the paper high, and its surface yielding texture and tone, especially if it were in excellent physical condition, a print could be sublime. "A friend of mine once said, 'The only way to get to know a Raphael drawing is to own one,'" Wagstaff later told a classroom of students. "In a funny way, that has a truth to it, because if you really have the drawing, you can pore over it. I cannot tell you the sensation that one misses, all of you who make photographs, when you put it behind glass."[24]

WAGSTAFF MAINTAINED THAT COLLECTING was in his genes, something that ran in his family. He would mention the uncle who was a serious book collector, the aunt who scoured the secondhand shops for treasures.[25] But there was something about Sam's obsessive collecting that seemed equally to come out of emotional deprivation. Photography provided Wagstaff an entirely undiscovered sphere in which to explore a new visual language, a history of processes and materials. He could traverse a subterranean world of private dealers and used bookstores and people who shared his interest in the peripheral and arcane. He could champion an unheralded cause and project an original point of view. Here was an entirely new community he wanted not so much to be a part of as to re-create on his own iconoclastic terms, with no obligation other than his belief in the medium—and his pleasure at looking at pictures.

Keith De Lellis, a private photography dealer in New York for many years before opening his gallery on Madison Avenue in 1997, started collecting and selling photographs in the early 1970s, when he was an enterprising teenager. He would venture into Manhattan from Queens, where he lived, and peruse the antique booksellers in the East Fifties for old photographs. He acquired early photographic prints for under a dollar and then resold them to museums and private collectors. He would type up lists of his collection and have his mother, a schoolteacher, mimeograph them. He'd send those to dealers as well as to curators at the Smithsonian or the Metropolitan Museum of Art. They became his clients.

De Lellis first encountered Wagstaff around this time in Argosy Books, a venerable store with a large inventory of old and rare books and prints. "I had no idea who he was, but he was wearing a chambray shirt and this flamboyant kind of Navajo Indian necklace in turquoise and silver," De Lellis recalled.[26] Not long after that, De Lellis met Wagstaff again at the Central Park West apartment of the dealers Allen and Hillary Weiner, who dealt in cameras and daguerreotypes and other nineteenth-century photography. Sam, De Lellis noted right away, "liked to get a bargain."

The photography world at that time remained a very small place—a ghetto in the art world, but for the teenage De Lellis, Sam's presence took it to another level altogether. With his associations with the Warhol crowd as well as society and museum people, "he made photography very fashionable, very chic," De Lellis said.[27]

Then there were Sam's surprisingly catholic tastes, which made him popular in all quarters of the photography world. At the Photographic Historical Society's fairs, he'd go table to table, equally excited about buying valuable nineteenth-century photographs or tintypes that cost only a couple of dollars as he was with a major purchase like the Hill and Adamson albums.

Daniel Wolf, who would later open what became for a time arguably the best photography gallery in New York, was an undergraduate at Bennington College in 1974. He had been interested in photography since high school, when he was an exchange student in Brittany and walked into an antique shop one day where he came across three albumen prints from the nineteenth century. He had never seen such arresting prints before. From that moment he was obsessed and, financed by his wealthy parents, he would go to Europe throughout his college years to buy nineteenth-century photographs. "I started to deal photographs because my dad told me that if I wanted to paint, which is what I did in college, I had to pay for the art classes. So I started selling photographs. I matted them up and put them in cardboard boxes and got a folding table and set up in front of the Metropolitan Museum and was able to sell a few hundred dollars of albumen albums over a weekend."[28]

Wolf kept all of his good photographic albums at his parents' apartment on Fifth Avenue. Already aware of Wagstaff's reputation in the small world of photography, he called Sam one day in 1974 to say he had some fine nineteenth-century material that might be of interest. When they met, Sam glommed on an album that Wolf thought was of no value. He had purchased it on the fly in Paris, running into a bookstore quickly on the way to the Metro. Asking if they had any albums, the proprietor pulled out these "photographs of Corot drawings," Wolf recalled. "I bought the album because it was only a dollar." Wagstaff stood with Wolf looking at the album and practically levitated. He told Wolf that it was an album of Corot *cliché verre*, a process in which nineteenth-century French artists drew or etched on smoked glass over a sheet of photographic paper, which was then exposed to light. "I had no idea what that was," Wolf said. "Of course Sam knew that period. He knew the Barbizon school, and he knew about Corot's friend Constant Dutilleux, the painter who encouraged him to experiment with *cliché verre*."[29] Sam asked him how much he wanted and Wolf put a high price on it, $700, for the album of approximately a dozen prints. Sam bought it on the spot. (Today an album of Corot *cliché verre* sells at auction for at least $1000 per print.)

Like De Lellis and Wolf, Harvey Shipley Miller, a young associate at a white-shoe law firm, had become a nineteenth-century photography enthusiast at a young age. He had completed an art history course at the Fogg Art Museum (while at Harvard Law School) with a focus on Milton Avery, and his interest in photography began when his boyfriend, Randall Plummer, dragged him to a show at the Robert Schoelkopf Gallery in 1974. Miller wrinkled his nose at the idea; he considered photography "a technical medium, a stepchild of the arts." When they got to the gallery, however, a show of work by Julia Margaret Cameron was just coming down. Several portraits were leaning against the wall, and one, a portrait of the astronomer Sir John Herschel, caught Miller's eye. "It looked like Rembrandt," he remembered. "That gaze in his eye, the light falling on the pupil, his otherworldly gaze, the white hair framed by the cap. It was extraordinary for me. I just flipped."[30]

They bought the photograph—their first—for $750. Soon after, they bought another Cameron from Schoelkopf, a signed portrait of the poet Alfred Lord Tennyson. Next, they bought a Kootz edition of *The Pencil of Nature* by William Henry Fox Talbot—one of the inventors of photography—for $5000 and then *The Sun Pictures*, also by Fox Talbot, for another $5000. These figures for photographic editions were astronomical in the early 1970s, but the Miller-Plummer photography collection was now underway.[31]

That year Miller had seen a small catalog of the rare books and albums being sold by George Rinhart and soon he was buying photographs from Rinhart as well. One day Miller and Plummer were walking through a Photographica fair at the Statler Hilton Hotel with George Rinhart, who introduced them to Sam Wagstaff. Rinhart had thus begun to play his best collectors—including Wagstaff, Arnold Crane, and Harvey Miller and Randall Plummer—against one another. When Rinhart acquired any new group of photographs or albums to sell, he would rotate the first choice among them. If one did not accept his prices, he would mention that the others were lined up right behind.

In the midst of the Photographica tables at the Statler Hilton, Wagstaff pulled Miller and Plummer aside. "We have to stick together," he told them. "The collectors have to stick together." He stared at the two of them and said, "The dealers lie."[32]

Over the years, Miller found Sam a reassuring presence at those trade fairs on the outskirts of the world of photography, where "tchotchke hounds" sold postcards and Civil War paraphernalia, territory that Sam was happy to mine precisely because no one of his background would look for treasure there. Miller considered Wagstaff unusually generous with his knowledge and supportive in their mutual pursuit of photographs. "He was highly educated, and his voice, his bearing, his thinking was so to the manor born and very, very sophisticated, but also very elegant," Miller said. "On occasions when we had coffee together, I would have iced coffee and he'd just have a cup of hot water with lemon."[33]

Even though Wagstaff became more immersed in photography and the motley cast of characters it brought into his life, he did not abandon his old friends and acquaintances so much as he tried to convert them. "When he started collecting photography, he was like a kid with new toys," his neighbor Klaus Kertess said. "He'd knock on my door and ask if I wanted to see some photographs. What little I learned about photography, I learned from Sam essentially. He was collecting these amazing nineteenth-century photographs. We'd have a couple of lines of coke and there'd be this big cardboard box with thousands of dollars worth of photographs and Sam would pull them out one by one, and show them to me, talk about them, then put them back again."[34]

Sam and Robert were in Paris in the summer of 1974 scavenging photographs and albums at flea markets such as the Marché aux Puces, at rare-book stands such as Tex-Braun, and from the booksellers along the Seine, educating themselves about French photographers of the nineteenth century as they went along. The painters Brice and Helen Marden happened to be in Paris at the same time. Brice Marden had connections to both Sam and Robert; he had befriended Robert at Max's Kansas City and had since taken up residence in the building next door to Mapplethorpe's on Bond Street; Sam had bought Marden's work from Klaus Kertess. "Sam and Robert and Helen and myself, we were all staying in the Hotel la Louisiane in Paris," Marden said. "They came in from a day where they had bought all these pictures. They were showing us these incredible old photographs. They were both really excited. This was when I started to have some inkling of Sam."[35]

Even as increasing attention was being paid to photography in the early 1970s, the art world continued to condescend to what it considered an applied art. Marden himself couldn't quite reconcile the loss of Wagstaff as a champion of his own brand of avant-garde work. "To lose someone like that to photography hurt," as Marden put it. He and others worried that if too many collectors like Sam turned to photography, it would kill the market for drawings and other less expensive work that younger artists depended on for income.[36]

WHILE IN LONDON TO attend photography auctions that October, Wagstaff made a purchase of such stunning audacity that it resulted in international controversy. On the block at Sotheby's on October 18 was an album of ninety-four portraits by Julia Margaret Cameron. The artist herself had assembled the album as a gift to her friend Sir John Herschel, which made it an object of unique historical significance. The gavel at Sotheby's came down on Sam's bid for the "Herschel album," as it was called, at an unprecedented £52,000 pounds—about $130,000, an astounding sum for photography in 1974.

Julia Margaret Cameron, now a towering figure in the history of photography, is known for portraits that reflect the period in which she worked and the artists with whom she associated and photographed, among them John Millais, Dante Gabriel Rossetti, and William Holman Hunt, the trio of founders of the Pre-Raphaelite Brotherhood. She did not take up photography until the 1860s, at the age of forty-eight. Her husband, a retired jurist, went to Ceylon on business, leaving her behind at the family home on the Isle of Wight. Her daughter and son-in-law gave her a camera: "It may amuse you, Mother, to try photography during your solitude at Freshwater Bay," her daughter told her.[37]

Embracing the field, Cameron said about her intentions as a photographer: "My aspirations are to ennoble Photography and to secure for it the character and uses of High Art by combining the real and Ideal and sacrificing nothing of the Truth by all possible devotion to Poetry and Beauty."[38]

All the negatives of the portraits in the Herschel album had been lost, which underscored the singularity of these nineteenth-century prints, increasing their value. In addition, the album was assembled and annotated in the artist's own hand as a gift to a pioneer in photography— Herschel had invented hypo (a chemical used in the process of photographic film development), coined the terms "negative" and "positive" to distinguish developed film from photographic prints, and had been a friend of Fox Talbot.[39] Besides the photographs, the binding itself—a panel of solid oak with a large medallion of carved foliage—was a beautifully crafted object. Finally, the album included an unpublished letter in which Mrs. Cameron issued a handwritten defense of what critics referred to as her "blurred style."

News of Sam's purchase of the Herschel album rippled through the art world on both sides of the Atlantic. The London art market in general was depressed, partly because of the Arab oil embargo and the resulting precipitous drop in stock prices, and the sale of the album at Sotheby's and one or two other photographs at Christie's that same day came as a surprise—a daunting one—to those who had dismissed photography as a negligible art world category.

In the United Kingdom, cultural objects more than fifty years of age and valued above specified financial thresholds require a license for export. The rules for exporting art are designed, according to the Arts

Council of England, to balance the need to keep nationally important objects in the country with the rights of owners and the importance of encouraging a thriving art trade. As Wagstaff applied for the license in order to bring his prize acquisition home to the States, newspaper reports of the sale of the Herschel album to a foreigner had prompted a swell of indignation in some curatorial quarters of London. "The 52,000 pound album, with its portraits of Tennyson, Browning and Herschel, is of major importance to historians," the *International Herald Tribune* declared. "It is equally important to art historians: By studying Mrs. Cameron's portraits of her parlor maid, Mary Hillier, posing as a Madonna in various attitudes, one learns a lot about the climate of the time that made pre-Raphaelite art possible."[40] The album, which had never before attracted much attention, was being appreciated for its major artistic significance to the British Empire only now that an American was poised to own it.

Behind the organized resistance to Sam's purchase, according to Philippe Garner, the auctioneer for the sale that day, was Colin Ford, the photography curator of London's National Portrait Gallery. Ford began a fund-raising campaign to match the price Wagstaff had paid. It reached its goal within months, and Sam's license was denied.[41] "Sam had mixed feelings about losing the Herschel album," Garner recalled decades after his gavel came down on Wagstaff's bid. "For a brief time it was his, and that surely gave him a buzz. But having secured his prize, Sam had a huge bill to pay. He became pragmatic about the situation. In a sense the stopping of the license, the efforts to save this historic album for the nation, and the attendant publicity were a vindication of the very cause that he had championed."[42]

Sam's consternation soon turned into excitement over new opportunities, as well as relief at not having to spend $130,000 all at once. "It probably empowered him," Daniel Wolf said. "He was generating heat. His mission was to educate. If that got in the newspapers, it fell into part of his agenda."[43]

The loss of the Hershel album also led to his discovery of the work of Nadar and to Sam's meeting André Jammes, a Parisian antiquarian book dealer who had begun collecting photographs in 1955. With his wife, Jammes had assembled one of the most important private collections of photographs anywhere, concentrating on the nineteenth century and in particular early French photography, early photographic albums, photographically illustrated books, and the history of photomechanical processes. Because he had started collecting so early, he had no competition, and because of his knowledge he was able to acquire a great many works long before anyone understood their value.

"The fact is that he did not know Nadar's work," Jammes remembered about first meeting Sam.[44] At the time, Jammes had in his possession the Braive collection, which consisted of the surviving core of Nadar's personal archive, well over three hundred pictures and many of the unique proof prints for his definitive works—extraordinary portraits made in the 1850s and '60s of a constellation of such renowned European artists as Sarah Bernhardt, Gustave Doré, Victor Hugo, Franz Liszt, Edouard Manet, Jean-François Millet, and George Sand, as well as his self-portraits. "It took Sam a long time to decide to buy my collection of Nadar works. He returned several times to view it, each time maintaining a strange silence. He then reviewed the holdings of the Bibliothèque Nationale that includes prints of every kind."[45]

The Bibliothèque Nationale is the French equivalent of the United States Library of Congress. When there is more than one print made of any photograph, French law requires a copy to be submitted to the Depot Legal, a kind of copyright repository at the Bibliothèque. Every picture by Nadar, as well as Le Gray, Atget, Marville, and many other notable French photographers, is filed there. Anyone can make an appointment to look through the pictures, and this is where Sam familiarized himself with Nadar's entire body of work.

Sam responded to what he considered in Nadar an absence of style. He read it as the truth of the thing itself, unadorned, allowing the subject to simply be. This is what he meant when he wrote in his Guggenheim recommendation for Enrico Natali that "no point of view takes a great picture." Nadar's portraits of the artists, writers, poets, actors, and patrons of the arts in Paris in the nineteenth century were made in his modest studio without any adornments or props. They are among the simplest and most straightforward studio portraits in the history of that genre. Nadar photographed his accomplished subjects following the tenets of realism that dominated painting of the period. The resulting images reject the exaggerated emotion and artifice of romanticism, instead presenting their subjects in a natural manner, absent any visual embellishment. In his portrait of Sarah Bernhardt, for example, the actress is portrayed not in a theatrical role but rather as herself, out of costume. Nadar's work is distinct from that of Cameron, whose more interpretive portraits reflect the Pre-Raphaelite ideals of her own circle. Cameron used her subjects to represent mythic figures or to illustrate emotional states of being. She would photograph a subject in period dress, bathed in a poetic light to evoke a distant history, a higher ideal. Cameron's subjects, like Nadar's, were accomplished; indeed, while the portraits Cameron made represent a pantheon of artistic and literary giants of nineteenth-century Victorian England, Nadar's body of work composes a parallel set of the luminaries in arts and letters of nineteenth-century Second Empire France, and the work of both photographers has come to define a time and a place, an attitude and a sensibility. Nevertheless, each body of work announces the distinct visual signature of its photographer.

When Wagstaff was forced to give up the Herschel album, he purchased the collection of more than three hundred Nadars from André Jammes. Sam would later come to regard these Nadars as the greatest assemblage of pictures of nineteenth-century photography.[46] Nadar was indeed the big game that Sam had reeled in for Robert, who began to refer to Nadar in his own portraiture. In a 1978 letter to Anne MacDonald, who by then had divorced Richard Manoogian, shed his surname and moved from Detroit to San Francisco, Sam would mention an exhibit of Nadar portraits borrowed from his collection for a show at the Stanford University Art Museum. "Rather dry but beautiful," he wrote. "Robert once told an interviewer that they were his main source of inspiration for portraits. They're clean so that they're not his total inspiration! But then, what is?"[47]

LUXE, CALME, ET VOLUPTE

Sentimentality is a failure of feeling.

—WALLACE STEVENS[1]

R EALIZING THAT HE COULD NO LONGER ACQUIRE PHOTO-graphs and albums of quality and rarity by the likes of Frederick Evans, David Octavius Hill, or Nadar to merely store in boxes or stack on the floor of his dilapidated Bond Street loft, Wagstaff became concerned about responsible conservation. As a former museum curator, he worried about the leaks in his ceiling; there were no climate controls in his loft; he did not have the proper flat files or filing cabinets. "Sam's loft was outrageous. There was no order in it to speak of," Klaus Kertess said. "So there'd be these cardboard boxes around him and they'd have these photographs in them. Don't forget, Sam's idea of cooking a meal was putting a hamburger on top of the burner itself."[2]

It became apparent that Wagstaff's loft was a dangerous environment for his increasingly valuable collection of photographs and albums, never mind the other works in his possession—the Vuillard, the James

Ensor, the Andy Warhol, and the Tony Smith *Throne* that stood in the center of the loft. He thus began an active search for a new place to live.

In 1975, Sam was fifty-three, and he enjoyed strolls along Fifth Avenue. So many of the landmarks along this great thoroughfare, the centerpiece of Manhattan, brought back fond memories for him. A century before, the great white marble arch at the entrance of Washington Square—the start of the avenue—had been commissioned by a forebear in Janet Rhinelander Stewart's family, his mother's friend; the Empire State Building at 34th Street towered into view farther north, while the New York Public Library at 42nd Street with its beautiful Beaux Arts façade demarcated the line between north and south in Manhattan. The grand and storied Plaza Hotel presided in the neighborhood in which he grew up. That great citadel of civilization, the Metropolitan Museum of Art, where he passed many hours while as a student at the nearby Institute of Fine Arts, anchored Fifth Avenue on the Upper East Side. It began the stretch known as Museum Mile, which also boasted the Guggenheim Museum, a striking white spiral monument designed by Frank Lloyd Wright. All cornerstones of a civilized world—art, literature, and the architecture that once harkened the future. With Sam's turn to photography, the Flatiron building, another landmark on Fifth Avenue, had taken on new meaning, its bold triangular shape now a symbol of the different world he was living in—a photographed world—reminding him of Steichen every time he ambled by.

Fifth Avenue has been a mecca for tourists, who join New Yorkers in shopping at such fashionable emporiums as Bergdorf Goodman, Saks Fifth Avenue, and Tiffany & Company. It also has a geographic function, serving as the border between the East Side and the West Side. Ultimately, though, it is the so-called gold coast along Central Park— the thirty or so blocks lined with exclusive apartment buildings of rusticated limestone and an old-world refinement—that represented the apogee of urban grandeur during the twentieth century.

At its south end, however, the avenue has a different kind of residential intimacy. The boulevard starts at Washington Square, the very heart of Greenwich Village, and just a few steps north of the square sits One Fifth Avenue, a voluptuous Art Deco building. The building's ceremonial twin-vaulted awnings stretch across the sidewalk from the entrance to the street. Its imposing two-story lobby is paneled in mahogany, the couches and chairs arranged in the manner of a hotel lounge. In fact, Harvey Wiley Corbett, the chief architect at Helmle, Corbett and Harrison, designed One Fifth Avenue, which opened in 1929 as a residential hotel, the building's chief function until 1975. When Wagstaff learned that the owners were converting the hotel into apartments, he took the leap from the derelict bohemia of Bond Street to the top of the mountain—a penthouse apartment—at the very base of Fifth Avenue.

Sam could be spontaneous in his daily activities, even impulsive, as reflected in his purchase of nineteenth-century photographic albums. But his choices were just as often the product of an intricate, underlying calculus that balanced good judgment, refined taste, and deep intuition with a basic resistance to expectations. One Fifth Avenue, at the corner of 8th Street, stands proudly downtown. It could not be further in spirit from the silver-plated, four-digit addresses uptown along Central Park, such as 1040 Fifth Avenue, at 85th Street, where Mrs. John F. Kennedy settled not long after the assassination of the President. In 1975, possessing a four-digit address on Fifth Avenue was a pedigree in its own right. Perhaps, then, only Sam would fully understand his own inside joke of acquiring the first single-digit address on so grand and reputable an avenue—another nose-thumbing gesture at his uptown brethren.

One Fifth Avenue was stylish, an address itself with balance and poise; and, in another fitting symmetry of which he was likely not aware, his mother's will had clearly stated that Sam was to receive "one-fifth" of her estate, as did his sister, Judith. Between the siblings it was an even share, but only on paper: Olga had released thousands of shares of Newhall Land and Farming stock to Sam in the last years of her life, providing him a good deal more than his sister received; on the other hand, Sam's niece, Judy, who had become close to her grandmother in the last years of her life, was left the three-fifths. One-fifth of his mother's estate was enough of a financial cushion—nearly one million dollars is what he had written to Robert—for Sam not to think twice about buying a penthouse at One Fifth Avenue.

Part of the impetus for the move was Wagstaff's increasing visibility in the field of photography—as a collector, as an advocate, and as a not-so-behind-the-scenes patron of Robert Mapplethorpe. His base of operation had to support the increasing visibility of his reputation, a suitable environment to which to invite anyone of prominence to look at his photographs. Of course, in keeping with his iconoclastic profile, his new apartment would in no way resemble the "fancy pants" stuffiness and pretense of the gold coast uptown. He was asserting his belief in photography as a serious art form; he was tailoring his public image to bolster the credibility of his collection; and he was choosing to live in a manner more in keeping with his age (and, whether he acknowledged it or not, with his pedigree). The presence of a doorman at the entrance provided a layer of exclusivity, even if the ambience was downtown casual. And the views—the World Trade Center from one window, the Brooklyn and Manhattan bridges out another, and Washington Square Park just below—could not help but impress.

Around the time of his move, Wagstaff wrote to Thomas Messer, director of the Guggenheim Museum, to propose an exhibition of works from his growing, if nascent collection, along with photographs from the collection of Arnold Crane, a Chicago lawyer who had begun to collect photographs a decade before. "As you know, photography is at a strange new place," Wagstaff wrote to Messer. "For the last several years there has been a growing awareness of it by many, like myself, who treated it as worse than a secondary consideration, third, or fourth, even after graphics, on the higher scale of art excellence. But photography is not a secondary consideration. It is a thing unto itself and of its own excellence."[3] It would be months before Messer responded with apologies not only for his tardiness in getting back to Sam, but for his curatorial staff's indifference to photography in general, writing, that the Guggenheim did not want to go in that direction—at least yet.[4]

Meanwhile, New York had become nearly insolvent. As the nation's largest city teetered on the brink of bankruptcy, its diminutive mayor, Abe Beame, and Governor Hugh Carey appealed to President Gerald Ford to provide federal funds that could prevent default. When the President refused, the *Daily News* ran an instantly famous newspaper headline: "Ford to City: Drop Dead." (Ford never actually said that; the headline was written after he denied the request for federal funds to save the city). Despite the scrambling of politicians in the city and Albany, the state capital, to find a way to avoid default, the timing of Wagstaff's move to One Fifth Avenue was in a personal sense financially propitious: he bought at the bottom of the market. Once again, true to his ability to find a bargain, Sam purchased the penthouse (apartment 27B) for $25,480; at the same time, he purchased another unit in the building (apartment 8JJ) as a proper storage facility for the photographs in his collection; for that second unit he paid $7750. By today's standards the price of Sam's apartments is nothing short of quaint; at the time, however, the cost of these apartments fell somewhere between a bargain and a deal. (By way of comparison, the next year the price of a two-bedroom apartment in the San Remo on Central Park West, arguably then a more desirable building, was $36,000.)

In conceiving the environment for his new apartment, Sam took many cues from his frequent expeditions to the suburban home of his good friends Tony and Jane Smith. Their daughter Kiki Smith speaks fondly of Sam's visits when she was a teenager: "We loved it when Sam came because he just had this beautiful voice and he was just a beautiful man to be around," she said, adding how much she enjoyed it when he spontaneously burst into a song by Cole Porter. Sam often brought his young artist friends out to South Orange, New Jersey, to meet the Smiths. "Mike Heizer was someone that both my parents liked," Kiki Smith said. Her father, the sculptor, "was very fond of him and his work. And Richard Tuttle he was very fond of, and Gordon Newton certainly came to visit us because of Sam."[5]

Tony Smith had studied architecture and worked for years in the offices of Frank Lloyd Wright as a project director on several commissions. Eventually, he set up his own architectural practice and among the twenty or so residences he designed was one for Betty Parsons, an art dealer, on Long Island. In the 1950s, he taught in art schools throughout New York City. Another of Smith's close friends was Tennessee Williams, who in fact had been the best man at his and Jane's wedding in California in 1943. Considering Smith's background, it is surprising that his success had not come earlier in his life. The issue of Smith's late blooming was addressed in the 1967 *Time* magazine cover story following his show at the Wadsworth Atheneum:

> [Clement] Greenberg complains that the days of the great innovators are gone, that pop, op and minimal are not true avant-garde art, but merely "novelty art." The only thing that can save high art, he continues, is long periods of gestation. What's needed is for the "larger art public to stop breathing down its neck." In Smith's case, however, the argument is academic—because he has already spent some 30 years, in a manner of speaking, gestating.[6]

Wagstaff, too, had spent a long time gestating before reaching his mature form, and, no doubt, his late blooming was part of a bond he felt with Tony, who served perhaps even an inspiration for him.

While the Smith residence in South Orange sat in a row of suburban houses on an average middle-class street, the façade concealed the modernist—or minimalist—simplicity of its interior. It was Tony's childhood home, which he had stripped bare—white walls, almost no furniture, little or no art. Sam followed suit, stripping his new apartment to an essentially functional environment: the walls were painted white and the flooring he installed was wall-to-wall white linoleum; the apartment was at the top of the tallest building in the neighborhood, so his views were unobstructed and the rooms were bathed in light. Sam loved the light, often bringing it to the attention of his guests. He installed a large prism, which in daylight created rainbows of color against the white walls.

Never one for conventional domestic objects, Sam positioned several tall avocado plants throughout the apartment in stainless-steel pots. The few pieces of furniture were purely functional: two low stainless-steel tubular chairs, armless, with white cushions, and a glass and steel table against the wall. He continued the practice of sleeping on a mattress on the floor in the bedroom. Sam never hung pictures on the wall. Instead, he would lean them against the wall on the floor, sometimes framed, or stack them vertically against one another.

Sam, at the age of four, with his parents, Mr. and Mrs. Samuel
Jones Wagstaff Sr. New York City, 1926

Sam's paternal
grandfather,
Alfred Wagstaff,
"The Colonel"
*Courtesy of
Thomas L. Jefferson*

Sam's maternal
grandfather,
Arthur Piorkowski
*Courtesy of
Thomas L. Jefferson*

Sam's mother, Mrs. Donald V. Newhall (née Olga Piorkowska)

Courtesy of Thomas L. Jefferson

Sam's father, Sam Sr.
Courtesy of Thomas L. Jefferson

Sam's stepfather,
Donald V. Newhall
*Courtesy of Thomas L.
Jefferson*

Sam's stepfather,
Donald V. Newhall,
in later years
*The Getty Research
Institute, Los Angeles
(2005.M.46);
by permission of
Thomas L. Jefferson*

Sam's uncle,
David Wagstaff,
in costume for the
Beaux Arts Ball
of 1916

*The Getty Research
Institute, Los Angeles
(2005.M.46); by
permission of Thomas L.
Jefferson*

An illustration for an
advertisement in a 1918 issue
of *Harper's Bazaar* by Sam's
mother, Olga Piorkowska
Thomas, before she married
his father.

*The New York Public Library,
General Research Division*

The Wagstaff
family home,
"Tahlulah,"
in West Islip, on
the south shore of
Long Island

*Courtesy of
the West Islip
Historical Society*

Sam at
about two

*Courtesy of
Thomas L.
Jefferson*

Sam with his
sister, Judith

*Courtesy of
Thomas L.
Jefferson*

Sam in Majorca,
about eleven
years old

*Courtesy of
Thomas L.
Jefferson*

Sam, top row center, among the literary magazine staff his senior year at Hotchkiss. He was the picture editor.

By permission of the Hotchkiss School

Sam, the "deb's delight," late 1940s
*Courtesy of Dimitri Levas;
by permission of Thomas L. Jefferson*

Lt. (j.g.) Sam Wagstaff, U.S. Navy, c. 1944
*Courtesy of Dimitri Levas;
by permission of Thomas L. Jefferson*

Sam at an opening, Wadsworth Atheneum, mid-1960s

Courtesy of The Wadsworth Atheneum Museum of Art

Sam with Tony Smith at the Wadsworth Atheneum, mid-1960s

Courtesy of The Wadsworth Atheneum Museum of Art

Sam Wagstaff, curator of painting, prints and drawings, in his office at the Wadsworth Atheneum, mid-1960s

Courtesy of The Wadsworth Atheneum Museum of Art

Dragged Mass Displacement, by Michael Heizer, during
its installation at the Detroit Institute of Arts, 1971

Courtesy of The Detroit Institute of Arts;
by permission of Michael Heizer

Gallery shot, "Black, White, and Gray," the first museum
exhibition of minimal art organized by Sam at the Wadsworth
Atheneum, 1964

Courtesy of the Wadsworth Atheneum Museum of Art

Sam in his apartment at Lafayette Towers, Detroit, c. 1970

Enrico Natali

Sam with
Enrico Natali in
New Hampshire,
c. 1971
*Courtesy of
Enrico Natali*

Sam with
Anne MacDonald
Manoogian, c. 1971
*Courtesy of
Anne MacDonald*

Mark Kaminsky, photographed by Sam Wagstaff
in Formentera, 1975

The Getty Research Institute, Los Angeles (2005.M.46)

Chuck Howard with
George Platt Lynes
(back to camera), c. 1949

*The Kinsey Institute; by
permission of George P. Lynes II*

Jim Crawford, c. 1969
Jim Crawford

Richard de Menocal, c. 1950

Robert Mapplethorpe not long before meeting Sam, c. 1971

Gerard Malanga

John Waddell was another art patron prompted by Wagstaff to start collecting photographs in the late 1970s. Waddell acknowledged his confusion about the decor of Sam's apartment: "It was a high-end New York City apartment which was effectively unfurnished," he said. "Open the refrigerator, and you would find nothing but a bottle of champagne and a bottle of ketchup."[7]

Besides *Throne*, which had dominated his Bond Street loft, Sam owned another sizable work by Tony Smith: *Die*, which had been installed for a time on the front steps of the Detroit Institute of Arts (today, this 1962 work resides in the Whitney Museum's collection).[8] *Die*, a six-foot steel cube, is painted with black automotive paint. As Tony Smith explained, it is six feet high—tall enough for a person to stand in; it is six feet wide—wide enough for a person to lie down in; and it is six feet deep—a "final" resting place at "six feet under." Sam turned his new apartment into an equivalent of *Die*, a kind of white cube inside which his daily life could transpire with little requirement for maintenance. It suggested the white simplicity of the gallery space. The design anticipated by several years a trend in Manhattan real estate in which dozens of factory buildings farther downtown were converted to apartments or lofts that came to look like residential versions of the white box gallery.

ONLY A YEAR AFTER his "aha" moment about photography, Sam's reputation had taken hold in the auction houses that organized photography sales both in London and New York. So few people were interested in photography that Sam Wagstaff's name came to represent scholarship, taste, and passion about the medium. Nonetheless, in 1975, photography was still underrated. Sam was becoming something of a bellwether, writing his own rules about what was important in photography and influencing the specialists at the auction houses and their auctioneers, as well as the few galleries that represented photography. What is Sam Wagstaff up to? they wondered. What does he know that we don't?

Perhaps spurred on partly by Wagstaff, interest in nineteenth-century photography was increasing at the London auction houses, not least because of the kerfuffle over the Herschel album, by Julia Margaret Cameron, that resulted from his attempted purchase. After that, albums that for generations had been considered useless heirlooms, stored away in attics in Britain and France, were being dusted off and brought in for appraisal. Britain's economy was in a downward spiral—long strikes for essential services were crippling London and the gentry were, as they always seemed to be doing, fretting about their fortunes. Wagstaff's Herschel album incident attracted a surfeit of unearthed new material for the big London auction houses; the old families were raiding their attics for nineteenth-century photographs.

These early photography auctions acquainted Sam and a select few other collectors with such unfamiliar names as Peter Henry Emerson, whose nineteenth-century British landscapes and lyrical scenes of rural life evoke French realist paintings; Roger Fenton, the official British photographer of the Crimean War, whose pictures resemble those of the American Civil War by Mathew Brady and Timothy O'Sullivan; and Gustave Le Gray, whose seascapes and landscapes are optically precise and yet filled with such painterly tonal ambiguities that in 1857 the *Journal of the Photographic Society* wrote, "We stop with astonishment before M. Le Gray's *Sea and Sky*, the most successful seizure of water and cloud yet attempted."[9] These obscure photographers of the nineteenth century were at the time known only to experts. For Wagstaff, however, the auction house became an unofficial classroom; in the first two years of his attendance at the photography auctions, he had purchased twelve prints by Emerson, fifty-five by Fenton, and twenty-nine by Le Gray.

Among the auction house specialists who quickly realized that Wagstaff was a singular photography collector was Ann Horton of Sotheby's (then known in New York as Sotheby's Park Bernet). Horton had started work there in 1972 as a specialist in impressionist painting, but three years later, because of the growing interest in "fine-art" photography, she was asked to take over the area of photography. Until then, Sotheby's had put on sales of photographs in New York once every five years or so; there had never been enough photographs of serious value to justify them more frequently. Sotheby's had been also following a museum model that folded photography into the category of "rare books and prints." It would not be until 1977 that Horton was able to convince Sotheby's that there was enough public interest—and photographic material—to establish an autonomous photography department. By then Horton knew about the great numbers of nineteenth-century photographs Wagstaff was acquiring at the auctions in London and from two private dealers in Paris, André Jammes and Gerard Levy. Soon enough he would make her acquaintance and start attending the auctions at Sotheby's as well. "Sam had complete confidence in his own eye," Horton said. "He had personality and style. Once he even wrote me a little note thanking me for doing the Baron de Meyer sale. It was wonderful and I was so amazed. He must have picked up those manners in boarding school. I was so proud to have him in my field."[10]

At the same time, however, Horton never knew quite what to expect when Sam arrived for a private viewing before an auction. Sometimes he was forthcoming about what he was interested in; at others he was subtle and more calculated; often enough, she found him to be genuinely kind. But Sam was known to enjoy a few lines of cocaine when feasting his eyes on new work to heighten his pleasure and cerebral clarity. He was not always even-keeled, and he occasionally snapped at her if she couldn't answer a question on the spot.[11]

After graduating from Bennington, Daniel Wolf had started selling nineteenth-century photography in the back room of an antique book dealer on Madison Avenue; the first show he mounted was a series of waterfalls by the American painter and photographer William Henry Jackson. Wolf fell into the small and exclusive group of collectors and dealers from New York who attended the photography auctions in London. Among them were Paul Walter, who ran his family's industrial electronics firm and had started collecting after seeing the beautifully detailed pictures Felice Beato had taken in India; John Waddell, who would specialize in photographs between the world wars; Pierre Apraxine, curator of the Gilman Paper Company Collection; Richard Pare, curator of the renowned Seagram Collection of Photographs; Harry Lunn of the Washington, D.C., gallery Graphics International; and

George Rinhart, who had sold Sam his first photographs. Wagstaff was the acknowledged ringleader of this rarefied group.

Together, these men became the defining forces in collecting fine art photography, establishing a legacy that endures to this day. Like Walter, Waddell, and Apraxine (for Howard Gilman), Wagstaff would sell his collection of photographs a decade later to a major institution; in his case, it was the J. Paul Getty Museum, in Los Angeles, a purchase that launched that museum's collection of photographs, which is often cited today among the top three museum collections of photography in the world.

"We would sit around, fifteen or so of us every three months in London looking at this stuff, then going out to cafés and talking about it," Wolf said. "Sam would be there, Paul Walter, and Richard Pare. It was the history—and the language of the history—of photography being developed around those auctions."[12]

The auctions introduced a wealth of material to Wagstaff and his fellow collectors. They were a lively forum for the discussion, analysis, and delectation of photography—not unlike a graduate seminar at a fine university. The men did not know it at the time, but the activities and discussions of their group proved to be an incubator for the burgeoning international, multi-million-dollar photography market. Together they pondered the new names being introduced to them: Who is Felice Beato and how does he compare with John Thomson? How is Charles Marville related to Henri Le Secq, or Le Gray to Carleton Watkins? They would discuss the albums that had come up on the block that day, the techniques of the photographers, and the photographic processes and materials that defined the periods in which the photographs were made. Without quite realizing it, they were establishing an unofficial ranking system—a pecking order, if you will—for these nineteenth-century photographers based on their collective judgment and their individual tastes.

The photographers to which they gravitated are of course of paramount significance today. Felice Beato and John Thomson both represent the finest examples of nineteenth-century photographs made by outsiders inside China, India, Japan, and Egypt; Marville's handsome photographs document the public buildings and civic spaces of mid-nineteenth-century Paris before they disappeared in the transformation of the city by Baron Haussmann; and Le Secq meticulously documented the historical monuments in nineteenth-century France. The work of Marville and Le Secq is among the most straightforward—and, as a result, most important—visual records of the architecture and sculpture of what remained of the ancien régime. Of course Eugène Atget would follow them and arguably eclipse them both with his simple, and inadvertently poetic images of Parisian streets and the gardens of the great ancien régime chateaux. The American Watkins photographed the Western landscape in the late nineteenth century, often for purposes of geological survey; his pictures exemplify the medium's capacity to represent the world in optical facsimile, as well as the artist's ability to capture breathtaking beauty with the camera.

All this photographic work has in common a documentation of the actual world and subject matter that remains of great historic value. Immediately, though, it is a record elevated by the fact that the "photographed world" was new and the medium itself was a revelation—these artists were seeing the world before them for the first time in photographic terms. They were framing it for the eyes of others, while also mastering a variety of new techniques, materials, and processes, from the glass plate to the waxed paper negative, from the calotype to the collodion print and the albumen print. Each technique had properties that changed the look of the photograph, so these were pictures of discovery and wonder for the photographers themselves. Wagstaff had an eye for this magical quality that still resided in the images.

Shortly before Wagstaff moved to One Fifth Avenue in 1975, Clark Worswick, an expert on Asian art, visited him at his Bond Street loft. Worswick had been sent at the suggestion of his boss, Alan Wardwell, the director of Asia House. Sam pulled out a very rare album he had just acquired either at auction or from a private dealer—he wouldn't say. They were photographs of Madura, an Indonesian island near Java, including rare pictures of the Great Pagoda there, all of which very much impressed Worswick. He said, "They were taken in 1858 by Linneaus Tripe, printed in calotypes—very large calotypes 15 by 12 inches. Maybe there were two sets in all of England." [13]

Not long after that, Worswick joined the group of photography collectors and dealers in London. At the very first auction Worswick attended there, he recalled an introduction between Sam and another collector, Dan Berley, who was not part of the group but had been purchasing twentieth-century photography since the 1960s. Berley had formed a small press with Lee Witkin of the Witkin Gallery in 1969. Berley and Sam established that they were both from New York. Berley asked Sam, typically dressed down for auction in his T-shirt and jeans, what part of town he was from. "Oh, I live on the Bowery," answered Sam, just before the first round of bidding that day. One photograph started at £7000. "It kept going, and going, and going," Worswick said. "Sam finally outbid everyone at some outrageous sum. Afterward, Berley, who was the underbidder, went up to Sam, looked him up and down and he said, 'That's pretty good for a guy who lives on the Bowery.'" [14]

Paul Walter, who had been a collector of Indian art for years, had met Sam as he expanded his art collecting into photography. His electronics business required frequent travel to Europe, so Sam persuaded him to go to the auctions while in London, as well as to put up his hand and bid on the things that he liked. [15] While there was competition at auction among these collectors, there was camaraderie as well. If several of them expressed interest in a particular group of pictures, they figured out a way for one to do the bidding and acquire the lot, and later to divide the cache among them. For example, when several albums of work by Alfred Capel-Cure, [16] a nineteenth-century British photographer who made architectural studies of country houses, came up for sale, no one wanted all the nearly 100 pictures. According to Paul Walter, he agreed to go in with Wagstaff and several other dealers on purchasing the albums. "Later they came to my apartment and we laid the photographs out on the floor," Walter said. "We each took turns picking out the ones we wanted until they were all gone." [17]

Despite the camaraderie, Wolf, the youngest member of this clique, felt that he and the other dealers were on the low end of the totem pole. As a dealer, he could not afford to offend any of the collectors in the bunch. Once, a very important image, *Houses of Parliament Under Construction* by Roger Fenton, came on the block. Wolf believed this salt print from around 1858 was a masterpiece of architectural photography, and he found himself in a bidding war with Richard Pare from the Seagram Collection. Wolf outbid him and bought the picture for $3000, more than he had ever spent on a single photograph. Pare told Wolf that he had been instructed to buy that very picture and requested that Wolf, a dealer, sell it to him at no profit. "I had to do it," Wolf said, explaining that Phyllis Lambert, to whom Pare answered at the Seagram Collection, was his only real client. (Lambert was responsible for persuading her father, Samuel Bronfman, to hire Ludwig Mies van der Rohe to design the famous Seagram Building.) "It was not even an issue. If I were to own the picture, I would lose my gallery."[18]

Wagstaff was not above the same kind of intimidation in pursuit of what he wanted. The young dealer Keith De Lellis once found himself embroiled in a bidding war with Sam over a Man Ray photograph of butterflies, a color photograph from the 1930s. "It was absolutely fantastic. It was such a beautiful print," De Lellis said. "I remember wanting it in the worst way and of course Sam wanted it, too." Wagstaff slowly turned around during the bidding and gave De Lellis his most intimidating look. "My [bidding] hand kind of withered," he recalled. Wagstaff bought the image.[19]

Harry Lunn, a former CIA agent and the only member of this group not based in New York, had turned to photography in 1971 after seeing a print of Ansel Adams's *Moonrise, Hernandez, New Mexico* (1941). He mounted a show of Adams's work that same year at Graphics International, his gallery in Washington, D.C. He charged $150 per print, which had been made in editions, and the show brought in $10,000. (Ten years later, *Moonrise, Hernandez, New Mexico* would break all records for the price of a single photograph, at $71,000; Lunn's quiet representation of Adams's work had been the invisible hand behind the appreciation in value of that image.)

The auctions were fertile ground for dealers like Lunn. If you knew what you were looking at, there would be hundreds of lots, some with multiple albums in a single lot. If you had an eye and an idea about the history of photography, there were prints to be found of high aesthetic quality and genuine historic significance. Lunn was someone who understood that with patience came serious financial benefit. He was known to gather the Wagstaff band of collectors and dealers for lunch during the auctions in London. "Harry's idea was to get everybody so drunk that they wouldn't bid against him. He had an enormous capacity for liquor himself," Worswick said. "And he would share all the lots with his little group, and it would be impossible for anybody else to get anything."[20]

The rules of the photography market were really just being written, so it was never clear if the exploits of these men constituted illegal activity. And yet, "auction ring" is a term used to describe a form of market rigging, and it is indeed illegal. As those familiar with such auctions know, members of an auction ring agree beforehand to limit the bidding within their small group; only one in their group bids on the lot and then all of them divide it up among themselves afterward. Sam would let Harry know what he wanted and Harry would then monopolize the bidding. "So," Worswick said, "you were either friendly with Harry or you rarely bought anything."[21]

In Wagstaff's files are invoices from Harry Lunn in which he charges Sam for his share of the lots divided between the two of them. "Enclosed, as promised, is the memorandum on our various half-interest and related Sotheby deals over recent sales," Lunn writes in a letter from 1975, explicitly describing the result of several sales. "When you get a minute, please send me invoicing instructions on the seven Carleton Watkins prints. I will want to invoice the $8,500 price in dollars rather than in a mark or franc equivalent because of the shifting rates at the moment. By the way, it is fine with me if you want to disassemble the Beato album before we meet to divide it. It could save some time when we do the division."[22]

Their auction ring was a mutually beneficial structure. Initially, however, for Wagstaff it was not a matter of trying to manipulate the market to secure the future valuation of the work he was collecting;

rather, it served his interest only insofar as he was acquiring the best material for the least amount of money. Wagstaff may have convinced himself that his hands were clean because he wasn't a merchant; he was in it, as he believed, for love. Of course, he understood that all of this activity would prove to be a good investment and, true to his curatorial instincts, he loved the pictures. Still, he wanted to prove that photography was an important art form and he was intent on putting together a first-class collection. The ultimate financial value of his collection would simply be a useful by-product of his best intentions, but also a value that the art world would have to reckon with.

Wagstaff was buying serious work from only a handful of dealers: Rinhart in New York; Lunn in Washington, D.C.; and André Jammes, Gerard Levy, and Galerie Texbraun (successor to the rare-book stand he loved, Tex-Braun in Paris. But the auctions were another arena for him altogether. He genuinely loved them, treating each one as an event, a performance, with its own drama and choreography. He enjoyed the camaraderie and the attention. He brought a particular vigilance to each sale, not only perusing the catalog but every single lot, every single photograph. He was methodical, even compulsive, about making detailed notes in every one of his auction catalogs: for instance, he made calculations about how much money he was spending and he would figure out how much a lot of twenty pictures would cost per print and write it down. He created elaborate pricing matrices, and then he went from auction to auction, sitting through an entire sale, writing down not only the price for every single lot at gavel, but recording the name of the person who had the paddle; he also jotted down the name and telephone number of every new person he encountered at an auction.

G. Ray Hawkins was another dealer whom Wagstaff first met in 1975. A graduate student in the film department at UCLA, Hawkins had opened the first photography gallery in Los Angeles that year. He was banking on sales from the gallery to help finance his first feature film and made the first of many trips to New York to peddle photographs by West Coast photographers. In particular, he brought with him portraits by Edward S. Curtis of Native Americans in the Pacific Northwest, made in the early twentieth century. In that tiny community of fine art photography, Hawkins had heard about an important collector named Sam Wagstaff, and he called him up while in New York to introduce himself.

"I like Curtis, but I'm not interested in Curtis prints," Wagstaff said. "Now, if you ever find any *Vromans*. . . ."[23] This is how G. Ray Hawkins was introduced to the work of Adam Clark Vroman, whose primary subject had been the Pueblo in the Southwest at the turn of the twentieth century. Vroman's pictures document life among the Pueblos in a natural manner and with a visual intelligence that provides detail and information with an almost classical observation. He would prove to be one of Sam's favorites.

Upon Hawkins's return to Los Angeles, he garnered a useful tip about the gallery world: nothing sells in January. Hearing of the exhibition rental program offered by the Friends of Photography in Carmel, he called them up and was told that, by coincidence, their show of Vroman copy prints had just closed and was available to rent. He booked it for his gallery the following January. The pictures were not for sale but at least he would have something on the walls. Adam Clark Vroman had founded the Vroman bookstore, in Pasadena, today still the oldest independent bookstore in Southern California. His heirs, who had kept it going, were ecstatic to learn that a commercial gallery was interested in their relative's work, and offered Hawkins an additional twelve vintage Vroman prints to include in the exhibition. (A vintage print is one made by the photographer within a period soon after the negative was exposed. It's considered valuable because it's presumably closer to the original intention of the photographer; in addition, the use of the paper from the period in which the photographer lived adds layers of historical value.) They even assented to the idea of selling half of them. Hawkins called Wagstaff immediately to say he had come upon a group of original Vromans, directly from the family. "Send them to me," Sam said. Hawkins held one for himself and shipped the other eleven to New York. Sam selected the five he wanted, for which he paid $2000 each. The Vroman heirs were so encouraged by this quick sale that they decided to sell all of them, so Sam split the remaining six with Paul Walter. All told, Sam bought eight Vroman prints from Hawkins for $16,000.[24]

"In certain ways Sam was a very romantic collector," John Waddell said. "He could get lost in the moment of experience." Waddell had become interested in images of the early modernist period, made between 1918 and 1938, especially those with enough graphic power to "hold the wall." Waddell's late arrival among these early photography collectors, in 1979, did not handicap his ability to amass a singular collection of his own. "I didn't run with the nineteenth-century crowd," he said. "I didn't deem them particularly competitive with me."[25]

Waddell was interested primarily in photographs made between the two world wars and, at the time, little of that work surfaced at auction. Even though he did start attending the auctions he had better luck with two private photography dealers, Gene Prakapas in New York and Edwynn Houk in Chicago. Waddell was vigilant about getting the best possible deal, looking at hundreds of pictures by a single photographer before purchasing the one(s) he wanted; in addition he would ask the private dealer to price half a dozen of them at once for a basis of comparison. With that information he would try to eke out a bargain. Waddell was cerebral and strategic and he considered Wagstaff by comparison something of a pushover as a collector.

"Sam's eye really helped me to see new things," said Ann Horton, the photography expert at Sotheby's in New York. "He helped me to see Frederick Evans freshly. I don't think his eye was at all intellectual. John Waddell's, for example, was very intellectual. Sam was highly intelligent, and maybe unconsciously, after he decided he wanted a photograph, he would let his brain tell him it's okay."[26] For Sam, always, it was first and foremost about looking at the print and trusting the sensation he got from seeing. He was fluent in the language of the eye; for him, the impulse to know the world visually was equivalent to, if not drawn from, pure sexual desire. "Death fascinates me less than sex in photographs," he said, adding even more pointedly that some "images allow you to linger, allow you to return again and again to a special mind-place that is sexy in the best sense of the word—emotional, intellectual, and sensual."[27]

Sam would run his long fingers over a print to feel it and then point out an area of the photograph that served as counterpoint to another part of the frame; he might comment on a single tone or the overall luminosity or the intricacy of detail in the leaves of a tree or the bricks on a wall. His passion was evident to anyone who ever saw Sam looking at a photograph. "What Sam brought to collecting was an extraordinarily acute eye and a passion for photography that I think has been absolutely forgotten today," Worswick said. In many ways, Wagstaff brought the regard for detail and fine craftsmanship of a nineteenth-century connoisseur to a mid-to-late-twentieth-century world. "This is the man who set the aesthetic benchmarks for what's good in photography. It's just an extraordinary level that very, very few collectors have been able to reach."[28]

Wagstaff might have been first to draw attention to the idea of photography as a serious medium of collectible art, but, according to Daniel Wolf, "the real father of photography, for all of us, and especially Sam, is André Jammes. We are all students of André Jammes. He was everybody's star in the sky."[29] Not long after Wagstaff moved into One Fifth Avenue, André Jammes came to New York and Sam gave him a party in his new apartment. Jammes was an old-school Frenchman who adhered to strict social etiquette. Wagstaff, who had spent enough time in Paris in his life to know that there were layers of distinction for the French that even he didn't understand, was nervous about hosting Jammes. His apartment could impress, but it was idiosyncratic and not properly furnished. He was able to gather a fine group of guests: John Szarkowski, the most pedigreed citizen in the photography community in New York; the Austrian-born Lisette Model, the legendary photographer; the Hungarian-born André Kertész, another renowned photographer, who lived across the street; and a host of well-heeled collectors, such as Paul Walter and Pierre Apraxine. Many of the guests, however, were younger artists and photographers, including Mapplethorpe, and together they composed something of a motley crew.

That evening Wagstaff put out a beautiful silver bowl filled with caviar. He also served very good champagne. Jammes felt duly honored, but Paul Walter remembered the reaction of some of Sam's younger friends at the party who were not used to seeing him put on such "fancy pants" airs. "Everybody said, What is this? Look at all that caviar," Walter said. "I said, well, this is André *Jammes*. You don't understand. Sam has bought a lot of photographs from him and there are a lot more he expects to buy, so he is trying to treat him right."[30]

BY THE FALL OF 1975, word had made its way through the art world that photography was being monetized. The market phenomenon is what generated the most visible public dialogue about photography yet, in both the art world and the press. That September, *Art in America* presented an all-day symposium called Collecting the Photograph, at Lincoln Center.[31] Wagstaff was on one panel to talk about private collections, and he was in excellent company: Szarkowski spoke about the function of a photography collection in an art museum; Peter Bunnell, director of the Princeton Art Museum, spoke about the photography collection in the context of teaching art history at the university; Weston Naef spoke about photography in the context of an Old Masters collection; and Harry Lunn spoke about the "image" marketplace.

Meanwhile, magazine articles were debating photography's importance as a fine art. In November 1975, Andy Warhol's *Interview* published an entire issue on photography. "Is Photography Art?" was the title of an article that gathered answers from a variety of art world denizens. Robert Hughes, the art critic of *Time*, said the question was resolved by the photographs themselves: "A great thing about this whole photography being art [debate] is its sudden emergence into the sale rooms. But the fact that photography has become collectible has got nothing to do with whether they are works of art or not." Lee Witkin wryly observed that, whether the medium is paint, watercolor, or the camera, "art is what a human being produces in any form. The right human being." This article drew on artists from a variety of disciplines as well. The British painter Francis Bacon conjured an image of all of the "sepia-colored people" in those nineteenth-century photographs, musing that they are all dead, "which adds poignancy," he said. "Whether the fact that time has worked on them has made them more poignant, I don't know." Louis Malle, the film director, said that photography is the art of stopping time, which, as a filmmaker, fascinated him. "It's trying to grab moments and fixing them which is what we're all after."[32]

Henry Geldzahler, curator of twentieth-century art at the Metropolitan Museum, offered an impish anecdote about a course on aesthetics he took while majoring in art history at Yale. "One week the question was, Is photography a science or an art? And the session went on for an hour and later in the week for another hour and I finally couldn't stand it anymore and I raised my arm and . . . said, 'I always thought it was a hobby.' And that cracked the class up and ended the discussion." John Richardson, the Picasso biographer, was equally dismissive about photography, saying "artists make excellent photographers—Degas, Eakins, Samaras, Hockney—but photographers seldom make good artists." Peter Schub, a photographers' agent, said that the existing photography galleries didn't really know how to cope with photography as an art form because no one was really knowledgeable enough about photography, but cited as exceptions "John Szarkowski, the curator of photography of the Museum of Modern Art, and Sam Wagstaff, the collector."[33]

Given the fact that Warhol and Wagstaff had been friends and known each other since the early 1960s, it was no surprise that Sam was featured in that *Interview* issue as well. An article called "The Wagstaff Collection: A Slideshow by Sam Wagstaff," assembled by Chris Hemphill, drew heavily from the presentation Sam made at the *Art in America* symposium two months earlier. The magazine printed four pages of photographs from Sam's collection. "Photography collecting is my vice," Sam was quoted as saying. "I suppose I could also say I'm an ecstatic. I can't explain it to myself but I go ahead willy-nilly anyway."[34]

Among the pictures *Interview* published from Wagstaff's collection was *Circus Artists* by August Sander, the German photographer whose portraits made in the early twentieth century constitute a methodical record of what he considered to be the archetypes of German society. His subjects are shown in context of their professions—the baker, the banker, or the merchant—in pictures assertively descriptive and precise; the subjects are often presented head to toe, whether sitting or standing. *Circus Artists* is a group portrait of performers out of costume and sitting outside during a break. Each distinctive face confronts the viewer with a deep, unflinching gaze. The random choice of other pictures published from his collection—Man Ray, Thomas Annan, Charles Aubry, Heinrich Kuhn—offers a clue to Sam's sensibility, which favored originality, idiosyncrasy, pure visual description, and surprise.

In the article, Wagstaff draws a comparison of the new interest in photography by collectors and curators in 1975 with the period in Paris between 1850 and 1875, "when the vogue for Italian primitive painting began and one could pick up for virtually nothing some of the greatest paintings that had ever been painted, but which were relegated under the still denigratory name of 'primitives.' "[35]

When this particular issue of *Interview* came out, Wagstaff was already a fixture in the photography world, as both an earnest collector and a shepherd of Mapplethorpe's nicely evolving career. Not to be outdone, the twenty-eight-year-old Mapplethorpe had a presence in this same issue—a full-page photograph of a banana across the frame, a studded leather key chain around the center dangling an array of keys. Visually the picture evokes the graphic surrealism of Man Ray; it also reflects that moment in the street culture of gay life, when keys worn on the left indicated you were sexually dominant, on the right, submissive.

Although Warhol didn't much care for Mapplethorpe at first and for many years maintained a cool distance from him,[37] the editors at *Interview* were giving him assignments on a regular basis. He made portraits of any number of young European aristocrats, including Rebecca Fraser, daughter of Lady Antonia and Sir Hugh Fraser; Erskine Guinness; Diane de Beauvau-Craon, and the Lambton sisters, Isabella and Rose; he also made a portrait of Henry Geldzahler and David Hockney on Fire Island. And, of course, he continued to photograph his muse, Patti Smith.

Smith's career as a musician by that time had admirably soared in the public sphere with the release of her 1975 album *Horses*; she was not only a poet but also, now, a rock star. Mapplethorpe's soon-to-be-iconic portrait of Patti on the cover of *Horses* was taken against a white wall in Wagstaff's new apartment at One Fifth Avenue. She wears a white shirt, black suit pants, and very thin suspenders, with a suit jacket thrown over her shoulders—a very suave gambit, so androgynous, elegant, and feral. A little bit of upscale minimalism for the downtown punk rocker. Perhaps there was even a sexual fantasy being played out between the two of them artistically as Patti affected a seductive man-boy pose, which served, simultaneously, the transgressive impulses of the rock musician to defy the expectations of her fans.

Interview published in early 1976 another portrait of Patti by Robert with the caption: "Now chic: Patti Smith, rock star, by Robert Mapplethorpe, art photographer." The picture accompanied an interview with Smith by Maxime de la Falaise McKendry, and the introduction to the interview defined the moment for Smith: "Now, one can't open *Time, Newsweek, Vogue*, et al., without running into Patti's aint-I-bad image, always framed by an ecstatic review of her premiere rock-and-roll record, *Horses*, released by Clive Davis' hot Arista label."[37]

Once again Sam Wagstaff found himself at the center of the avant-garde. Patti Smith and Robert Mapplethorpe had become emblematic of the *Interview* gestalt, both of them alumni, so to speak, of the back room of Max's Kansas City, and both affecting an urban hauteur in their respective art forms that was sexy and playful, but tough. Rene Ricard would later write about Patti and Robert in *Art in America*: "Their friendship is their masterpiece. . . . Mapplethorpe photos are always beautiful, but a Mapplethorpe photo of Patti Smith is, well, history."[38]

Not long after Sam and Robert met, it became clear that the young artist was not one for a serious conversation about literature. So Sam would go out to dinner with Patti and the two of them would discuss books. Sam encouraged her writing and then, of course, the idea that she could be a musician. At one point early on, Patti, who had very little money, spoke of her desire to make a pilgrimage to the poet Rimbaud's grave in southern France. Sam volunteered to help finance her trip, giving her just enough money to put the dream within reach. (Sam would also finance the first single by the Patti Smith Group, "Hey Joe"/"Piss Factory," in 1974.) This followed the same pattern in which Wagstaff supported so many other young artists he believed in: he wasn't going to make it so easy that they didn't have to work toward their goal, but he wanted to give them enough incentive to believe it was possible.

Robert was the only young artist for whom Sam consistently broke that pattern, making it possible for him not to worry about money at all. Sam never withdrew his financial assistance or his commitment, but he did pursue satisfactions of his own that were contrived to some extent to keep Robert on his toes.

Mark Kaminsky, the handsome young blond Wagstaff had picked up on the subway, was still in the picture. He had been completing a degree in architecture at the State University of New York at Buffalo and now he had become something of a fixture in Sam's apartment. For Sam, physical attraction was sustained only with his belief in someone's native artistic talent. Mark aspired to be an architect and Sam knew something about architecture. But there was also a certain built-in limit to Sam's affections. While Mark had the training, and also genuine talent, Sam sensed early on that he was never going to be the next Ludwig Mies van der Rohe.

Wagstaff had lived in the Mies towers in Detroit. It was Wagstaff's idea to have *Die*, Tony Smith's six-foot black cube, installed in the public plaza in front of the Seagram Building, the Mies-designed tower on Park Avenue. In the late 1960s, Sam had approached Philip Johnson, who had collaborated with Mies on the building, to facilitate the request. While Johnson is thought to have built the first glass house, in 1949, the idea had come directly from Mies, who began his design of the Farnsworth House in 1947. Mies's Farnsworth House and Johnson's Glass House both might be seen in pure minimalist terms: the structure is the design; there are no decorative flourishes; everything is pared down to its essential form, the thing itself—shades of Wagstaff's own exhibition "Black, White, and Gray."

Not surprisingly, Sam now had the idea of building a glass house on the roof above his new apartment at One Fifth Avenue. He put Mark Kaminsky to work on the design and put in motion the laborious stages of obtaining approval from the co-op board of One Fifth Avenue and also from the New York City Landmarks Commission.

All of this was underway when Wagstaff took Mark Kaminsky on a European vacation in the summer of 1975. Along the way they stopped for a while in Majorca, where Sam was at enough of a remove from Robert's territorial attitude about his work to feel comfortable taking his own pictures. Sam had been photographing by now for several years, mostly on vacation, out of Robert's purview, at the beach in Oakleyville, where he continued to photograph a variety of nude young men.

Wagstaff took a great many pictures of Kaminsky in Majorca and on the nearby island of Formentera. Indeed, Mark was a golden boy— toned, well-proportioned, and healthy. He was the all-American ver- sion of Sam's usual template of primal attraction, closer, in fact, to Chuck Howard than the gaunt, hard-edged toughness of Gordon Newton or Mapplethorpe. In some of the pictures, Mark is naked among the rocks, standing in a cove along the seashore, or lying like Ophelia in the still water. Some of the poses recall those in photographs by George Platt Lynes, while others are more idealized, like those of F. Holland Day. There are other pictures in which Sam photographed Mark in an urban setting, dressed in black, holding a bouquet of yellow flowers, standing under a black umbrella. These are portraits of the Cecil Beaton school, full of romantic pretense, beautiful though they are. Sam clearly had some feeling for Mark. Whether Mark was clothed or naked, the pic- tures have a seriousness about them, as if Sam were bestowing an honor on him, recognizing his universal beauty, as if for the ages.[39]

In one letter to Robert from the Isla de Majorca, Sam expresses his pleasure to be back there after so many years, describing in elaborate detail a small town on the west coast of the island called Deya (Deia), right by the sea, with steep cliffs and few beaches, where he swam off the rocks and waded in calmer waters in tucked-away coves. There were olive orchards, where, according to one farmer Sam spoke with in Spanish, the trees were two thousand years old. "I hope I get some good pictures of them," he writes. Picasso once lived in the house next door to the small hotel where they were staying. Robert Graves, the writer, lived a mile or so away. Sam lamented the tourism in Palma, where he had lived for two years as a boy, but then he was reassured that once he got to the more rural parts of the island, the old charm and provincial Iberian magic were still there. "Very simple life—swimming, lots of sun, walking up and down cliffs, eating well, getting brown, very tired at night, lots of sleep, used up seven rolls of film—have to get more."

The letter, however, never mentions Mark. Robert was aware of

Mark, but he did not take him, or Sam's feelings about him, seriously enough to be threatened. As far as Robert was concerned, Mark was not an artist and certainly not a photographer. If anything, Sam's picture taking aroused Robert's jealousy more than the proximity of some attractive young man. For Sam and Robert both, attractive young men came and went as a matter of course. Nothing so obvious was going to threaten their relationship.

"Don't know whether you'd like it here," Sam writes to Robert—his so-called dearest Mufflet. "It's rather primitive and very simple and just the perfect place to vegetate for awhile—not unlike Oakleyville minus the sweeters, sundrenched and full of nature. Hope to move on in a few days to some other beaches and then to Ibiza, then to a smaller island called Formentera, where I've never been. Hope you're well and happy, sweet thing. I love you and miss you. It feels good to have you to think about. Many Monkey Hugs from Majorca. Yours, Sam"[40]

He is the poet, he's the one who doolies and duties

in the sand dunes on the empty beach so no one sees.

He will swim past all the landmarks of the heart.

—FRANK O'HARA[1]

PART THREE

THE FINE ART
OF LONGING

Gerald Incandela, mid-1970s
Courtesy of Gerald Incandela

THE INAMORATO

W AGSTAFF'S ASCENT IN THE PHOTOGRAPHY WORLD HAD been exponential, and by middecade, he found himself operating as something of a one-man institution. He initiated a routine in which his mornings were spent fielding various requests: from museums to borrow works for exhibition; from editors and reporters; from photographers, who were writing him from all over the country to show him their work; or from institutions inviting him to lecture on photography, among them the Smithsonian, the San Antonio Museum Association, the Claremont Colleges outside Los Angeles, the Albright Knox Art Gallery in Buffalo, Pratt Institute, and the Friends of American Arts at Yale.

All this attention had begun when the Metropolitan Museum of Art asked him to lend his Nadar portrait of Alfonse Daudet, among the group he had acquired from André Jammes, for its 1975 show about impressionism. Soon after that exhibit, he received a letter from the Wellesley College museum asking him to lend two Baron von Gloedens for a show about F. Holland Day. For a show at the Asia Society entitled "The Last Empire: Photography and British India," he lent Clark Worswick two photographs by Samuel Bourne, of Bourne and Shepherd, still the oldest running photographic studio in the world, and another by Colin Murray. That year a letter from Harold Pfister of the National Portrait Gallery at the Smithsonian, regarding an exhibition they planned to do on the daguerreotype, provides a clue about an awareness in curatorial circles of Sam's growing expertise about photography: "Your interest in this field has been pointed out to us and I would be happy to explain further our intentions and receive whatever advice you might wish to offer."[2]

Now in keeping with his regular schedule, Sam went to London for the auctions in March 1976, happily mining troves of undiscovered photographs and albums as they materialized from the recesses of the collective European attic. The new community of collectors and dealers following in his wake provided welcome camaraderie. Some of them— Paul Walter, George Rinhart, and, later, John Waddell and Pierre Apraxine—also happened to be gay, adding another layer to the private language of their unique cabal. Sam was at the center of this new phenomenon, and he relished the momentum that his own activities created for the growing interest in photography.

Although the jokes about Sam's parsimonious streak persisted among his friends, he proceeded, unfazed, his characteristic style of idiosyncrasy never failing to impress. Clark Worswick remembered someone at auction in London asking Sam why he didn't stay at the Westbury, a luxury hotel in Mayfair, where Paul Walter stayed. "I stay in modest hotels because the money I save I think of as money I can buy pictures with," Sam replied. "So I'll look at pictures and say, 'This is one night at the Westbury. This next one is two nights at the Westbury.'"[3] He preferred to spend his money on timeless objects. Even when his choice of object seemed impetuous and the amount he spent unprecedented, his decisions were rarely, if ever, foolish. So he scrimped at the somewhat threadbare Hotel Constantine, a bed-and-breakfast on the Old Brompton Road, where he and Robert both preferred to stay while in London, not coincidentally near the gay bar district in Earl's Court, and in particular the Colehern, a leather bar popular with an international clientele.

Sotheby's and Christie's scheduled their triannual photography sales within days of each other, and Sam was in London that week to attend both. After one morning auction he went to see what was on the wall at Nigel Greenwood Inc. Ltd., a gallery known for showing emerging artists, such as Gilbert & George, and American artists such as Bruce Nauman and Ed Ruscha. At Nigel's, Sam ran into an acquaintance, the filmmaker Derek Jarman, whom he had known from overlapping circles in both London and New York. Unaware of Sam's recent turn to photography, Jarman was delighted to hear that he was in town to buy photographs at the London auctions. He urged Sam to go look at the work of his former boyfriend, the twenty-four-year-old Gerald Incandela.

Sam telephoned Incandela almost immediately after running into Derek Jarman and went to see his work a day or two later. Gerald was tall and dark-haired, with a poetic air about him. Raised in French Tunisia and of Italian descent, he had studied art history in Paris, where he had refined his European sensibility to an aesthetic bordering on the Proustian. The technique he used for printing his photographic landscapes, still lifes and portraits was thoroughly original. After the photosensitized paper was exposed to the negative, he brushed developer (or emulsion) onto the paper in the manner of paint, allowing glimpses of the photographic image to emerge in sweeping brushstrokes and leaving other sections of the paper blank. The interplay of positive and negative space and the use of the artist's hand in the application of the photographic chemical left the impression of a pencil-drawn image rather than a photographed one.

Perhaps Gerald's photographs reminded Sam of the *cliché verre* by Corot he had purchased from Daniel Wolf, which blurred the line between the drawn image on glass and the print that resulted from its exposure directly onto photographic paper. Maybe he responded to the successful interplay of photography and painting, or the lyrical effect of the persistently emergent image, or the application process of the emulsion itself that was a visible component of the finished piece. Whatever the reason, Sam was clearly impressed. He bought several of these photographs during that March trip to London, the beginning of his support of Gerald's work as an artist.

At the time, Gerald was living in Clapham Common with his boyfriend, Thilo von Watzdorf, a thirty-two-year-old specialist in nineteenth-century art at Sotheby's. Well regarded, he had risen rapidly within the organization and was now seated on the board of directors. Von Watzdorf had been responsible for several important Sotheby's sales of Ballets Russes costumes from the Diaghilev and de Basil Ballet Foundation in the late 1960s. The sales were reported to be glittering social occasions not forgotten by anyone who attended.[4]

Gerald had been living with Thilo for two years, and their life together was financially secure and socially correct—in stark contrast to the threadbare bohemian existence Gerald had endured with Derek Jarman. Jarman's theatrical performances were staged in the underground art world of London and his Super 8 short films were shown in noncommercial venues that yielded virtually no income. Jarman had had one commercial windfall, as the set designer for Ken Russell's film *The Devils* in 1971, but that income had long been used up. Gerald and Derek had moved from place to place, managing to house-sit for a stretch in a friend's flat on Sloane Square near King's Road, a convenient fulcrum of homosexual activity with gay bars and active cruising on the street—a lure for each of them that had only taxed their relationship.

The circle Gerald and Derek had inhabited in Swingin' London was not unlike the back-room crowd at Max's Kansas City in New York—artists, rockers, fashion designers, and drag queens who animated their daily activities with an antic, theatrical, sexually ambiguous, and decidedly urban flamboyance. Andrew Logan, an artist around whom a great deal of social activity swirled, launched the first Alternative Miss World competition in London in 1972, a beauty contest conceived to highlight imagination and costume over native good looks. As a contestant in one of the first competitions, Gerald took the stage as "Miss Synthetic," appearing naked under a plastic see-through frock. The event attracted the likes of Leigh Bowery, Tim Curry, Malcolm McLaren, Vivienne Westwood, and Zandra Rhodes. In fact, David Hockney was one of the judges. Alternative Miss World, produced a dozen times over the years and the subject of a 2011 documentary, *The British Guide to Showing Off,*

might well have been a spiritual prototype for Wigstock, an annual out-
door drag festival that began in New York's East Village in 1988.

Jarman, who would go on to make the films *Sebastiane* (1976), in
which Gerald appeared, *Caravaggio* (1986), and *Wittgenstein* (1993), had
given Gerald his first camera as encouragement for his young lover to
"find" himself as an artist. Even after they broke up, Jarman continued
to encourage Gerald's career. Gerald remembered his ex-lover calling
him to say that Sam Wagstaff, who was about to ring him up, could
likely change his life. The parallels between Sam's introductions to
Mapplethorpe and Incandela are conspicuous: a former boyfriend making the connection, each time offering Sam a deeper invitation into a
city's contemporary art world demimonde.

On that chilly March afternoon, Sam arrived at Gerald's house in
Clapham Common. It was a weekday and Thilo was at work. Gerald,
generally watchful and soft-spoken, was struck by Sam's formidable
appearance when he first opened the door. Feeling a little uncertain in
the presence of the older collector, he led Sam inside. Instinctively Sam
assessed the sophistication of the cozy double parlor: a Rauschenberg
tire was situated in the fireplace and lit from within, a red Warhol self-
portrait hung on the wall, an authentic silk screen on canvas. It was
clear that Thilo, the art expert at Sotheby's, had acquired the work and
also that Thilo must have been supporting Gerald. Gerald politely laid
out his 20-×-24 prints on the coffee table in front of the couch—a Donald Judd steel cube. Sam felt immediately at home sitting with Gerald on
that cold day in London, surrounded by some excellent contemporary
work by New York artists, looking at the young artist's photographs
in this snug little drawing room with its charming french doors, and
falling almost predictably in love. The feeling would ignite an ardent
courtship—and, of course, mentorship—that would continue on both
sides of the Atlantic for the next two years.

One of the first images by Incandela that Wagstaff bought is a com-
posite portrait of Thilo, his boyfriend, dressed in a business suit and
sitting in a chair in that very parlor of their home, Thilo's mother standing next to him with a glass of wine in one hand and a cigarette held
theatrically to her face in the other; Thilo's father is in the adjoining

parlor wearing a suit and reading the paper. Incandela is reflected in a mirror with longish dark hair, standing behind the camera.

Thilo's mother was a titled princess, and his father a close relative of Queen Juliana of the Netherlands. By the mid-1970s, John Waddell was involved with Thierry Millerand, Thilo's former boyfriend. Millerand brought Waddell to meet Thilo, and Waddell remembered "passing through a dense haze of marijuana smoke, arriving at this great over-stuffed couch with a lot of pillows, in which I found a mellow young Tunisian, Gerald Incandela." Gerald would have spent holidays with Thilo and his cousin, Beatrix (who became queen in the 1980s), at the Royal Palace in the Hague.[5]

Today, *Thilo and His Parents* clearly prefigures by several years the photographic tableaux of David Hockney, in which scenes are constructed with multiple Polaroid images. But when Gerald made this piece, no one else was constructing scenes out of multiple photographs, nor were they painting the image on paper with photographic fixer. Thilo was upset that Gerald sold so personal a picture to a stranger, but greater infractions were to come from Wagstaff and Incandela.

Sam set out to persuade Gerald to move to New York, an essential step, he asserted, in launching his career as an artist. There were several obstacles: the first was Gerald's relationship with Thilo; the second was that, while Sam was an attractive and compelling and powerful art world figure, Gerald was not falling in love with him; and third, Gerald was terrified of flying. None of these encumbrances seemed to weaken Sam's resolve.

Sam's idea was, just as he had with Mapplethorpe, to set Gerald up in an apartment in New York, introduce him to other artists and dealers, and buy his photographs as he created them on a monthly basis. Sam figured this strategy would bolster Gerald's confidence and encourage his productivity. During the proceeding year, Sam sometimes wrote Gerald twice a day from New York. He made transatlantic calls regularly, an exorbitance in those days and out of character for a man who hated to spend money on anything but art—and Robert. Once again, however, Sam was able to openly integrate his love of the artist with his love of the art.

Gerald could come across as indecisive. It was not that he was unsure of what he was doing as an artist, or that he was unclear about how he should be shaping his life; he was someone who proceeded very much from instinct, and in this case his instinct was to hold back. Sam's attention was flattering, and his counsel was valuable, but the intensity of the older man's affection overwhelmed him and, instinctively, he recoiled. "There was an attraction, but not a physical attraction," Gerald recalled. "Sometimes when you think you are two people who understand each other, there is a closeness somehow. It's just understanding life at a higher level." But for all Sam's efforts at emotional intimacy, Gerald held himself at a certain remove. "It was romantic," Gerald said, "but romantic love is not necessarily physical love."[6]

During the courtship, Sam revealed to Gerald a side of himself often hidden behind the persona of leather-clad iconoclast and avatar of youth culture he had cultivated since taking up with Robert. Sam flew to London several times that year for the auctions, and while he continued to don his downtown Manhattan uniform—studded leather motorcycle jacket, T-shirt, jeans, and sneakers—his sensitivities were more genteel, expressing, for example, an appreciation for the fine Louis XVI era tea service while he and Gerald had tea, praising the integrity of the craft, the wit of the pattern, the beauty of the line, its exemplification of the period's neoclassical ideals. Walking down the street in London, he was capable of summoning charming and arcane anecdotes about British history. Passing St. Paul's Cathedral might prompt him to mention the architect Sir Christopher Wren's secret association with Freemasonry; crossing Bedford Square in Blooms-bury on the way to the British Museum would conjure the wonderfully scandalous Lady Ottoline Morrell, the patron of the avant-garde in her day and the inspiration for Hermione Roddice in D. H. Lawrence's *Women in Love*.

One of Incandela's photographs, a seascape, had reminded Wagstaff of the work of Gustave Le Gray, so Sam took Gerald to look at the Le Grays at the Victoria and Albert Museum. Gerald liked this side of Sam, describing it as "quiet nobility," evident to him in the way Sam recognized the poetic in simple daily activities and expressed nostalgia for what was meaningful in history. "Sam would, for example, appreciate a picture of lace, a Rayogram of lace," Gerald said. "He would get such pleasure. That's where we could come together, too. My education at that point was more European—we look at the past, and history, and we have more old buildings, old objects, which still can be appreciated, and not just dismissed because of modernism all of a sudden. He made me look at life from a higher point of view."[7]

While Wagstaff's attraction to Mapplethorpe had been animal, spiritual, even aesthetic, Gerald brought out some truly romantic strain in Sam's personality, tapping into the sensibility that early on had been cultivated from Olga's standard of taste in the fine domestic objects made of china, porcelain, and silver he was surrounded by as a child, the European painting he was introduced to early in his life, and the centuries-old architectural treasures he admired throughout Europe as a student. Sam still regarded these encounters with a nostalgic—and, to Gerald, a poetic—response. While Robert, the free-spirited, rough-hewn young artist, summoned unbridled animal passion, Gerald was a different kind of madeleine. In one letter to Gerald, dated simply "Sunday" but written a few months after they first met, Sam wrote with the fever of Goethe's young Werther:

Dear, dear Gérald,

It was nice talking to you last night all sleepy and warm in bed. You were sweet not to be irked by being woken up at such an hour. Hope you could snooze again. It's always a little different from what one expects, what one's been thinking, how one remembers, isn't it for you, too?, a phone conversation. I want to jump out of the phone and kiss you.[8]

Sam's impetuous, surprisingly adolescent infatuation stands in contrast to his otherwise worldly cultivation. The image of wanting to jump out of the phone to kiss Gerald is, in itself, so innocent, honest, and touching as to be beyond judgment; the mere fact of it, though, written by a man of fifty-four, displays an unexpected dissociation between his emotional development and his natural age. He goes on to express his insecurity about what is transpiring for him, and, yet, disavows that his insecurity is the very condition of his emotional state:

> *It seems so dry yet it corrects the memory which sometimes gets too influenced by "I" and loses the "you," though that's what it dwells on, and fears that the "we" isn't happening and never will, though it knows its [sic] happened already. I guess I'm just selfish and impatient—the pessimistic optimist. It makes me think of a crazy Rodgers & Hart song, which goes:*

> *"Unrequited love's a bore,*
> *And I've got it pretty bad . . .*

Here, Sam includes several more lines of the song that express the melancholy pleasure of his sadness, the romance of his longing, the feeling of uncertainty, of being lost, like a babe in the woods. Then, as if he were not the one to be citing the lines, as if the song wrote itself into his letter, he disavows its very meaning and intention:

> *Well, I certainly don't think of myself in those terms. It's sort of a cute song, don't you think?*[9]

Wagstaff was blatant and unrelenting in his effort to drive a wedge between Gerald and his lover, Thilo. The first time Sam was invited to dinner at Clapham Common he brought a bottle of Chateau d'Yquem, his favorite wine. It was an extravagant gesture that Thilo could see brought with it romantic designs: Thilo felt that Sam, the dinner guest, was drawing a line in the sand in his own home. Sam became convinced that Thilo did not really love Gerald, asserting on more than one occasion that Thilo perceived Gerald more as a possession than a person. Repeatedly Sam asked Gerald what he got out of his relationship with Thilo, claiming that Thilo thought of Gerald's work as a hobby. This may have been an unfair assessment, since Thilo bought Gerald the enlarger he used to make his prints in the basement of their house. "You can't be an artist as long as you live this lie," Sam wrote him.[10]

Between the several trips Sam made to London in 1976, in which he attended the auctions and spent most of his remaining time with Gerald, he resorted to a bit of treachery. In the 1960s he had been close to a Parisian art dealer named Jean Chauvelin, whose gallery specialized in the Russian avant-garde. Sam knew that, because of Thilo's position at Sotheby's and his knowledge of Russian constructivism, he and Chauvelin were more than acquainted. So he wrote a letter to Gerald that he put in an envelope addressed to Chauvelin in Paris. In the letter he had referred to a moment between Gerald and himself that a reader would likely construe as having been sexually intimate. Thilo does not remember receiving a call from Chauvelin about the letter, but Gerald remembers hearing about it and confronting Sam. Sam claimed it was an absentminded mistake, but it only hardened Gerald's resolve to resist Sam's entreaties.

All of this was written in the stars, according to Gar Osten, an astrologer Wagstaff had commissioned to do a "progressed" reading of all planetary aspects of his astrological chart of 1975–1976—a single-spaced, thirteen-page letter with elaborate month-by-month predictions. Osten, who at the time was writing a book called *The Astrological Chart of the United States from 1776 to 2141*, had a reputation for accurate predictions about occurrences of historic notice, anticipating, for example, the exact date President Nixon would be hospitalized for phlebitis, or Nelson Rockefeller's rise from governor of New York to the vice presidency. Osten's reading anticipates Sam's infatuation with Gerald, writing in his description for March 1976: "Your mind will be abrupt, whimsical and fanciful. And you will be liable to meet with those in this late winter period who will affect you magnetically, and you will be liable to act indiscreetly and impulsively and will later regret the action."[11]

AS SOCIAL HISTORIANS HAVE copiously documented, the 1970s introduced a host of threats to conventional monogamy in the straight world. Countless doors were opened to heterosexual experimentation— wife-swapping parties in the suburbs, heterosexual orgy clubs such as Plato's Retreat and the Hellfire Club in downtown Manhattan. In post-

Stonewall gay New York, too, the promise of casual, consensual sex was barely ever a wink and a smile away, and gay couples contended with the issue of monogamy not as a given at all but as something indisputably optional.

It's in this complicated context that Wagstaff and Mapplethorpe's relationship has to be understood. For both of them, their relationship occupied a primary place. And yet the emotional grounds were determined, fundamentally, by Robert's promiscuity. Not that Sam was monogamous, but he had been forced to accept Robert's terms in order to establish equal footing. Unlike Robert, who rarely got emotionally involved with his sexual partners, Sam fell easily into a more intimate pattern with his liaisons. If Robert had avowed his fidelity, Sam might well have been happily monogamous.

In that regard there's a certain sense of strain in much of Sam's behavior with Gerald, too, a forced openness about promiscuity that did not come so naturally. For instance, in one letter to Gerald, Sam tries to be nonchalant about Gerald's sexual activities with others:

> Hello, it was so nice (easy) to talk to you this A.M. (your P.M.) and to hear that you'd been naughty—partly that blond I bet, the chubby cute one with the come-on grin—Yes, no? . . . You are naughty and you know it, which is great. To think of someone giving you enjoyment. Horny may not be the exact word but it's close. I don't mean I want to watch, but that it's good to know that you're the animal that you are, Monkey, Happy monkey with a monkey grin. You're very beautiful, Gerald, in so many directions; you must surprise yourself even—every day, some new craziness.[12]

Sam managed his own promiscuity with old-school reserve. Initially he presented himself as single to Gerald, talking about his relationship with Robert only in terms of Mapplethorpe's career and his work. Mark Kaminsky was still around, too, and, had Gerald known about him, it would have looked—as it did to any outsider at the time—as if Mark were Sam's official boyfriend.

Sam rented a house for a month that summer of 1976 in Fire Island

Pines, a little over a mile east of the much sleepier Oakleyville along the barrier island and an entire civilization apart. For stylish debauchery there had been Havana in the 1950s, and Ibiza in the 1960s, but at that moment for gay men in America, Fire Island Pines was something of a Dionysian Mount Olympus—a center of power and, arguably, unparalleled sexual splendor that garnered social cachet from the list of denizens and summer residents throughout the 1970s: fashion designers Calvin Klein and Perry Ellis, the record mogul David Geffen, the Hollywood executive Barry Diller, the Broadway director and choreographer Michael Bennett, the director, choreographer, and actor Tommy Tune, the aristocrat Egon von Furstenberg, the male model Joe McDonald, as well as an endless stream of artists and writers, well-placed art critics, book editors, magazine reporters, art directors, photographers, set designers, actors, singers, dancers, and waiters.

In the playground of gay culture in 1970s Manhattan, gay men wove their activities through the broader fabric of heterosexual life, but at Fire Island Pines the straight world was edited out almost entirely. Women visited only rarely and straight men almost never. By 1976 the Pines, as it is called, which also happens to be an anagram for "penis," was the exclusive preserve of gay men. It offered a utopian promise of brotherly communal spirit that often proved more a mirage. The generally lascivious vibe in the community approached hysteria and frenzy before sunset on any given day, as handsome men began frolicking in various states of undress in the enchanted setting of the affectionately named Meat Rack, a stretch of scrub forest in the sand dunes between the Pines and its equally gay but less luxurious neighbor, Cherry Grove, where the men of the community roamed the bushes for sexual thrills. On any of the boardwalks that functioned like streets in this place without cars, a young man would amble by in a red Speedo and sunglasses—chiseled face, muscled, well-proportioned body, genitals carefully outlined under fabric. Then, a minute later, another one would pass, eclipsing the pulchritude of the first. And, then, again, and again, endlessly, until something approaching overload occurred in the nervous system for anyone walking along the boardwalks. The concentration of attractive men on this single sliver of island created a phenomenon of romantic longing that ricocheted from one stranger to the next, along with persistent free-floating lust, only to leave so many residents and guests, alike, lonelier and more frustrated than when they first arrived.

Sam always seemed to find himself at the center of a historic moment, whether escaping the Fascists at the start of the Spanish Civil War, landing at Omaha Beach in Normandy on D-Day, being among the first to identify minimalism, attending Woodstock, anticipating photography as the next important focus of the art world, or meeting Robert Mapplethorpe at the dawn of gay liberation in New York. Sam may have rented the house in the Pines that August as a present for Robert, who hated the austere tranquillity of Oakleyville, but it didn't escape him that as a gay man of his time Fire Island Pines was the most desirable place to be. The house was typical of the simple modernist style of that community, built mostly in the 1950s and '60s, made of naturally weathering slatted cedar that in the sun turns light silver gray. The two-story home had four bedrooms; the living room was off a glass-enclosed atrium and it opened onto a pool deck that overlooked the ocean. Mark Kaminsky stayed with Sam at the house the entire month and Robert came out to the beach for long weekends, often bringing guests with him—one weekend, for example, it was Patti Smith, who was by then already rock-star famous.

Steven Aronson was another houseguest that month. Robert was supposed to meet him at the ferry slip—everyone arrived by boat from the "mainland" of Long Island—but he was delayed and Aronson, his two-hundred-pound Newfoundland in tow, was obliged to find his own way to the house. The door was unlocked and he walked in, calling out hello. Looking up at the two-story atrium, he noticed a basket chair suspended from the ceiling. Sam was naked in the basket chair with a young man in flagrante delicto. A resident of the Pines would not have found this a surprising scene to happen upon. "It was certainly a side of Sam I had never seen before," Aronson said. "But he was a gentleman and he was going to remain a host, even, and called down to me from near the ceiling, 'Yours is the second bedroom on the left.'" The boy in the chair with Sam, Aronson soon learned, was Mark Kaminsky.[13]

Mapplethorpe arrived later that day with Peter Berlin, a gay porn star. As Aronson described it, there was no food in the house, and the weekend "was as boring as it was creepy. I saw neither hide nor hair of any of them again. We kept wildly different hours—they slept all day and hunted all night." But, on Sunday, when Maxime de la Falaise arrived bringing not only lunch but Princess Diane de Beauvau-Craon and Sam LeTulle in tow, "they all got up for that!" The previous night would have been spent at the Meat Rack or at the Ice Palace, an all-night disco in Cherry Grove. Robert didn't pay the slightest bit of attention to Mark Kaminsky all weekend. As far as Aronson could tell, Robert's attitude about Mark was dismissive, as if he were "something the cat dragged in."[14]

Sam may have liked having Mark around, but in the end he proved more of a diversion than what might have been called a serious flame. Mark was certainly attractive and he possessed enough ambition about being an architect to complete his degree, but Sam's romantic interest had already been diverted by Gerald.

Earlier that summer, on the Fourth of July, Paul Walter, who lived on East 82nd Street, had a party on his terrace to watch the tall ships regatta sail into New York on the occasion of the U.S. Bicentennial. Sam brought Mark Kaminsky. Later that evening, Sam invited the crowd downtown to watch the Macy's fireworks on his roof at One Fifth Avenue. When Kaminsky told Walter about his design for the glass house, Walter was impressed that Sam was attempting to nurture the young architect's talent with so ambitious a project; he also found himself a little smitten.

Not long after, Paul Walter and Mark Kaminsky met again. Mark said he was planning to visit friends in Germany and hoping to make a stop in Morocco. Paul was going to be in Paris around the same time, and mentioned provocatively that he had a standing invitation from Christopher "Kip" Forbes to stay at the mansion of his father, publisher Malcolm Forbes, in Tangiers. He suggested Mark might meet him in Paris and go from there to Morocco. Mark ended up doing just that.

Sensing that his own days with Wagstaff were numbered, Mark sent Sam a postcard from Morocco, explaining that he was there with Paul Walter. Sam was relieved for the most part; his affections had transferred to Gerald Incandela, and he didn't know how he was going to end his affair with Mark. Still, the mischievous child in Sam couldn't wait for Walter to get back to New York; he wanted to make him squirm over the betrayal.

"Why, you snake," Sam said at the start of their first phone conversation when Walter returned from Morocco. But as soon as Walter began to stammer, Sam just laughed. "Oh, Mark's such a sweet guy," he said. He claimed he was not at all upset and hoped that the two had had a good time.[15] Soon after that trip Kaminsky moved in with Paul Walter. Several years later, Steven Aronson was visiting a friend who had bought a triplex in Midtown and divided it into three apartments. Paul Walter had purchased one of the floors and had moved in with Mark Kaminsky. "The name rang a faint bell," Aronson said, "and then, clang! I remembered—the boy in the basket!" Aronson later met Mark again at Paul Walter's, in Southampton, and saw that he had other qualities aside from being quite nice-looking, describing him as "intelligent, and just plain nice."[16] (Mark Kaminsky and Paul Walter would live together for seventeen years, until Mark's death from AIDS in 1993 at the age of thirty-nine.)

Meanwhile, Sam was positioning Incandela in the art world. During Sam's second trip to London in 1976, he called his friend Robert Fraser, who had owned the art gallery where Yoko Ono had the show at which she met John Lennon. Sam brought Robert Fraser over to see Gerald's work. Fraser was known as "Groovy Bob" because of his association with the Beatles and the Rolling Stones and so many other jet-set figures. In 1969 he had been arrested for drugs and was forced to close his gallery. After serving time in prison, he had returned to London to reconstruct his life. The next year Fraser would give Gerald a one-man show at the Bologna Art Fair. "It was Robert Fraser's public return in the art world," Gerald said.[17]

SAM HAD PURCHASED JACKSON POLLOCK'S *The Deep* in 1969, hoping, as we have seen, that the Detroit Institute of Arts would buy it. He paid Lee Krasner, the artist's widow, $190,000 for it. Once he returned to New York, he was fastidious about securing the painting a home appropriate to its stature and significance—it was the last Pollock drip painting. In 1974, he put it on the market through Xavier Fourcade of the Fourcade, Droll Gallery and sold it to his friend, Dominique De Menil, with the express understanding that the painting would end up as a gift from the Menil Foundation to the new French modern art museum, the Centre National d'Arte Contemporain Georges Pompidou. Two years later he received the final payment for the full $700,000 price. He was resolute about shepherding it to an institution of international reputation, where it would be cared for and exhibited and viewed by millions of people. Nevertheless, his investment in the Pollock had more than tripled in five years. He was not interested in having his ownership of the painting known or in having his fingerprints anywhere visible on the sale. The provenance of the painting issued by Fourcade, Droll listed only two previous collections: Lee Krasner Pollock and "Private Collection New York."

With the $700,000 sale of the Pollock, Sam recovered his seemingly extravagant investments: the Hill and Adamson album he had purchased for $215,000 in 1974; the Nadars he bought from André Jammes after the Julia Margaret Cameron Herschel album fell through; and his two apartments at One Fifth Avenue. There was enough left over for him to feel free to invest in Incandela's future as an artist in New York.

As Sam's campaign to bring Gerald to New York intensified, his activities in the photography world deepened. That year Boston University invited him to become a member of the board of visitors for the department of art history. Carl Chiarenza, chairman of the department of fine arts, wrote him about an expansion of the university's PhD programs in art history that was to include photography: "You are one of a small group of individuals chosen to help us in our efforts to build an outstanding program using the unique resources available in our community."

During this period, he fielded requests from journalists, such as one from Douglas Davis, the art critic of *Newsweek*, who was writing an article on the origins of photography up through the Photo-Secession.[18] Or the one from Andy Grundberg, picture editor of *Modern Photogra-*

phy, asking whether the magazine could reproduce several panoramas in his collection for an article about that genre.[19]

But the finest acknowledgement of the respect Sam was garnering in the photography world that year came from the director of the department of photographs at the Museum of Modern Art, John Szarkowski, the leading arbiter in the field, who invited Sam to sit on the museum's Committee on Photography, which was responsible for approving and providing funds for acquisitions for the museum's collection of photographs. The Museum of Modern Art was considered the "judgment seat" of photography,[20] and members of that committee included Beaumont Newhall, the preeminent photography historian and the first curator of photography at the museum, and Monroe Wheeler, the longtime MoMA official and intimate of George Platt Lynes.

The meetings of the Photographs Committee were heady affairs. With a stentorian voice and droll wit, Szarkowski assumed the role of professor to that choice little group of intellectuals; the committee members were often joined by museum trustees, such as Shirley C. Burden, Mrs. John D. (Blanchette) Rockefeller, John Parkinson III, and Arthur M. Bullowa. Two young women whose names were to become prominent in the field also sat in those committee meetings. In 1976, Susan Kismaric had just been hired to run the study center in the Department of Photographs. Kismaric, who would eventually become a curator in the department, was made acting director in 1980 while Szarkowski was on sabbatical. In a conversation with Wagstaff before one meeting, she mentioned that among the potential acquisitions on the agenda that day was a picture from an ongoing project by Nicholas Nixon, a now well-known series begun in 1975 in which he photographed his wife and three sisters-in-law together every year (for over thirty years) in a chronicle of time that shows, among other things, how the women aged. Kismaric, who was always nervous before this intimidating group, showed Sam the picture and explained the project to him. "So what?" he said stingingly. In recounting the episode many years later, Kismaric reflected with some amusement, "Well, you could say so what about anything, I guess."[21]

Maria Morris Hambourg started as an intern in 1975, and Szarkowski would later hire her to begin work on the Atget photographs in the museum's collection. She sat in the Photographs Committee meetings as well. Later, in 1985, she would join the staff of the Metropolitan Museum of Art and become the founding curator of its Department of Photographs. Her first impression of Sam in those meetings at MoMA was memorable—"very handsome, rakish, and outspoken." She could tell he was clearly informed, not in the least intimidated by the sometimes cantankerous Szarkowski during the meetings. "What I liked about Sam so much, aside from just witnessing this sort of grace and authority, was his contentious nature," Hambourg said. Sam had no qualms about challenging Szarkowski's ideas, and Hambourg got the impression that Szarkowski found it somewhat refreshing, as if they were "parries from another fencer who was just as good."[22] Even though Sam took it all seriously enough, it didn't prevent him from attending black-tie affairs at the Museum of Modern Art wearing a tuxedo, an unironed white shirt, and white sneakers.

Wagstaff continued to reconstruct his role as a curator. Just as artists sought his attention and support in the 1960s, he was now fielding requests from photographers who had gotten wind of his collection and wanted him to buy their work. It had started in 1975, when Harold Edgerton, a professor of electrical engineering at the Massachusetts Institute of Technology, sent Sam a letter describing his photographic work as technical and scientific.[23] Edgerton made photographs with a device called the stroboscope that isolates natural properties during physical action. Sam would later write that Edgerton's famous photograph of a drop of milk creating a liquid corona "is *the* photograph of the 20th century as Warhol's soup can is *the* painting."[24]

Photographers were coming to see him by referral as well. Ellen Brooks, a young artist from California who had studied with Robert Heinecken at UCLA, did not consider herself a traditional photographer, even though she used photographs in a material way. One of her early wall installations, *Adolescent Piece*, consisted of seventeen life-sized (104 inches × 48 inches) photographic portraits of nude preadolescent children, each one sitting or standing in front of a cloth backdrop. Brooks came to New York in 1976 with a set of 20-×-24 prints from this series and made the rounds to galleries. Holly Solomon, who had opened a gallery in SoHo the previous year, liked the work and suggested that Brooks go see Sam Wagstaff.

Brooks was the same age as Mapplethorpe. She was somewhat overwhelmed walking into Wagstaff's spare, all-white apartment with its dazzling view of the city. "He had a pink Oxford cloth shirt on," she remembered. "I never liked pink shirts."[25] Yet, his looks, height, and voice made her nervous until they sat down and he started to talk about her work. He insisted that her portraits of the naked children were not prurient, pornographic, or shocking, as some people might think; in fact, he saw them as beautiful, classical, and respectful of the subjects. He bought seven prints, at $240 apiece.

Soon afterward, Wagstaff and Brooks had dinner downstairs at One Fifth, an Art Deco restaurant in Sam's building that had become a new art world hangout. Joining them was Lynn Davis, who had worked with Berenice Abbott as an apprentice. Davis was supporting herself as a photojournalist for *Time* and *Esquire*. Her own work, though, like Mapplethorpe's, focused on formal nude portraits. She met Robert when a magazine put out by Fotofolio, which published high-quality postcards with pictures by important photographers, wanted to publish an article about her, and they asked her to pick two photographers to include in the feature. In another magazine she had seen one of Robert's photographs, *Mr. 10½*, an image of the genitals of porn star Mark Stevens displayed on a block like a slab of beef. She proposed Mapplethorpe, along with Peter Hujar, another friend, as the two other photographers.[26]

Davis and Mapplethorpe then started going to galleries and museum shows together on a regular basis. She would visit Robert on Bond Street and they would gossip and discuss their own work or the work of others. Robert had native knowledge and good visual instincts, Lynn said. "He was ferocious. And the way that he was ferocious isn't how other people might think. He was ferocious about his work, in his interest to try, to look, to see, and to put things together. He had his own refined point of view very early on."[27]

As Lynn was getting to know Robert, they would visit Sam in his apartment. Sam was always enthusiastically showing them new pictures, which were all over his apartment "in boxes, in piles, leaning against the wall," Lynn recalled. He showed them early-nineteenth-century photographs, which didn't interest her that much. "It was almost more interesting to me that his cupboards were full of sprouts," she said. "Sam grew his own sprouts. There were maybe four or five flats of sprouts. He had them in his cupboard. Sprouts! He ate them."[28]

Davis understood that Wagstaff was a strong presence in Mapplethorpe's life, but for years, as close as she and Robert had become, she had no idea that Sam and Robert had anything approximating a romantic relationship—or that Sam was supporting Robert. She was under the impression that Sam, because of his interest in photography, was only a patron of his work—once, Robert showed her a photograph he had just made and told her that Sam had bought it. She saw it as a true collaboration of mentor and protégé. Lynn was aware that Robert and Sam were in contact every single day, talking about what Robert was working on, what Sam was collecting, or what they had gone to see in galleries, but it looked to her as though Robert was supporting himself with assignments from *Interview* or private portrait commissions. "When I met Robert, he was already living on Bond Street," Lynn said. "I just assumed he had earned the money to buy Bond Street. I knew that whenever Robert and I would go out to eat, we would go to the bank and he would come out with an envelope full of cash."[29]

One day that fall Judy Linn brought Elaine Mayes to meet Sam. Elaine Mayes had photographed the music scene in San Francisco and was now shooting musicians in New York. Sam had brought out some calotypes by Fox Talbot, talking about how beautiful the prints were and the aesthetics of aging on different kinds of papers. Mayes asked him what he thought of C-prints, then the most common process for printing color photography. Wagstaff didn't think they were stable and that with time the color would very likely fade, but he said, "Oh, they'll be like calotypes in a hundred years. Don't worry about it," reassuring her that fading color would tie the print to the period in which it was made, only adding historic value to the photograph.[30]

Wagstaff began to organize soirees in which these young photographers would gather in his apartment. They were considered fun because he provided drinks, cocaine, and marijuana, and he would bring out the photographs he had been acquiring for everyone to look at and discuss. Even though Sam collected a great deal of nineteenth-century material, it wasn't necessarily his goal to focus on historic photographs. Often he would say that there just wasn't much contemporary work that caught his attention, but he was buying work from Robert Mapplethorpe, of course, and also Gerald Incandela, Judy Linn, Ellen Brooks, and Elaine Mayes.

Mayes remembered one of these soirees at which Wagstaff took people up to the roof of his building. Everyone admired the view. He said that he liked living on the top floor and then described his plans for the glass house with the roof garden, which had been thwarted by the building's co-op board and the landmark commission. Mayes asked why the roof was so important to him. "So I can show my artist friends the view," he said.[31]

One day during the holiday season Wagstaff, Judy Linn, and Elaine Mayes were walking along Houston Street. It had gotten very cold and a man was lying down on the sidewalk, huddled without a jacket and clearly freezing. Sam went over to him, kneeled down, and asked him if he needed help. The man couldn't respond. Sam thought he should call someone and make sure the man had shelter for the night. The scene made an indelible impression on Elaine: "His concern, his talking to the man and going over and feeling responsible, always endeared me to Sam, because he didn't have a sense of boundaries about where he belonged in a public sense. And that's even more of a patron, a person who cares for other people and takes care of other people."[32]

While the impulse to help a man on the street in need is only human, it was not something Wagstaff did as a matter of course. He always seemed to be a man on a mission, self-assured, independent, now providing something of a community for these young photographers, not only support for their work but an environment in which to discuss photographs and share information. He had surrounded himself with artists, once again, amid his frenetic pursuit of rare and fine photographs. And yet, in the realm of his emotional life, he might have been experiencing some vacancy, a familiar sense of longing. Sam was in love with Gerald Incandela, but his love was not being readily reciprocated. Robert was a strong presence in his life on a daily basis, but affection was not an accessible component of their unique attachment. Mark Kaminsky had gone to live with Paul Walter, so even the physical warmth of another person was no longer immediately at hand. Of course, Olga had died. The gesture of reaching out to a man in the cold has metaphorical resonance in the context of these absences.

One night around Christmas 1976 Paul Walter and Mapplethorpe were having dinner together at Max's Kansas City. It was obvious by then to both of them that Sam's obsession with Gerald was not going away. Sam had begun scouting apartments for Gerald. "Sam was just crazy about him, and Robert was terrified," Walter said. Robert interrogated Walter about Gerald all evening: Who is this guy? What's he like? What does Sam see in him? Is he a good photographer? Robert was afraid that his days were numbered. What was he going to do? "Finally," Walter said, "Robert told me he was just going to have to find himself a new rich boyfriend."[33]

Soon after that, Robert wrote Sam a handwritten note on Christmas red paper:

Dear Sammi,

Merry Christmas old thing—all the monkey hugs this wumper can bring. Thank you for making my life a lot easier and Happier.
I still love you,

Robert[34]

ELEVEN

LET THE GAMES BEGIN

This book is about pleasure, the pleasure of looking and the
pleasure of seeing, like watching people dancing through an
open window. They seem a little mad at first, until you realize
they hear the song that you are watching.

—SAM WAGSTAFF[1]

ALTHOUGH ROBERT MAPPLETHORPE'S WORK HAD BECOME
exclusively photographic by 1976, he did not want to be
defined as a photographer. Robert may have been working in the
medium of photography, but he was exploring sexuality in his work
with a vision that transcended the form. As his partner and advocate,
Wagstaff understood that the gallery system in the 1970s still relied on
convictions about the integrity of the artist, so he thought it would be a
mistake for Robert to be represented by one of the few photography galleries that had opened in New York. After all, Andy Warhol, who made
repeated use of the photographic image, was considered an "artist," not
a "photographer." Certainly Robert was not going to let the lingering
stigma about the medium relegate him to the photography ghetto.

While it may have appeared that Mapplethorpe—with Wagstaff's guidance—orchestrated his first major exhibition in a SoHo art gallery with strategy and calculation, in fact serendipity played the first hand for him. The show's genesis began at a party in December 1975 given by Norman Fischer, a high-minded drug dealer and art collector who lived in a penthouse apartment above Abingdon Square in the West Village.[2] Many of Fischer's clients were artists who were more than willing to barter their artwork for drugs. Robert paid for marijuana and cocaine with photographs, and Fischer liked his work enough to hang half a dozen portraits on his living room wall. One of the guests at Fischer's party that night was a young artist named Ed Shostak, who was struck by Robert's pictures: "They were beautiful," Shostak remembered. "Pictures of British aristocrats, taken outdoors. I had never seen anything like them before."[3]

Shostak was represented by Holly Solomon, and he and Solomon spent a good deal of time together, going to exhibits and talking about artists. Solomon, a short and swank platinum blonde, was known for her theatrical mannerisms and sartorial wit. Already a well-known New York collector of pop art before she opened her SoHo gallery, she had been given the affectionate, if sarcastic, sobriquet "Pop Princess" in the press. The morning after Norman Fischer's party, Ed left a message for Holly with David Boyce, her gallery assistant, about Robert Mapplethorpe's work and suggested that she make an appointment to see it.

In the downtown orbit of Manhattan in the 1970s, there persisted a romantic idea about the artist as urban deity. Making art was regarded as a noble pursuit surrounded by an almost mystical aura, and not thought to be dictated by money. The artist's studio was an inviolate preserve where inspiration succeeded to exploration, where an idea or an impulse could be nurtured into a perfectly crafted object.

The New York art world was still a small and incestuous community. Common wisdom granted the artist the freedom to live by his own rules, often at the expense of material comfort or social decorum. These artists were surrounded by art dealers, critics, and museum curators, and together they constituted more of a metropolitan hamlet than what was later to become a locus of industry and international commerce.

Artists had easy access to dealers; their work was put on the walls of galleries; barely a handful of critics wrote about the art itself; and some enlightened or connected people bought it. Occasionally a curator would anoint one with a museum show; a few mythic reputations were made. But the artist's success, unlike the national celebrity of a movie star or an occasional writer, such as Truman Capote or Norman Mailer, was circumscribed within a few stratified cultural precincts of New York. Aside from Warhol and Pollock—rare exceptions who would become household names in their own time—there was little recognition on the national stage for the visual arts. The primary reward was the respect of one's peers.

The photography world remained a barely acknowledged ghetto within that circumscribed domain. In May 1976, the burgeoning medium experienced something of a setback as a result of "William Eggleston's Guide," the first one-man show of color photographs at the Museum of Modern Art. Eggleston's saturated color photographs— snippets of an unusually observed, idiomatic Americana—ran counter to the black-and-white orthodoxy of fine-art photography at the time, and the show, organized by John Szarkowski, was uniformly panned by critics. Once again, however, critics were not versed in the language of the photographic image; they had not yet spent time anatomizing the medium itself—never mind its history of light on film, an impression on paper, a vocabulary of tones and shapes and juxtaposition and depth on a flat surface. In addition, at the time, color was a separate language altogether. The subject in the frame—a car, a tricycle, an industrial building—was not the only element to define the image, but the perceptual concerns were often overshadowed by it. "Mr. Szarkowski throws all caution to the winds and speaks of Mr. Eggleston's pictures as 'perfect,'" Hilton Kramer wrote in *The New York Times*. "Perfect? Perfectly banal, perhaps. Perfectly boring, certainly."[4] Kramer missed the point. Eggleston's focus on buildings or cars or individuals in context of their daily lives was not exactly the meaning of his work. Perception—as much as the act of documentation—was close to the subject, but that was a difficult idea to contend with in 1976.

Since MoMA was the most visible and highly regarded platform for photography in the art world, the reaction to the Eggleston show was thought of as a critical slap in the face to the medium. No one at the time imagined that Eggleston would later come to be regarded as a pioneer in color photography, and one of the most consequential and influential artists of his era.

Back in 1969, Holly and her husband, Horace, a wealthy business-man who ran an industrial products supply company, had been pioneers, too: they arrived in SoHo just as artists had begun taking over aban-doned commercial buildings, turning industrial lofts into working stu-dios that doubled as living spaces. The Solomons "commissioned" the artist Gordon Matta-Clark to renovate an empty loft on Greene Street, which then became a vital alternative artists' space for poetry readings, concerts, and performances. It attracted an art world crowd that included Warhol, Jasper Johns, Dennis Oppenheim, Bruce Nauman, and Sigmar Polke.

Holly later claimed that she opened 98 Greene Street Loft, as it was called, in SoHo "because it was far enough downtown that it wouldn't upset my in-laws."⁵ But she took to SoHo, and in 1975 she opened her gallery on West Broadway, when Castelli and Sonnabend were two of the few other galleries in the neighborhood. Among the first artists Holly exhibited were Laurie Anderson, Mary Heilmann, Gordon Matta-Clark, Ed Shostak, and Will Wegman.

By the first week of 1976, Shostak's phone message about Map-plethorpe was buried somewhere on David Boyce's desk. Shostak called the gallery again to ask what Holly thought of the pictures, and Boyce apologetically called Robert immediately, making an appointment the following day. So, on January 5, Boyce walked over to Robert's Bond Street loft to look for himself. While he perused several spiral-bound portfolios of photographs, Robert offered an occasional comment in what Boyce described as a manner "as spare as the composition and lighting of the images I was paging through—still lifes, portraits, and a few landscapes." Robert then slid two more bound books toward him, explaining that these were his "dirty" pictures. Robert sat sprawled in a Stickley armchair like a transgressive little boy, watching as Boyce leafed through the male nudes. "In the silence between us, the smoke from his Kool cigarette curled upward, undisturbed," Boyce later wrote. He forced himself to regard the sexual images with the same objective criteria as the nonsexual images, "despite the minute hint of naughty glee that glinted in Robert's eye."[6]

Boyce was convinced that the images were good enough to show Solomon, and the following week she and Ed Shostak paid a visit to Robert's studio. When it came to painting, sculpture, and conceptual work, Holly was confident in her judgment, but she knew very little about photography. In fact, the idea of photography as an art form unsettled her. Still, she could see that his photographs were "handsome." She later told David Boyce that while she was not keen on the "dirty pictures," she thought his portraiture might be a worthwhile addition to the gallery.[7] "I recognized that Robert was an artist," she said. She knew he was eager for representation, but before she would commit to giving him a show, she wanted to test his ability to work with people. So she commissioned Robert to do her portrait.[8]

In the mid-1960s, when she decided to have her first portrait done, she had approached Richard Avedon, but found his fee of $12,000 to be unconscionable. She already owned a Warhol *Marilyn*, so her next stop was Warhol. Warhol took Holly to Times Square and, just as he had with Ethel Scull, began feeding quarters into a photo booth. She posed for the automatic camera doing facial exercises she had learned while studying acting with Lee Strasberg. Warhol's *Holly Solomon*, a nine-paneled yellow, violet, and green silk screen of a single image from that photo-booth session, was first exhibited in Boston in 1966 (thirty-five years later it would sell at Christie's for $2 million). "I wanted to be Brigitte Bardot, I wanted to be Jeanne Moreau, and Marilyn Monroe all packed into one," Solomon said, indulging a fantasy about her Warhol portrait. Still, her intentions were equally serious: "What no one really understood about Andy at the time was that he was a great artist. . . . When Andy did a photograph, when Lichtenstein did a painting or a drawing, they understood that medium and the new vocabulary that they were adding to it."[9]

Now the full weight of Mapplethorpe's ambition was bearing down on him. After all, Holly Solomon had had her portrait done by not only

Warhol but also Roy Lichtenstein (Eli Broad would later pay $2.5 million for the latter portrait, called *I . . . I'm Sorry?* in 1995).[10] Robert had already photographed some well-known individuals, including, most recently, Princess Margaret and Arnold Schwarzenegger, who was just gaining recognition as a bodybuilder before the movie *Pumping Iron* made him famous. But his commission for Holly Solomon felt like a refined hazing ritual for entrance to a very select fraternity of artists. If he succeeded, his photograph would hang in her apartment alongside Warhol and Lichtenstein; he would have a show in her gallery. Indeed, he would be leaving the photography ghetto behind.

Robert told Sam about the commission right away, and Sam's encouraging reaction helped to make clear what the implications of the assignment were. Sam had canny insights about everyone in the art world and, while there is no documentation of their discussions about the commission, he knew enough about Holly's place in New York's social hierarchy to understand what she was likely to expect from her portrait.

Robert approached the project with his usual combination of insecurity, self-possession, natural charm, and elfin mischief. He photographed Holly in the bedroom of her luxurious Sutton Place apartment wearing white silk pajamas. The portrait he presented to her was a beautifully framed triptych in which she appears in stages of reclining on the bed. In the final picture, her head is thrown back on the cushions, the graceful line of her neck perfectly arched, a lighted cigarette in her hand, sprawled across her king-sized bed with her feet elevated comfortably on a pillow. She assumes the come-hither pose of a great movie star—Jean Harlow, say, in a Hollywood publicity still by George Hurrell—and Robert captured her platinum-blonde luminosity with delicacy and style. While the final frame has echoes of *Sunset Boulevard*, with Holly as a Norma Desmond figure whose beauty and celebrity is on the wane, the photograph itself is intimate and somewhat homespun, with wrinkles in the bedspread, the pattern on the fabric of the pillows matching the wallpaper, and dramatic lighting that retains a natural mood. The composition is formal and elegant, her pose verging on the erotic, and the sequence is unapologetically honest about its homage to—and parody of—Hollywood glamour.

Solomon understood that as an art object Mapplethorpe's triptych was based on a set of conceptual ideas that reference artwork outside of photography: the three pictures graduate in depth consecutively, suggesting the graphic geometry of pop art; the sequential action alludes to motion, as in the frames of a movie reel; the multiple images echo the grids of Warhol. Of course, Robert had seen the narrative sequences of Duane Michals and the time-action studies of Eadweard Muybridge, influences evident in the triptych as well, giving his portrait of Holly Solomon one foot in the history of art, the other in the history of photography.

Not surprisingly, Holly loved the portrait. She found Robert soft-spoken, gentle, perceptive, and kind, and she was impressed with his professional, meticulous, and sensitive approach to the shoot. Yet the general prejudices about photography as a second-rate art form and her lack of knowledge about its history continued to give her pause. Meanwhile, Robert waged his own campaign. He began to pay visits to the gallery in the late afternoon before closing time. He would linger around the front desk, striking up casual conversations with Boyce while waiting to go in to Holly's office. It was Holly who pointed out to David that Robert seemed to like him. "Robert had a charming friskiness about him, a devilishness that could be interpreted in several ways," Boyce said. "Some men on the make speak with a sly double entendre; Robert looked with one."[11]

Finally, Mapplethorpe asked Boyce out. They went to dinner in the West Village and then returned to Robert's loft on Bond Street, where they had sex for the first time. David knew from the "dirty" pictures that Robert's predilections included sadomasochistic role-playing and even bondage, but, with him, Robert turned out to be a gentle and easy lover, responsive and passionate, open and sharing. Lying together afterward, Boyce remembered, "Robert nuzzled my ear softly, saying, 'See, you didn't get tied up.'"[12]

Meanwhile, events in the art world were conspiring in Robert's favor. Several reputable art galleries had begun to take on the select representation of photographic work. Uptown, Marlborough Gallery had had a great success with an Avedon show, which featured a mural-sized group portrait of Andy Warhol's Factory entourage—with nudity—and attracted a crowd of three thousand people to its opening. At the same time, Castelli Graphics uptown hired Marvin Heiferman from Light Gallery to run its newly realized photography program. The prestigious Sidney Janis Gallery, which handled the abstract expressionists in the 1950s and pop artists in the 1960s, mounted its first all-photography show in late 1975, "Women of Photography: An Historical Survey," when the San Francisco Museum of Modern Art, which organized the exhibition, couldn't place it in a New York museum.[13] The Robert Schoelkopf Gallery on Madison Avenue had begun to devote one of its two floors to photography and hired Marcuse Pfeifer to run the operation. And Sonnabend Gallery, Holly's neighbor in SoHo, was about to publish a portfolio of photographs by David Hockney. Holly considered these galleries her community of peers as well as competitors, and the encroachment of "the photograph" on solid art world soil was another sign that her consideration of Mapplethorpe was in keeping with the zeitgeist.

Even though Sam had nothing to do with Robert's introduction to Holly, he would play a significant role in her decision to give him a show. "Sam Wagstaff was considered a great photography collector," Holly said. "I wouldn't have touched Robert without Sam. And there were others like me who felt the same way."[14]

After deliberating for months Holly finally scheduled a show of Robert's work to open on February 5, 1977, but she refused to exhibit his "dirty" pictures. Robert went directly to The Kitchen, an alternative space for video artists and experimental composers and performers, and proposed that they show his "X-rated" work in tandem with the Holly Solomon Gallery show. The board agreed.[15]

Robert designed a single invitation for the simultaneous exhibitions, a diptych with two nearly identical photographs of his hand holding a pen and writing the word "pictures" on a piece of paper; in the first frame his hand is bare; in the second he is wearing a fingerless leather motorcycle glove. Under the first is printed "Holly Solomon Gallery" and under the second, "The Kitchen," with their respective addresses; the announcement for the opening and the date underline both venues.

Robert never abandoned the importance of the frame that encased his photographs. The frame had been an integral component of his early assemblages and collages. He had elaborate frames built for the photographs for these two shows, each carefully constructed and made of silk. "Each frame was $1200 to $2000 and you sold the photograph for $150," Holly said. "If someone bought it framed, I would charge $150 for the photograph, plus the cost of the frame. So Robert got $75 and I got a big $75 for all that work."[16]

Sam was involved in every stage of the installation process. Holly regarded him as a sweet and elegant man but eventually complained that he was acting like an intrusive "Jewish mother." She was annoyed by his badgering phone calls throughout the day while they were hanging the show.[17]

On the wall at Holly Solomon Gallery were Mapplethorpe's portraits made on commission or on assignment, or as a result of his personal friendships, including Princess Margaret on the beach in Mustique with a bottle of Beefeater gin in front of her, Arnold Schwarzenegger, Patti Smith, Harry Lunn, and a wide swath of the New York demimonde. The opening at Holly Solomon drew a large crowd of uptown friends as well as a menagerie of SoHo artists, downtown Bohemians, gay men, and drag queens.

Farther downtown, at the Kitchen, his X-rated pictures included *Mr. 10½*, among the other pictures of men in various stages of nudity, sexual arousal, and leather-clad bondage—presented with uniform studio lighting and precise photographic resolution. The sexual content of the images created a dramatic counterpoint to the elegance of the silk frames, emphasizing the tension between erotic provocation and classical resolution. Robert aimed for the finest photographic detail of line and light and tone, making the subject more formally delectable. That same tension exists in Edward Weston's many studies of the female nude figure and other natural forms, a technical perfection that matches the erotics of a classical ideal.

Reaction to the X-rated pictures was double-edged. Some were appalled, but the gay men in attendance were titillated and thrilled. Mapplethorpe embodied the deep current of sexual change then rising to the surface by capturing homosexual carnality in classical form. He drew on his own native desire, coupled with serious artistic ambition, to eternalize erotic longing in aesthetic terms. That duality of high and low—technical perfection, aesthetic idealization, unflinching homo-erotic desire, and not a little wit—may indeed have been what defined "gay sensibility" in the 1970s.

Germano Celant, who would later become a senior curator at the Guggenheim Museum, attended both shows. He understood that it was a very powerful gesture for Robert to "come out" in his erotic photo-graphs, not only as a person but an artist. Other artists at the time—for example, Jasper Johns, Robert Rauschenberg, Andy Warhol—were gay, but they were hardly forthcoming about their sexual identity. "Mapplethorpe definitely collected pornography," Celant said. "But these images were a completely different input in the art world, as works of art. And that is what makes his work so radical. After that, it became easy. A lot of people started doing it. But in the beginning he was the one who forced the galleries to show his work."[18] While it was never Robert's intention to split his work into two arbitrary groupings, it would prove a beneficial strategy throughout his career. According to Mapplethorpe's biographer, Patricia Morrisroe, "the X-rated material gave him notoriety, but it was the PG pictures that made money."[19]

Sam treated Robert's art world debut as the occasion for a coming-out party for Robert and for himself—or, in the parlance of his patrician past, a debutante ball. It was a grand black-tie affair. Two hundred guests took over One Fifth, the restaurant in Sam's building, a setting that carried an aura of immediate chic as the modishly upscale, stylish and, yet, still essentially downtown replacement for the Max's Kansas City crowd. Also, it was gaining a reputation then as a favorite night spot for the cast of *Saturday Night Live*. One Fifth had the feel of a period Art Deco dining room aboard a great ocean liner of the 1920s: white-tiled walls, mirrored columns, white linen tablecloths, French wicker café chairs, black ashtrays, and waiters in white tails. Not only was Sam right at home—on the ground floor of his own apartment building—but the restaurant's allusions to an expat continental sophistication had resonances of Olga and Majorca and the ocean liners on which he had made crossings as a child. (In fact, the restaurant had obtained its permanent decor—the chairs and other accoutrements—from the Cunard cruise ship *Caronia*.)

Robert wore a velvet dinner jacket to his party. The guest list ran the gamut from the mannered swank of Diana Vreeland, the editor of *Vogue*, to the slatternly Danny Fields, manager of Iggy Pop and the Ramones. It also included the fashion designer Halston; the jewelry designer Elsa Peretti; British heiresses Catherine Guinness and Caterine Milinaire; artists Neil Jenney, Judy Linn, Lynn Davis; art world friends Klaus Kertess, Mario Amaya, and Charles Cowles; photography collectors Harry Lunn, Paul Walter, and George Rinhart; and Robert's friends and acquaintances David Croland, Bob Colacello, and Fran Lebowitz.

"All these people, and Diane von Furstenberg was there with this young actor and weightlifter by the name of Arnold Schwarzenegger," George Rinhart said, describing Robert's excitement as they stood together perusing the guests. Robert was positively gleeful when he showed George the jewel-studded bar pin made of platinum he was wearing on the breast of his jacket. "See what Sammy gave me?" Robert said. "Well, that's awfully nice," Rinhart said to Robert, winking at Sam, who stood beside him beaming.[20]

Ed Shostak was there with his friend Neil Jenney. "It was a fabulous party," Shostak said, observing that the combination of guests in that restaurant had the kind of energy and outré glamour that would help create Robert's reputation in the art world as an enfant terrible.[21] Not everybody, however, thought it was an appropriate celebration. Fran Lebowitz, then a writer for Andy Warhol's *Interview*, respected the pursuit of art as something pure and true. She had known Robert as a struggling artist in the back room of Max's Kansas City and considered the occasion not as the beginning of his legitimacy, but as the end. "I thought the party was a joke," she said, likening Robert in that context to a once rebellious girl "showing you her big diamond ring and telling you she's marrying a rich doctor and moving to Greenwich, Connecticut." Lebowitz was appalled even before she arrived, because the people she knew who drove taxis and waited on tables had already called her up wondering how they could get an invitation.

Those who scored one arrived dressed to the nines. "How was it possible that all these people who were starving to death had dinner jackets?"[22]

Wagstaff's belief in Mapplethorpe's work had not wavered in the five years since they met, and he could not have ordained a better public launch for Robert's career than the dual shows at Holly Solomon Gallery and The Kitchen. It was pleasurable for him to watch Robert take this step into the art world. Robert's evolving persona seemed only to further tickle the bad-boy impulses in Sam. Robert's personality took on the same profound contrasts found in his work—sweet, seductive and graceful, with an aura of menace that conjured the most forbidden corners of sexual desire. "Robert was the 1970s leather-clad equivalent of the great dandies and decadents of the late nineteenth-century—Beardsley, Oscar Wilde, Huysmans," Philippe Garner, the Sotheby's auctioneer, would later say.[23]

The party was reaching its effervescent peak when the host quietly slipped out, stopping on the way to his own apartment on the top floor to visit Patti in the apartment she and Allen Lanier had recently taken in the building. Patti had been bedridden for several weeks after a serious fall off the stage during a concert in Tampa, Florida. Her reputation as a punk rocker had taken off, and Sam was quite amused, too, at the "ain't I bad" persona that was fueling her newly acquired fame. After filling her in on the success of Robert's exhibits and the festivities downstairs, Sam called it a night and went upstairs. Clearly the evening was a triumph for Robert, but equally for Sam.

The following day Paul Walter sent a bouquet of flowers to Sam, and a separate bouquet of tulips to Robert. Later that year, Sam would show Paul Walter a diptych Robert had made of a spray of tulips in a black vase, beautifully situated and dramatically lighted with a new quartz studio lamp and taken with the Hasselblad Sam had bought him, one tulip bending away from the rest and touching the side of the frame. "I wasn't exactly in and out of Robert's studio every single day, but I'd never seen any flowers there before," Paul Walter said, referring to the congratulatory tulips he had sent. "And I had never seen any flower pictures before by Robert."[24]

———

SOON AFTER ROBERT'S SUCCESSFUL exhibits, Sam could barely contain his pleasure about another personal victory: Gerald Incandela had agreed, finally, to come to New York. The biggest hurdle had been Gerald's fear of flying, a terror so great that, during the summers, going with Thilo to Greece or Italy, Gerald had to travel instead by train, boat, and car. At Sam's suggestion, he had started to see a therapist in London to address his fear of flying, which helped him make the decision to travel by plane to New York in the spring of 1977.

While Gerald was also undergoing hypnosis to overcome his terror of flying, Sam was contemplating another uncanny forecast in Gar Osten's elaborate astrological reading of his chart:

> *Was particularly interested in the new photographic direction of your life and this is simply a further extension of the artistic, creative influence of Neptune which has been transiting your 10th House of public life since way back in early 1964 [when "Black, White, and Gray" opened]. Your own natal Neptune, which governs photography, is positioned in your 7th House in Leo and it is ready for a transit of Saturn in the next year (October of 1976, beginning) and this could well bring an exhibition of some kind which would be important and rewarding in many ways. This could lead to publication of some kind in book form or through some other communications field, which would bring you considerable recognition personally.*[25]

A phone call came early in the spring as if cued directly from the configuration of the planets in Sam's chart. Jane Livingston, the chief curator at the Corcoran Gallery of Art in Washington, D.C., was interested in mounting a major show of photographs from Sam's collection.

When Livingston arrived at the Corcoran in 1975, after eight years as a curator at the Los Angeles County Museum of Art, one of her ambitions was to develop a curatorial program for photography. In early 1977 she began thinking about a symposium that would examine photography's evolving status within the art community, hoping to bring together curators, critics, and collectors at the top of the field. It was her idea to mount an exhibition of photographs from Wagstaff's collection in tandem with the symposium; the photography market being established by Sam and his fellow collectors was becoming a credible indication of the growing status of photography in the art world.

Wagstaff had already made a great impression on Livingston when they first met. She had already known him by reputation as the curator who showed Tony Smith's work before anyone else, and she happened to be dining with Tony Smith at the fashionable Russian Tea Room on West 57th Street one day in the early 1970s. "Sam came up to us and he was wearing this velvet shirt and turquoise and silver necklace and he was this dazzling man," she said. "He was in a great mood, with this huge smile. He had just come from some kind of a retreat, a sort of Buddhist meditation thing." [26] Livingston had since followed with curiosity Sam's turn to photography and his growing reputation in the field.

Not long after her phone call, she arrived at Sam's apartment to discuss the Corcoran show. The absence of furniture surprised her—like many before her, she had the impression that he had just moved in. After a long discussion about her ideas for the exhibition of photographs from his collection and about the symposium that she envisioned at the Corcoran, which was scheduled for the following February, Jane returned to Washington, leaving the selection process for the show entirely to Sam. The project would occupy his time and attention for the rest of the year.

Wagstaff had never been the subject of an exhibition. The decisions facing him would be uncharacteristically autobiographical. He would have to arrive at an organizing principle for the great variety of work in his collection. He would have to break down the collection into categories representing the scope of the medium itself, grouping pictures by genre, historic period, printing method and materials, and individual photographer. Only in the act of looking at the collection as a whole would he come to some understanding of what the photographs meant to him, and, by extension, what his choices reflected about his sensibility, his knowledge, his judgment, and his taste.

He was humbled, and a little uneasy, to be considered in the role of an artist. He revered "artists," exalted them above everyone else, including himself. But this prospect was also in violation of an unspoken taboo of his class: it was vulgar to put one's own name forward conspicuously in connection with social status or personal achievement. On the other hand, the fact that it was a collection of objects never before given much respect or credibility in the arena of art provided a counterweight to any assertion of personal accomplishment. He could approach the show as a cause. The "photograph" remained still an art world stepchild, and it delighted Sam to flaunt his regard for it in the face of those who had never taken it seriously. He would soon tell a *People* magazine reporter who interviewed him for the show that he "looked on photography as an underdog. It wasn't getting its day in court." [27]

Perhaps prompted by Gar Osten's astrological forecast, Sam set out to publish a book of photographs that would accompany the exhibition. The task would not be easy. He approached Lustrum Press, run by the photographer Ralph Gibson, but Gibson published only monographs of individual photographers. The few other publishers he approached declined, citing the cost of publishing a book of work by so many photographers from periods throughout the history of the medium, which would require too many variations in the printing process.

Ralph Gibson referred Sam to his business partner, Arne Lewis, who had a graphic design studio on East 12th Street, four blocks from Sam's apartment. After an initial meeting, Sam hired Arne to design and produce the book, enabling Sam to publish it under his own imprint. He called the imprint Gray Press—a look back to his first exhibition as a curator, "Black, White, and Gray," perhaps, or a reference to photography's mostly black-and-white history. He would pay Lewis $2500, and the printing itself cost $7000. [28]

Pulling together the show and the book gave Sam a new lens through which to enjoy and assess his collection. The momentum was made that much sweeter by Gerald Incandela's arrival for a three-week stay on May 1, 1977. Sam took a taxi to the airport to greet him. Nothing could have been more glamorous for the young artist on his first trip across the Atlantic than an introduction to New York by way of Sam's "minimalist" apartment. The first thing Gerald noticed was the bouquet of fresh pink peonies on a little table by the window. "And, then, the hazy sunset out the window over the Hudson River made me think of a Turner painting." Sam's sense of moment was animated by the stylish tone of his preparations, his anticipation of Gerald's arrival evident in the extravagance he allowed himself only selectively: fresh flowers, as well as, according to Incandela, "cocaine and champagne and caviar."[29]

Gerald had agreed to come to New York with some trepidation. Sam was more than twice his age, they didn't know each other that well, and their connection was still undefined. Wary of the prospect of spending three weeks as a guest in Sam's apartment, Gerald made arrangements to stay with Robert Woolley, the head of decorative arts at Sotheby's, and Woolley's boyfriend, Jeffrey Childs, an antiques dealer, at their apartment on upper Fifth Avenue. Woolley was a friend and colleague of Thilo's, which put Gerald on more familiar ground. In any case, the only bed in Sam's apartment was a thin futon where he slept on the floor between two avocado plants, an accommodation that would not have suited Gerald's more traditional tendencies. Sam accepted Gerald's arrangement without a fight.

Sam was in very good shape for a man in his fifties; the muscles of his body were taut still, but his face had acquired a handsome rugged crag-giness and his eyebrows were bushier than they had ever been. The golden-boy looks that had once defined his youth were transforming him into something else. Perhaps his tastes were evolving too. Certainly what attracted Sam to Gerald cannot be found in the template of his other attractions. There was nothing gritty about Gerald, who was tall, with jet-black hair and fair skin. He had a poetic air about him. He spoke with a quiet consideration that had as much to do with his artistic tem-perament as his discomfort with English.

It had been almost a year since Sam had begun his campaign to con-vince Gerald that he should be living in New York. Almost immediately after his arrival, Gerald began proving him right: in fact, he loved the pulse and vitality of the city. The spectacular orientation from Sam hardly tempered these perceptions. During long walks, Sam pointed out details on buildings he particularly liked and offered up the history and lore of one neighborhood after another. One of Sam's favorite places was Grand Army Plaza at the corner of Fifth Avenue and 59th Street: he and Gerald stood with their backs to the prosaic General Motors Building and looked across Fifth Avenue at the Plaza Hotel—later designated a national historic landmark—standing against its backdrop of glass skyscrapers like the tallest French Renaissance chateau in existence. Cabs and limousines pulled up to the grand entrance behind the Pulitzer Fountain on the leafy plaza in front; hansoms drawn by often festooned horses lined the street near the entrance to Central Park, where Augustus Saint-Gaudens's bronze monument of General Sherman on his horse stands guard; the more subdued but posh Sherry-Netherland Hotel arose to their right with its elegant sidewalk clock at the corner. So many people rushed by that it was hard for them to stand still without being jostled. "This is New York for me," Sam told Gerald. He may have distilled his own manner of living and being to an essential modernist austerity, but he never seemed to lose his affinity for the New York of Edith Wharton and Henry James, a city life that still possessed the gentility of European customs and tastes. This was the neighborhood of Sam's childhood; he noted that in the previous century a section of Central Park along 59th Street had been deeded to the city by the Wagstaff family.

Sam took Gerald with him everywhere. He introduced him to, among others, Tony Smith, Klaus Kertess, Paul Walter, Barbara Jakobson, Holly Solomon, and Daniel Wolf. He brought Gerald to a dinner party at the home of John Szarkowski in honor of the photographer Brassaï. "Sam made me look at life from a higher point of view," Gerald said of his first days in New York at Sam's side. "To look at the world from above. I didn't know about all of this. I wasn't exposed to it before. It was like being high."[30]

With Sam's help Gerald set out to find a place to live, and, in less than two weeks he signed a lease on a one-bedroom apartment with a large terrace in the East Twenties. The plan was that Gerald would go back to London to pack up his things and return the following week to begin his new life in New York. Yet despite an uneventful flight from London (for which he had been hypnotized and which he survived taking sedatives), his terror of flying consumed him all over again. He felt as if he arrived in New York having climbed up a very tall ladder, and the prospect of flying back to London made it seem impossible to climb back down. Sam took him to a therapist on Park Avenue, who offered the insight that no celestial being was hovering in the skies waiting to scratch Gerald's name out of the big book the minute he boarded a plane. "He was right," Gerald said. "How pretentious of me to think that God is going to make the plane fall out of the sky because I am in it."[31]

Conditioned by his therapy, Gerald returned to London, said good-bye to Thilo, and, at the age of twenty-five, moved to New York. Sam subsidized his relocation and set up a familiar financial arrangement: he supported Gerald, buying every picture he produced, giving him an incentive to work that fully honored his dignity. Gerald started out by making three or so pictures a month: Sam paid $500 each.

It was common knowledge among Sam's circle that he and Robert were a couple, so Gerald's presence caused some confusion and generated a good deal of gossip. But Gerald believed that Sam never considered it a choice between him and Robert. "Robert and Sam were very close and talked a couple of times a day," Gerald said. "Sex between the two of them was over. I think Robert knew that I had no intention of taking Sam away from him, but he was worried all the same. And I was also worried about the inevitable professional rivalry and felt at a disadvantage in the territory of those two pros."[32]

"Sam's attachment to Robert was umbilical, no matter what, no matter who," said Barbara Jakobson, who understood that Sam and Robert were the kind of lovers who had ended the sexual side of the love affair but continued their life together. Of course, Robert's promiscuity was countered by Sam's devotion to Gerald, and the ambiguity of Sam and Gerald's relationship didn't help. "When Sam became infatuated with Gerald Incandela, Robert was jealous and disdainful," Jakobson said.[33]

He may have been threatening to Robert, but Gerald, a young and inexperienced foreigner newly arrived in the great metropolis, was for the most part guileless and vulnerable. He didn't always know how to navigate his position. With one gesture, Sam had opened up to him a sphere of access and influence that would have taken any other young artist years, if at all, to reach. While the affection and attention Sam showered on Gerald was openhearted and well meaning, it left Gerald uncertain about what it required in return. His affection for Sam was still not developing into romantic sensation, or even sexual attraction. Sam once told Gerald that the only thing he couldn't bear was to have disappointed someone. Gerald didn't want Sam to feel like a disappointment around him, but it seemed inevitable. "I was in that position of saying no and I felt bad about it," Gerald said. "Being in a position of not giving. It felt cruel." Nevertheless, Gerald felt a genuine closeness between them and a natural ease around Sam, as if they were "soul mates for that moment."[34]

That summer the two spent a good deal of time together sitting around Sam's white apartment with the dappled, ever-changing daylight, getting stoned and selecting pictures for the Corcoran show. Judy Linn's sister, Nancy, worked for Sam as a curatorial assistant, maintaining the photography files and records in his eighth-floor apartment. Sam would summon her with requests to look at all the pictures by William James Stillman, or Frank Meadow Sutcliffe, or William Henry Fox Talbot. Then Gerald and Sam would pore over them, one by one, Sam delighted to have a captive audience, one who would marvel aloud at the tones in an albumen print or the empty space in a composition or the precise detail of a brick wall in 1840s Britain.

"He was giving me a crash course in the history of photography as well as seeking my reaction to all the pictures he would show me," Gerald recalled. When showing photographs to fellow collectors, other curators, or friends, Sam would inform them about what they were looking at. When he showed photographs to Michael Heizer, Tony Smith, Robert Mapplethorpe, or Gerald Incandela, he was seeking their reaction. "Sam had tremendous curiosity and respect for the 'artist's eye.' Of course that didn't mean that he wouldn't test it or provoke it to then be marveled by what we told him."[35]

Gerald remembered Nancy Linn coming upstairs with four to six black boxes of Nadar prints. He and Sam would sit on the floor with more than three hundred vintage prints spread out all around them. "I knew by then who Nadar was," Gerald remembered. "I was very impressed that he had so many."[36] Nadar's portraits are characterized by simplicity, honest expressions, natural lighting, and a clarity of visual description that set a standard and made Nadar the single most important influence on portraiture throughout the history of photography. Nadar's effect is evident in the work of August Sander, Berenice Abbott, Alfred Stieglitz, Richard Avedon, Peter Hujar, and the earlier portraits of Robert Mapplethorpe. The Nadar portraits in Sam's collection provide an added layer of cultural amusement, if not historical weight, from his subjects—the actress Sarah Bernhardt as Lady Macbeth, the writers Victor Hugo and George Sand, the composer Franz Liszt, the Barbizon school painter Jean-François Millet, among so many others. And yet Sam settled for only two pictures by Nadar for his book of photographs, a single brooding self-portrait and an uncharacteristic non-portrait made inside the dark Paris catacombs—the former a salt print, the latter albumen.

As it turned out, Sam did not place the Nadars on the same spread: the figure by Nadar in the catacombs faces a picture by Mapplethorpe of a leather-masked man squatting in a bunker next to a metal ladder. The visual similarities explain the pairing: in both pictures a single figure is cast in chiaroscuro light and set in an industrial enclosure. The differences lie in facts known to the viewer: the pictures were taken over a century apart, one documenting a worker in the catacombs of Paris, the other a man on a sexual escapade in Sausalito, California. In both cases, Sam opted for the less obvious and the more idiosyncratic example of the photographer's work over the historically sound or typical curatorial choice. He was pairing pictures that worked together according to his own eye. "Art, like chess, is a game of personal opinion, and probably only important for oneself as long as it is really personal," Sam would later write about the photographs he assembled. "Also, I have found that it's best to make up one's own rules, wherever possible."[37]

In Sam's volume, which was titled *A Book of Photographs from the Collection of Sam Wagstaff*, another spread includes a 1934 publicity still of the actress Marta Eggerth in *My Heart Calls You*, next to a photograph of a modest room with bright hazy sunlight pouring through the windows. Marta Eggerth is sitting on a bench in profile in a gauzy white dress with one leg up and her head flung back; this picture might very well have been the template for Robert's portrait of Holly Solomon. The anonymous publicity still and the sunlit room, by Judy Linn, seem to have nothing in common in terms of subject matter, composition, or genre. Gerald remembered "Sam's big love for shimmering light,"[38] which is one explanation for the logic of this pairing: both are luminescent, one animated by studio light shining through the transparent fabric of the dress, the other radiating sunlight through the screens on the windows. Neither picture draws from the historical canon, but together they are a lesson in light on film, luminosity on paper, and each one has a shimmering presence both sensory and pleasurable.

Not that Sam ignored the canon, still something of a mutable construction in the mid-1970s; so many discoveries were being made at the auction houses of Europe that would alter and revise the history of photography. While one spread in the book, for example, pairs the work of Walker Evans and Robert Frank, neither photographer had quite yet reached the apotheosis of his canonization. Other spreads are given to individual photographers such as Roger Fenton, August Sander, Frederick Evans, and Gustave Le Gray. In most cases they are not signature images by those photographers, but neither are they any less important given their photographic resonance.

Perhaps above all others, Sam loved Gustave Le Gray, the nineteenth-century French photographer and teacher of Charles Negre, Henri Le Secq, and Nadar. In his treatise of 1852, Le Gray wrote, "It is my deepest wish that photography, instead of falling within the domain of industry, of commerce, will be included among the arts. That is its sole, true place, and it is in that direction that I shall always endeavor to guide it."[39] One of the two Le Gray pictures in the book is a seascape in which the sky dominates most of the frame. Clouds are composed of subtle tonal gradations and vast empty spaces, and underscored by the photographically precise horizon line at the bottom of the picture. The image is thoroughly modern, almost a century ahead of its time in the purity of its compositional structure, the "minimalist" absence of subject, and its painterly elocution. On the facing page Sam placed a military maneuver on a vast field, the silhouettes of the men and the horses in the distance rendered with solid shading in place of precise photographic detail, giving it the quality of a drawing. "Sam liked the nineteenth century and preferred it when it looked modern or ahead of its time," Gerald said. "The fact that Le Gray was working, I think officially, for the emperor of France might have added some cachet."[40]

Two portraits by Baron von Gloeden are also in the book. Each young boy stares directly into the camera with eyes so penetrating that they seem to be boring holes into the viewer. These are not the naked and languorous Sicilian boys one expects in the turn-of-the-century pictures by von Gloeden; here the subjects' intense staring is a kind of sexual confrontation that appealed to Sam's own erotic tastes.

Sam was cognizant of the signature images of important photographers, but in a provocation that suggests something close to a zen koan, he wrote of his own idiosyncratic selection of photographs: "I make no pronouncements, no predictions. I'm not making a public statement. I only say 'this thing exists.' "[41]

When hanging a show of paintings, one can make a painting look good or bad on the wall depending on the work it is placed next to. With that in mind, Gerald and Sam moved pictures around on the floor in the process of pairing photographs for the book. In one spread, a vertical triptych is placed next to a horizontal diptych. The triptych, by an anonymous photographer in a plate from *Practical Poses for the Practical Artist* (1912), shows a young woman's hands at her waist, first from the front, then the back, and finally holding a clasp. The images graduate in depth from top to bottom in the same way that Mapplethorpe's triptych of Holly Solomon graduates in depth from the first picture to the last. They might also have been templates for triptychs that Sam made from the pictures he had secretly taken on Fire Island several years earlier. The diptych on the right, by George Hewitt from 1905, is called *Mrs. Hewitt Reading, Left; Mrs. Hewitt Going Upstairs, Right*. They show intimate sequential moments in an older woman's quiet evening ritual that Gerald suggested had resonance for Sam of his mother and his grandmother, referring to it as Sam's madeleine. It was the kind of moment he longed for as a child—the safety and comfort of his mother close at hand at night—but that was denied to him during his years in boarding school.

"I don't remember who thought about putting the hippopotamus next to the Lewis Carroll, but we were in full accord and somehow the fun we were having together made it happen," Gerald said,[42] implying that there might have been no deeper intention than the fact that they were stoned. He was referring to the picture of a frowning Alice Liddell, the little girl on whom Lewis Carroll modeled his eponymous heroine, which shares a spread with one of a hippopotamus in the zoo.

Jane Livingston appreciated Sam's definitive and quirky way of juxtaposing images, describing the entire process of working with him as harmonious and celebratory. "The only tension I remember was that Gerald Incandela was with Sam all of the time, and Robert part of the time, and it was sometimes a little strained only because Robert would have wanted more participation in everything, but he sort of hung back. Gerald was always very sweet, unobtrusive."[43]

It was unclear to both Gerald and Robert what Sam was thinking when it came to the cover of the book. Sam remained noncommittal until September, as he and Gerald continued to make selections for the book. Then Sam would transport the pictures in a portfolio box to Arne Lewis's nearby studio. Sam was characteristically cavalier with the prints, letting Lewis stack them casually on a table in the middle of the room. Lewis, however, would spot each print meticulously—removing white spots or crease marks by adding tone—and then set each one up on an easel and photograph it to make working prints for layout purposes. When a 1907 blue-tinted cyanotype by Edward S. Curtis fell off the easel onto the floor, the print was creased, but Arne was able to spot it out for the purpose of reproduction. "It didn't seem very important to Sam," he remembered.[44]

The book's trim size was eleven inches square. Many of the photographs are printed to their exact size, designated as such in each caption. The book was printed in sixteen-page signatures, or forms, as is the custom of book production. Because it was printed in duotone, the different forms were printed in different colors: some with black and brown inks, others with black and blue inks, others, black on black inks. It would not have made sense to put two pictures printed with different colored inks on the same spread, so some of Sam's choices for pairings had to be altered to accommodate the duotone colors of each signature.

Lewis also kept pressing Sam to decide on the cover picture, but, even before that decision, Sam was emphatic about the color he wanted for the cover. "I showed him a lot of colors that I thought would work but he insisted on peachy pink, a color he was particularly fond of." Lewis said. "I think the most important thing about the book really for him was the peachy pink."[45]

Sam's provocative nature was never more pronounced than in the rivalry he set up between Robert and Gerald over the cover of his book. Which one would be given that honor? He lorded the decision over them with a strain of sadistic intent, perhaps in reaction to the manner in which he felt an absence of affection—whether emotional or physical—from each of them. He understood the inordinate power he had over both of them and he was quite comfortable reminding them of it in just this way.

Sam's love for Robert was both deep and complicated, their connection inviolate, his belief in him as an artist bordering on the sacred. So much had been consistently forgiven: Robert's disregard for Sam's enthusiasms and his insensitivity to Sam's needs and the promiscuity that ended their sexual relationship all seemed to be granted a kind of lifetime impunity. At the same time Sam was in love with Gerald, and yet that love was still without consummation. It was unclear how long he would wait to have sex with him. "If love lives on hope, and dies with it again," Corneille writes in *Le Cid*. "Your heart is freed, as your hope is dead." Sam's hope was not interminable.

Sexual attraction follows its own logic, of course, but Gerald also felt that he couldn't completely trust Sam, not because Sam was older and so much more accomplished, but because of his relationship with Robert. Sam and Robert had their own private language; in person or on the phone, in front of other people or alone, they often communicated excitedly in an almost indecipherable baby talk. It always left Gerald feeling excluded. "It's difficult to bond with somebody if you feel that they already have a very strong bond with somebody else."[46]

Robert would invariably stop by while Gerald and Sam were looking at pictures, and after he left Sam would muse, as if with satisfaction, that Robert seemed a little jealous and worried. Gerald assumed all along that the cover image would probably be from the nineteenth century. According to Gerald, it never occurred to him that one of his own pictures was under consideration. But Paul Walter remembered that Gerald was hoping to be on the cover while Robert was worried that he himself wouldn't be. Walter recalled that the tension was palpable.[47] So did John Waddell: "Gerald had an incredible aesthetic sensibility. Gerald was an artist," he said, explaining why he believed Sam had included Gerald in the process of selecting the photographs for the show and the book. "Sam was going to put Gerald's picture on the cover of the book," Waddell remembered, "and Robert was very upset."[48]

While the cover decision was playing out as a protracted drama, Robert had introduced Sam to Jared Bark, who had been framing Robert's photographs. Bark's frame shop was in a loft building on Wooster Street in SoHo, owned by Weston Naef, the curator of photography at the Met. (Paula Cooper's gallery was in the same building). During the summer of 1977, Sam brought dozens of photographs at a time to Bark's studio to make decisions about the framing of the work for the Corcoran show. Sam would arrive at the end of the day and for several hours they would look at each picture to decide on the matte and the frame. "Most of our moldings were hardwood moldings," Bark recalled. "There were a variety of American hardwoods—cherry, walnut, maple, and a variety of papers and matte board, silk and other materials we could choose for the matting. The profile range was fairly limited—simple modern profiles, by and large, and all natural finishes."[49]

When working on larger exhibitions of this type, it was Bark's experience that curators made a single choice of frame for all the pieces in a show. "Sam, however, was intent on framing each photograph as an individual work," Bark said. So they would place a single photograph on the table and consider the type of wood, the profile of the frame, and the matting options. Bark was struck by the way Sam stood and stared at an image on the table, like an eagle eyeing a rabbit far below on the plain. "He would fix the piece in his eye and the intensity of his concentration was impressive," Bark said. "Seldom was I able to collaborate with someone whose intentions were so high to get each one right."[50]

Sam took a break from the entire book enterprise by renting in

August 1977 the same Fire Island Pines house he had rented the previous summer. The most stylish manner of transport from Manhattan to Fire Island was then the seaplane, a tiny mosquito of aeronautical design that only seated five people, plus the pilot, taking off and landing on water. Passengers boarded the seaplane at the 23rd Street pier on the East River. The windows were open on either side as the propeller revved up and the plane glided away from the pier, then picked up speed and caught the air, lifting off in a seesaw ascent. The rapidly increasing altitude could be dizzying—and frightening, according to Gerald—as the towers of the city receded, like the sensation of an amusement park ride that is thrilling and threatening, at once. In those days the plane flew over the neatly lined houses in one well-organized Long Island suburb after another and, in less than twenty minutes, it sailed back down, bobbing to and fro in the soft breezes of the Great South Bay. The handful of passengers climbed out of the cabin and down into the water, wading to the shores of paradise in shorts and bare feet, bags on their shoulders, roughing it in a way that only money can buy. The fastest escape from the city—and the most fun—was certainly a vast improvement on the lumbering Long Island Rail Road, and another of the rare extravagances Sam didn't seem to mind indulging himself in for the sake of Gerald.

Sam was hoping it would help Gerald further overcome his fear of flying, but Gerald experienced too much anxiety and nausea during the flight to appreciate the efficiency—if not the glamour—of the seaplane. Still, both were glad to be on Fire Island. Robert arrived later and all three stayed there together off and on during the month. Patti came to stay for a weekend, and Sam couldn't have been happier to treat it as a kind of family retreat.

The beach at Fire Island is pristine and deceptively simple, all straight lines and all white sand and rolling, if not occasionally jagged waves—the quintessential minimalism of nature. Their house was modern and comfortable, and Sam was content to sit out by the pool and make his way through E. F. Benson's *Mapp and Lucia* novels, an amusing entertainment about social climbing among Britain's landed gentry in the 1920s and '30s. Its elegant bitchery cloaked in double entendres was just the kind of social satire that characterized Sam's own sense of humor, an intelligent and knowing lampoon of the class in which he grew up on this side of the Atlantic—the "fancy pants" he liked so much to deride. All the pretense, pomp, and circumstance, and material extravagance that he repudiated on one level he nonetheless cherished as representative of quality and substance. In fact, he used the term "fancy pants" in self-mockery as much as he applied it in derision of others. Soon after he finished the books, Sam gave George Rinhart a copy of the compendium volume, *Make Way for Lucia*; urging him to read it, Sam claimed with his own inherent snobbery that Lucia, the main character, a social climber of some intelligence who was at times very good company but generally insufferable, reminded him of Rinhart. Sam equated himself with the Lady Adele, the Countess of Brixton, a witty and insightful student of human nature. "From then on we would play Mapp and Lucia to each other," Rinhart said, indicating an increasingly playful level of intimacy between them. "Lucia was known for her baby talk, and so Sam and I would go on and on and on in baby talk when no one else was around."[51]

The song "I Need a Man" by Grace Jones, the hard-edged Jamaican model–turned–disco chanteuse, was playing everywhere in 1977, and not without irony in the Pines, but Sam's favorite song on Fire Island that summer was "Native New Yorker," by Odyssey, a jazzy, calypso-infused disco hit with a cool, breezy rhythm. Sam rarely offered that he had been in the Glee Club at Yale, but he would burst into song whenever "Native New Yorker" was playing, substituting his own pointed words over the lyrics about unrequited love in the refrain.[52]

While the underlying tension between Gerald and Robert was not manifest as a general dynamic in the house, they played out a less formal, but perhaps equally disquieting, version of the *Mapp and Lucia* comedy of manners throughout the month, a kind of quietly simmering disdain incited in no small way by the machinations of "Lady Adele" Wagstaff. On one occasion Sam, Gerald, and Robert were sitting and eating at Botel's café in Pines Harbor, an afternoon ritual in which they naturally participated in a local pastime of watching the seemingly endless parade of bare-chested men on their way to the local grocery store and commenting on those who caught one's eye. Gerald was wearing a coral necklace that Thilo had given him. At one point, Robert flashed a half-mocking smile and asked him if he was a hippie. "Let's say that day, on a scale from one to ten, the apparent hostility coming from Robert was only three," Gerald said.[53]

Back in the city in September, Sam went to Arne Lewis and handed him a diptych of tulips by Robert Mapplethorpe. "This is what I want on the cover," he said. Lewis did not think it was the best choice and suggested other options, but Sam waved them away. This is the picture, he repeated, one full frame on the front, the second full frame on the back. It was the end of the discussion.

Tulips, New York (1977) is a mannered study of shape and structure in velvety black, white, and gray.[54] In the image on the front cover, nearly two dozen tulips rise out of a cylindrical black vase and fan across the frame in a balletic arc, one single tulip bowing to the left and brushing against the side of the picture—as if the lone stem echoes the arc formed by the entire bouquet. The bouquet is situated in a composition of frames within frames, hard edges against organic forms; the symmetry, delicacy, logic, and order add up to an elegant and poetic photograph. Flowers are nature's nerve endings, but they are also the sexual organs of a plant, and Robert photographed the tulips as if they were tingling with sensation, the single drooping flower protruding off to the left as if in semiarousal. The front cover of *A Book of Photographs from the Collection of Sam Wagstaff* is a still life of flowers, as casual in its simplicity as it is formal in composition, graceful in gesture, and debonair in tone. The back-cover image is mostly pure black background, with the petals of only a few tulips popping into the frame in close-up, one the drooping flower from the full bouquet, as if reaching from the front cover to the back.

These were the congratulatory tulips Paul Walter sent on the occasion of Robert's first official exhibition. By choosing this picture for the cover, Wagstaff places Robert Mapplethorpe as the contemporary link to the vast history of photography sampled inside. At the same time, the flowers were also a commemorative bouquet for Olga, standing in for the bouquets that Sam photographed in her apartment on the day she died. This book in fact gave material form to Sam's rebirth after Olga's passing. Although he had organized innumerable exhibitions over the years, each reflecting his judgment in service of the work of an artist or an idea about art making, *A Book of Photographs* is the first true representation of himself, his name stamped on the cover. It was as if he gave to the public a bouquet of fresh-cut tulips—albeit hard-edged in lighting and tone—the most sentimental public gesture he had ever allowed. Mapplethorpe was, of course, happy with the choice. The months leading up to it had been tortuous, the suspense eating at him. "If Gerald had a possibility of having the cover for the book," Judy Linn said, "Robert would have killed him."[55]

For his part, Gerald came to believe that it was the right choice, but he was naturally disappointed. For one thing, he did not like the way Sam had handled it. It was also the first time that Sam had profoundly disappointed him. "Sam kept saying, 'I don't know, I don't know,' and then it was a fait accompli," Gerald said. "I realized then, as I always suspected, that his alliance was with Robert first and foremost, and even if it was fair enough I had lost my trust in an ally."[56]

Perhaps in consolation, Sam gave Gerald the first copy of the book, and noted its order in the print run ("1/1, 500") next to his inscription on the title page:

For Smarty Pants with many, many thanks for all the help without which this would have been a lot less fun (and much more work) to do. I hope there will be more. With love and admiration that you're almost as smart as I am, Sam[57]

A P L A U S E

It's not that Velasquez is better than Rembrandt, but that Velasquez makes Rembrandt better.

—SAM WAGSTAFF[1]

PRESIDING AT A CANDLELIT TABLE, DASHING IN A PROPER TUXEDO, and basking in the limelight, Sam Wagstaff surveyed a room of more than two hundred people seated at tables spread throughout the main gallery of the Corcoran Gallery of Art in Washington, D.C. He was the guest of honor at this black-tie dinner on February 4, 1978, which celebrated the opening of "Photographs from the Collection of Sam Wagstaff." The evening felt like a fitting tribute to his enterprise of the last five years. Sitting nearby in a black velvet gown was Joan Mondale, wife of the vice president of the United States, who had been snidely dubbed "Joan of Art" by the media for her advocacy. Also present was the conservative Republican Senator Barry Goldwater, who told a reporter before dinner that he had "been a photographer for forty years," adding that he had published books of his photographs,[2] although we must presume none that had reflected the historic scope or the aesthetic reach of the one Wagstaff had just produced.

Scattered around the room were Sam's intimates and familiar friends:

Robert, Gerald, Judy Linn, Elaine Mayes, and Jane Smith, who came with her daughter Seton. There were also Paul Walter and Harry Lunn. Wider art world orbits were represented, too, by attendees like Walter Hopps, then curator of the Smithsonian's National Collection of Fine Arts, and Barbara Jakobson. And, despite his reservations about Susan Sontag's new book, *On Photography*,[3] Sam understood that the presence of one of the few serious cultural critics and thinkers to have gained notoriety in popular culture gave the evening just that much more intellectual heft. At the same time, the event served as a cotillion, of sorts, for Sam's arrival as a figure of veneration, not in the manner of the society balls of his youth at which his name and social position gave his presence legitimacy, but because of the art he had chosen to forward that was now being recognized by a national institution, reflecting the substance of his vision—and an earned gravitas.

It was exactly one year since the party Wagstaff had thrown at One Fifth to honor Mapplethorpe's first official foray into the art world. Paul Richard, the art critic of *The Washington Post*, led his review of *Photographs from the Collection of Sam Wagstaff* with this tongue-in-cheek conclusion:

> Around 250 guests from the White House and the Congress, the diplomatic corps, corporation boardrooms and the posher streets of Georgetown will attend the seated dinner. The ladies in their gowns, the men in their tuxedos, will—by their very presence among those small, machine-made pictures—be sending us a message. The collecting of photography is socially acceptable; the Establishment approves of photography-as-art.[4]

After so many years falling short of his own expectations—not only the aspirations imposed on him by Olga, but also the humiliations of being passed over in Hartford and forced out in Detroit—Sam had now become exactly the person he thought he should be. The unique role he was creating for himself eclipsed any success he could have attained had he been appointed, say, director of the Wadsworth Atheneum. He could look around the room and feel that he had made a name for himself on his own terms, with an immanent originality that reflected his artistic sensibility—and it was being embraced by those socially prominent and politically powerful alike. "There crackles round [Wagstaff] an air of dissipation but the Establishment is willing to overlook such static," commented Richard in the *Post*. "He has art credentials few photography collectors can match."[5]

The exhibition was mounted in the huge galleries of the Corcoran—spacious, Beaux Arts rooms with skylights designed by Ernest Flagg in the late nineteenth century—which had never before been used for photography. After Sam had chosen the photographs, Jane Livingston worked with him on the installation. "We weren't so careful then about moderating light on rare photographs, so the show simply glowed and scintillated," she later recalled, acknowledging a time before conservators cautioned about the damage caused by direct sunlight on a photographic print.[6]

Sam was intent on introducing work that had been overlooked or underrated by historians. He took the exhibition as an occasion to educate others about what he himself had been discovering, and he gave innumerable slide lectures about the photographs in the show. More than just a description of the pictures, it was a manifesto for photography as a formidable medium in the realm of fine art. The show would be traveling on to half a dozen other museums around the country, and he wanted people to embrace it on the correct terms. He wanted it to be understood that photography was not simply an invention that resulted in a practical application but one that sprang from the intelligence of the species in an ongoing evolution of consciousness.

Sam's art historical background was never more in evidence than when he talked about photographs, working out their place in the evolution of art. There were several pictures by Charles Marville in the exhibition, for example. One, *View from the Bridge of Saints-Peres, Paris*, a salt print (circa 1854), shows a stone quarry in the snow on the banks of the Seine. Several horse-drawn carts sit idle, except for the slight blur from the movement of the horses. A curved ramp rises gracefully in the center of the frame from the riverbank below to the level of the street. The snow leaves a mottled pattern on the piles of stone along the river.

"Mind you, this again is about ten years before French impressionism really gets its stride," he said during the slide show, referring to the pattern of snow as it anticipated that movement in painting. "This [picture] always makes me think of seeing a new painter. It's like a new eye. One thing that we haven't been able to do yet with photography strongly enough, I think, is to pewter our eye down to the point where we know hundreds of photographers the way we know hundreds of painters. It's going to be a lot more fun when we can do that."[7]

Among his favorites was the nineteenth-century photographer William James Stillman, sometimes called an American Pre-Raphaelite for the precise, almost scientific clarity of his images and the aestheticized view of his subjects. One picture in the show, *Interior of the Parthenon* (1869), centers on a freestanding row of Doric columns; the loose marble bricks of what once composed the floor of the great ruin are articulated in fine detail. "He is really the king of foregrounds," Sam said during a presentation of the pictures to a class of art students at Pratt Institute, pointing out the canny use of sunlight against the ruins. "This is about as classy a photograph as was taken by an American in 1869."[8]

Wagstaff's technical command of the materials and the processes in the evolution of photography could not have been more assured in his selection. It was, in fact, one of the underpinnings of the show. The process of making a print determined the look of the photograph, and Sam wanted to emphasize the differences between one method and another. He knew every type of printing process; he could identify a print made from a wet collodion glass-plate negative, or draw the fine distinctions between a calotype and a salt print.

The exhibition presented carbon prints by Adolphe Braun and Thomas Annan, calotypes by Hill and Adamson and William Henry Fox Talbot, albumen prints by Edouard Denis Baldus and Baron von Gloeden, and photogravure prints by Peter Henry Emerson. There was a salt print by Froissart, another little-known French photographer, whose *Flood at Lyon* (1856) is a beautiful third- or fourth-floor view out a window at the bend in a river, the row of buildings forming a graceful crescent along the promenade, and three stands of leafy trees with delicate trunks in the foreground. The etched precision of detail in the buildings and the trees is countered with an otherworldly mist rising from the water across the entire promenade. A peculiar and lyrical calm suffuses the image and obscures the fact that it is not a lovely French cityscape but a documentation of a small natural disaster.

Sam particularly admired a picture of the Countess de Castiglione called *Scherzo di Follia* (Game of Madness; 1863–1866), by Pierre-Louis Pierson, now one of the most famous portraits in the history of photography. She holds a square mask up to her face, leaving only one of her eyes, like a camera lens, visible. The countess, the mistress of Napoleon III, who might be considered the original Cindy Sherman, collaborated with Pierson to construct photographs in many guises with a nod to the artifice of the creation. The Metropolitan Museum of Art owned a later print, but there were only two known early prints: Sam owned one and Richard Avedon the other. "I might compare Sam to Diana Vreeland," Incandela said. "She identified the 'style' icons and he, the nineteenth-century-photography 'icons.' In that way he would be responsible for the portrait of the Countess de Castiglione's rise to stardom."⁹

One of the most formally resolved photographs in the show was a platinum print by Frank Meadow Sutcliffe. In *Natives* (circa 1890), three naked boys linger on the prow of a boat propped up on land at the water's edge. Two are photographed leaning against the boat, their backs to the camera, and the other is seated on the boat in profile. It looks to be a spontaneous moment of reverie and youthful camaraderie, but each boy strikes a pose consistent with the conventions of the academic nude. Sutcliffe photographed scenes of daily life in the seaside town of Whitby, England, where he lived, with the intent of universalizing just such ordinary moments. He made a series of photographs of the local boys frolicking naked in the river, the most famous of which is *Water Rats* (1886). Given its male nudity, the image created a brief controversy in Whitby. *Natives*, the picture in Sam's collection, is poetic in mood, composition, and tonal subtlety, and reminiscent of the 3-×-5-inch Thomas Eakins photograph, also in Sam's show: *Students at a Swimming Hole* (1883), for which he had paid $9000.

Vernal Fall, 350 Feet, Yosemite Valley, Cal., No. 44 (circa 1864–1866), is a majestic albumen print by Carleton Watkins, in which the dense waterfall mist appears as a solid white sheet dropping from a great height. The rocks on either side form a set of patterns that appear almost too mechanical for nature. "This is what a high style American eye saw in 1865," Sam said about Watkins's waterfall, referring to his subtle abstractions of nature.[10] And Sam made the same observation about William Rau, who documented the Pennsylvania Rail Road at the turn of the century. *Main Line and Low Grade Tracks at Parkesburg* (1906) is a bromide print showing the train tracks as Rau stood between the rails and likely photographed from the back of a train. It is a study in two-point perspective as the firm parallel lines cut through an intricate pattern of gravel on the rail bed and shoot straight out toward the viewer with controlled graphic drama. Sam thought that this picture, too, reflected "what a high style American eye saw" in the first years of the twentieth century.

George Barker was an American photographer who extensively documented Niagara Falls in the late nineteenth century. *Niagara Falls, 1888* is a dramatic photograph looking up at the falls as the cascading water crashes with great force on the huge boulders in the foreground. It is a study in bold blacks and whites as much as it is evidence of the majesty—and the violence—of nature. Sam made a wry comment about twentieth-century photography when discussing this photograph: "I think we can see where people like Ansel Adams, the idea of nature as MGM spectacular, began way back then," he said, disparaging the already canonized photographer. "One can get an inkling of the hipness of the aesthetic of a period like 1886 when you see photographs like these. They weren't all stupid, those people."[11]

The twentieth century was amply represented as well. Included in the show was a striking solarized study of a male torso by Man Ray, made in 1933. Man Ray, the Dada artist who moved from New York to Paris in the early 1920s and aligned himself with Marcel Duchamp, had a flourishing commercial career later in that decade. His introduction to Paul Poiret, the acclaimed designer, during a fashion assignment for *Vanity Fair* would lead to the accidental, if inauspicious, birth of the rayograph, the term he used for his solarized pictures. Man Ray made his first rayographs while developing images of the designer's work.

The penumbra that surrounded the photographed object in his rayographs was seen then as a symbol of transformation beyond actual recorded form. Even today the effect suggests an aura of experimentation and imagination. The figure in Man Ray's *Male Torso* is frozen in the bold black outline of his own solarized shape, the highlights and shadows that caress his body adding an erotic charge to the electrified image.

The exhibit richly reflected Sam's fascination with perceptual titillation, particularly evident in so many twentieth-century pictures that explore visual abstraction. The solarization in the Man Ray print is one example, but another, less obvious one is the only Walker Evans image displayed. *Liberté, Promenade Deck, Port Forward* (1958) is a study in shape and form and light. An outer wall on the upper deck of a ship takes up most of the composition; a walking figure is silhouetted on the far right and framed in the bold stark outline of a doorway. Sunlight splashes the wall in a simple patterned highlight. The layers of shapes— a rectangular window, two boxed cabinet doors with small circles in the center—break up the solid expanse of wall with an asymmetrical geometry. Evans created a study of pattern and shape on a wall with sunlight and shadow, a departure from the straightforward objects so characteristic of his work. "It is not what one is looking for in Walker Evans," Sam said during the slide show. "It is maybe not what you want to be told about Walker Evans, but it is also Walker Evans."[12]

Sam's slide-show lecture became an extension of his show; it was an animated meditation on his evolving philosophy in photography and in his own enterprise of collecting it. "The people who have a background of art have an enormous amount of prejudice to get through to the point where we recognize photography as also an extremely important manifestation of the invention of the human mind as expressed through the eyes," he said. "We acknowledge that to painting, we acknowledge that to architecture, we acknowledge that to sculpture, but I am not really sure that we acknowledge that to photography. As a matter of fact I am goddamn sure that we don't acknowledge it, because we don't even know who the hell the photographers are."[13]

Photography remained merely a speck in the broad sweep—from

cave drawings to Greek sculpture to Italian frescoes to French neoclassical painting—of art history, coming at the tail end of a long continuum. Throughout much of its infancy, the photographic image had not been read in the language of the eye but rather in the realm of the mechanical and the scientific. Its ability to show empirical proof gave it endless forensic possibility. A photograph may have been magical in the early days, just as so many inventions are at first, like television in the 1940s or cell phones in the 1990s, but the awe photography inspired in its early years went as far only as its ability to record the parameters of the actual world. Still to come was an understanding of its promise as a medium of expression and revelation, as well as artistic manipulation.

Sam said in his lecture that he would like to be able to "pewter our eye down to the point where we know hundreds of photographers the way we know hundreds of painters" (with his memorable but to-the-point new usage of "pewter" as a verb). By this, he invoked the legacy of his first mentor in art history, Richard Offner, with whom he had studied pre-Renaissance Italian art at the Institute of Fine Arts in the late 1950s. Offner had been devoted to the practice of connoisseurship, inherited from Bernard Berenson. Berenson himself described connoisseurship as "the comparison of works of art with a view to determining their reciprocal relationship." The modern view of the connoisseur tends to be pejorative—a kind of superficial perfectionist in search of the best of a species of object for his own aesthetic pleasure and the status of exclusive ownership. But the practice of connoisseurship that Offner adapted from Berenson, and that Sam was taught, employed a serious methodology for examining works of art. Sam brought that same rigorous approach to the field of photography: he exposed himself to as much of its history as he could and learned to distinguish one photographer from another; he studied the photographic processes that evolved with each new technology during the nineteenth century and into the twentieth; he became versed in the different photographic genres—whether the portrait, the landscape, or the chronicle—and got to know how different photographers approached the same kind of subject matter; and he came to identify the characteristics that distinguished American photographers from, say, French or British ones. This very intimate knowledge suffused the selection process for "Photographs from the Collection of Sam Wagstaff."

A critic seldom seems to be able to express so precisely what the artist—or, in this case, the curator—intended, but the Paul Richard review that appeared in *The Washington Post* does exactly that. "Because photographs are made mechanically, and because they aren't unique, collectors once dismissed them as lesser works of art. If that prejudice has faded, it is, in part, because so much abstract painting now seems increasingly thin gruel. That photographs tell stories, that they document the instant, is no longer held against them," observed Richards, further noting that, in the Corcoran exhibit, while there are works by Eakins, Degas, Walker Evans, Robert Frank, and many other masters, "Sam Wagstaff is the artist that one most remembers after looking at this show."[14]

SAM ORCHESTRATED A SLIGHTLY perverse, if also captious, side-show in tandem with the exhibition of photographs from his collection at the Corcoran. In two adjacent first-flour galleries, Sam, melding his personal life and his professional judgment, chose to exhibit work by Robert Mapplethorpe and Gerald Incandela. "Sam had a huge bad-boy streak," Jane Livingston said about the Mapplethorpe/Incandela rooms, describing the expression of glee on Sam's face: "I just remember his laugh, the quality of his laugh. It was so funny, those dimples and that smile."[15] Certainly Sam wanted to showcase contemporary work he thought was important, and Robert and Gerald more than qualified. He could have chosen other photographers, too, male and female alike, to make a larger statement about emerging artists, but this act of pitting Cain against Abel played the two acolytes off each other in a gesture at once generous and sadistic.

As the chief curator, Livingston had a responsibility to the Corcoran and was not, therefore, one to indulge Sam's whim to exhibit Robert and Gerald's work had she believed his decision was based on some personal agenda. "I would never have agreed to show any work that I didn't think was good, or I didn't think was important," she said. "I was very stubborn and stainless about that sort of thing, so I had no trouble putting Gerald's photographs on those walls, you know. I thought: This is the real deal. I could see that Gerald was an artist, so it wasn't embarrassing in that way."[16]

Livingston's timing in mounting a show from Sam's collection—in fact, the very idea of a show of work by a private collector—was ideal, as were her instincts about what was taking place in the art world. She brought to photography an understanding of the trajectory of art making that led up to the new interest in the medium in the mid-1970s, just as Sam did as a former curator of contemporary art.

At that time the presiding authority in the field of photography was John Szarkowski, director of photography at the Museum of Modern Art, and Livingston was as respectful of him as anyone. While Szarkowski upheld the canon established by Beaumont Newhall, he was the keeper of the hierarchy and conferred importance on any number of contemporary photographers, adding to the canon, in particular, the work of Diane Arbus, Lee Friedlander, Garry Winogrand, and William Eggleston. Now the Corcoran exhibition demonstrated that Wagstaff's seminal role as a collector was becoming increasingly influential in the field Szarkowski dominated.

In contrast to Szarkowki's Mark Twain–like American prairie classicism, Wagstaff's sensibility took on the outrageousness of Lord Byron. As a private collector, Sam was bound only to his own beliefs and desires, which led to acquisitions that were sexier, more provocative, and further afield than the very un-Byron-like mandates of MoMA. "I am showing you a lot of these things just to show you that there is an alternative to Stieglitz, Steichen, Strand, etc.," he would say during his slide-show lecture, as much a comment on Szarkowski's vision as on the exhibition itself. "There are a lot of people who are worth looking at, who don't get shown."[17] Despite choices that appeared to some impetuous, the exhibition was hardly lacking in rigor. Wagstaff dipped in and out of the American tradition with what Livingston called "the typical imperiousness and the confidence of his own vision." He made it acceptable to bestow value on the underrated, or the amateur. "Sam was more of an underground figure," Livingston said. "You know, he wasn't an official curator, and he wasn't a writer. John took himself very, very seriously. And Sam never did that."[18]

For Livingston, Szarkowski's influence was undeniable. There were figures she would not have understood, much less championed, without his insights, photographers like Minor White or Frederick Sommer. "But the way I approached it, when I finally came around to the *New York School* [her 1992 book, which examines a period in photography between 1936 and 1963], which I think is probably my most important contribution to the field, I didn't get that from John Szarkowski, in terms of understanding that it was an unwritten chapter of photographic history," she said, "I got much more from Sam and Harry [Lunn] and Robert [Mapplethorpe]."[19] In the late 1970s, the Museum of Modern Art did in fact acquire two photographs by Gerald Incandela, and even though it eventually acquired *Tulips*, Szarkowski himself never did endorse the work of Robert Mapplethorpe. Still, Livingston stood by her decision to show the work of both photographers after Sam proposed it.

While in Washington, the "family"—Sam, Robert, and Gerald—all stayed as guests in the grand Georgetown home of Mary Swift, a friend of Livingston and a patron of the arts who helped support the photography program at the Corcoran. Swift enjoyed having artists around and was known to throw some grand and raucous parties. Robert first showed Livingston his collection of X-rated pictures, which he now referred to as his "X portfolio," in a bedroom at Mary Swift's house. The only thing Swift remembers now about their stay in her house was the X portfolio that Robert had inadvertently left behind. "There were pictures of Robert and Sam fucking," an eighty-five-year-old Swift much later recalled.[20]

The threesome that frolicked on Fire Island would play out their intense dynamic on a much larger stage in the capital city. Gerald had wisely sensed that Sam's affections would be temporary and Robert would always be the central character in Sam's life, yet Robert was understandably irritated about sharing such a visible platform with Gerald. Still, emotionally and professionally, it was a biblical drama in so many ways, carrying overtones of incest, and Gerald feared that Robert would eventually exact his revenge. While Gerald was overwhelmed with his good fortune—a show of his work at a major museum in Washington less than a year after arriving, ingénuelike, in the United States—it felt like his association with Sam had become a game of chess: one wrong move could be the end. Articulating a fear that Mapplethorpe seemed not to share, he mused yet later: "I was afraid to be perceived as Sam Wagstaff's boyfriend," he said. "I wanted people to take me seriously on my own."[21]

As Livingston remembered it, there was no question that Robert was going to have the last word. Gerald appeared to her in that context as something like Sam's "courtesan." There was a big contrast with Robert, who, she said, "was so amazingly opportunistic and ambitious. Robert had to scramble for everything he got. He was a real paradox. He didn't have anything like the basic inner confidence that Sam did, because Sam was such a patrician, but Robert had his own built-in confidence, too." Although he was clearly from the other side of the tracks, it was evident to Livingston that Robert knew who he was, and "he didn't take any shit from anybody. He had a real confidence in his own eye, and his own vision, and I think that's why Sam respected him so much. I think Sam learned a lot from Robert."[22]

THREE WEEKS AFTER THE opening of "Photographs from the Collection of Sam Wagstaff," the Corcoran hosted a two-day symposium entitled Photography: Where We Are.[23] Over the course of the weekend of February 25, 1978, Livingston presided over a series of presentations and panels. The introduction to the symposium by Peter Bunnell, director of the Princeton Art Museum, set the tone while echoing the Paul Richard review in *The Washington Post*: "It's not without reason to say that for those of us who have been involved with photography for a decade or perhaps two . . . it's hard to accept and to understand the rapidity with which this medium has blossomed into the general cultural consciousness of our civilization."

Sam was on a panel about collecting. He suggested in his presentation that the growing regard for art photography coincided with the deaths of *Look* magazine, in 1971, and *Life* magazine the following year.

"We're now free to receive photographs with a different kind of dignity," he said, and proceeded to speak for almost half an hour with a fair amount of logic and insight: "When I started to look at photography, I suppose I thought that photographs were the underdog and that made them more attractive because it meant that one could do something about them. I had visions of myself as being a walking sandwich board for photography which, god only knows, there had been lots of other people who were . . . long before me (I'm Johnny-come-lately in all of this). It has been very exciting to put together a group of images which I often feel should really have been bought by public institutions. But the public institutions weren't bidding at Sotheby's or Christie's or at the dealers."[24]

With an almost prescient understanding of the new world of interest in the medium that would follow, he continued: "That will come. . . . Photography seems to demand that very quiet place. Photography is the least decorative of all the arts. We can certainly say that it 'don't' hold the wall terribly well.' "[25] At least not yet.

During the question-and-answer session, one audience member, John Coplans, who had recently stepped down as editor of *Artforum* and would become an important photographer himself in the 1980s, added some drama to the panel by challenging the speakers with something of an admonition, suggesting that photography collecting was becoming its own precinct of exclusivity: "We were hoping to make photography more accessible, like the Farm Security Administration pictures, for example," he said. "But, instead, collecting is only making it less accessible. Collecting has become speculative. Photographs are commanding phenomenal prices—$12,000 for a single photograph."[26]

Wagstaff responded from the stage by asking him what his point was. Coplans said that he expected the panelists to be more honest about their investment interest in photography as a motivating factor in collecting.

Harry Lunn, the photography dealer, walked up to a microphone stand in the audience and, in his characteristic gentlemanly calm, proceeded to puncture Coplans's hypocrisy. "John, whom I know and to whom I've sold things, would not touch a Farm Security Administration print," Lunn said, staring Coplans down several rows away. "Mr. Coplans, who has a very distinguished collection of Western landscape photographs, you've only bought the finest, John. You wouldn't take anything less and why should you? . . . But, to feign horror at a $12,000 photograph, of which there are not many. . . . $12,000 is the cost of an ordinary Milton Avery watercolor, of which there are hundreds in existence. No one is writhing in horror at the fact that Milton Avery was struggling hand to mouth in the 1930s."[27]

A year earlier, Sam had bought the Lewis Carroll print of Alice Liddell for $10,000 at auction. Lunn stood at the microphone and pointed out that only three prints of Alice Liddell were in existence and that Sam purchased an exquisite photograph of great rarity and great beauty. He underscored his point as only a fine dealer could: "Why shouldn't it in the year 1977 or 1978 command the price of $10,000?"[28]

The next day, with her unassailably strict urbane demeanor, authoritative voice, and precise diction, Susan Sontag, still slender, her handsome features animated by a single streak of gray in her shoulder-length black hair, took the podium. "The discourse about photography is not very distinguished, doesn't have any great models, and is generally thought to be of poor quality," she began. She cited Walter Benjamin as the only example of lucid twentieth-century analysis about the medium. While the attempt to validate photography as an art form had been a theme since the 1840s, the low quality of current photography criticism derived from what she identified as a general defensiveness associated with photography throughout its history: "Photography, it seems to me, from the beginning is one of the most characteristically and continuously defensive of all art-making activities. This kind of defensiveness, which takes the form of an aggressive desire to defend photography, has foreclosed a lot of interesting possibilities. We haven't had time to develop canons of criticism."[29] She chastised the photography world for centering the discourse on the sterile question "Is it Art?" and then asserted that obviously it was and it was time to move forward.

Sontag went on to discuss the commodification of photography, exemplified by the exhibition of works from Wagstaff's very collection upstairs. "We're not talking about a theoretical discourse within the aesthetics of photography or a disinterested critical discussion. But we're talking about an activity where money is at stake, where lots of money can be made, and where promoting photography—the photograph—as a valuable and, when possible, a unique object" becomes the central element to a great deal of critical discourse.[30] Even Sontag's *On Photography* was, in her own words, written as a polemic about the "problematics" of photography as a phenomenon and did not attempt a critical examination of photography as art.

Would money become a determining factor in concluding a photographer's significance? No better or more immediate target of this concern existed than the show of Wagstaff's collection upstairs—proof that "money talks." So many photographers in the exhibit were unknown and, because of their place on the wall of the museum, new attention was going to be paid to them. Was that because Wagstaff wanted, Sontag wondered, to drive up the value of that work? It was not an unreasonable question, although it should not have overshadowed Sam's earnest motivation to apply his knowledge, judgment, and taste—his purity of vision—to his acquisition of photographs, guided by his belief in the transformative nature of art.

Following Sontag, Rosalind Krauss, the editor of *October*, a cultural journal that was just beginning to publish the French poststructural theorists, took the stage and laid out the foundation for what would become postmodern art theory. Krauss spoke with an intellectual intensity that matched Sontag's. Her presentation could not have provided a more fitting riposte to Sontag's plea for a higher level of discourse about photography. Krauss anatomized the work of Stieglitz in pure art historical terms with the kind of crackling intelligence and airtight logic that leaves no room for argument, and, perhaps, no air in the room.[31] ("Spare me smart Jewish girls with their typewriters," quipped Clement Greenberg, the legendary critic of modernism, to Krauss, his most influential disciple, in 1974.)[32] During a group panel following her talk, Krauss also injected the photography market into this public palaver: "Collectors have an investment in museums, with their antiquarian, synoptic attitude about collecting photography," she said, again singling out the Wagstaff collection upstairs as an example of the museum legitimizing his judgment as a collector, which only increases the monetary value—and, in turn, potentially skews the historical importance—of the objects.[33] Not that she was wrong, in general, but the target of her censure was Sam Wagstaff, and he was not an exemplar of market-driven collecting. History would show that the market followed his lead.

The final speaker, Hilton Kramer, art critic of *The New York Times*, asserted that the defensive battle about whether or not photography is art had already been won. The thesis of his talk lamented the "museumization of photography," referring to the collection and exhibition of every kind of photography by large museums, which blurred the aesthetic distinctions that still needed to be made about photography (a cloaked dagger meant for John Szarkowski as a result of his 1976 William Eggleston show). Museums have "lightened the burden of photography by making it clear how easy and accessible the photography aesthetic is," he said. "Photography is now part of the great aesthetic ooze, where everything in a category is art once you attend to it as art."[34]

FOLLOWING ITS RUN IN D.C., the exhibition came to Wagstaff's doorstep: the show opened at New York University's Grey Art Gallery on Washington Square, literally around the corner from his apartment (the satellite exhibits of work by Incandela and Mapplethorpe did not continue, however).[35] Robert Littman, the gallery director, gave Sam free rein to hang the show as he wanted. Sam, not unappreciative of the media attention, wrote to his good friend Anne MacDonald, now living in Marin County, north of San Francisco, with her new husband, Wayne Walker, a football player and local television sportscaster: "The whole photography petard on which I've been hoisting myself recently is also fun. Did you see me in *People* magazine (April 17) and now four pages in *The New York Times* Sunday magazine section (June 11) just in time for the opening of my show here June 13. Who needs it? But it keeps me laughing (at myself). It's all Robert's fault. He got me into it."[36]

In many ways, Sam was not entirely being genuine with a throw-away quip like "Who needs it?" He may have privately looked down on

People and mocked his own pleasure at the media attention, but he reveled in it all the same. In the 1960s, Sam had been the subject of local newspaper articles in Hartford and Detroit, but this kind of coverage was different. He had crossed over to a national level of exposure and had become adept at capturing the respectable press as well as the weekly tabloids like *People*. In February it had been *The Washington Post;* now a review of the Grey Art Gallery show appeared in *The New York Times:*

> In short, this exhibition and collection seems to be the work not of a historian but of an esthete who believes (with Francis Bacon) that there is no true beauty without a little strangeness in the proportions. It juxtaposes the commonplace and even, at times, the perverse with the rare and wonderful in a way that fills the Grey Gallery with a shimmering, strange, romantic beauty. . . .[37]

The reviewer went on to speculate that because Wagstaff included photographs otherwise conspicuously absent in surveys by noted photohistorians Beaumont Newhall and Helmut Gernsheim, other histories of photography were now viable.

In September 1978, during the exhibition's run at the Seattle Art Museum, *American Photographer* ran an article by its editor, Owen Edwards, entitled "The Collector Who Would Be King." It provided insight into Sam's growing reputation:

> With a mixture of scholarly intent, egoism, and a sense of magisterial responsibility, Wagstaff seems determined, even anxious, to have people see his collection as exemplary. . . . Though Wagstaff claims he no longer gets first refusal from dealers, the level of activity indicates he is not so much a surfer on the crest of photography's wave as a factor in the rising tide itself.[38]

Perhaps the most resonant and ultimately validating praise came early on from the most highly regarded sources, not in the high-end social world but in the photographic realm. In a March 7, 1978, letter,

John Szarkowski had interjected a compliment about *A Book of Photographs from the Collection of Sam Wagstaff*" after a little MoMA Photographs-Committee business: "Your book gets better and better with each visit. Again, my sincerest congratulations."[39]

With the exhibition, the book, and the critical response, Wagstaff had indeed entered a dialogue with art history. Nevertheless, over the years he gave less importance to his curatorial judgment than the personal pleasure he derived from his activities as a collector. "So I'm a bit of a spoiled brat, so what?" Sam told the admiring Paul Richard, the art critic for the *Post*: "The only way to buy is to buy things you like. Gustave Le Gray made those pictures in the 1850s. He's the greatest photographer of all, the best that there has been, and the textbooks hardly mention him. It's like leaving Rembrandt out of a history of Western art."[40]

Although the note from Szarkowski had served as a kind of personal seal of institutional approval, Wagstaff by no means had abandoned his own standards. But the note from Richard Avedon, the most famous and revered photographer of that time, both within the field of fashion and among the cultural elite, must have given Wagstaff a soupçon of personal satisfaction that had nothing to do with historic imperatives: "[I] just saw your book yesterday. It's an absolutely beautiful collection. I'm particularly envious of the Cameron and admiring of many others. Best wishes, Dick."[41]

THIRTEEN

BACK TO POMPEII

Weeeee . . . I am in love with life and me and my angel's dust
and I am the golden boy and I thank my angel's dust because
it's the most wonderful wonder in the world it helps me make
me want to flyyyyyyyyyy! . . .

—LARRY KRAMER, *FAGGOTS*[1]

O NLY FOUR MONTHS AFTER THE WAGSTAFF TRIUMPH AT
the Corcoran, an exhibition called "The Male Nude: A
Survey in Photography," opened at the Marcuse Pfeifer Gallery on a
very respectable strip of Madison Avenue, only blocks away from the
Whitney Museum and Sotheby Parke-Bernet.[2] The ambitious show fea-
tured the works of more than seventy-five photographers, including
Eugène Atget, Heinrich Kuhn, Edward S. Curtis, F. Holland Day,
Baron Wilhelm von Gloeden, Imogen Cunningham, and Minor White,
as well as such contemporary photographers as Lynn Davis, Peter
Hujar, and David Hockney. Included were several portraits by Robert
Mapplethorpe of Marcus Leatherdale and Robert Sherman.

"Of all the fascinating things I learned while putting this exhibition
together, the most conspicuous is that the subject of the male nude is still
a controversial one, even if we believe that this particular decade is more

liberal, liberated, libertine," wrote Marcuse Pfeifer in the exhibition catalog, published a year after she mounted the show.[3] Her comments reflected that current social attitudes toward homosexuality had progressed since Stonewall, but there was, at best, ambivalence. "Had this exhibition included the female nude I feel certain that I would never have encountered such a diversity of negative responses."

Ostensibly, the male body was displayed for direct visual contemplation, like figure drawings in which the eye follows every line to understand the shape of a thigh, the curl of a finger, or the volume of a penis. The penis had rarely before been seen with such photographic clarity on the walls of a proper gallery, but surely that cannot be the explanation for so many reviewers to conclude that the show was homosexual-themed. "There is especially something to be said for old-fashioned prudery when the unclothed human body is a man's body," Gene Thornton wrote in *The New York Times*. "There is something disconcerting about the sight of a man's naked body being presented primarily as a sexual object."[4] Perhaps most surprising about Thornton's review was not his homophobic comments, but the fact that the *Times,* which, until 1963 had used the word "pervert" in place of "homosexual," and which refused to countenance the word "gay" until 1987, had reviewed the show at all.

Marcuse Pfeifer's interest in mounting a show of male nudes at her gallery was not to present men as sex objects. Instead, Pfeifer, a lesbian, was making a feminist inquiry about an imbalance notable throughout art history, and just as strong in photography as in older mediums: the ubiquity of the female nude figure and the scarcity of the male one. Of course, photography was born in the Victorian era, when fig leaves had to be placed over male genitalia in statuary throughout England. However, as it turned out, even in contemporary photography, the male nude proved a tricky subject.

The majority of photographs in the show were hardly erotic. One-third of the photographs were made by women; many others by heterosexual men. The subjects appear in so many different contexts, from walking in the woods to sitting on a couch, from standing on a boat in a river to entering a room on crutches. Even the Mapplethorpe pictures in the show fall into the benign genre of portraiture.

The critical reaction to this exhibit reflected a high level of heterosexual male discomfort about looking at other men naked. The sub-
liminal fear manifested in the reviews suggested that simply to gaze
upon a naked man implied a longing to touch—or was the fear summoned in the dread of self-comparison to the subjects in the pictures?
Either way, disavowing the male nude as a viable subject for aesthetic
contemplation only underscored an American taboo about homosexuality, which remained powerfully in force near the end of the twentieth
century.

"The nude is a matter of convention," Ben Lifson wrote stiffly in, of
all places, the open-minded, alternative-thinking *Village Voice*. "In
photography it's difficult because everyday experience doesn't readily
proffer naked people, to say nothing of men with phallic symbols
between their legs; a nude in a photograph is presumed naked in order
to be photographed. The male nude is harder still; a man's body doesn't
lend itself to abstraction like a woman's."[5]

John Ashbery, the eminent poet, whose relationship with his life
partner, David Kermani, dates back to the early 1970s, leveled a disparaging opinion as well, which might have reflected the attitudes of the
era more than his own evolving thinking on the subject. "When is a
nude not a nude? When it is male," he wrote in his review in *New York*
magazine. "Nude women seem to be in their natural state; men, for
some reason, merely look undressed."[6]

In *Art in America*, the ever-witty Rene Ricard offered a campy twist
on male nudity, although with a few veiled prejudices of his own:
"Women are the traditionally decorative half of humanity and men the
functional. . . . But, don't men's genitals have a certain anomalously decorative look, like an accessory thrown in to be amusing, to decorate the
finished product like an earring? I think it's the tacked-on look that
bothers people."[7]

The sanest voice in this irritable chorus was that of a woman, Vicki
Goldberg, whose *Saturday Review* piece concluded the male nude was
"essentially homeless." She acknowledged that the male figure evokes
neither "reverence nor fondness," and that public acceptance was a long
way off. "Women's frank appreciation, however, might be rearranging

matters; it would be splendid, and ironic, if women were the ones to restore men's sense of the beauty and dignity of their bodies."[8]

As homosexuality became more visible in the late 1970s, Robert Mapplethorpe's name contributed to the changing public perception of gay men, and perhaps it was his presence in "The Male Nude" that underscored the profound unease displayed by the largely male critics. At the same time, the outward manifestations of an expanding gay culture—the increasing size of the annual gay pride parade, the profusion of gay bars and back rooms, the popularity of disco music, and so on—made for a Pompeii-like atmosphere. In fact, to be gay in New York in 1978 was to experience a freewheeling kind of social cachet unprecedented, it would be safe to say, in American history. On the other hand, untold numbers of gay men, even in New York City, remained painfully in the closet and homosexuality had by no means shed its taboo status. The very thought of two men kissing continued to repulse the general public. Nevertheless, in many circles of Manhattan being gay had begun to assume a new brand of chic. For many it seemed that the social leper had suddenly become the most desirable guest at the party.

A primary cause of this new chic was Studio 54, which had opened in 1977, and within two years had become the most glamorous nightclub in the world—anointed "the world's top celebrity disco" by *People*, an incessant bacchanal that was covered nightly in the *New York Post*. This was the unlikely result of a door policy of reverse exclusion that privileged attractive, stylish gay men because "they make the dance floor hot," explained Steve Rubell, the gay co-owner. The policy also allowed the selective admission of celebrities, straight and gay alike, arriving in proper evening attire—Andy Warhol, Liza Minnelli, Bianca Jagger, Halston, Calvin Klein, Margaret Trudeau, and Margaux Hemingway, among others. With its emphasis on a certain high-toned beauty and style, which seemed a modern incarnation of the nightclub milieu Wagstaff had been familiar with in his own youth, Studio 54 came to epitomize a carnival of visual taste and celebrity glamour.

Wagstaff, who was brought up to expect a place at the top of any guest list, nonetheless spent a lifetime grappling with the complication of his homosexuality. During his twenties and thirties, he harbored an awareness that, should his "secret" get out, it could be his ruination. It had taken years for him to make the necessary emotional accommodations in concocting a furtive, if stylish, double life; later, once he met Mapplethorpe, it was still a struggle to retire the partition between his public persona and his innate desires. He may never have shed the guilt and shame, even when he began to live openly as a gay man, and despite Mapplethorpe's fervent assistance. So, on an occasional stop at Studio 54, it was not just surprising but disorienting for Sam to now be considered socially desirable precisely because he was gay. Given his handsome bearing and his social and professional standing, he fit right in, looking as if the club had been designed for people like him. Although he could snort a few lines of cocaine and be happily distracted by all the gym-toned, half-naked men writhing like sweaty monkeys under the blinking disco lights, he couldn't escape his unease about the sudden trendiness of his sexuality. "I think Sam was very buttoned up before he met Robert, a real high WASP," Paul Walter said. "After his mother died he may have opened up a little bit more, too, less worried about the publicity."[9] But Sam's residual awkwardness about being openly gay never really subsided, even if, at times, he seemed to reflect a defiant air about it.

In this climate, gay men were dancing together with abandon, thumbing their noses at victimhood to overdetermined disco anthems such as "I Will Survive," "I Love the Night Life," and "Last Dance." Frank Rich would later write in *Esquire* about the "homosexualization" of America during this period, describing disco music at Studio 54 in particular, as "music for the bodies, not the brain or heart, and the bodies in view were well kept."[10] Many of those gay men undulating on the dance floor at Studio 54 were the same ones who spent summer weekends in Fire Island Pines, where the "boy next door" aesthetic was cultivated to an A-list chic. By the late 1970s, many gay men in New York had outgrown both the nature-hippie look of social rebellion and the construction-worker paradigm of masculine sexuality defined by the disco group the Village People, opting instead for stylish haircuts and trim, well-defined bodies that emulated the healthy, athletic, successful veneer of the Ivy-league heterosexual.

Self-Portraits, Sam Wagstaff, 1973
The Getty Research Institute, Los Angeles (2005.M.46)

Sam on the beach in Oakleyville, Fire Island, photographed by Robert Mapplethorpe, summer 1972

The Getty Research Institute, Los Angeles (2005.M.46)

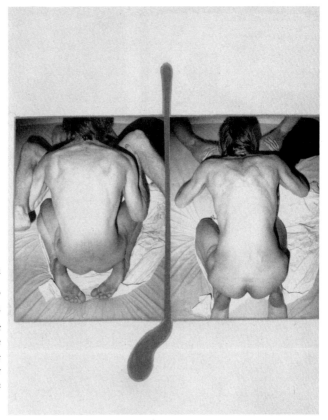

Untitled (Sam and Robert), c. 1972

The Robert Mapplethorpe Foundation; used by permission

Sam and Robert at One Fifth, the restaurant, mid-1970s

Alan Kleinberg

Robert Mapplethorpe with Patti Smith before meeting Sam, 1970

Norman Seeff

Sam photographed
by Robert
Mapplethorpe, 1973

*The Robert
Mapplethorpe Foundation;
used by permission*

Soon after his mother died
in 1973, Sam took this
photograph of Patti Smith
wearing Olga's boa

*The Getty Research Institute,
Los Angeles (2005.M.46)*

Sam in his apartment at
One Fifth Avenue, New York, 1976
Arnold Newman/Getty Images

Auctioneer Philippe Garner presides over the sale of the Herschel album by Julia Margaret Cameron, at Sotheby's in London on October 18, 1974. The gavel came down on Sam's bid of $130,000.

Courtesy of Philippe Garner

Harry Lunn at the Lee Witkin auction estate sale, Sotheby's, 1985

Jonathan Becker

Daniel Wolf photographed
by Andy Warhol, 1982
Andy Warhol/Artists
Rights Society

John Waddell, late 1970s
Courtesy of John Waddell

George Rinhart, c. 1980
Courtesy of George Rinhart

Paul F. Walter, 1970s
John M. Hall; courtesy of Paul F. Walter

Sam at a party in New York,
c. 1980

*Catherine Steinmann;
courtesy of George Rinhart*

Sam in an updated
television appearance

Sam dancing
with Barbara
Jakobson at
MoMA's Party
in the Garden,
1980s

*Courtesy
of Barbara
Jakobson*

Sam with his cat Teenangel, at home in 1984
Harris Fogel

Sam, center, with his sister,
Judith Jefferson, at the wedding
of his niece, left, at the St. Regis
Hotel, New York, 1978
Courtesy of Judy Jefferson

Sam at a friend's flat in
London, mid-1970s

Sam at the Lee Witkin estate sale Sotheby's, 1985

Jonathan Becker

Sam acquired Jackson Pollock's 1953 painting *The Deep* in 1969. He sold it to the Centre Pompidou in Paris in 1974.

Musee National d'Art Moderne, Centre Pompidou, Paris; photograph by Jacques Faujour. Source: Art Resource New York

Tulips, one panel from a Mapplethorpe diptych used on the front and back covers of *A Book of Photographs from the Collection of Sam Wagstaff.* This 1977 diptych sold at auction at Christie's in 2005 for $156,000.

Sam owned one of three versions of *Die,* by Tony Smith

National Gallery of Art; by permission of The Tony Smith Foundation

Sam's "aha" moment about photography occurred when he first saw *The Flatiron* (1904), by Edward Steichen, on exhibit at the Metropolitan Museum of Art in 1973.

Alfred Stieglitz Collection, The Metropolitan Museum of Art. Source: Art Resource, New York

Nude, Fire Island, New York (c. 1973), by Sam Wagstaff

The Getty Research Institute, Los Angeles (2005.M.46)

Thomas (1986), by Robert Mapplethorpe

The Robert Mapplethorpe Foundation; used by permission

Sam in front of a Frank Stella painting, mid-1960s

Ira Rosenberg; courtesy of Dimitri Levas

By then as well, the gay men of the Pines had formed a quietly powerful network that later came to be referred to as the "gay mafia." Many of them were respectfully employed in positions of influence in their fields—particularly in the worlds of media, fashion, and advertising—and it was possible for them to use their gay sensibility to define the look and the mores of the time. Calvin Klein and Perry Ellis, for example, both hovered at the top of fashion with a sartorial minimalism that might as well have derived from the simple lines and pastel colors of the beach, the sand, and the sky on Fire Island; however both men maintained a strict separation between their private lives and their public labels, remaining publicly in the closet.

For the most part, Sam could take the Pines or leave it. He rented the oceanfront house each August for several years ostensibly for Robert, and for a short period the novelty of such unabashed sexual behavior in so concentrated an environment was its own thrill. But Sam was happier when he sequestered himself in Oakleyville, the little hamlet tucked into the woods a short distance west on Fire Island—an eternity away from the frenzy and the glitz of the Pines. With his predilection for the art world ethos of John Cage and the "consciousness of being," Sam could be perfectly content walking on the beach alone and looking for the nails that had washed ashore from merchant ships sunk long ago at sea. Sam sometimes rented a house in Oakleyville during other parts of the year, one that he would eventually buy. As a guest one weekend, Pierre Apraxine asked about a cup filled with these nails on the window ledge. Sam explained that in the 1850s, land-based pirates on the island made beach fires at night to lure the cargo ships to shore; they would loot the ships and destroy them and the ships would wash out to sea. Folklore had it that this was how Fire Island got its name." Sam suggested they take a walk at sunset and look for the nails. Even though it was difficult at first, because the nails were so tiny and the waves kept washing over the sand, Apraxine became rather good at finding them.

Robert also professed ambivalence for the libertine atmosphere of Fire Island Pines. He told an interviewer that he had a love-hate relationship with the Pines. "If I'm not there I think I'm missing something and when I'm there, I'm not sure it's really what I want," he said. "It's hard for me to be relaxed. It's sexually obsessive, and in that situation it's hard for me to think of anything else but that."[12]

All the openness about being gay didn't come smoothly, so, despite the homoerotic content of Mapplethorpe's more controversial images, he was careful not to be identified as a gay-themed artist. Even as Studio 54 was opening its doors, a national backlash to this seemingly conspicuous subculture had emerged with a virulence that was nasty. Anita Bryant, a television singer and Tropicana Orange Juice spokeswoman, led a successful 1977 drive to repeal a Miami city ordinance that banned workplace discrimination based on sexual orientation, in the process turning it into a national campaign against gay rights. More tragically, the following year, Harvey Milk, an openly gay member of the Board of Supervisors of San Francisco, was assassinated by a former colleague.

Such events only reinforced Sam's discomfort in talking openly about his sexuality. Sex and romance were subjects for intimate conversations with friends or in letters to the object of his affection. He did not hide his relationship with Robert, but neither did he feel at ease when it was discussed in a public arena. "A lifelong bachelor" is how Sam is described in the *People* profile in 1978.[13] In another six-page profile that year, in *American Photographer*, the only mention of Sam's life partner is a description of "a friend, photographer Robert Mapplethorpe," who took him to an exhibition, "The Painterly Photograph," which first turned him on to photography.[14]

Gay cultural influence, however, continued to grow as the 1970s waned. The media had showered great affection, for instance, on Bette Midler's Broadway hit *Clams on the Half Shell Revue* which first brought camp to the mainstream, another example of the popularization of a style and manner that had catapulted itself directly out of the gay community. Clive Barnes's review in *The New York Times* was mixed, although "when everything is said and done," he wrote, "by heck, New York is still her town and she is still its best Bette."[15]

For the majority of gay men in New York, however, the Pines–Studio 54 circuit was but a narrow slice of gay reality. The heart of gay life resided "by heck" downtown, out of sight and after hours: the dingy art bar called the Bar in the East Village and the speakeasy-flavored

Julius in the West Village; the more menacing leather bars farther west along the Hudson River, where gay men in their black leather jackets and construction boots made the rounds from Keller's at the corner of Christopher and West streets to the Cock Ring, the Ramrod, the Eagle, the Stud, and the Anvil—the last of which, for all of its dank squalor, had acquired a singular veneer of Weimar-era sophistication. And then there was that much more sinister S&M labyrinth of recreational bondage and degradation called the Mineshaft.

While Mapplethorpe dabbled in the uptown world of glamour and occasionally made an appearance at Studio 54, he would cruise the West Street bars by midnight almost every night. The atmosphere of sexual menace was further deepened by the extended parking area for commercial trucks under the elevated West Side Highway alongside West Street, known as "the trucks." Many gay men would skulk in the shadows between the vehicles while cruising for anonymous sexual activity.

Typical of the way many urban gay men partitioned their social lives and their sexual escapades, Robert would arrange two-tiered evenings, going to concerts, openings, or to dinner with friends in the earlier part of the evening, saving the midnight hour for cruising the bars. "Robert and Sam and I would go to Da Silvano for dinner," recalled Barbara Jakobson, who had recently commissioned Mapplethorpe to do a series of portraits of art dealers for a book she was writing about the burgeoning art scene in SoHo.[16] Da Silvano was a small Italian restaurant where dealers like Leo Castelli or Holly Solomon often dined with artists or collectors. "At the time I had a little yellow Volkswagen convertible and I would drive it downtown," Jakobson said. "After dinner Robert would ask me to drop him off at a respectable distance from the Mineshaft."[17] He was not one to be seen in the predatory atmosphere of the sexual hunt alighting from so cheerful a car driven by a woman. Robert went to the bars, which were always packed by midnight, not only to find sexual partners but also models to photograph.

One night at the Mineshaft, Robert noticed an interesting-looking young man with alopecia, an autoimmune disease that causes the loss of all body hair. His name was Robert Sherman, and Mapplethorpe introduced himself, handed him his phone number, and said he would like to photograph him. Sherman, barely twenty-three and newly arrived from the suburbs of Connecticut, thought Mapplethorpe a little menacing. Only weeks later, at the urging of friends who told him how famous the photographer was, did he call. They made a date to meet again at the Mineshaft at midnight, and Mapplethorpe lured him back to his loft. They had sex and went to sleep. Then, as the sun was coming up, Robert roused his trick and said he wanted to photograph him in the early morning light. The now famous picture, which appears in the "Male Nude" exhibition catalog, shows Sherman crouched naked in a geometric pattern of light and shadows from the fire escape out the window reflected against the white wall behind him.[18]

Wagstaff, meanwhile, would go home alone after those dinners. By 1979, Sam had become a very busy, very lonely man. He was no longer spending time with Gerald Incandela. In the two years that Gerald had been in New York, they had never once slept together and Sam's ardor had begun to run its course. By then Gerald was enjoying some success, with two shows of his own work, at Barbara Gladstone's first gallery and at Charles Cowles. Not long after Gerald had arrived in New York, Sam made the introduction to John Szarkowski at the Museum of Modern Art. Encouragingly, Szarkowski later visited Gerald in his studio and bought another photograph, a study of New York's Metropolitan Life Building, which he would put on exhibit at MoMA several years later.[19]

Not long after the 1978 Corcoran show, Sam had announced to Gerald he was going to stop "his patronage." He was very pleasant about it and, in fact, Gerald agreed that—given the frustration he had caused Sam, as well as the discomfort Sam had created in Gerald—it was only fair. Sam had bought Gerald a photograph by Frank Meadow Sutcliffe, another image from the water series that included *Natives*, the picture in Sam's show and book. When Sam told Gerald he was withdrawing his financial support, Gerald returned the Sutcliffe. That, too, he felt, was only fair.

Although Sam had a broad circle of friends and acquaintances, the promise of a steady partner who provided both physical and emotional intimacy seemed ever more remote. The price of involving himself with men half his age was becoming clear on those nights when, after dinner, he watched Robert go off to the bars, then went home alone.

Sam's longing for an intimate, romantic world he could share with an exclusive partner had never gone away. The secret languages Sam always created with his *inamorati* were similar to the private language he consistently tried to decode in art—from minimalism and land art to mail art and photography. His collections, too, were private preserves in which the semiotic language of a species of object could be explored in depth, be they West Somali Dogon sculpture, early Italian Renaissance paintings, or French lithographs of the nineteenth century. This intimate, exclusive preserve still faintly coruscated now and then in the comfort of his quasi-familial routines with Robert, their frequent dinners and daily calls. Over the phone Robert would recount his adventures of the previous evening and report on the success or the failure of his trick as a photographic subject to his increasingly voyeuristic partner. (Whether Sam's voyeurism was erotic or aesthetic—if that distinction can even be drawn—remains something of a conundrum.) If they hadn't dined together, Sam would tell Robert about his evening, too, whether he had gone out with Harry Lunn, or to a dinner party at Weston and Mary Neaf's SoHo loft, or to one of Mrs. Stewart's salons on Park Avenue; he might have gone to the opera with Jane Smith or to an opening of photographs by Martin Munkacsi at Daniel Wolf Gallery; or he might have invited John Waddell over to look at some new pictures. If Sam was feeling particularly wicked, he would drop the name of some famous person he had sat next to at dinner, just to taunt Robert, reminding him of what he was missing. They would gossip and then they would strategize.

Often enough, he and Robert went to parties or events together, stoking Mapplethorpe's reputation as the enfant terrible blessed by Sam Wagstaff. Sometimes they would attend openings at MoMA, Robert wearing his requisite studded leather motorcycle jacket and leather chaps over Levi's, Sam dressed not as severely in a pair of leather pants. Photography was only the latest secret language Sam was decoding and translating for the public, and Robert its very personification.

Meanwhile, Mapplethorpe's male nude studies embodied the deep current of social—and sexual—change powerfully rising to the surface of the era. Robert was trying to eternalize erotic longing in aesthetic terms. Photographing his conquests in the morning light allowed the lingering physical passion and tactile experience of the night before to inform his scrutiny of the subject in the clear light of day. The camera gave him a measure of distance to see his subject openly, more objectively, without embarrassment. Often Robert spoke of loving his subjects while he was photographing them, even if he didn't love them, much less know them or recall their names, afterward. "I can fall in love with the subject and not be personally involved," he later told Janet Kardon, director of the Institute of Contemporary Art in Philadelphia.[20] Robert once described making love and taking pictures, both, as forms of losing himself: "When I have sex with someone I forget who I am. For a minute, I even forget I'm human. It's the same thing when I'm behind the camera. I forget I exist."[21]

EARLIER IN THE YEAR, only two weeks after Sam's show of photographs from his collection had opened at the Corcoran Gallery of Art in Washington, D.C, another show, "Photographs from the Collection of Robert Mapplethorpe," opened at the University Art Museum at Berkeley, on February 17, 1978. All along, Robert had been collecting photographs, too, often going to auction with Sam and buying work alongside him. Robert did not always have the means to buy what he wanted, but Sam often surprised him later with a gift. As a testimony of this munificence, Robert had accumulated more than five hundred vintage photographs in his own collection by 1978, a good many given to him by Sam. There were seventy-two photographs from his collection in the Berkeley Art Museum show, including work by Berenice Abbott, Julia Margaret Cameron, Francis Bruguière, Baron Adolph De Meyer, Peter Henry Emerson, Frederick Evans, Roger Fenton, Lewis Hine, Eadweard Muybridge, Man Ray, Frank Meadow Sutcliffe, Edward Steichen, Carleton Watkins, and Minor White.

Jim Elliott, named director of the University Art Museum at Berkeley in 1976, was someone Wagstaff knew quite well. Both had been candidates for the position of director of the Wadsworth Atheneum a decade before. When

Elliott was given the Atheneum position and became Sam's boss, they remained friends. And when Elliott and his wife bought the house next door to Sam Green's in Oakleyville, Wagstaff became a regular guest, often staying there, too, when they were away. No doubt Sam had a strong hand in orchestrating the show of work from Robert's collection in Berkeley. Sam's goal, of course, was to forward the idea that Robert Mapplethorpe was not only an artist but also a connoisseur with a high-minded platform of knowledge about the history of photography; this would add gravitas to Robert's growing reputation as an enfant terrible.

During this period, Wagstaff was interviewed about his own collection for Spanish television. He took the opportunity to speak not only about how he first turned to photography but to emphasize Mapplethorpe's influence on him. "I think I would not have been so eager to join the fray, to join a completely unknown situation—of course, beginning from zero is the fun place to be, it is the thin ice," Sam told the interviewer, referring to his own metaphor for new forms of art and aesthetic ideas that are untested by time.

> I don't think I would have felt quite so sure of myself had I not had Robert's eye right behind me. He has—for the totality of photography—a very crisp way of looking at it, a sure way of looking at it. I have always counted on his eye to help me. Luckily, we agreed most of the time. He has helped me enormously and, I assume, I helped him. I had the first collection of Nadar in the United States. I was very pleased when Robert gave an interview and someone said you do a lot of portraits. Who is your favorite photographer? And, he said Nadar.[22]

When the show of Mapplethorpe's collection of photographs came down a month later, he left them on loan to the University Art Museum, until 1982, when he put them—perhaps one-fifth of the photographs he owned—up at auction at Sotheby's.

In the fall of 1978, "Photographs from the Collection of Sam Wagstaff" traveled to the Berkeley museum, as well, and Sam had gone to the Bay Area for the opening. Elliott's decision to take the Corcoran show of Wagstaff's photographs had an air of cronyism about it to begin with, but the association between the two collectors—Sam and Robert—presented an overt conflict of interest, in particular, since both were given shows at the same museum in the same year.

While Sam was in San Francisco for the opening of his own show, he had dinner with members of the Newhall family, his steprelatives. A few nights later, he brought them to a party thrown in his honor by his good friend Anne MacDonald, who had been living in Marin County with her new husband since leaving Detroit. A letter Sam sent thanking her lays the groundwork for what Robert would later venture in his well-known photographs of a female bodybuilder named Lisa Lyon:

> *You really have to do your jock book. I loved hearing you talk about it. You'll do it very well I know and don't you dare talk yourself out of it on the grounds that you don't or can't write. Your dinnertime outline sounded OK to me and then nobody else could do it the way you can do it. A woman writing about sports, who woulda thunk it— that's just the point, a new point of view and yours. Do it, damn it. . . . Robert loved the idea of doing pictures and I think could help you make it have a very different look from the usual press photo look.*[23]

By the time the show of works from his collection opened at Berkeley, Mapplethorpe had been regularly shuttling back and forth between New York and San Francisco. Concurrently, an exhibition of his own photographs had been scheduled at Simon Lowinsky Gallery in San Francisco. The gallery refused to show eighteen of the pictures Robert wanted to exhibit, some from the sexually explicit group exhibited at The Kitchen in 1977. Not unmindful of publicity, Robert took his complaint to *The Advocate*, a national gay newspaper; the resulting article brought attention to the show at Lowinsky, which presented the more palatable work, just as Holly Solomon had in 1977—flowers, portraits, and the milder male nudes.[24] But, as a result of the censorship of "gay imagery," Jim Elliott linked Robert up with 80 Langton Street, a nonprofit gallery, which happily took on a hastily arranged show of Robert's X-rated pictures: "Censored" opened one month later, on March 20, 1978. A consummate showman, Mapplethorpe used *Self Portrait with Whip* (1978)—a now famous photograph in which he appears bent over with bare buttocks and a leather whip inserted in his anus, like the tail of an animal—on the invitation. "Sex without the camera is sexier," Mapplethorpe told Robert McDonald of *The Advocate*, who reviewed the show. "Sex is the highest art form. . . . It has a magic in it comparable to the magic in great art."[25]

Meanwhile, Robert had become enamored of San Francisco, the beautiful hills and the candy-colored Victorian houses vibrating in the sharp California sunlight. The Castro District, like the West Village in New York, was filled with gay bars of every variety, and gay men cruised them at all hours. People there were friendlier and less socially stratified by profession and class than Robert had become used to. The atmosphere was more playful and accepting than the serious intensity brought to cruising the West Street bars in New York. A sense of humor was evident throughout the gay subculture in San Francisco, from the hamburger hangout off Castro Street called Hot and Hunky to the disco called Dance Your Ass Off.

During his visits, Robert hardly sequestered himself to the Castro, where the crowds overflowed the bars along the street. He socialized regularly with Anne MacDonald, even after Sam had returned to New York. She thought nothing of going shopping with him for clothes or throwing an impromptu dinner party for him. After dinner, Anne would drive Robert back to his hotel and wait while he changed out of his green velvet jacket and jeans into full leather regalia, often including chaps with only a jockstrap on underneath, and then drive him to the Castro or to Folsom Street, a more hardcore strip of gay bars, given its emphasis on leather and sadomasochism. "He had his spots where he wanted to be dropped off," she recalled, which were usually several blocks from the bar he was heading to. She watched him as he walked away, his bare buttocks framed in leather chaps, and then, mischievously, trailed him in the car until he approached the bar. "Then I would put the window down, and I'd yell out, 'Bye, sweetie. Don't come home too late, Robert, darling.' "[26]

IF MALE NUDES WERE not being embraced by largely male art critics, such remonstrations did not seem to be hurting Robert's career. In fact, the public censure may have actually had an inverse effect, as in the *cause de scandale* that provides a luster of notoriety to someone's reputation. In March 1979, the International Center of Photography mounted "Trade-Off," a show of work by Lynn Davis and Robert Mapplethorpe. This young institution was then on Fifth Avenue and 94th Street, housed in an elegant neo-Georgian mansion on Museum Mile built in 1915 for Willard Straight, an American diplomat and publisher, and his wife, the former Dorothy Payne Whitney. The galleries in fact were the size of parlors. William Ewing had become director of exhibitions at ICP after arriving from Montreal in 1977. "I saw quickly that MoMA had an authority that was unquestioned," Ewing said; "so I was keen to do something at ICP which would look further afield."[27] He began a program that he called "New Directions."

Initially, he had invited Lynn Davis to do the exhibition; she suggested including Robert Mapplethorpe and Peter Hujar, since all three of them had been photographing the nude body and making portraits. Hujar declined because he did not want to be compared with any other photographer. But Mapplethorpe was game, and "Trade-Off" became a show of portraits of twenty individuals, each photographed by both Lynn and Robert. "We'd hang them more or less in pairs and see how they stacked up against each other," as Ewing described the show's intentions. "Perhaps there would be a gender effect, perhaps not . . . more interesting was the question of their individual sensibilities."[28]

Mapplethorpe and Davis asked Ewing himself to be photographed for the show. "They shrewdly recognized that if I went through the process I'd have a better understanding of it," recalled Ewing, who was tall, slender, dignified, and always in a jacket and tie. "And that was true. I remember Lynn's nervous agitation and how hard she worked at it . . . whereas Robert was cool, smooth, and it was almost over before it was started. Also, I saw that Lynn's portrait wasn't flattering whereas Robert's was. A good lesson."[29]

On Davis's part, the exhibition was fun to put together, at least until they began the installation. The collaborative spirit disappeared the moment Wagstaff showed up. "He tried to get all of Robert's pictures in the very best positions in the room," Lynn said. "I was dumbstruck."[30] Finally, Bill Ewing had to step in and insist that both artists were shown to the best effect. Although put off by what she saw as Wagstaff's blatant chauvinism, she found herself admiring how "Sam moved Robert out into the world in a way that was really interesting. He totally believed in him."[31]

Because of Mapplethorpe's growing reputation, the evening of the show's opening party seemed to belong to him. Davis knew almost nobody, but she was happy for Robert. "He had a following by then," she said. "All the gay community came out."[32]

Mapplethorpe was friendly with Carol Squiers, a writer for *Artforum*. Ewing asked her to write a catalog essay for "Trade-Off."[33] The essay she wrote referred to the gay subject matter in Mapplethorpe's work: "Mapplethorpe extends this tradition of forging and chronicling a public posture for gay men, although he has been known thus far for a purely sexual delineation."[34] Robert got furious. "He said he wasn't going to be ghettoized, and said that it wasn't true," Squiers recalled. She understood his logic about not wanting to be ghettoized, but his patent denial of his gay subject matter—and by default his own community—was striking.[35] Robert did not permit the essay to be published.

The same month as the ICP show with Lynn Davis, Mapplethorpe, then thirty-two, had his first solo exhibition at Robert Miller Gallery. Miller, an elegant figure in the art world, owned the blue-chip gallery with his wife, Betsy, with whom he lived, along with their three children, on the Upper East Side; he also kept a boyfriend in a separate apartment. Miller had first approached Mapplethorpe after his shows at Holly Solomon and The Kitchen; in keeping with the direction of other galleries, Miller wanted to bring photographers into his stable alongside the painters and sculptors he already represented, artists as diverse as Lee Krasner, Alice Neel, Milton Resnick, and Louise Bourgeois. Mapplethorpe would be in good company; his work was moving uptown.

Mapplethorpe was honorable with Holly Solomon when leaving her gallery, meeting with her to explain his logic in moving to an uptown gallery that would provide him broader exposure. He thanked her for representing him with the gift of a print, *Self Portrait with Whip*. He inscribed it in colored pencil: "To Holly and Horace." Although it was not exactly to Solomon's taste, and her husband found it more of a hostile gesture than one of gratitude, she already understood by then, as Robert did, that the photograph would only increase in value with the years. (In fact, it sold at her 2002 estate sale for $26,400.) While their relationship had gotten prickly before his departure, Solomon continued to appreciate Robert's charm and recognize his talent as an artist. Still, she had never quite warmed to his "unsavory" behavior, or to the "avaricious" pressure he put on her to sell his work.[36]

The show at Robert Miller, called "Contact," consisted of Mapplethorpe's sex pictures, portraits, and flowers.[37] One elaborately framed triptych was particularly shocking on the walls of an exclusive gallery at Fifth Avenue and 57th Street: *Jim and Tom, Sausalito* (1977) consists of three images of two leather-clad men, one standing and urinating into the mouth of the other, who kneels before him. The press reacted to the show angrily—even ferociously—barely ever referring directly to this set of images. For example, Ben Lifson repudiated the work in *The Village Voice*: "Everything about the show is hostile. Mapplethorpe's subjects—fleshy, overblown, aestheticized flowers; fashionable people; gay men in costumes and rites of sadomasochism—exist within a closed circle."[38] In *The New York Times*, Hilton Kramer sagely wrote that the "real interest of this show lies not so much in 'art' as in the way it somewhat redraws the boundaries of public taste." Nonetheless, Kramer could not hide his discomfort, adding, "After Helmut Newton, perhaps Mr. Mapplethorpe's [work] was the next logical step. But it gives one the creeps, all the same."[39] Vicki Goldberg, this time in *New York*, delivered a levelheaded observation, acknowledging that Mapplethorpe's S&M pictures could "turn a brown paper wrapper blue," but adding that he photographed "with a purity of technique and design that is positively elegant," maybe "too elegant for his own good."[40] All the media attention, despite the tone of calumny, fomented interest in Mapplethorpe's work, sending his prices soaring.

Ever protective of Mapplethorpe, Wagstaff also understood that the critical reaction would create intrigue and counseled—no doubt having learned from his own experience—that it would serve his career well.

Never mind that Wagstaff, ever the provocateur, loved the idea of infamy for his affectionately nicknamed "Wumper."

For an earlier interview she'd conducted with Robert, Carol Squiers had asked him how he felt about the critical reaction to his photographs. "Finally, it works in my favor, I suppose," he said. "And I have a lot of good people on my side. A lot of people that I respect like the pictures, which is nice because you have to have someone that you're playing to."[41]

Squiers, with straight dark hair cut to the line of her chin, had about her a Brechtian intensity that could be easily countered by her Dorothy Parker–like tales, given sarcastic emphasis with her Chicagoan accent. When she first met Mapplethorpe, she was nervously afraid that she'd be greeted by bondage apparatus hanging from the ceiling of his loft; instead, there was only tasteful mission-style furniture—along with a few skulls here and there as homey appurtenances. After that interview, she and Mapplethorpe started hanging out, going to gallery openings, dinner, parties, and downtown nightspots. She found Robert to be "very nice and very kind, and very nonthreatening; with an inquisitive mind, he was keenly observant and insightful about people."[42] There were times when his insecurity made his delivery halting and indirect, but she appreciated his vulnerability. And he was fun, he loved to gossip, and he had a wry sense of humor. "He had these fabulous cheekbones. He was very thin and lithe, just very sexy," she said. He had always been open about his homosexuality with her, even though "he would make jokes about the two of us having sex"—which had added to her confusion about his reaction to her essay for "Trade-off."[43]

Their evenings invariably began at Robert's loft, where they would smoke a joint before venturing out. One night they were meeting Sam for dinner at One Fifth, a fifteen-minute walk from Bond Street. Robert took his time getting dressed and he and Squiers had gotten stoned and then distracted by one thing and another, causing them to arrive for dinner half an hour late. She recalled that Sam was visibly angry, scolding them like a parent.

"Sam loomed very large with Robert, even when he wasn't around," Squiers said.[44] Often, when she arrived at Robert's loft, he prefaced the evening by saying that Sam was not happy he was going out. It seemed that, wherever they were going, Sam always expected Robert to stop by first. Squiers had the impression that Sam's possessiveness irritated Robert, but she was aware of their deep bond and the ways each benefited from the other. She saw them as a modern version of Fred Astaire and Ginger Rogers: "Sam gave Robert class and Robert gave Sam sex appeal."[45]

One night in October 1979, Mapplethorpe and Marcus Leatherdale, his studio manager and sometime model, stopped by Carol's tiny studio on Thompson Street to pick her up. (Mapplethorpe had met Leatherdale at a gallery opening in San Francisco and persuaded him, almost in Wagstaff style, to move to New York; for a brief time they were also lovers.) When Robert and Leatherdale arrived, Squiers was watching TV coverage of Pope John Paul II's first visit to the United States. The three of them ended up together on her bed, although only to watch the Pope say mass at Yankee Stadium. Robert and Marcus were stretched out in head-to-toe leather regalia on either side of Squiers, sandwiching her in the middle, the Pope's face on the small screen framed by two pairs of leather boots at the end of her bed.

———

BY 1979, MAPPLETHORPE MAY have remained Sam's "Wumpers," his "Monkey," but Mapplethorpe was becoming a name, an abstraction, an idea. Sam continued to monitor Robert's career as if his growing reputation were the relationship itself. The romance and intimacy Sam once experienced with Robert was now subsumed by the enterprise of securing Mapplethorpe's place in the art world firmament. Whether it was an act of sublimation, Robert's role as a surrogate for Sam's unfulfilled desires to become an artist himself was no longer a relevant question.

Although Wagstaff's reputation as a curator had already been established as far as Europe in the 1960s, it was evolving there further now in the context of photography. Mapplethorpe's reputation was growing internationally as well because of Sam's advocacy. In June 1979 Sam was in Italy for the exhibition of photographs from his own collection at the Venezia la Fotografia, a photography festival that included exhibitions throughout Venice. An international audience now embraced Sam's aesthetic, even if it did not always comprehend the subtleties of his message about photography. "I felt that people were missing his point, which was that great images are everywhere," said Bill Ewing, who helped Sam hang the show in Venice and, afterward, in Turin. "He showed stuff from the flea market, anonymous material, just great pictures. His show seemed to be saying, 'Forget the canon—look around you, it's everywhere.' But people wrongly said, 'Ah, this is the new canon. These are the new masterpieces.'"[46]

Wagstaff's European trip was also a chance to promote Mapplethorpe to a new community of curators and gallery owners, such as Galerie Jurka, in Amsterdam. "I followed him around Europe maybe a month later," Ewing said, "and wherever I went people would say, 'Sam Wagstaff was just here.' And then six months later I'd get an invitation from that place for a Mapplethorpe show."[47]

It was impossible to be an art aficionado or a photography connoisseur—much less a gay man—by the end of the decade without being aware of Robert Mapplethorpe. Besides the four shows in New York and the three in San Francisco, Mapplethorpe also had a show in Amsterdam, and another in Paris, in 1979. Despite his growing prominence, Robert still needed Sam to arrange some of these shows and was aware of his dependence. The Galerie Jurka published a catalog for one Mapplethorpe exhibition, in April 1979, which Robert inscribed to Sam: "For Sam, You made all this possible. Love, Robert '79."

He could be tyrannized by Sam's parental attitude and overbearing personality and he could resent the inequity that money had early on introduced into their relationship, but the two still had a deep connection. Robert felt implicitly understood by Sam, his so-called Scorpio soul mate—as an artist, as an individual, and as a gay man. Sam's presence in his life was as comforting and grounding as it was at times enervating. Perhaps Robert could not fully understand how a fifty-eight-year-old man experienced the world, in general, but Sam's increasingly existential loneliness surely did not escape him.

Even though Gerald had ceased to be a regular presence in Sam's life, Robert still harbored a deep resentment about him, projecting onto Gerald the anger he should have directed toward Sam for manipulating the two younger men so skillfully. It was not so much that Sam had fallen in love with Gerald; rather, Sam had brought the same amount of respect to Gerald's work. The entire episode surrounding the Corcoran show and the book of photographs had been a trial of anxiety. Gerald was gone, but there was always the terrifying possibility that another young artist might come along and catch Sam's eye.

One night during one of his visits to San Francisco, Robert went to the Stud, a notorious Folsom Street leather bar, where he met a tall, wiry young man named Jim Nelson. Nelson made his living doing makeup at Elizabeth Arden. He became Robert's playmate for several evenings, engaging in any sexual challenge Robert seemed to throw his way. While he wore black leather and kinky paraphernalia to the bars at night, the tough outer skin of sadomasochistic detachment could not mask the delicate Southern flower into which he startlingly blossomed at moments of excitement or distress. He could be histrionic, flailing his arms about and exaggerating his Texas drawl at the drop of a ten-gallon hat.

Regardless of his fragility and lack of cultural sophistication, Nelson had what gay men call "natural talent"; he was nice looking and well endowed. By the end of this particular trip to the Bay Area, Robert came to the conclusion that not only would Sam like Jim Nelson, but that he could be the solution to the Gerald problem—that is, a potential young, attractive, and talented artist who might conceivably alienate Sam's affections once again.

Robert arranged for Jim Nelson to come to New York to meet Sam. Sam Green told Patricia Morrisroe that the rumor in their circle was that Robert had sent Jim to New York overnight express. "That's how Jim arrived at Sam's door—air freight."[48] The image of Sam meeting Jim for the first time conjures a scene in the movie *The Boys in the Band* in which Harold, the guest of honor, opens the front door to see a handsome, gift-wrapped blond hustler named Cowboy Tex, played by Robert La Tourneaux, who says he's the present for the birthday boy. Jim turned out to be quite a gift: he moved in and lived with Sam for the rest of his life.

FOURTEEN

THE ARRIVISTE

The process of photographing is a pleasure: eyes open,
receptive, sensing, and at some point, connecting. It's
thrilling to be outside your mind, your eyes far ahead of
your thoughts.

—HENRY WESSEL[1]

L ESS THAN ONE MONTH BEFORE THE PRESIDENTIAL ELEC-
tion that would usher Jimmy Carter out of office after a single
term, Dick Cavett devoted the entire half hour of his nationally tele-
vised PBS program to the subject of photography. Sam Wagstaff was
his sole guest for the evening.

With its theme song taken from *Candide*, by Leonard Bernstein, *The
Dick Cavett Show* was an intellectual counterpoint to the frothy TV talk
shows of that period, such as Johnny Carson or Merv Griffin. On the
evening of October 17, 1980, Cavett wasted no time with an opening
monologue, walking out onto the stage from behind the curtain, staring
into the camera, and getting right to the point: "Tastemakers have
treated the art of photography as a kind of bastard child of the arts," he
began. "Painting and sculpture everyone always says, of course, are in

a class by themselves, and some people dismiss photography as just a lot of snapshots. But, then, times have been a-changing."[2]

By the turn of the decade, more than half a dozen serious galleries in New York were showing photography exclusively, while blue-chip galleries such as Sidney Janis, Marlborough, and Robert Miller were now regularly mounting photography shows between painting and sculpture exhibits. By then Richard Avedon, known for his fashion photographs and his celebrity portraits for *Vogue*, had made the spectacular crossing from the world of commerce to a major exhibition at the Metropolitan Museum of Art—personifying the migration of the medium into the most exalted precinct of the art world.

Dick Cavett was exactly the kind of person whom sophisticated New Yorkers were delighted to sit next to at a dinner party. He was charismatic, urbane, and handsome, with a relaxed conversational manner. His comments were informed and substantive, his questions delivered with an often wry willingness to be amused. He was expert at the well-timed, dryer-than-a-martini aside, and he volleyed effortlessly with a formidable and challenging roster of guests on his show over the years: Gore Vidal, William F. Buckley Jr., Norman Mailer, Susan Sontag, even Christine Jorgensen, the first anatomically transgendered individual. But the challenge Wagstaff's appearance presented was that the subject of photography was not the most entertaining television fare. In fact, Cavett ran into some awkwardness describing his guest, a fellow Yalie. Sam was not easy to define in the arena of television shorthand, where a writer was a writer, a politician a politician, and celebrities had national reputations that preceded them. "Sam Wagstaff, my guest, is a preeminent collector of photographs," Cavett said, pausing as if to listen for the sound of channels changing across the country. "Collections of photographs have become valuable and important and are taking a new place—maybe a rightful place—in museums, homes, and the hearts of America. I think that would be what he would hope to help do. Welcome an interesting man—Sam Wagstaff."

Eschewing leather and perhaps even feeling somewhat intimidated by the unfamiliar protocol of a TV appearance, Sam walked out on stage in a proper suit and tie, his hair well cut, his gait unusually stiff. When he sat down and began speaking, his voice tightened at the bottom of his throat and remained a flattened monotone throughout the entire show. The playfulness that usually animated his personality was clearly shackled by self-consciousness in front of an audience, with the glare of the lights and under the scrutiny of multiple TV cameras. He came across as a staid museum director, a solemn bank president, or even a close-to-the-vest international arms expert, as if he were channeling his grandfather, Arthur Piorkowski, the American representative of a German steel syndicate. Sam had asked John Waddell, who had insisted he buy a new suit for the occasion, if he would mind taping the show. Waddell agreed so that Sam could watch it later. "Afterward, I told Sam that he certainly seemed a 'fancy pants.'"[3]

Nonetheless, Sam managed to rise to his own kind of eloquence, walking the audience through a slide-show presentation about photography and launching into a kind of disquisition on the photographic surface. At one point he cited the difference between viewing a painting in reproduction and seeing the real thing, describing the surface texture that provides so much information in a painting, and in which so much of the magic resides. He used Van Gogh as an example, referring to the significance of his mad brushstroke, which seems to disappear in reproduction. "In the same way photography, the surface of the paper, the different kinds of papers, how the surface is treated, is very important so that a reproduction of it is always a diminution of it, is always a lesser thing."

He chose a provocative image to open the presentation: *Students at a Swimming Hole* (1883), by Thomas Eakins. It was a cheeky gesture to show a picture that displayed male genitalia on television—bait, perhaps, for the irritable photography critics who had responded so badly to the recent male nude exhibitions in New York. But Sam couched it in relevant art historical detail, never bringing up the fact that the boys standing on a ridge at the edge of a lake were naked. "It looks like a snapshot but if you look closely every single figure is posed," he said. "By nature of the length of time necessary to take that photo [in 1883] they had to stand still for a certain length of time. It is more or less a sketch for a rather famous painting, which is in Fort Worth, called *The Water Hole* or something. . . ." (He meant *Swimming*.)

Only two or three prints of the image exist, he explained, so this one from his own collection was very valuable. In particular, he said, an Eakins photograph is viewed in the marketplace in the same way as a Man Ray—a photograph by a painter. "I have a couple of photographs by Degas and they are treated by people in art as a handwritten sketch might be, a hand drawn sketch by the artist," Sam said. "An Eakins is worth probably about $10,000."

"For a pitcha?" Cavett asked in mock disbelief.

"You're not buying a *pitcha*," Sam said, gamely. "You're buying an *Eakins*." He went on to say that he had recently found a Mathew Brady photograph at the well-known Argosy Book Store, for which he paid ten dollars, and not long after a dealer offered him a thousand for it. "I don't do that every day," he said. "I don't want to come off as Mr. Smarty Pants."

When showing a portrait of a Navajo boy by Karl Moon, from 1907, Sam said that the two great American photographic subjects were Indians and Abraham Lincoln. And when he showed a picture from his Corcoran exhibit by Lewis Carroll called *Girl on a Sofa* (circa 1859), thought to be a scowling Alice Liddell, Dick Cavett observed that she looked like "an angry Lolita." It had since been discovered, Sam then revealed, that the subject was actually a little boy. "I can remember feeling like that when I had to have my picture taken at that age," Sam said, not even cracking a smile.

Only as Cavett thanked him at the end of the show did Sam finally flash his winning smile, as if relieved that it was over. The success for him had been not just that he managed to get through it with his dignity, but that it constituted another breakthrough, bringing his advocacy of photography to its largest platform yet.

SEVERAL MONTHS LATER, THE G. Ray Hawkins Gallery in Los Angeles sold a single photograph, Ansel Adams's *Moonrise, Hernandez, New Mexico* for $71,000—tens of thousands of dollars higher than any photograph had ever commanded in the marketplace. *Moonrise* is a sweeping view of the Western landscape in the light of early evening, the town of Hernandez in the foreground dwarfed by the distant snow-capped mountains, a gleaming white moon hovering above a band of silver clouds in an enormous black sky. It was an atypically large print at the time—39 by 55 inches. The sale sent tremors through the photography art world, with reverberations and deep confusion in the art world at large. With a single sale, art photography became a subject of intense public focus. The sale of *Moonrise* attracted the kind of attention that could establish a market for photography well beyond Sam's select little auction ring, one that was launched into a stratosphere previously occupied only by painting. (Twenty-five years later, in 2006, Sotheby's would auction a print of *Moonrise* for $609,600—a figure in keeping with the inflation of the market.) Although he played a big role in its ultimate valuation, Sam, in fact, never thought much of Adams's work, comparing his overwrought Western landscapes to movie sets on the MGM lot.

In April 1981, Daniel Wolf Gallery mounted "Walker Evans and Robert Frank: An Essay on Influence."[4] In twenty-five or so pairings of the two men's images, this now historic exhibition presented a visual meditation on the differences and the similarities in their work, as well as on the nature of influence itself. The idea of the show seemed so perfectly obvious once it was presented that the logic fell into place, as if the intricate clockwork of history had been all along hiding in plain sight.

The visual geometry and descriptive clarity of Walker Evans's photographs of American life are often equated with clear-eyed objectivity. His 1938 *American Photographs*, the exhibition catalog from his first show at MoMA (it was also MoMA's first-ever one-person photography show), is a seminal document.[5] Because of it, photography as proof, or documentation of the actual world, came to be regarded as a defining principle of the medium's art making practice. In the exhibition catalog, Tod Papageorge, who had originated the show at the Yale Art Museum, wrote that Evans could find beauty in anything, whether a chair, the façade of a building, or a hand-painted commercial sign: "Our dominant sense of his work, however, is not that it is simply beautiful, but that, in the act of so precisely naming the world, the photographer has divested it of its usual, customary values, and granted it a new meaning—that of having-been-truly-seen."[6]

Eight years after immigrating to the United States, the Swiss-born Robert Frank traveled across the country photographing the people, the places, and the kinds of events that reflected America as he experienced it—with a foreigner's second sense. He took Evans's *American Photographs* with him as a kind of visual and spiritual guide, but Frank's approach to his subject matter was nothing like that of his mentor. Frank would liberate the photographic image from Evans's compositional tidiness and emotional distance, and while his documentation of America was no less factual, he incorporated into the image his own emotional experience of the spontaneous activity he was photographing. Several years after that transcontinental trip, Frank published *The Americans,* one of the most influential photography books of the twentieth century.[7]

The dual work reflected Daniel Wolf's instructive approach to exhibitions at his 57th Street gallery. His was perhaps the most distinguished of all the photography galleries in New York at the time, not only because of the quality and historical import of the work he presented; Wolf wanted to inform people about the history of photography. "If you went to Daniel Wolf's gallery and you paid attention to what he was doing, you would really know something," said Carol Squiers, who was by then writing about photography for *The Village Voice.* "Daniel Wolf really educated the East Coast audience about nineteenth-century photography. He had such a great eye that the point at which I really understood nineteenth-century photography was when he did a Carleton Watkins show. It's one of the best shows I've ever seen. And I can only imagine that Sam Wagstaff's habits of collecting—as well as Paul Walter's habits of collecting and those of a few other people, like André Jammes—must have had some kind of influence on Daniel."[8]

All the photographs in the Walker Evans/Robert Frank show were on loan from Harry Lunn. His fellow photography dealer George Rinhart was involved in those acquisitions, and Wagstaff plays a role in the story, too. As we have seen, these three men were at the center of the auction group that had established the marketplace for photography in the first place.

Seven years earlier, Rinhart had visited Walker Evans at his home in Old Lyme, Connecticut. When Evans pulled out a set of original prints from *American Photographs*, Rinhart understood their significance and, on the spot, offered him more than $10,000 for fifty prints, provided that he signed them. Evans, who needed the money, obliged. In 1974, $200 for a print was hardly an insult, even for Walker Evans.

As soon as Rinhart returned to Manhattan, he proudly invited Wagstaff over to take a peak at his conquest. As Sam looked through the prints, he knew he was holding in his hands some of "the most important pictures in the corpus of twentieth-century photography."[9]

In a letter Sam once wrote to Bob Bishop, a young photographer, he described the very qualities he admired about Bishop's photographs that characterized his essential response to Walker Evans's work and that seemed to explain his standard refrain about photography: "No point of view takes a great picture." Asking Bishop what he thought of Eliot Porter and the Sierra Club books, Sam wrote, "I personally find your work better, cleaner, less arty, closer to something simple in nature, the dumb, just-being-there feeling of it, the ecstasy of seeing what is as it is rather than the personal satisfaction of clever composition or cropping according to modernist art considerations. In that sense I must say I admire your classicality."[10]

Sam had articulated his philosophy about photography's ability to represent the actual world, exemplified in the work he so admired of Le Gray, Nadar, Adam Clark Vroman, and the two Evanses—Frederick and Walker. Sam's point parallels one of John Szarkowski's essential guiding beliefs about the photograph: "more convincingly than any other kind of picture, a photograph evokes the tangible presence of reality. . . . The photographer's vision convinces us to the degree that the photographer hides his hand."[11]

In other words, there is no greater mystery than the truth revealed. It was then hardly a surprise that Sam was enthralled with the Walker Evans prints. "Your choice, a thousand dollars apiece," Rinhart said.[12] That day Sam bought at least ten—the number Rinhart had to sell to recoup his

$10,000 investment. While Sam was willing to pay $50,000 for all of them, the dealer, understandably, held on to a good many for himself.

It was becoming evident, however, that at a certain juncture the tables had turned and Rinhart was now following Sam's lead. "Since Sam was so turned on by Walker Evans, I thought I should go up and try to buy all of his work," Rinhart said. Returning to Old Lyme, Rinhart offered Evans $100,000 for the entire inventory of his studio. "In an odd way, it was once again Sam Wagstaff," Rinhart said. "That's what led me to do it."[13] Evans, who was not in very good physical health, accepted Rinhart's offer.[14] Once again, Rinhart prevailed upon Evans to sign as many of the 5500 prints as he could. While there is some question about the veracity of Rinhart's assertion, Walker Evans did sign a portion of them, despite the fact that his signature at times was illegible.[15] The next year, around the time of Evans's death, Rinhart sold Harry Lunn the entire collection, save for a few choice signed pictures, for $250,000. (It would turn out to be a good deal for Lunn as well: in 2005, a single Walker Evans image, *The Breakfast Room at Belle Grove Plantation* from 1935, sold for $195,000.)

Soon, Lunn would also purchase more than 700 signed Robert Frank prints. The origin of this sale is serendipitous. In 1975, Marilyn Penn, a young Manhattanite, started taking pictures. Her husband, Arthur, a lawyer, thought that if his wife wanted to be a photographer, they should learn something about the history of photography. He hired Clark Worswick at the Asia Society to assemble a photography collection for them. Within two years Worswick had amassed 40,000 prints for the Penns, mostly in batches of albums or entire collections. Curiously, Penn's only proviso was that no single image could cost more than one dollar.

Late in 1977, Paul Katz, a former photography curator at the Marlborough Gallery, told Arthur Penn that Robert Frank, who had turned to filmmaking, was selling the rights to all his prints, but a deal with Tennyson Schad, the owner of Light Gallery, had fallen through. Penn bought the rights to all 3100 images, including the original prints for *The Americans*. Frank had 1600 prints and proceeded to print the additional 1500 to complete the deal. The photographer signed each print, and Penn paid him $300,000.

Harry Lunn quickly convinced Penn that Frank's reputation, already well established in photography circles, would grow only if some of the prints were kept in circulation. Penn and Paul Katz, by then partners in a publishing venture called Pennwick, agreed to sell Harry Lunn 150 pictures by Robert Frank each year in tranches—$40,000 one year, $50,000 the next year, over the course of four or five years. By 1981, Harry Lunn owned more than 700 signed pictures by Robert Frank, for which he had paid $250,000—the same amount he had given George Rinhart for the entire Walker Evans collection.

Although the idea of the show at the Daniel Wolf Gallery of work by Evans and Frank was Papageorge's, it would not have been possible without Lunn's magnanimous, if strategic, loan of the images. By this point, Lunn was becoming instrumental in the placement of important work in private collections, galleries, and museums. In 2011 Judy Keller, the chief curator of photographs at the Getty Museum, would give a lecture called "Circa 1970: "The Invention of the Photography Market," that began "I would like to talk about just three men, all of them Americans—the dealer Harry Lunn, the collector Samuel Wagstaff Jr., and the artist Robert Mapplethorpe—who, among them, and with great enthusiasm, created the sales structure, the connoisseurship credentials, and the raucous glamour that make up the persistent lure of the photography market."[16]

If Harry Lunn's fingerprints are now visible all over the history of photography, it was Wagstaff's counsel that gave him the confidence to build his Washington, D.C., gallery into a singularly influential one. "I think knowing Sam and getting drawn into Sam's world was very, very important to Harry," recalled Jane Livingston, who saw the relationship between Harry Lunn and Sam as a formative one. "I think that they learned from each other—not in the same way as with Robert and Sam, but in a comparable way."[17]

ONE MONTH AFTER THE Walker Evans/Robert Frank show, Robert Mapplethorpe's show "Black Males" opened at the nearby Robert Miller Gallery in New York. Later, the show moved to Harry Lunn's gallery and Lunn copublished three concurrent portfolios by Mapplethorpe: *X*, consisting of homosexual sadomasochistic imagery; *Y*, which are floral still lifes; and *Z*, the nude portraits of African-American men, taken from "Black Males." Lunn represented Mapplethorpe's work outside New York, often arranging shows in galleries elsewhere in the United States and in Europe in tandem—and sharing commissions—with Robert Miller Gallery, which continued to be Mapplethorpe's sole U.S. representative. Howard Read, Mapplethorpe's dealer at Robert Miller Gallery, sold all twenty pictures in the show—the 30-X-30 prints for $2000 each, the 30-X-40 prints for $2500. *Man in Polyester Suit* was in that show, a torso shot from the chest to the knees of a man in a three-piece suit, his elephantine penis dangling out of his open fly. "Black Males" was Robert's most successful show to date—commercially, certainly, if not also critically.

Mapplethorpe rendered African-American men in terms of erotic desirability, and both critics and scholars have argued about the racially complex issues raised by his photographs—especially the matter of stereotyping black men with large penises. The fact that Mapplethorpe was genuinely attracted to black men added a psychological dimension to the socially double-edged implications of the work. Does his work place the black male form on a pedestal, or does it merely objectify these men in service of the pleasure of the privileged? In an essay written for the show when it was mounted at Galerie Jurka in Amsterdam, Edmund White wrote, "There are those liberationists, of course, who would say that whenever a white desires a black some sort of 'racism' is occurring." But White suggests that such assertions do not always hold up to the individual case "because sexual desire, finally, is a form of love . . . not love in the sense of sustained social responsibility but love as passion, as appetite, as irrepressible yearning."[18]

One day when the show was still in New York, Malcolm Forbes, whose business magazine was known then as "the Capitalist Tool," came into Robert Miller Gallery wearing his summer whites. Betsy Wittenborn Miller, who co-owned the gallery with her husband, happened to be sitting at the front desk. "I'd like to buy the Mapplethorpe portfolio," he said to her. Forbes was married and had five grown children, but it was an open secret that, like Mrs. Miller's own husband, he had a sexual predilection for young men. While Mrs. Miller knew which of the three portfolios he wanted, it embarrassed her to have to ask him to specify. He bought the *X* portfolio.[19]

John Waddell remembered being at the gallery one Saturday morning to look at photographs with Howard Read. "The phone would ring every hour or so and Howard would say, 'It's Robert again,'" Waddell said. Both men knew all too well that Robert was calling Read throughout the run to find out about the progress of sales. "He had Howard dancing on the head of a pin."[20] Robert was accused of avarice and unseemly self-promotion on many occasions, but he offered his own explanation. "I had to sell a lot of photographs to make the kind of money a painter made from selling just one painting," he told his biographer.[21]

The Millers were known for hosting lavish buffets after openings at the gallery, with eighty or so people in their apartment. At the dinner for "Black Males," Betsy Miller was surprised to hear Sam leveling a vehement defense of the United States military. He remained proud of his presence at Omaha Beach on D-Day as a Navy lieutenant, and there was an honored tradition of military service in Sam's family. Still, Betsy Miller found Sam's attitude about the military incongruous with her sense of him as a downtown art world figure and as a gay man— particularly when she heard him declare that he had no respect for those who did not fulfill their obligation to serve in the armed forces. How could this square with a man who had grown his hair long, worn beads, smoked pot regularly, attended Woodstock, followed the practices of Gurdjieff, and engaged in the various disciplines of the occult? How did he overlook this judgment regarding Robert, who had been of draftable age but did not serve in the era of the Vietnam war? By now, people in the art world who knew Sam understood that he was not an easy character to pigeonhole. Clearly the privileged bohemian was still wrestling with his patrician legacy.

That fall, as the excess of the Reagan era began, another influential show of photographs opened. The Museum of Modern Art exhibit on Eugène Atget elevated him to the stature of a deity among artists. In its sensibility, rigor, and scope, as well as in its purity of feeling, the body of Atget's photographs of Paris and its environs over thirty years focuses on the streets, buildings, village squares, monuments, the chateaux, their gardens and statuary, the flora of the countryside, all with unadorned photographic description and precision of detail, composing in effect a portrait of the French sensibility of the late nineteenth and early twentieth centuries. Atget's work is breathtaking. And so was "The Work of Atget: Old France," the first of four exhibitions that MoMA planned to present of this photographer's work.[22]

The opening night gala was one of those grand events at the Museum of Modern Art that Sam so enjoyed. He attended in his uniform of a tuxedo with an unironed shirt and a pair of white sneakers. The ground floor of the museum was turned into a lavish party space with full bars, passed hors d'oeuvre, and even a pianist at a grand piano.

The Atget exhibitions and the four volumes published in conjunction with them might be considered the pinnacle of John Szarkowski's distinguished career. Szarkowski and Maria Morris Hambourg had been tasked with making order out of the five thousand photographs Berenice Abbott had salvaged from Atget's studio in 1927, and which the museum had purchased from Abbott in 1968. It was a genuine labor of love, an homage to photography itself. "Atget represented to John the very best of photography for many reasons, not least of which is that Atget seemingly saw a purpose for his work that had nothing to do with creating art, but rather, a moral purpose," said Susan Kismaric, the MoMA curator.[23] No better testimony to this conclusion exists than in the poetic description put forward by Szarkowski in his introduction to the first exhibition catalog: "As a way of beginning, one might compare the art of photography to the act of pointing. All of us, even the best-mannered of us, occasionally point, and it must be true that some of us point to more interesting facts, events, circumstances, and configurations than others." Here, Szarkowski revealed something of the foundation of his own thinking about the nature of photography, no matter who is making photographs. Of course he was so inspired by Atget, of whom he speaks specifically in this next passage: "The talented practitioner of the new discipline would perform with a special grace, sense of timing, narrative sweep, and wit, thus endowing the act not merely with intelligence, but with that quality of formal rigor that identifies a work of art, so that we would be uncertain, when remembering the adventure of the tour, how much our pleasure and sense of enlargement had come from the things pointed to and how much from a pattern created by the pointer."[24]

Four years earlier, Wagstaff had acquired a historical manuscript about Atget by Pierre MacOrlan, an influential French film and photography critic, who published *Atget Photographe de Paris*, the first book on the photographer, in 1930. He provided the manuscript to John Szarkowski when he was beginning to organize the shows. "I do very much appreciate your thoughtfulness in entrusting to us this very interesting document," Szarkowski wrote thanking Sam.[25]

THE ATGET SHOW OPENED one month before Wagstaff's sixtieth birthday. By then, perhaps the most anomalous arrangement in Sam's life, Jim Nelson had been living with Sam for two years, since his arrival from San Francisco. Although Robert's idea had been to distract Sam from Gerald by delivering Nelson to his doorstep, the younger man had become, in Klaus Kertess's view, the trick that wouldn't leave.[26]

The relationship was nothing like any of Sam's previous romantic connections. First with Robert, then with Mark and later Gerald, Sam had willingly—and even aggressively—shepherded his beau of the moment around, determined that he would meet everyone Sam knew in New York. But Jim was more of a backstreet relationship; it would never occur to Sam to bring him to a party at, say, the Robert Millers. In fact, many people in Sam's life did not even know of Jim's existence, but those who did agreed that Jim was the last person anyone would have expected Sam to be involved with. Nevertheless, enough of his friends recognized that there were benefits for Sam in keeping Jim around.

People found a sweetness about Jim and recognized his genuine kindness. He was almost as tall as Sam, and he always seemed to be smiling and upbeat. Yet he could be childlike and insecure, as if compelled to tailor his behavior to the expectation of others or to the particular situation he found himself in. For most people in Sam's orbit, Jim left the impression that he was willing to be defined by whomever it was he was speaking to in the moment or, in the case of Sam, living with. "He struck me as being somewhat innocent in a world in which Sam was otherwise swimming with the sharks," John Waddell said. "With Sam, Jim was fawning, almost worshipful. He talked about Sam with a certain wonderment. It's entirely possible that even after the passage of quite a few years, Sam might have appreciated that."[27]

Sam also appreciated the transformation in his home life once Jim moved in. Sam never cooked—unless one counted those infamous burgers cooked directly on the burner—and for so many years he had rarely ever thought of eating at home. To Sam's amazement, Jim regularly shopped for food and whipped up dinners. Even some of his closer friends acknowledged an unlikely benefit for Sam: "Sam was just thrilled because he was saving so much money," Paul Walter said. "He told me this, not having to go to restaurants all the time. 'This Jim's great. He cooks. I'm saving all this money.' "[28]

Anne MacDonald concluded that Sam had reached a point in his life when he wanted to have something of a wife. "Jim never went out," she said. "He was probably at home tatting those doilies—he really created a home for Sam. He didn't want to go out. He said to Sam, 'If this is your thing, you go out; you want to do that.' He really didn't even seem to care if Sam was faithful or not."[29]

It turned out that after years of his almost monastic daily existence, Sam liked having someone around to make him comfortable and tend to his needs. While Robert provided Sam with a deep, familial conspiratorial purpose and an entire ethos of artistic engagement, their relationship did not transpire on the level of daily domestic comfort. Sam's friends, for their part, tended to see his relationship with Jim as an unhealthy power imbalance. Jim provided physical tenderness but fundamentally he took care of Sam's domestic needs. "I don't want to sound demeaning of Jim, because I think he was genuinely a nice person, but it's a bit like the close relation one has with a butler," Pierre Apraxine said. "Servants don't judge. You can be who you are. I think for Sam, it was a kind of pre-retirement."[30]

When Jim did go out with Sam or Sam's friends, often it led to calamity. Sam brought Jim with him to London one year for the photo auctions but on a day when he had some commitments, asked George Rinhart to take Jim to lunch. After the meal, George and Jim walked along Bond Street, going in and out of the antique shops. They stopped in one little place filled with porcelain figurines. Jim got so excited by their refinement in miniature that his arms started flailing about, and he knocked over a small *objet* worth $600. The proprietor asked Jim how he intended to pay for it, but Jim didn't have any money and he started to cry. The proprietor locked the door, and in order to secure their departure Rinhart had to shell out the money. When they returned to the hotel, George expected Sam to reimburse him, but Sam, parsimonious, as ever, casually dismissed it as Jim's obligation. Jim was forced to pay George back gradually. George, who had done a good deed by putting up the money to begin with and ended up being penalized in the process of the lesson Sam was teaching Jim, came to dismiss Jim as "a very dizzy queen, and awkward. I was not a fan."[31]

Meanwhile, Robert found Jim an utter annoyance, but he didn't let the relationship unsettle him the way Sam's bond with Gerald had. For one thing, Jim was not an artist; for another, Robert had new romantic preoccupations of his own. He was now involved with Milton Moore—the "Man in Polyester Suit," and he was in love. Robert took an apartment around the corner from his loft so the two of them could live together outside the daily activities of his studio. It was a deep and tortured relationship: Milton had emotional problems that were only compounded by a homosexual relationship and Robert, who was physically obsessed with Milton, was less than sensitive to his psychological turmoil. It lasted not much longer than a year or so. Robert then took up with Jack Walls, another black man; this time he was able to sustain a much longer, if also troubled relationship.

As Robert's connections with black men grew, accounts of his racism proliferated, to the point that people who worked in the studio recounted his verbal abuse and sexual humiliation of boyfriends and models. "Robert's obsession with blacks was a little scary, a little on the edge," said Diego Cortez, who included Robert's photographs in a show at PS 1, a contemporary art space in Queens, in 1981. For the most part, Mapplethorpe's images of African-American men are reverential. He renders them in terms of classical sculptural form and erotic desirability. He photographed some black men on pedestals, idealizing others in elegant poses, arranging their limbs and their genitals just so. "Basically the work reads [as] pure," Cortez concluded. "Sometimes art goes beyond the artist's own narrow-mindedness."[32]

THE YEAR 1981 SEEMED to be one of canonization in photography—Ansel Adams, Eugène Atget, Walker Evans, and Robert Frank. Even Sam's own *violon d'Ingres*, Robert Mapplethorpe, was being unofficially canonized, in his own lifetime, if not by John Szarkowski and the Museum of Modern Art, then certainly by the social currents of the day and the forces of the market. Meanwhile, an entirely new strain of photographic art making was appearing in galleries downtown.

The year before, Metro Pictures, a new SoHo gallery, had mounted "Untitled Film Stills," a body of photographs by a young artist named Cindy Sherman. The show had garnered a lot of *sotto voce* interest. Sherman's 8-×-10 black-and-white pictures looked like Hollywood film stills of the 1950s and '60s, and she was the star in each one. In a series of elaborate and almost virtuoso games of dress-up, she replicated the circumscribed range of female archetypes presented to her generation on the big screen, from which a young girl was able to model—or to obfuscate—an identity of her own. In contrast to Mapplethorpe's carefully crafted, finely detailed, studio-lighted subjects, Sherman utilized the visual vocabulary of the modest black-and-white photographs of the era in which she grew up to record her makeshift and, yet, evocative cinematic tableaux. Sherman's work, then, was an exercise in self-portraiture as much as it marked the beginning of a new direction: an exploration of the very idea of representation and identity in the medium of photography, interrogating the way identity is constructed by the cultural forces all around us. She managed to strike that chord with pictures that were novel, kitschy, campy, and fun.

The moment was ripe. Photography was about to undergo a rigorous, necessary, and unforgiving examination by a new generation of artists, scholars, and critics challenging the medium's fidelity to fact, its role in constructing social realities, and its new status as an art world commodity. "The camera never lies" had become the singular anti-trope of a new artistic practice. Whether or not Sherman had in mind Roland Barthes, Michel Foucault, and the other French postmodern structuralist philosophers and cultural critics, she was immediately embraced by those who did.

Sherrie Levine, another artist showing at Metro Pictures, had stirred the pot the previous year with a much more adversarial show, "After Walker Evans," which consisted of her copies of Evans's pictures. She had rephotographed them directly from a catalog of his work. This "appropriation art" was the newest version of the Duchamp "readymade," of Dada mockery of the preciousness of the art object, and of the fluxus recontextualization of everyday objects. Levine's rephotographed Walker Evans pictures were twice removed from the original print, framed in museum style, and appeared exactly like Evans photographs on the wall. Only they weren't. They were Sherrie Levine photographs. The work debunked the commodity value of the singular print, vintage and otherwise. The Walker Evans estate, which Harry Lunn had been advising since his own purchase of the Evans material in 1975, bought every picture in the show so that Levine could not sell them in competition with original prints. Harry Lunn was thinking ahead.

The philosophical underpinnings for this new photographic strain were expressed in 1981 in Douglas Crimp's article "The Museum's Old/ The Library's New Subject." In this seminal postmodern tract, Crimp, the managing editor of *October*, extrapolates from Roland Barthes's manifesto "The Death of the Author" the notion that ideas or even works of art that reside in the world are properly authorless—that they should no longer be tethered to the author or the artist who first presented them. Crimp's essay cites the creation of the department of photography at the New York Public Library in order to identify a shift in focus from the subject-based categorization of photographs to a new classification by artist, which, he argues, inappropriately privileges the photographer:

And thus the list goes on, as urban poverty becomes Jacob Riis and Lewis Hine; portraits *of* Delacroix and Manet become portraits *by* Nadar and Carjat; Dior's New Look becomes Irving Penn; and World War II becomes Robert Capa; for if photography was invented in 1839, it was only *discovered* in the 1960s and 1970s. . . .

Books about Egypt will literally be torn apart so that photographs by Francis Frith may be framed and placed on the walls of museums. Once there, photographs will never look the same. Whereas we may formerly have looked at Cartier-Bresson's photographs for the information they conveyed about the revolution in China or the Civil War in Spain, we will now look at them for what they tell us about the artist's style of expression.[33]

All along, Wagstaff had been buying historically grounded albums of the nineteenth century as examples of photographic achievement, and, then dismantling them and sharing the lot with his fellow collectors. Certainly he was not buying an album with views of Paris, say, but of photographs by Atget; he was not interested in the documentation of Kelmscott Manor for the purposes of architectural record, but rather for the exquisite light and texture and tone in Frederick Evans's prints; he was taken not by a chronicle of travel scenes in India, but by the photographs of Felice Beato. He was among the first to change the conversation about photography from the subject to the image, from the chronicle of information to the language of the eye.

In the end, of course, even he would agree that the subject and the image cannot be separated, that a fine picture is the perfect marriage of what it is and how it looks. However, he had been perfectly content to forward the idea that the eye spoke first. And the vision that mattered, for Sam, belonged to an artist. The photographer may hide his hand, the more artfully the better, but wasn't that hand really the secret ingredient?

It did not help that the emerging postmodern bloc of critical thinking cast Robert Mapplethorpe in enemy territory. Robert's work was purely photographic, aesthetic; it had become increasingly valuable in the art market; and his sexual objectification of the body, despite the points it may have won for being unconventionally male-focused—and, more radically, homoerotic—did not sit well with the postmodern critique of power relations between artists and their subjects. With these three strikes against him, Mapplethorpe's form of modernism and his authorial vision would be seen as retrograde. In this new atmosphere of procrustean political and cultural righteousness, theory threatened to topple narrative, history, and artistic individuality.

Sam failed to be amused by the new postmodern turn of thought—what would, in fact, become the stance of the 1980s—and he was not shy about instigating a dialogue about it among his own intellectual and photographic set. He held fast to his instinctive responses, even as they were beginning to seem out of sync with the events unfolding around him. On February 13, 1980, he had sent John Szarkowski a letter, enclosing an article by Roland Barthes:

> *Don't know if you see the U of C Berkeley mag, but, if not, thought you might enjoy hot-shot Barthes' piece on Avedon. It seems to me that for the portraits the word "corpse" is right-on—a joint show with Jerry Liebling's might prove the point. Why is Barthes considered the* ne plus ultra *of today's hip thought on seeing? That's not a question I'm asking you to answer. It's just a statement of disbelief. As Barney Newman said when he first saw Bob Rauschenberg's abstract paintings, "Some of these guys think it's easy." He certainly never had any reason to back away from that crack.*[34]

WHILE BOTH UPTOWN AND downtown the art world raged on, its various factions dueling in print, on the walls, and in person—modernists versus postmodernists, painters versus photographers, feminists versus chauvinists—another kind of meeting took place on August 11, 1981, at 2 Fifth Avenue, a massive pile of white bricks that stood across the street from Wagstaff's soaring Art Deco residence. Larry Kramer, the host, who was the screenwriter and producer of

Ken Russell's 1970 film, *Women in Love*, based on the D. H. Lawrence masterpiece, and, more recently, the author of *Faggots*, a scathing 1978 novel about the viciousness of the gay world, had urgently summoned the author Edmund White, the curator Henry Geldzahler, and sixty other leading figures of the gay community to his apartment. The meeting had been largely prompted by a July 3 article in *The New York Times*[35] (following several pieces in the gay newspaper the *New York Native*),[36] in which the reporter, Dr. Lawrence Altman, described a new illness that was cropping up among gay men in New York and San Francisco: "Doctors in New York and California have diagnosed among homosexual men forty-one cases of a rare and often rapidly fatal form of cancer," he reported. "Eight of the victims died less than twenty-four months after the diagnosis was made." The article further reported that the cause of the outbreak was unknown, but that the sudden appearance of the cancer, Kaposi's sarcoma, had prompted a medical investigation that could "lead to determining the causes of more common cancers."[37]

The men who gathered that evening faced a terrifying abyss of ignorance and social neglect. No one knew what to call the disease, much less what caused it and how to prevent exposure to it. There was as much denial in the gay community about its existence, combined with a fear that such an epidemic might curtail sexual behavior, as there was panic about who was next to be diagnosed. In *The Gay Metropolis*, Charles Kaiser would compare being gay at the beginning of the AIDS epidemic to standing without a helmet at the front lines in a war: "Friends are falling all around you but no one even knows where the bullets are coming from. There are no weapons to defend yourself, no medicine for the wounded, and if you want to flee, when you start running you won't know whether your wounds are fatal—or nonexistent."[38]

Wagstaff must have also read the article about the strange new cancer in *The New York Times*, or at least heard about it, since that summer the news spread rapidly on Fire Island and in Greenwich Village. Still, he was oblivious of the historic meeting across the street from his penthouse, which would result in the creation of the Gay Men's Health Crisis. Still handsome and congenitally trim, Wagstaff had by this time acquired the weathered visage of a somewhat rumpled, elegant, gray eminence. He had traveled far from his childhood uptown and the repressive atmosphere of his patrician family, managing to free himself of the internalized stigma—indeed, the stench of disgust—around the very idea of his homosexuality. We know that early on he found a way to navigate the feelings that dared not speak their name with a manner of behavior that would not betray his secret, a burden he carried well into his forties, until he no longer had to be so vigilant about protecting his professional or social reputation. But the amount of pain, fear, deception, guilt, and shame the closeted homosexual endured throughout those years must have been summoned all at once in the spasms of dread that surfaced with the news of the "homosexual cancer," as it was being called at the beginning, before it was given the name GRID (Gay Related Immune Deficiency) and then, finally, AIDS. For so many gay men in Manhattan, the menace of this new medical threat came with an air of retribution about it. Could this be the devastating result of such hedonistic abandon in the 1970s—unbridled sexual activity with incalculable numbers of partners, multiple antibiotic treatments for syphilis and gonorrhea, continual recreational use of marijuana, cocaine, and other pleasure-stimulating drugs, and the unabashed flaunting of homosexual identity? Sam was now in the line of fire of an unnamed enemy. Perhaps it summoned the residual pain and guilt of his earlier years, but he did not yet feel directly vulnerable, even though it is likely that he had already been exposed.

For one human being to love another, that is perhaps the most difficult of all our tasks.

—RAINER MARIE RILKE[1]

NOCTURNE

Jim Nelson on Fire Island

FIFTEEN

THE PICTURES
GENERATION

S AM WAGSTAFF COMMENTED ON NUMEROUS OCCASIONS
that he had turned to photography because, after minimalism,
painting had nowhere to go. "To be frank, I got cranky about the '6os.
I got to Tony Smith, to Agnes Martin, to Walter De Maria, but then my
interest lagged," he told *The Washington Post* in 1978. "Nothing took
me farther, until I found photography and again turned on."[2] By 1982,
however, painting, which had languished for a decade, was back—only
now with an existential chip on its shoulder. SoHo had become the center of aesthetic discovery and commercial impudence for a thoroughly
revivified art world.

The artists being touted in SoHo included the American neo-
expressionists Julian Schnabel and David Salle; the Italians Sandro Chia
and Francesco Clemente; and the Germans Georg Baselitz, A. R.
Penck, and Markus Lupertz. Their neo-expressionist paintings took on
an almost hieroglyphic approach to figuration, and Wagstaff, hyperalert
to new trends, was watching, just as interested as everyone else in find-

ing out why neo-expressionism had arrived as a *coup de foudre*. It wasn't only the neo-expressionists who embraced a more rollicking and emotionally volatile aesthetic: the graffiti artists Jean-Michel Basquiat and Keith Haring had taken their primitive street iconography directly to the stretched canvas on the gallery wall. At the same time, the "pictures generation" artists, such as Cindy Sherman, Sherrie Levine, and Richard Prince, were constantly tweaking "reality," challenging conventional photography to something of a duel. So much was going on, and so little sense being made of it, that the money alone being spent conferred an instant hierarchy of importance on these artists.

SoHo was no more than a ten-minute remove from Sam's apartment—through Washington Square and down LaGuardia Place, which, south of Houston Street, turned into a suddenly burgeoning West Broadway. The focus of activity was situated at 420 West Broadway, the renovated cast-iron bulwark that was home to the galleries of Leo Castelli, Ileana Sonnabend, Andre Emmerich, John Weber, and Charles Cowles. The address pulsed with the gravitas, say, of a museum of contemporary art, acquiring additional fairy dust through its links to Warhol and gathering the same white-hot intensity of the Factory in its era. As the number of galleries in the surrounding blocks multiplied— from Paula Cooper to Barbara Gladstone, Metro Pictures, Marlborough Greene Street, Annina Nosei, and Tony Shafrazi—spending a weekend afternoon in SoHo was the new version of the Madison Avenue "Saturday route" of the 1960s. In SoHo, the crowds appeared younger; looking at art was fun and, at least on the surface, more egalitarian. Even the restaurants were cooler and more casual. Adding to this fashionable mix were a handful of avant-garde clothing shops, such as Agnes B. and Betsey Johnson, while Turpan Sanders sold well-designed items for the home you didn't know you wanted until you saw them. West Broadway crackled with energy. Crowds poured out of the galleries and into the streets. Campy sidewalk performance artists sprouted as well like the Steinettes, a Jewish girl group with ironically teased hair whose witty songs had names like "Lunch Hour Love Affair" that were sung in harmonic homage to the Ronettes.

With a new sense of expectation in the air, the art world was alive again. As if to echo the tenor of the neighborhood, one multicolored wall-sized mural at West Broadway and Broome Street declared, "I Am the Best Artist." While Rene Moncada, the artist responsible for the mural, was largely ignored by the art world, his mural seemed to speak for every artist who lived in the neighborhood.

"In my memory, 1982 is a pivotal moment when artistic trends that had been coalescing over the previous five years or so finally cohered," wrote Lynn Zelevansky, the director since 2009 of the Carnegie Museum of Art.[3] She and others have noted the shift away from the cooler, more idea-centric ethos of conceptual art, toward a more materialist focus on visual impact as the 1980s marched forward. The artistic legacy of John Cage—the consciousness of being—that had meant so much to Sam for the moment seemed diminished, indiscernible in the heady and acutely monetized art scene of that new era.

Still, Sam understood that something vital and important was taking place, and he visited these new galleries in SoHo, talking to the dealers he knew as he made his rounds. Paula Cooper, a pioneer in SoHo, had opened her gallery in the 1960s, originally in a third-floor space on Prince Street. Sam had come to see her then to put a sculpture he owned by Mark di Suvero on consignment, which she was able to sell. She also represented Lynda Benglis, whom Sam included in a show at the Detroit Institute of Arts—the first time Benglis showed any work in a museum. "He was so elegant and patrician and it was surprising in the art world then," Cooper said. "It wasn't that he was so incredibly establishment or anything," but in that context she found him to be "a refreshing surprise."[4]

By the early 1980s she had moved her gallery to a larger ground-floor space on Wooster Street. Cooper was aware of the shift in the art world, which was becoming a cruder place, incorporating more mercantile attitudes and practices. "It must have horrified Sam, or anyone who had any idea of what art was and how it should be dealt with and treated and shown," she said.[5]

Da Silvano and Ballato were the restaurants of choice for the established dealers and collectors in the neighborhood, but a stylish new restaurant had everyone talking: founded by three alums of One Fifth, the

Odeon opened in late 1980, replacing One Fifth to eventually become the Max's Kansas City of that decade. Keith McNally, his brother, Brian, and Lynn Wagenknecht, who later married Keith, bought a former 1930s cafeteria at West Broadway and Thomas Street, installing a big red neon sign with Art Deco letters spelling "The Odeon" in front and keeping the one that spelled "Cafeteria" on the side street. Inside, they struck just the right chord, retaining the interior's unadorned utilitarian simplicity while adding a few classic Parisian flourishes worthy of the iconic La Coupole—framed mirrors above the tables along the wall, for example, so diners could observe everybody in the room. The original globe lanterns hung from the ceiling and cast a buttery glow that twinkled in the ribbed frosted glass dividers between the leather booths. A large electric clock by the bar was ringed with a neon light that changed colors. The new owners kept the terrazzo tiled floor and the wooden venetian blinds, and added a long, burnished mahogany bar. The tables were covered in white linen; New Wave music shared time with old Billie Holiday standards; and a persistent cloud of cigarette smoke hovered over the room each evening. Every night of the week the restaurant was packed with a downtown cultural demimonde that brought just the right degree of flamboyance to what many thought to be the best ongoing party in New York. Not surprisingly, Robert and Sam ate there often, together and separately, either with Ingrid Sischy, the editor of *Artforum*, and Amy Sullivan, her girlfriend, who ran Agnes B., Jane (Mrs. Tony) Smith, or Brice and Helen Marden, among others.

On any given night Julian Schnabel could be seen as well at the Odeon, along with Mary Boone, David Salle, and Ross Bleckner. Andy Warhol's entourage often included Jean-Michel Basquiat and Paige Powell, who worked for *Interview* and would order Andy's food for him because he didn't like to talk. When Andy did say something, it would be with deadpan wit: Robert Longo, another prominent young artist, might walk by wearing dark glasses, going to his table in the back of the restaurant, and Andy would say, "There goes Robert Loooongooo." David Hockney and Henry Geldzahler could be seen at a large round table surrounded by attractive young men. The list of regulars included Hollywood stars, *Saturday Night Live* cast members, and fashion designers—Richard Gere, Robert De Niro, John Belushi, Dan Aykroyd, Diane von Furstenberg. The young publisher Morgan Entrekin stopped by often, along with the equally young, as yet unpublished writer Jay McInerney, whose 1984 novel *Bright Lights, Big City* would memorialize the restaurant in tone just as Dawn Powell had written about the Stork Club or Gay Talese had written about Elaine's.

In McInerney's roman à clef one could read about the endless lines of cocaine with which people "powdered their noses" in the Odeon's bathrooms downstairs. Amy Sullivan remembered how brazen Mapplethorpe was, not even bothering to leave the table to take a snort. He periodically reached for the little colored disc in his jacket, lifted the tiny spoon to his nose, and took a hit—in full view of the group of people he was dining with. When *Bright Lights* was about to be published, the Random House lawyer asked McInerney whether the establishment actually existed. When MacInerney confirmed that indeed it did, the lawyer asserted that they would be sued if he didn't take out every passage that mentions cocaine use. "I'm sure they won't care," McInerney said. The artwork had just been delivered for the cover of the book, depicting the Odeon at night with its glowing red neon signs. "Gary Fisketjon, my editor, suggested that I just talk to the owners," McInerney said. When he met with Keith McNally to explain the situation and show him the artwork, McNally said, "Great. No problem."[6]

On April 17, 1982, *New York* published what would become a legendary cover story. "The New Queen of the Art Scene," by Anthony Haden-Guest, was an anatomy of Mary Boone's meteoric rise from a young assistant at Klaus Kertess's Bykert Gallery to the owner of, first, her own small gallery at 420 West Broadway and, then, at the age of thirty, relocating to a larger eponymous gallery across the street.[7] The article opens with a Balzacian scene that captures the generational shift in the art world, as Boone had taken on sole representation of Julian Schnabel while sharing a show with Leo Castelli: "Tacking past each other in opposing flotillas, like eccentric sailboats, the huge canvases crossed West Broadway. Leo Castelli passed them by with barely a glance. 'Julian,' he crooned to a young man in a worn leather jacket. 'Mary,'" before bestowing on each of them a "magisterial peck on the cheek."[8]

The canvases were being transferred from Leo Castelli's gallery to Mary Boone's, and both dealers are credited for what became known as the "Schnabel phenomenon." To anoint Schnabel with a show in his gallery served Leo Castelli, the most influential art dealer on both sides of the Atlantic, well, confirming again his reputation for identifying the next big thing—in this case neo-expressionism—and prolonging his relevance for another few years. For Boone, Castelli's imprimatur on this young artist was tantamount to a blessing by the Pope, affirming her new prominence and granting her gallery instant blue-chip status. By 1982 Boone, with the smoldering allure of her compact height, dark features, expensive clothing, and dominatrix heels, had no compunction about slapping a Reaganomic price tag of $60,000 on a Schnabel.

Robert Hughes, the renowned art critic for *Time*, would over the years assert his antipathy toward everything Julian Schnabel represented, as when he consistently referred to the artist's work as "supply-side aesthetics." His vitriol for Schnabel and other artwork of that period, which he considered disingenuous at best, is summed up with clarity and passion in his *The Shock of the New*: "What has our culture lost in 1980 that the avant-garde had in 1890? Ebullience, idealism, confidence, the belief that there was plenty of territory to explore, and above all the sense that art, in the most disinterested and noble way, could find the necessary metaphors by which a radically changing culture could be explained to its inhabitants."[9] Reviewing Schnabel's first show at Mary Boone's gallery in April 1981, Hilton Kramer wrote in *The New York Times* that after minimalism, the busy-ness of Schnabel's work accounts for so much of its appeal: "For eyes starved by the austere nourishments of minimal art, Mr. Schnabel's work provides the pictorial equivalent of a junk-food binge. It is understandable, therefore, if it causes a certain amount of indigestion in the process."[10]

Today it is possible to see in the regurgitative imagery of the neo-expressionists a host of metaphors that seem to define the period. Capitalism was running amok and these artists manifested the rupture occurring before their very eyes between commerce and value—Julian Schnabel's broken plates, David Salle's fractured images, Barbara Kruger's lacerating epithets, and so on—even as they themselves succumbed to the seductions of the period and hugely benefited from the financial free-for-all.

David Hockney, the blond, bespectacled, often whimsically dressed Englishman, was quietly going about his own highly regarded work and continuing to show his lyrical, representational paintings at Andre Emmerich's' gallery in SoHo. He came to New York often from his home in Los Angeles for extended stays while designing stage sets for productions like Parade, a program of three early-twentieth-century French works at the Metropolitan Opera. Sam knew David Hockney through Henry Geldzahler and occasionally Sam and David would talk about photography, a medium Hockney had been exploring in his own work for some years. The two men saw eye to eye on the charged relationship between painting and photography. "I would be always a bit provocative," Hockney said of his stance toward photography. Whenever he found himself in a conversation about the supposed death throes of painting, Hockney would counter, "No, it's photography that's changing. That's what's really is going on. 'Painting is dying' assumed photography was going on just being the same."[11]

Wagstaff, of course, agreed. In the context of photography's ascendance in the 1970s, painting had been lying low. But now that painting was thriving again, it was photography that seemed to be undergoing some growing pains. In the early 1980s, the idea that a straightforward black-and-white photograph might approximate something called objective reality, or that simple documentation of the actual world could be expressive of human experience, was officially *retardataire*. In this new postmodern climate, a Walker Evans picture of, say, a Depression-era gas station was no longer a meaningful work in its own right; in order for it to qualify as art, it seemed, an analysis of its social implications was required. A straightforward aesthetic reading of the picture was considered naïve, according to the pervasive influence of academic theory and literary deconstruction.

For Sam, there was no getting around it: the new postmodern bloc of artists and critics repudiated everything that he and John Szarkowski—and Beaumont Newhall before them—had accomplished. Perhaps even worse, Wagstaff himself was being lumped into the intellectually vilified category of authority referred to as "the patriarchy." As a collector, Sam's motives were being questioned because he had had such a strong hand in creating the market for photographs. He was an easy target for postmodern critics who indicted any commerce-driven enterprise, such as the one that had succeeded in fetishizing and, therefore, commodifying "the photograph." Sam had always been in the vanguard of cultural thought; now the sirocco winds that seemed to shift the very nature of culture had caught up with him, and he was cast among the retrograde old guard.

Writing in *Afterimage*, an art journal published by the Visual Studies Workshop, the art historian and photography critic Abigail Solomon-Godeau, who had studied with Rosalind Krauss and was a strict adherent of postmodern thinking and its characteristic abstruse locutions, used the occasion of the 1983 publication of *The Art of French Calotype*,[12] a serious art historical survey, to level a moralizing salvo at its earnest and highly respected authors. In her essay, "Calotypomania: The Gourmet Guide to Nineteenth-Century Photography," she cited in particular co-author, André Jammes, the French photography collector and rare book dealer, to exemplify the taint of commerce in the realm of the fine arts. Graciously acknowledging that his activities as a collector rescued thousands of nineteenth-century photographs for posterity and that his own exhibitions and publications provided something equal to a public service, she swiftly embarked on a snide—if elegant—evisceration of his most recent project: "Thus, while *The Art of French Calotype*, by Jammes and the art historian Eugenia Parry Janis, can be said to represent the *summa* of Jammes' activities, it is less a work of scholarship than a pedantic work of public relations, an elaborate gloss on the patrician sensibility of Jammes and an upholstered exercise in photographic *gourmandise*."[13]

In that scolding turn of phrase, she indicted the circle of collectors that included Wagstaff, Howard Gilman, Harry Lunn, Phyllis Lambert, John Waddell, and Paul Walter, all of whom had been canny in their calculations of the emerging photography market. To suggest that these collectors were motivated solely by their interest in a good investment is to minimize the significance of their discerning eyes, and their sense of moral obligation to preserve for the sake of history objects that offer evidence of an evolving civilization. Their collections were composed of the finest examples of the photographic image in existence, made with the highest technical achievement of any given period. As a collector, Wagstaff said, "I didn't give a damn whether photography appreciated or not—I appreciated it."[14]

By 1982, Sam and his cohorts were in fact that much wealthier because of their photography collections, yet their influence had clearly begun to wane. The new photographic work being shown by the SoHo galleries or written about in *October, Artforum*, and *Afterimage* emerged as a dire challenge to the descriptive photography found in their private collections. It was perhaps only cold comfort that their collections were considered slightly less retrograde than the Department of Photographs at the Museum of Modern Art, most often branded the epicenter of entrenched institutional thinking. That April, Andy Grundberg reported in *The New York Times* that photography was suffering a setback and attributed its rise in popularity to a mere economic bubble that had inevitably burst:

> It is time to declare the photography "boom" officially over. The economic hard times that have fallen elsewhere have fallen on photography, too. The watchword for the 80's is retrenchment, and its signs are manifest. The medium's halcyon days in the late 70's were fed essentially by a hothouse investment climate, but today the bloom is off the collecting market place.[15]

SAM WAS A SERIOUS COLLECTOR—but a serial collector as well. Collecting was always a visceral activity for him. Whether it was the West Somali Dogon sculpture or the Native American early Mimbres pots he once collected in the 1960s, he went in full bore. These expressive artifacts taught him about different cultures, reflecting native rituals for him to contemplate, with actual materials from the region that could be touched. They offered a new visual language he could translate in a private, interior world of his own. For Sam, the launch of each collection represented a new, elaborate puzzle that would yield clues, slowly, though ineluctably, until one day, the pieces would have fallen into place. As soon as an entire universe had been revealed to him whole, he would start over again with a new species of object to relish and decode.

When Sam had turned to photography, it created for him a private universe on a more massive scale than any he had explored before. As he mastered the signature subjects of individual nineteenth-century photographic artists, ascertaining the differences between a Frank Meadow Sutcliffe or a Peter Henry Emerson, an Atget or a Marville, and then traversed into the twentieth, assaying the particularities of a Dorothea Lange or a Walker Evans, the contours of a new world would manifest, often thrillingly. As we have seen, Sam familiarized himself with the chronology of technological advancements that had altered the way photographs of a particular era looked, and he learned to trace the evolution of the medium in different genres, like portraiture, from Nadar to August Sander, Man Ray, Richard Avedon, Peter Hujar—on to Robert Mapplethorpe. Or landscape photography, from Carleton Watkins and Timothy O'Sullivan to Ansel Adams. There was a history and a photographic iconography to understand, a story to tell about how the world was portrayed through the camera, in light on film, exposed over minutes and, then, eventually, in seconds. From that private universe, he was able to exercise both his authority and mastery of a new subject. Such rarefied knowledge conferred immense respect but it also seemed to isolate him in a creative chrysalis: he could reside privately with the pieces of the puzzle and, publicly, be acclaimed as master of its meaning or significance. Learning about the history of photography and deriving pleasure from looking at the photographs was the best way for him to learn, as simply as it sounds, about his own eye, to refine his sensibility, to come to know himself. Letting his eyes roam a picture, he could say, Yes, this makes sense to me; as in, I recognize in this work not only something true about the world and something true about life, but something essential about myself. Know thy culture, know thyself.

On a deeper, more atavistic level, collecting photography enabled Sam to acknowledge the psychosexual desires that for so long he had to suppress, at least until he met Robert in 1972. The art historian Michael Lobel writes that in order to cope with the cultural prohibitions against homosexual activity, "gay men have often produced a certain erotics of secrecy—whether located in the deployment and recognition of the subtle signs of cruising, or in the furtive excitement of tea-room sex."[16] Looking at photographs, Sam could identify and mentally catalog details about an era, a culture, or the nature of experience itself that were lost on the general public. He could admire an object, then whisk it away into his own private realm, where it was granted a new personal meaning in a "closet" of his own.

After a decade of collecting photographs, Sam had achieved both personal satisfaction and a widely acknowledged admiration. The exhibition of photographs from his collection had traveled to seventeen museums in the United States and Europe alone; he had been hugely instrumental in photography's widespread recognition among curatorial ranks and in the marketplace. He sat on the Photographs Committee at MoMA, as well as the Visiting Committee of the Department of Prints and Photographs at the Met. Even though new critical winds now threatened to undermine this little revolution, his confidence in his own taste—in the essential rightness of his eye—never wavered. And yet as 1982 turned into 1983, Sam had begun to lose interest.

No more revealing example of this can be found than in his relationship with Robert, for him the personification of photographic art making and through whom Sam had gotten as close as he would ever become to being an artist himself. This relationship glued him to photography, yet Robert was less and less glued to Sam. In 1982, Robert had ten one-man exhibitions alone; his reputation was growing in Europe faster even than in the United States. By 1983, he had come of age, recognized as a star in the firmament of the New York art world, and he no longer needed a mentor. A long parade of celebrities clamored to his studio to sit for their portraits: Susan Sarandon, Richard Gere, Philip Johnson, Julian Schnabel, Cindy Sherman, Andy Warhol, among them. There, too, was Sam's mission, so to speak, accomplished. Pleased, yet at the same time slightly dismissive, Sam sent Robert a card on which he taped the printed word "YIPPEE" in bold letters emblazoned across the top and wrote, "My Muffin is getting very, very fame-iss [sic]. Monkey hugs and lots of love, Sam."[17]

Nevertheless, Sam and Robert continued to talk by phone at length once or twice a day. Robert's studio employees would overhear tender and intimate baby talk on Robert's end of the call. But then, all of a sudden, he would lash out at Sam, annoyed by some comment or demand. Their relationship had devolved into a benevolent father and his contemptuous son.

Wagstaff continued to buy vintage photographs at auction. The color work defining contemporary photography in the galleries at that time—that of William Eggleston, Stephen Shore, Joel Sternfeld, Jan Groover, or Joel Meyerowitz—left Sam cold. But there were a few contemporary photographers he still championed, like the work of Joel-Peter Witkin, for example, whose ghoulish vanitas photographs, with grotesque figures, dead animals, skulls, and other shocking instruments and objects captivated him. Witkin's work shared a still-life photographic precision with Mapplethorpe's, but the differences perhaps suggest more of a comparison between Freud and Jung: Mapplethorpe's live human subjects were photographed with an overt sculptural eroticism; Witkin's live subjects share space with moribund objects and draw on archetypal symbolism.

Perhaps Sam's enthusiasm for photography waned just as it was wrested from the graces of the avant-garde, since, increasingly, it was being embraced by a broader audience—the museumgoing, poster-buying public at large. Despite the fact that this was to some extent the result of Sam's own doing, there seemed to be an inverse relationship between mainstream approbation and his own personal passion. Given his expensive lifestyle—even despite impecunious appearances—and the fact that he was not actively earning money, he was beginning to dip into his principal. Thus, one day, when Daniel Wolf asked Sam if he would ever consider selling his photography collection, he responded, surprisingly, that he might.[18]

"LADY LISA LYON," a show of Mapplethorpe's photographs opened in March 1983 at Leo Castelli Gallery in SoHo. Lisa Lyon considered her bodybuilding in the context of performance art. Robert had met her at a party in SoHo in 1979, the same year Patti Smith left New York. Smith had reached a level of fame in the world of rock 'n' roll that had begun to take a psychic toll, and perhaps that was one reason she chose to sequester herself in Detroit and focus more of her energy on marriage and motherhood. Before she moved, however, she released an album called *Wave*; the cover picture, taken once more by Robert in Sam's apartment, shows Patti in a white dress with two white doves perched on her hands. It was the last time Robert and Sam would see her for many years: Patti and her husband, Fred Sonic Smith, one of the founders of the MC5, would make a clean break from her life in New York.

Bruce Chatwin later described Robert's first meeting with Lisa Lyon in terms that made his captivation clear. "Robert liked her quivering lip and glittering eyes. He liked the mop of loose black curls that made her look like an Old Testament heroine. He liked her leather jacket and her tight rubber black pants. It was obvious that her body was superlative—small, supple, svelte, without an ounce of surplus fat, and so very different from the sinewy torsos of the ladies in muscle magazines."[19]

When Robert photographed Lisa in his loft the next day, she arrived wearing a miniskirt, thigh-high leather boots and a wide-brimmed hat decorated with feathers. She was a muscular woman and he photographed her in the feathery hat as she flexed her biceps. "I had never seen a woman like that before," he said. "It was like looking at someone from another planet."[20] He had said the same thing about Patti when they first met.

Accordingly, Lisa, who was from a well-off family in Beverly Hills, became a photographic muse for Robert in a series of pictures made over two years, in the studio and outside. She appears nude at times, clothed at others, sometimes in full dress, her muscled body at odds with the evening gowns and the boas and the leather regalia. Robert saw the project as a photographic novel without a real story line—an abstract tale that goes in and out of fantasy. They worked on it together—she as a performance artist and Robert as a photographic artist—in what Robert considered a constructive, mutually beneficial collaboration. For a time they were inseparable and traveled to Joshua Tree and Palm Springs, the Caribbean, and Paris. They had a brief sexual romance, outlasted by a much longer photographic collaboration.

"One of the points I'm making in photography is being a sculptor without having to spend all the time modeling with your hands. That's much too archaic for me," Robert said in a filmed interview in 1984. "Lisa as a bodybuilder is sculpting with her body. That's one of the reasons we worked so well together. . . . Inventing sculpture myself with the camera—that's when photography is really exciting."[21]

Robert's homosexuality wasn't an obstacle for Lisa. She was enthralled with him, regardless. "Everybody loved Robert in a weird way," she said, acknowledging that he was easily capable of creating enemies, too, with his "cruel and nasty" behavior, but "you had to forgive him, because he was a genius, a visionary, a revolutionary; he did things other people would never dream of doing, violated every taboo. Wasn't it William Blake who said, 'The road of excess leads to the palace of wisdom'?"[22]

In one picture Lisa wears a wedding dress and a veil, and holds a bouquet of white daffodils against her chest. She is seen from the side, head turned toward the camera with an expression as beseeching as it is bewitching, resolute but searching. There is a symmetry between this image and the one of Patti wearing a summery white dress with the doves. Could it be that Robert was presenting both Patti and Lisa in symbolic anticipation of marriage to him? He dedicated the accompanying book, *Lady Lisa Lyon*, to Patti, perhaps less a gesture of love than what might be considered a wish to rub in her face his displeasure at being abandoned.

For the most part, Sam found Robert's pictures of Lisa Lyon uninteresting. Certainly the work was not what Sam had in mind when he had encouraged Anne MacDonald to pursue her "jock book" in 1978 and suggested that Robert, who loved the idea, shoot the pictures. MacDonald's idea and Sam's enthusiasm for it might well have inspired Robert to proceed with photographing Lisa, the "jock," and turning the series into a book. Sam's foreword to *Lady Lisa Lyon* is telling; the opening paragraph borders on an incoherence that does little to obfuscate his contempt for Robert's fascination with Lisa, and for the entire enterprise:

> This whirlwind tour of one lady's anatomy, and other eccentricities, is just the latest Mapplethorpe provocation in his ongoing series of provocative documents in praise of the Life of Riley. With a new, self-made woman available for all seasons, the shy pornographer has decided to take a series of carom shots off her revised femininity. . . .[23]

However, the Lisa Lyon pictures are not as good as Mapplethorpe's pictures of Patti Smith, so perhaps Sam felt that Lyon was an unworthy surrogate. In Robert's pictures of Patti, their communion is obvious and emanates a solemnity that borders on the religious. Robert's pictures of Lisa—with their overdetermined poses and theatrical costumes—never quite get beyond the level of artifice. Clearly Sam harbored sadness about Patti's absence, and maybe that—more than the lack of authenticity and the absence of emotional articulation—accounts for his cranky song about the Lisa Lyon pictures.

The year before *Lady Lisa Lyon* was published, Sam had written Patti in Detroit on the occasion of the birth of her son, Jackson. It was a chatty letter on a tall slender note card in his kinetic and barely legible script; he placed the card inside an announcement for a publication of Rimbaud poems with drawings by Peter Thompson:

> *How nice to have your announcement about your son. Hope mother and child are doing famously. . . .*
>
> *Still being the photo collector. My show ends up at the Petit Palais in Paris for the month of November, its 17th stop.*
>
> *Robert is off to L.A. for a week to do poster photos for Richard Gere's latest movie. He's just bought himself a large format camera and has begun to do color in earnest—House & Garden covers have been ordered then some new sculpture 3 crosses filled with carpeting,*

red, white & blue, & 2 colored mirror ones—Catholicism doesn't
die easily.

One of his younger brothers, Eddy, who wants to be a photog,
too, is working for him. Robert has suggested he change his name if
he really wants to enter the fray. As you see, the world here continues.
Miss you.[24]

Love and hugs, Sam.

The letter came back unopened, stamped "Return to Sender."

SIXTEEN

WHISPERS OF
THE MUSE

Photography is the common language of modern history.
It's everywhere; and everyone, in some way, understands it.

—HOLLAND COTTER[1]

A S THE PHOTOGRAPHY MARKET WAS DRYING UP IN THE
early 1980s, Daniel Wolf spoke with several collectors about
the idea of selling their collections. Some of them, like Wagstaff, had
registered interest, at least theoretically. As he sat at his desk in his 57th
Street gallery on the morning of March 4, 1983, Wolf saw an article in
The New York Times announcing the appointment of John Walsh as the
new director of the Getty Museum in Los Angeles. The *Times* reported
that Walsh would be responsible "for the growth of the Getty Museum's
collections, which have been very much strengthened in the last few
months and which may eventually move into new areas."[1] It was well-
known that the Getty's endowment of $1.2 billion had made it the richest
museum in the world. With the appointment of Walsh, who had most
recently been a curator of painting at Boston's Museum of Fine Arts, it

would begin a new round of acquisitions. All of a sudden, Wolf's idea took on structure and purpose.

John Walsh, forty-five, fair-haired and trim, with the bearing of a refined scholar, and Daniel Wolf, not yet thirty, with dark hair and a quiet intensity, sat on the same committee for Phillips Exeter Academy, the preparatory school from which they both graduated. They had run into each other often enough at art events to be on familiar terms. Wolf knew that the Getty had ambitions to compete with the best museums in the world and the absence of a department of photographs was a conspicuous omission. He waited two weeks before calling Walsh and inviting him to stop by the gallery. When they met, Wolf told Walsh about the consortium of photography collections he could put together for the Getty. As an example of the quality of material he was talking about, he brought out the Overstone album, by Julia Margaret Cameron, for which he had paid $64,000 at auction; consisting of 113 albumen silver prints, it included portraits of the poets Robert Browning, Alfred Lord Tennyson, and Sir Henry Taylor; the artists William Holman Hunt, a founder of the Pre-Raphaelite Brotherhood, and G. F. Watts; and other portraits representing states of being, with titles such as *Peace*, *Love*, *Sadness*, and *Contemplation* or with fanciful titles like *The Five Foolish Virgins* and *The Five Wise Virgins*, in which Cameron's august friends or aristocratic relatives were posed with poetic gestures in diaphanous light. "This is the market," Wolf said.[2] Walsh looked through the historic album thoughtfully.

Several months later, the anxiously anticipated phone call came from Walsh to say that the Getty board had made available funds to purchase the best private collections of photographs in the world. It was a development that would have international reverberations for photography, altering the composition of curatorial respect for the medium as well as the market's valuation of the photograph.

Wolf went immediately to Wagstaff to obtain his official consent to proceed to sell his collection in June 1983, although he would not reveal the buyer, and acknowledged a price had not yet been offered, nor would he say that other collections would be packaged together for the sale. Neither did he tell Arnold Crane, the Chicago lawyer who had assem-

bled his collection by meeting with individual photographers throughout the late 1960s and '70s, and buying entire bodies of their work. The
third collection Wolf had in mind, however, that of André and Marie-
Thérèse Jammes, consisted of seminal nineteenth-century material, and
its procurement would require substantial intuition and acumen on the
part of Wolf.

Wolf made a trip to Paris specifically to meet with Jammes. "I told
him I have a person who wants to buy his entire collection," Wolf
recalled. Jammes just said no. Despondent, Wolf retreated to a café to
ponder the situation. "André was the first collector and the most brilliant," Wolf explained. "Nobody had the intellect that André had,
because he came from the school of old France that acknowledges
enlightenment. He was a book dealer, so he had all of the tactile knowledge of these books as well as the intellectual history. There was nobody
like him. He was everybody's star in the sky. A wonderful human being,
as well. And clever and wicked. Way ahead of everybody."[3]

Knowing Jammes and his standards as well as Wolf did, he decided
to try one more approach: full disclosure. "Nobody knows who this
buyer is except me," Daniel told Jammes. "Then I told him the whole
story, about all the collections, about who the buyer was, and again I
asked him if he would sell. And he said yes." André Jammes was the
only one of the three collectors who knew that the buyer was the Getty
Museum, and that his collection was in very good company among the
others in the sale.[4]

Wolf, who had a serious, close-to-the-vest manner, was further
energized as he circled the globe for the Getty in search of supplemen-
tary photographs in smaller collections to round out the sale. "It was
great fun, the year of my life," he said. Besides relying on his own
knowledge, he was also getting expert advice from Weston Naef, the
curator of prints and photographs at the Metropolitan Museum. Walsh
had been a curator at the Met before going to Boston, and Naef had
started out there as his intern. From the beginning, it was obvious to
Walsh that Naef was going places: "I'd get into an elevator, and there
would be Weston with a quiet old man wearing a beret, and he'd say,
'Oh, John, I'd like you to meet André Kertész.'"[5]

Now, Naef was quietly advising the Getty as well, suggesting and evaluating additional purchases of photographs; this was a bald conflict of interest and ethical breach for a Met curator, but it soon served his own carefully thought out career plans.[6] Anticipating that the Getty would prove successful in its quest to acquire these private collections, Walsh offered Naef a position to set up the Getty's photography department and become its chief curator, which he readily accepted. He left one of the world's most important museums for an institution whose reputation at the time was based only on its enormous endowment. "That challenge was one that I could not resist," Naef later told the *Los Angeles Times*.[7]

By late 1983, Wolf had bundled not only three major private photography collections but also rare and choice individual prints and albums from a variety of other international sources—a blind trust, of sorts, not unlike the way an equity fund is put together. Before he went back to Walsh to begin negotiating the price, Wolf spent a week with Wagstaff evaluating every picture in his collection to assign a dollar amount to the whole thing. "It was a wonderful process because I got to see everything Sam had bought," Wolf said.[8]

Every morning, the two would meet in Wagstaff's eighth-floor apartment at One Fifth Avenue and look through pictures well into the afternoon. Anne Ehrenkranz, Sam's archivist, pulled the photographs out of drawers, sometimes even crawling on her hands and knees to reach for boxes of prints or albums. Wagstaff and Wolf would discuss every image in aesthetic terms, appraise the condition, quality, and rarity of the print, and then assign each one a market value. "I'd say this one is $1600 and he'd say okay," Wolf recalled. "It wasn't hard because the range of value at the time was very limited. $2000 was a lot of money for a print then and many of the pictures were in the $1000 to $3000 range." Nevertheless, some approached $10,000.[9]

It would prove to be a marvelous experience for Sam to survey his entire collection, and to consider the significance of a decade's work. Given the more than six thousand pictures Sam had amassed, there were many that represented high points in photographic history—the Nadars, the Le Grays, the Le Secqs, the Balduses, and, of course, the Hill and

Adamson albums, as well as the Fox Talbots. Not all the photographs were of such an empyrean quality, however. Some were, Wolf noticed, "just okay faded pictures," the ones Sam had bought simply to satisfy his own curiosity. Name-brand photographers were hardly Sam's only quarry, as some of the pictures had been acquired as if a reflection of Sam's abiding belief that photography was not always about artistic perfection. Nobody had ever seen the artist before and Sam would buy it for the first time because "you don't know if you're ever going to come across it again."[10]

Wolf also noticed great variety in the representation of the actual world. Sam was after a quality of authenticity in the photographs he loved and collected—not just an accurate depiction of the scene, but some perceptual insight about the experience itself. In other words, "that dumb, just being there feeling" that Sam could not always adequately articulate was represented in many of the images. Authentic experience is one of the most elusive characteristics to identify in formal terms. Photography has the ability to take you to the actual moment, rendering the simultaneous experiences of once having been there then with being there right now.

In sheer financial terms for Sam, photography would prove to be a far more prudent investment than the stock market, which remained, at best, static in a prolonged bearish retreat throughout the 1970s and early 1980s. Indeed, no financial advisers to either Mr. and Mrs. Samuel Jones Wagstaff Sr. or to Mr. and Mrs. Donald V. Newhall could have realized such a healthy return during this period. The value of photography had increased almost exponentially, so much so that Sam and Daniel concluded that Wagstaff's collection could now be handsomely assessed at approximately $5 million.

IT WOULD BE MONTHS before Wolf would come back with an actual offer, so Sam had some time to contemplate his next step. Although Jim Nelson worked all day as a hair and makeup artist for *As the World Turns*, a long-running soap opera, he also fulfilled an unspoken obligation to take care of domestic necessities. John Waddell remembers Jim "as sweet, mindless, gushing, adoring, dizzy and innocent." It was clear to him that Jim couldn't engage Sam intellectually, but Sam did not seem bothered by it and was even visibly amused about the arrangement. His standard refrain whenever he was asked about the relationship was "Jim takes care of me." [11]

Sam would sit on the corduroy couch (a new addition since Jim had moved in) and play with the cats: Teenangel was a beautiful, pedigreed Russian blue that Robert had given him the year before, while Manny was a tiger-striped Irish fold. "He talked about kitties all the time," John Waddell recalled. "He loved kitties. He loved kitty pictures." [12] Sam had been collecting pictures of cats for years and, to the consternation of Robert, John Waddell, and others, threatened to organize an exhibition of his kitty pictures. The fact that cats as subjects were prone to cliché was precisely what amused Sam most about the prospect.

Harris Fogel, a young photographer whom Sam had met while giving a talk at Humboldt State University in Arcata, California, had recently moved to New York. One day while Sam was waiting to hear back from Daniel Wolf, Fogel stopped by to show Sam his new work. They sat on the couch while Sam thumbed through the pictures. When Fogel picked up Teenangel from the floor, he noticed the cat had been lying on a small matted print. Fogel recognized it as a photograph by August Sander.

"Is this the real thing?" he asked. "Is this what I think it is?" Sam just nodded, and Fogel was incredulous. "I was holding this piece of history and Sam was so nonchalant about the cat sitting on it," Fogel said. "I think he started laughing, petted the kitty, and said not to worry, look how soft Teenangel was. And that was that." [13]

As his photography collecting wound down, Sam's days became more leisurely. He would go out for long casual lunches with friends or acquaintances at neighborhood spots like One Fifth, the Cookery, which doubled as a jazz club in the evening, or Il Cantinori, a new art world haunt. Lately a nice-looking young man named Dimitri Levas had been spending a lot of time with Mapplethorpe at his studio, and one day Sam took him to lunch. Levas had moved to New York from San Francisco, first working at the Charles Cowles Gallery in SoHo and then for John Loring, the design director at Tiffany. He collected Italian decorative glass, something Mapplethorpe had also recently become interested in acquiring. Levas, enamored of Robert's reputation as a photographer and enfant terrible, had started bringing him collectible glass vases, often with flowers, to photograph. Soon Levas was helping Robert style his pictures, and the two would go on shopping excursions together in SoHo and uptown to buy Italian glass. The purpose of the lunch, Levas soon realized, was for Sam to vet him as a professional companion for Robert. Sam, who once had indirectly praised Levas's poster design for a Carleton Watkins show at Jeffrey Fraenkel Gallery in San Francisco, made sure to let him know what a privilege it was for him to be working and cavorting with Mapplethorpe. "Lunchtime with Sam was almost always about how great Robert was and what a unique person he was and how he'll never meet anyone else in his life like Robert. I mean, on and on and on," Levas said. "Robert was very charismatic. He was amazingly intelligent for someone who wasn't very well educated, and intuitively intelligent, and he knew how to glean things from people. So I think Sam wanted to check me out, to see if I was a good guy to be around Robert. I think he wanted to like me because Robert did, but I don't think he did."[14]

Robert may have outgrown the need for a mentor, but it didn't stop Sam from keeping close tabs on every aspect of his career. Betsy Evans had met Mapplethorpe during his show at the Simon Lowinsky Gallery in San Francisco. When she moved to New York and heard that Robert was looking for a studio manager, she went to see him. She might have come across as too prim for Robert; he told her there were other candidates and he would get back to her. But that night, to her surprise, he called with some urgency and asked her to meet him for lunch the next day at One Fifth. Sam was there, too, and she had the impression that his approval was required. She got the job and would work for Robert as his studio manager for two years.

On his frequent stops at Robert's studio, Sam would sometimes abandon his stately manner, jumping around and laughing gleefully, as if he were channeling a teenage version of himself. Robert would get annoyed, roll his eyes, and say disrespectful things to him in front of

Dimitri, Betsy, and others in the studio. It never appeared to faze Sam, at least on the surface. He maintained his posture as the benevolent father, whether out of patience and wisdom or impenetrable defenses. In fact, Robert's eruptions, his displays of contempt, could take on a darker quality. "I used to think of Sam and Robert as being like Brian Epstein and the Beatles," Howard Read, Robert's dealer at Robert Miller Gallery, told Patricia Morrisroe. "But after a while it became sad, because Sam would come into the gallery, and Robert would tell him, 'Shut up! You don't know what you're talking about.' "[15] At the same time, Dimitri and Betsy both recalled the patter of baby talk that would mark their conversations on the phone, often more than once a day.

After lunch, on his way back to his penthouse, Sam often stopped at his eighth-floor apartment, where he would sit with Anne Ehrenkranz, sometimes for an hour or more. Ehrenkranz had gone to Brearley and Smith—both of which Sam unfairly referred to as finishing schools— and was completing a master's at the Institute of Fine Arts, Sam's alma mater. She was married to a very successful attorney with whom she was raising four children in a lavish, art-filled apartment on the Upper East Side. Sam was not interested in talking about photography; instead, he chose to regale her with stories about his glamorous mother. He recalled that, as a child, he longed to live in a house as grand as the Van Rensselaers or recounted with not inconsiderable affection his adventures as a schoolboy in Majorca. He and Ehrenkranz would compare notes about the Institute of Fine Arts, Sam passing on the lessons he absorbed from his own mentor, Richard Offner, or art historical tidbits from his travels through the grand villas of Tuscany and Umbria or the duchal houses of the British countryside. Even though Sam was only in his early sixties, his nostalgic forays into a fabled past took on the quality of reveries that seemed to distance him from the idle present.[16]

For Ehrenkranz, Sam was still a force of nature, even if his face was getting craggier and his physical deportment assumed more and more the pallor of age. Sam retained a hardy façade, the AIDS virus he would later be diagnosed with undetected, still, not yet challenging his immune system or revealing any symptoms. But the menace was closing in all around him, and word spread that people he and Robert knew in the gay community and the art world were dying of the disease known then as GRID. Like so many others, Sam proceeded as if he were invincible. Gay men at the time largely ignored the threat of exposure, without regard to the entreaties of doctors and community activists to practice what was soon to be called "safe sex." Although it wasn't known at the time, up to five years could pass between the initial exposure to the virus and the first "opportunistic infection," a bout of serious illness that indicated the person was developing full-blown AIDS. And no one, including Sam, knew whether or not he had already been exposed to the virus.

As he reflected on his past to Ehrenkranz and others, too, Sam was also contemplating his future, observing the types of objects others in his midst were collecting. His friend and fellow collector John Waddell had recently moved into the neighborhood. Aside from collecting photographs, Waddell collected modernist decorative arts, and when Sam first visited the apartment, he admired a set of four floor lamps that Waddell had placed in a row against the back wall. Each was more than five feet tall, the shade a flat horizontal band of linen supported by three very slender iron rods coming to a triangular configuration at the base. Sam asked who designed them, and Waddell explained they had come from the famed Arizona Biltmore lobby and had been attributed to Frank Lloyd Wright. Sam was dubious. "I find it curious that Wright would have taken a triangle in plan," he said. "I would have expected him to take a square, for which there would have been four rods." Waddell said that Sam's hunch proved accurate; it was later confirmed that Warren McArthur, the brother of the hotel's architect, designed the lamps. "There wasn't a dealer, there wasn't a curator, there wasn't an expert who had ever said as much about those lamps as Sam did," Waddell said, underscoring a point about Sam's informed eye.[17]

Despite accommodating himself to a more sedentary way of life, Sam was still traveling to Europe for the auctions every year and making stops wherever Robert had a show. Decorative glass as a collectible was becoming much more in vogue; by then Robert had been collecting Murano glass by Venini. Philippe Garner, the meticulously elegant British auctioneer, was planning to conduct a Sotheby's sale in Monte Carlo

of glass by Emile Gallé, a French designer from the fin de siècle—
"flourishy, Beaux Arts–like, Proustian," he said, and had suggested to
Sam that it might be rewarding for him to view the sale. "Sam flew
down to Monte Carlo and invested his characteristic intense concentration in examining the glass, I am tempted to say, 'communing' with each
piece," Garner said. However, in the end, Italian glass just did not catch
his imagination.[18]

Then Garner had another idea. A colleague of his at Sotheby's, John
Culme, was a specialist in nineteenth-century English silver. Culme
could illuminate the social and historical contexts in which silverware
was produced and used, and why it was a valuable collectible object.
"Inevitably, photographs played an important part in that process as
vital visual evidence," Garner said, explaining that he had helped Culme
build a collection of photographs relating to silver—still-life subjects,
maker or retailer stock records, silversmiths' shopfronts, and so forth.
"As close colleagues at Sotheby's, we became familiar with one another's fields and with the key players," Garner explained, "so Sam was
well-known to John by reputation when I arranged the lunch."[19]

They met at Enzo Apicella's Pizza Condotti, an Italian restaurant
around the corner from Sotheby's in London. It was not long after a
Brooklyn Museum exhibition called "The Genius of Charles James,"
and Garner made reference to the fashion designer's celebrated satin
"eiderdown" opera jacket of 1937. Sam came out with a rejoinder to the
effect that this was "the first soft sculpture, well before Oldenburg"—a
wonderful instance, Garner thought, of the breadth of Sam's cultivation
and of his sharp, free-ranging appreciation of creativity across disciplines and conventional boundaries. Culme had been charmed, and Sam
was equally intrigued by Culme's expertise in silver.

THE GETTY MUSEUM OFFERED in early 1984 to pay in the range of
$20 million for the bundle of collections Daniel Wolf brought to their
doorstep. Sam would receive $4.6 million after Wolf took his commis-
sion. Once the sale was completed, however, he was shocked to learn
who the buyer was. Sam had assumed the interested party to be the

Harry Ransom Center at the University of Texas, which had acquired the very rare and historically important Gernsheim collection of photographs almost twenty years earlier. According to George Rinhart, Sam was particularly upset that his collection, so singular in historical significance, was now lumped together with others.[20] He felt his collection was the product of his own aesthetic sensibility, and its originality would defy any such merger. Perhaps, too, he expected the sale of his collection to be as much a provocation as his engagement with photography had been a decade earlier, and the fact that others chose to do the same thing at the same time took some of the thrill out of the gesture.

With the announcement that it had acquired those three private collections comprising eighteen thousand images, the Getty immediately, if not sensationally, distinguished itself with one of the foremost museum collections of photographs in the world. Of course, Walsh put photography in perspective when discussing the purchase in the *Los Angeles Times*: "By being able to move very quickly and quietly, we were able to make an extraordinarily favorable deal," he said. "We were able to get the whole works for less than the price of a moderately good Cezanne still life."[21]

The sale, wrote Andy Grundberg in *The New York Times*, "was more than unexpected; it was stunning. In one stroke the cash-rich California museum gobbled up the two most prestigious collections in private hands in this country, joined them with seven others to create a collection bigger than that of either the Metropolitan Museum of Art or the Museum of Modern Art." In fact, continued Grundberg, it "shifted the geographic center of photographic scholarship and connoisseurship in the direction of Malibu."[22]

Wagstaff's "vaunted" collection was described to include sixty-five hundred photographs, dating from 1839 paper prints by William Henry Fox Talbot, as well as signature images by Nadar, Hill and Adamson, Julia Margaret Cameron, and Carleton Watkins. "Blasphemy, thy name is Sam Wagstaff, Jr.," wrote Suzanne Muchnic in the *Los Angeles Times*. "The legendary collector of thousands of photographs, the urbane gentleman with an enchanted eye and a well-stocked bank account, the tall, slim, attractively graying New Yorker whose talent for spotting unknown artistry has been lauded across the country, has declared himself 'bored to death with photography.' "[23]

At least in print, Wagstaff seemed pleased that he had once again defied expectations. He admitted that classical photography had gotten under his skin and he loved it still, even though collecting it had over the years become less rewarding "than some of the crazier things," he told the *Los Angeles Times*. "To be contrary and a little cranky is fun sometimes—maybe all the time."[24]

Judy Keller, now the chief curator of photography at the Getty Museum, considers the Wagstaff collection the core of the museum's collection of photographs: "Not only because it is one of the largest, but because it has the greatest range in terms of the history it covers, as well as the number of photographers who are part of the canon and were a major part of what Sam considered important: the Julia Margaret Cameron holding, and Nadar, but, also, all of these other significant artists, like Gerald Incandela."[25]

Not every picture in Wagstaff's historic collection, however, made it to the Getty. He would keep most of his Mapplethorpes.

SEVENTEEN

THE GLIMMER
AND THE GLOOM

If a man has character, he has also his typical experience,
which always recurs.

—FRIEDRICH NIETZSCHE[1]

PIERRE APRAXINE ARRIVED AT SAM'S APARTMENT, LATELY FILLED
with silver objects, one day in early 1985. A serving cart held a
repoussé silver pitcher, in which the pattern had been intricately ham-
mered from the reverse side to create on the surface a delicate filigree in
relief; punch bowls with handles shaped into phantasmagorical figures;
and a tureen with ornately designed legs. Fanned out on the coffee table,
as if they were common knickknacks, were a set of butter knives by
Ball, Black, whose ivory handles were designed as sheaves of wheat;
beside them stood a Meriden silver-plated inkwell with ornamental cats'
heads on either side, and a Gorham dish in the shape of a canoe. More
silver objects sat on the windowsills. Even more occupied floor space
throughout the room, almost suggesting at first glance the look of a
pawnshop whose owner had run out of space instead of a modernist
Fifth Avenue penthouse. But then beams of sunlight spilled through the

windows into the apartment. "There was nothing but the silver and the sky and the white walls and the white floor, and then the Wagstaff furniture that had descended from the Colonel's farm in Central Park, a settee and two armchairs, and that's it," Apraxine said, describing the scene. "But, the light on the silver—it was the most elegant place I have ever been."[2]

Sam had known the tall and very refined Pierre Apraxine for almost twenty years. They first met in Brussels in the mid-1960s, when Apraxine worked as a curator for the Banque Lambert. Leon Lambert had commissioned Gordon Bunshaft of Skidmore, Owings and Merrill to design the bank's modern headquarters in Brussels and brought Apraxine on when the building was finished to catalog his art collection, add contemporary acquisitions, display the works, and serve as a kind of emissary to the art world throughout Europe. Sam met Pierre during one of his trips to Europe for the Wadsworth Atheneum. They would remain friendly over the years, but it was when Sam started his involvement with silver that he and Pierre became closer.

For Apraxine, who was born in Russia and educated in Belgium, Sam had long been an encouraging influence. Moving to New York in the early 1970s, Pierre relied on Sam a bit like an elder brother, a kind of "guru who doesn't say very much but nudges you here and there."[3] Very much in the manner of a playful elder brother, Sam would taunt Pierre about his Russian heritage, which he had been intent on distancing himself from on arrival in America. Perhaps it was that residual boarding-school sense of humor—turning the act of ribbing someone about a tender subject into gales of hilarity—that prompted Sam to further rub it in by sending Pierre touristy postcards with pictures of Leningrad or Moscow or showing him quaint photographs taken in the old country. Still, behind it all lay a genuine regard and affection. One day in Pierre's early years in New York, he received a phone call from Sam urging him to go to A la Vieille Russie, a legendary antique shop in the Sherry-Netherland Hotel that specializes in European, and particularly Russian, jewelry and crafts. They were selling a Russian box made during a tsarist-era revival of the peasants' crafts in 1890 or so, probably from Talashinko. "It's the most wonderful thing you ever saw!" Sam exclaimed. "You have to go and see it, you have to buy it."[4]

Pierre thought it was another of Sam's antics, but he went to look at it. He realized he had bid on the very same box at auction in London before he moved to New York. It had been too expensive even then, and now, in one of the most expensive antique stores in New York, the price had quadrupled. But, because Sam had insisted, Pierre bought it, and it still sits on a table in Pierre's West Village apartment, a reminder of Sam's presence in his life.

In the mid-1970s, after working as an adviser to the Museum of Modern Art, Apraxine was hired as curator of the Gilman Paper Company art collection. While surveying the holdings, he presented the idea of adding photographs to the collection and invoked the name of Sam Wagstaff, then just coming to prominence. Howard Gilman and his brother, Charles Gilman Jr., who were born and raised in New York, had inherited the largest privately held paper and building products company in the United States. Culturally minded and generous in their philanthropic support of the arts, they knew Sam's reputation and gave Apraxine free rein to acquire photographs.

Sam and Pierre would find themselves competing at auction on more than one occasion. At Sotheby's in London in 1977, not long after Pierre started collecting for the Gilman Collection, a set of photographs came up from Roger Fenton's personal "gray albums," thus named because Fenton mounted the prints on gray paper. One image, entitled *The Skeleton of an Ostrich*, attracted them both, but since Pierre had been given a set amount to spend at auction, Sam outbid him. On more than a few occasions Pierre would say, "It's always a pleasure to lose to Sam."

Occasionally, however, Sam would have his comeuppance. In 1981, G. Ray Hawkins consigned a photograph to Christie's by George Hurrell, a portrait of the virile matinee idol Ramon Novarro, bare-chested in the role of Ben-Hur. Hurrell inscribed the 1930 print on the back: "This is my first original vintage print of Ramon Novarro which launched my career in Hollywood. He and this photograph were responsible for getting my first job as portrait photographer in M.G.M. Studios in Culver City. George Hurrell." In fact, the picture was taken to resurrect Novarro's career; star of the 1920s, his Mexican accent had not been up to snuff in the new era of talking pictures. (Only later would his homosexuality come out in the newspaper reports of his violent murder in 1968 by two hustlers he had hired to come to his Laurel Canyon home for sex.)

Hawkins had paid $2000 for the print and $300 for the frame, but he didn't mind that Christie's modest estimate was set at $1000–1500. He knew the print was bound to command a much higher figure, and he sat at the back of the room as the bidding began. Sam, sitting in the front row, immediately raised his paddle at the opening figure of $500. Then, as if in a duel, Pierre, several rows back, raised his own paddle. The bidding volleyed back and forth between them, with several others jumping in periodically and upping the ante. Sam kept bidding, undaunted, until Pierre's final bid at $10,000 brought down the gavel.

It wasn't until 2005, eighteen years after Sam's death, that his influence on Apraxine—and Gilman—would come full circle. Just as the Wagstaff collection had been acquired by the J. Paul Getty Museum, the Metropolitan Museum purchased the Gilman Paper Company Collection,[5] by then "widely considered to be the most important private photography collection in the world."[6] The acquisition was as much a tribute to the eye of Pierre Apraxine as it was to the enterprise of the Gilman brothers. Malcolm Daniel, the Met's curator of photography, told the *Times* that it had been his department's priority for fifteen years to acquire the Gilman Collection: "It is undoubtedly the most important thing that has happened at the Met in the area of photography and is probably the most important thing that is likely ever to happen."[7] The Met's acquisition of the more than eighty-five hundred photographs in the Gilman collection made it in a single stroke "one of the world's preeminent institutions for 19th-century photographs."[8]

IT WAS LESS THAN a decade after Wagstaff and his cohort had begun to collect photographs that the major museums became competitive players in a race to acquire significant private photography collections. Gilman's was, in fact, the last of that group's big private collections to follow Wagstaff's into the hands of a large museum. Soon after the news of Sam's 1984 sale to the J. Paul Getty Museum, for example, Paul Walter pledged sixty pictures from his collection to the Museum of Modern Art. In May 1985, that museum mounted an exhibition of those images. The show was organized by John Szarkowski, then approaching sixty and still the reigning authority in the field, with the photographic masterworks ranging from the 1840s to the 1930s.[9]

Another important museum acquisition took place in 1987, when John Waddell's collection went to the Metropolitan Museum of Art. The acquisition was facilitated by a contribution of $1.8 million from the Ford Motor Company—at the time the largest corporate gift made to a museum in the United States for an acquisition. Known today as the Ford Motor Company Collection at the Met, it includes among the finest examples of avant-garde photographic work made between the world wars from the Dadaist, futurist, surrealist, and constructivist movements.[10]

The Waddell collection "is a brilliant reconstruction of a particularly complex epoch," Philippe de Montebello, the director of the Met, said when the acquisition was reported in *The New York Times*. "The collection is international in composition and thus mirrors the period when modern technology first made possible worldwide travel and communication."[11] Two years earlier, Sam had told Waddell that he had finally come to understand the focus of his friend's collection. "Sam was interested in a hundred and forty years of photography," Waddell said. "I was concentrating on about twenty-five years, and he said to me, 'You're doing the advent of modernism.'"[12]

The 1984 sale of Wagstaff's collection to the Getty included a stipulation that allowed him to proceed with four previously arranged exhibitions. The first would include 160 photographs to be shown initially at the International Center of Photography and then travel to museums around the country. So, in early 1985, emotionally divorced from photography and already married, as a collector, to silver, Sam still rose with some pleasure to the task of this prior commitment. "Photographs from the Sam Wagstaff Collection at the J. Paul Getty Museum," opened at the International Center for Photography in New York on

March 29.[13] On the announcement was Henri Cartier-Bresson's *Children's Party at the River* (1953). This photograph of a mother with a baby in her arms standing with several young girls in ballet tutus on the bank of a river recalled, uncharacteristically, an impressionist tableau by Degas or Monet, bringing it into the modernist twentieth century with cubist blocks of shadow and light. Sam considered it "one of the most delicious pictures Cartier-Bresson ever made."[14] Cartier-Bresson, considered the father of photojournalism, originated the term "the decisive moment," which identified the juncture at which an equal balance is struck between activity and observation: the photographer responds to something as it transpires in real time and choreographs his position, finding the visual geometry in the frame and setting the right exposure of light to film, rendering out of a spontaneous situation a marriage of subject and image, like two coils of DNA, inextricably linked. The result, then, is not just a moment in time caught by the camera but the timelessness of the moment expressed in visual form.

Dimitri Levas has kept the invitation for the preview of the show, on which Sam wrote, "Robert is going to hate this show because it's so silly so often, but you, being more mature than him, will be able to understand [that] it's stooping a tiny bit to conquer."[15] Of course, Sam was setting Dimitri up to show it to Robert, thrilled as usual to stir the pot with just such a provocation. Dimitri, who by that time had become one of Robert's closest friends, chose not to take the bait. At the same time, the note reflects Sam's more casual attitude about photography at that point. Stepping off his soapbox, he was presenting work he simply liked, without a complicated agenda. Gone was his drive to instruct the public about the history and importance of the medium.

On display were Sam's idiosyncratic, if waning enthusiasms of the moment, perhaps his afterthoughts about photography. One picture of the 1930s bank robbers Bonnie Parker and Clyde Barrow was taken by Barrow's uncle and characterized by Sam as "partaking of the aesthetics of shock."[16] The ostrich skeleton taken in 1852 by Roger Fenton—his small victory over Pierre Apraxine—was on display, an unexpected subject for the official British photographer of the Crimean War, known for his many portraits of Queen Victoria. For the most part, though, the exhibition registered as an instructive exercise in visual surprise, less in service of his advocacy of the medium than as a selection of things that Sam was pointing to as worthy of some attention—in keeping with Szarkowski's description of the act of pointing in his essay on Atget.

The New York Times Magazine published a five-page profile of Wagstaff on the occasion of this show, entitled "Collecting's Big Thrill Is the Chase." Margaret Loke, the author, asked the photography curators at MoMA and the Getty to weigh in on Wagstaff's accomplishment as a photography collector and aesthetic warrior. John Szarkowski acknowledged Sam's intuitive "recognition that there were many more interesting photographers than anyone had written monographs about and done exhibitions on. The example he set was extremely healthy and useful." And Weston Naef, perhaps as a way to minimize Szarkowski's hegemony in the field, posited that Sam "did more to stretch the character of interest in photography than anyone before him."[17]

The public acknowledgment of Sam's success as an arbiter in the field brought him genuine satisfaction, but by that time he was immersed in his new collection of silver. The ICP show, more than anything else, provided evidence that Sam now had a "one foot in and one foot out" relationship to photography. It was in effect a public swan song, which enabled him to move on to his new medium. "One of the things I enjoyed most about beginning to collect photography was that I was starting at zero," he told Loke in the *Times*. "In looking at silver, it's zero all over again."[18]

Nevertheless, the show provided a moment to look back on an achievement of Fitzcarraldian proportion—referring to the 1982 Werner Herzog film about a man, who, against all odds, moves a steamship over a mountain. Sam and the photography collectors with whom he had maintained close alliances had all started at zero and went on to amass collections that warranted acquisition by the likes of the Met and the Getty. These collections had begun as the single-minded pursuits of a small cadre of idiosyncratic individuals who competed with one another, at times colluded with each other, and generally nudged one another further in their mutual quest to define and capture photographic quarry spanning two centuries. That many of these early collectors happened to be gay is a detail of no small significance. Indeed, the sexuality of the collectors and curators who garnered such focus on photography—Sam Wagstaff, John Waddell, Paul Walter, Pierre Apraxine, Howard Gilman, not to mention the dealer George Rinhart (along with the very closeted, indeed married, Harry Lunn)—should not remain a mere footnote in art history.

WE MIGHT BEGIN BY noting once more that the rise of the gay rights movement in the early 1970s occurred simultaneously with the growing interest in photography as an equal among the arts. Indeed, gay men led the public charge for photography in the marketplace with their newly liberated sensibilities and willing gazes. Why didn't they gravitate to some other art form? Imagine what it felt like for Sam, or one of his friends, to be able to hold a picture in his hands and to let his eyes freely breathe in the image. It might have been, stereotypically, a picture of a male nude, or a Civil War battlefield, a ruin on a Greek hillside, a garden of the ancien régime in Paris, a palisade in a Western landscape, or sunlight on a bouquet of flowers at the turn of the last century. For Sam, it was an altogether new way of observing the reality in which he had been living for so long as an outsider (even if he was a privileged outsider). The act of looking at a photograph, itself an object with the taint of illegitimacy in aesthetic terms, took on the thrill of the illicit, becoming further eroticized by the knowledge that one was peering into a private reality. The unique print, the vintage paper, the artist's hand evident in an obsolete process, could be fetishized to the point of titillation.

Barbara Jakobson, who got to know Sam well during his run as a photography collector, was often shown his newest acquisitions, as well as Robert's, Paul Walter's, or Pierre Apraxine's. She saw from the beginning that the art of photography as an object of pursuit was so much more satisfying for these highly aestheticized men than painting. "The erotic component of a photograph is so palpable, whether it is a still life or a portrait, and it's been that way since the invention of the medium," she said. "Maybe that's what impelled collectors like them to go to such lengths."[19] Writing in *Artforum* when Wagstaff was already ten years dead, Bruce Hainley posited this connection between Sam's homosexuality and his passion for photography: "Wagstaff acknowledged collecting as an erotic drive akin to the size queen's," he wrote, adding that Wagstaff's collecting "also revealed the inextricable, if elusive, link between gay desire and the interminable pleasures of the gaze. I'm not sure which of the two came first."[20]

Photography was not alone among the arts, of course, in coaxing or arousing the homosexual imagination. For so many artists who were gay throughout the twentieth century, the crux of what constituted the "gay sensibility" began, promisingly though painfully, with alienation. Perhaps it was the need to create an entire alternate universe on canvas, or on the page, or the stage or in verse or with song that became the twentieth-century homosexual artist's progenitive urge. It proved to be quite a productive one. You remove the homosexual from the equation of culture and the arts and what do you have? "Which came first," quipped Paul Walter. "Culture or the homosexual?"[21]

Sam began his silver-buying spree in late 1984, when he purchased a silver coffeepot for $5000 at Butterfield and Butterfield auction house in San Francisco. Throughout 1985 and well into 1986, he would establish ongoing contact and correspondences with dealers across the country: from Judith Applegate Antiques in Dayville, Connecticut, for example, he bought four serving pieces by Shiebler for $4200; from Edward G. Wilson antiques in Philadelphia he spent $1075 on cutlery; from Carol Thomas in Palm Beach he paid $661.50 for spoons; and from Argentum in San Francisco he splurged on various bowls, a butter dish, napkin rings, and a serving spoon for $11,100.[22]

Before Sam's first silver purchase, however, he went to several auctions to acquaint himself with the field. At one of them, Ronald Hoffman, a Manhattan antique dealer, was bidding on "aesthetic silver," a movement in silver design in the 1870s and '80s that began in England and spread to Europe and the United States, inspired by Japanese art at the beginning of the Arts and Crafts movement in England.[23] "He came up to me, introduced himself, and told me that he liked what I was buying," Hoffman recalled. Sam took Hoffman's card, and two days later appeared at his shop.[24]

From the moment Sam walked through the door of Ronald Hoffman Antiques, he barraged Hoffman with what seemed like a million questions—what Hoffman liked about a particular object, why he bought it, what was it about the form, the workmanship, the pattern, the design. Hoffman would engage Sam in a tutorial about the characteristics that distinguished the pieces by Gorham from those of, say, Reed & Barton, or Meriden, or Shiebler. "He had a strong face, a very nice smile, a nice way about him," Hoffman said. "You immediately liked him. Otherwise, I wouldn't have answered all these questions, because that could drive an antique dealer crazy. But he was so interested in everything. And he would hold the object, fondle it, and you could see his mind thinking. . . . He wouldn't just pick, say, Tiffany."[25]

Sam's expeditions to Ronald Hoffman's antique emporium became a weekly occurrence, and his questions continued. Over time he would purchase thirteen items from Hoffman, including ladles, an ice cream spoon, an olive fork, a baby cup, and a Tiffany tray, spending $22,506 in the shop. After a while, he told Hoffman that if anything new came into his possession that might be of interest, to call right away and he would come by to take a look. While other collectors cared more about the weight of an object or the potential return on the investment, "Sam only notices quality," Hoffman told Nicholas Fox Weber for a 1986 article on Sam's silver collection in *House & Garden*. "If a piece has an odd twist in it that gives it extra zip, he bubbles. When he really loves something, he does a little dance."[26]

While it was true that, with any particular breed of object, the initial spark of attraction for Sam came from its visual qualities, his passion was riveted equally by being the first to recognize its value and, then, to salvage it from obscurity by elevating its importance in society. His homosexuality cannot be divorced from this enterprise; his sensitivity to the arcane or the disregarded was consistent with the impulse to find relief in the unconventional and the unexplored, insight from what had been overlooked, and to invent a parallel universe of symbols and meaning—such as camp, for example—in a society that had for so long rejected his kind. "Sam's passion for silver was an example of his canny collector's instinct for the next underappreciated thing," Barbara Jakobson said. "The beauty of American silver of this period rang a bell for him."[27]

Wagstaff would not be alive, of course, to witness the welter of gay rights decisions in the early part of the twenty-first century that rendered gay discrimination illegal—diminishing the alienation that homosexual men and women had historically felt. It is a question whether the resulting assimilation of gay people into the mainstream will diminish proportionately the aesthetic sensibility that had evolved in homosexual men as a result of their marginalized status across the arc of Wagstaff's own lifetime.

One of the first works of art that Sam bought, for example, was a floral painting by the American artist Charles Demuth, who was gay.[28] Describing Sam's apartment in Hartford in the 1960s, Richard Tuttle remembered "piles and piles of obscure, tantalizing art catalogs and scholarly pamphlets. And there was a great Charles Demuth Sam owned, though he couldn't afford even one."[29] Demuth, a protean stylist who seemed to absorb with skill and originality so many of the art movements of his lifetime, was perhaps best, a watercolorist. One watercolor, entitled *Cabaret Interior with Carl Van Vechten* (c. 1918), depicts a nightclub at the dawn of Prohibition. Like many of his figurative works, it conjures a utopian fantasy of social freedom evident in so much of the cultural output of the twentieth century that reflects the "homosexual aesthetic." Van Vechten, symbolizing the urbane homosexual of an era, converses with a woman at one table; a black man stands with a white man at the bar; a guitarist plays in the center of the scene as two male sailors dance in each other's arms.[30] This painting shows a particular kind of transgressive, yet sophisticated, social milieu in which modern music, lively drinking, serious conversation, racial diversity, and homosexuality are simply the mode, a vision that might well have foreshadowed the back room at Max's Kansas City fifty years later. Van Vechten, around whom the painting revolves, was an artist, photographer, and writer whose work fell short of his success in "pursuit of what might be called the extracurricular activities of modernism: knowing the right people, having the right things, above all being seen at the right places at the right time."[31]

Wagstaff, too, could be said to have partaken of the activities of modernism—knowing the right people, acquiring some very choice things, and finding himself so often in the right places at the right time. This is less a comparison with Van Vechten than a reflection of urban homosexual traits that applied to both of them and that had been absorbed into what constituted the "gay sensibility" throughout the twentieth century. In fact, Wagstaff personified many aspects of the gay sensibility—the decidedly attractive bon vivant, who appreciated fine things, refused to succumb to convention, indulged in his own pleasures, remained unapologetic about his behavior, and regarded art above almost everything else. With photography, Sam managed to become a ringleader for a small and select group of "highly aestheticized" gay men who saw a cultural opening and, like all pioneers, charged through it. By the time they were finished, their photography collections exemplified the "pointing"—in the most poetic Szarkowskian sense—to an entire visual record at its finest of the nineteenth and twentieth centuries, resulting in a seminal treasure of photographic excellence. Not only worth the time and the effort in terms of their handsomely rewarded investments, it was with pleasure as well as their foresight, their connoisseurship, and their regard for a civilized society that they left what was once considered a marginal form safely in the hands of the nation's most august art institutions, where it will be studied and enjoyed and argued over in perpetuity.

IN NEW YORK CITY in the mid-1980s, during the most frightening and painfully incontrovertible scourge on his community of urban homosexual men, Sam seemed to be averting his eyes by turning all his attention to the frothiest of decorative objects, "aesthetic silver." Once again, his new enthusiasm left everyone around him in a state of perplexity. Edmund White took a philosophical view of Sam's obsession with silver at that particular moment in his life, relating it to AIDS and the specter of dying. White drew analogy to a mutual friend, Bruce Chatwin, the bisexual writer, who had said on more than one occasion, perhaps apocryphally, that he contracted the AIDS virus from Sam Wagstaff. Chatwin developed a mania for collecting when he was dying of AIDS. "Bruce was buying so much stuff toward the end of his life that his wife would have to just take it back quietly the next day or they would have been ruined. It was something like an Egyptian urge to pile up goods to see you through into the next world. It was a very pharaonic kind of urge in both cases."[32]

Judy Linn saw it differently. No speculation could negate the sheer pleasure Sam derived from the elaborate and yet subtle detail in the craftsmanship, and also the whimsy—or what was referred to in the marijuana-smoking culture as the playful and consciousness-expanding "mind-fuck"—in the brilliance of design. "Teapots in the shape of spaceships," Linn said. "Ice buckets in the shape of icebergs with polar bears running around on it. Then you realize once you put ice in it there would be frost on the outside."[33]

It seems to be one of the inexplicable anomalies of human nature that those who have something unique to offer to society so often end up as victims of their own attributes. Visionaries have always endured the contempt of others. Artists who respond to their time as if with an instinctive understanding of the future have to endure an angry or indifferent world with patience or bitterness. Wagstaff's friends rolled their eyes over his sudden interest in silver, concluding it was just another delusional obsession. At this point in his life, he didn't much care what other people thought, but the alienation of the homosexual during the twentieth century resulted from just such a lack of understanding, if not blatant scorn. Among those who, in the context of their homosexuality, became victims of their attributes are Charles Demuth, Aaron Copland, Adrienne Rich, Tennessee Williams, George Cukor, James Baldwin (whom Norman Mailer called with veiled homophobia "too charming a writer to be major"),[34] Willa Cather, Langston Hughes, Edward Albee, Andy Warhol—all great figures whose contributions are essential to the cultural legacy of twentieth-century arts and letters, but who were discriminated against, often painfully, for their homosexuality, whether known or intuited.

Although the gay rights movement had made a dent in the wall of discrimination during the previous decade, by 1985 there were more than two thousand reported AIDS cases in New York City, and over one thousand deaths, mostly gay men, including legions of artists, writers, and musicians—the flowers of civilization. A visible pall had fallen on Manhattan's gay world. Young men walked the streets of the West Village looking like ghosts of themselves, emaciated, fragile, their faces sunken, their stares vacant, their gaits halting. Terror, dread, and grief had replaced the celebratory ease with which gay men had so recently manifested such youthful vitality, such collective joie de vivre. Every day another friend or acquaintance tested positive for the virus, or had been diagnosed with Kaposi's sarcoma or *Pneumocytis carinii* pneumonia, the other major opportunistic infection. Who would be next? everyone wondered. There were repeated protests throughout the city, demanding more federal funding of drug trials, more news reporting about the lack of research, and that, ultimately, attention be paid.

Nevertheless, the "gay cancer," now called AIDS, was being publicly thrown back in the faces of those who were ill as confirmation of God's retribution for their perversion. For example, the Southern Baptist televangelist Jerry Falwell: "AIDS is not just God's punishment for homosexuals, it is God's punishment for the society that tolerates homosexuals."[35] William F. Buckley Jr., the most respected intellectual on the right, wrote an op-ed piece in *The New York Times* in which he suggested that "everyone detected with AIDS should be tattooed in the upper forearm, to protect common-needle users, and on the buttocks, to prevent the victimization of other homosexuals."[36] Such public disdain—never mind stigmatization—rang out as an alarming reminder of the registration numbers tattooed on the arms of the people entering the Nazi death camps during the Holocaust.

The parallels between gay life in Berlin in the 1930s and New York in the 1980s cannot be denied. "The excitement that characterized Weimar culture stemmed in part from exuberant creativity and experimentation," writes Peter Gay in *Weimar Culture: The Outsider as Insider*. "But much of it was anxiety, fear, a rising sense of doom."[37]

Christopher Isherwood wrote about the artistically fertile but decadent Weimar culture in *The Berlin Stories* and elsewhere. In 1985 Isherwood was interviewed by Armistead Maupin for *The Village Voice*, and he spoke about the psychic damage wrought by invoking God's will on the people who had been exposed to the AIDS virus. "Fuck God's will," Isherwood said with righteous defiance. "God's will must be circumvented, if that's what it is."[38]

The Normal Heart, a play written by Larry Kramer, the founder of Gay Men's Health Crisis, opened that April in New York. A political screed of operatic intention, the play was a very welcome, badly needed acknowledgement in the cultural arena of rage and fear during an urgent crisis. Although many reviewers did not consider it a great play, they fully embraced its timing, its message, and its depth of feeling. When it opened on the West Coast later that year, the *Los Angeles Times* gave *The Normal Heart* a qualified rave. "It takes an angry man to write an angry play," wrote theater critic Dan Sullivan. He said it wasn't a good play but "it almost doesn't have time to be one, so intent is it on imparting its rage at the Establishment and in inspiring gays in the audience to stop playing victim—and to stop killing themselves."[39]

The Normal Heart played in New York at the Public Theater, not far from Wagstaff's apartment. Whether or not he saw the play, so ubiquitous was the media coverage and so prevalent were conversations about it in gay circles that it was clear the disease was getting much closer. In fact, it was during the run of this drama that Jim Nelson got sick and was diagnosed with an opportunistic infection from the AIDS virus.

Perhaps Sam found glimmers of comfort in the surface of silver, but by then he could no longer deny that the disease was something even he had to contend with. The next month, in May 1985, Sam bought a house on Fire Island, in Oakleyville, for which he paid the inflated price of $300,000. The house was near those of his old friends Jim Elliott and Sam Green, and he and Jim Nelson would spend most of the summer there. It was small, bare-bones, nothing much more than a beach shack with a rudimentary kitchen and bathroom. The roof leaked and the only area for lounging was a small screened-in porch surrounded by stalks of sea grasses and the natural shrubbery of the forest. While it suited Sam's monastic tendencies, Jim, who had grown quite accustomed to the creature comforts of a penthouse at One Fifth Avenue, took it upon himself to make the place more livable, hanging curtains, buying linens and proper kitchenware, and tending his garden of roses.

Sam was never comfortable talking about the AIDS epidemic, but Robert was in a state of obdurate denial. When Fran Lebowitz warned him about the danger he was putting himself in, her appeal fell on deaf ears. She had seen firsthand the kind of sexual behavior that took place in the bars frequented by Robert and others. Lebowitz was a very close friend of Peter Hujar, with whom she had once ventured late one evening to the Eagle's Nest, a leather bar along the West Street circuit. "I remember watching a man put his foot, wearing a boot, up another guy, and I turned to Peter right before I left, and said, 'This is not about sex, this is about death.' "[40]

Steven Aronson, who had known Robert since 1970, was also incredulous when, leaving a lunch party at Kenneth Jay Lane's apartment in 1985, Robert mused, "Gee, this AIDS stuff is pretty scary. I hope I don't get it." Of anyone in New York, Aronson thought, Robert was the likeliest to become infected.[41] Still, according to Mapplethorpe's biographer Patricia Morrisroe, when the socially ubiquitous Suzie Frankfurt urged Robert to pay attention to the health hazards of his sexual behavior, his response was delusional: "I'm not in a high-risk group," he said.[42] Everyone around him knew that Robert was gambling with his life. He might have privately understood the danger of his unrelenting sexual behavior in the very epicenter of the "gay plague," but he neither acknowledged it to anyone else nor curtailed his nocturnal habits.

By then Robert knew a great many accomplished people and could be seen at the most stylish places, often going to dinner at Mr. Chow on East 57th Street, the current preferred restaurant for the art world and—with its high ceilings, multiple levels, and cream-lacquered walls—arguably the most beautiful modern room in which to dine in Manhattan. A lively mix of gay and straight art stars congregated there. A group portrait taken at Mr. Chow by Michael Halsband is a telling "moveable feast" of mid-1980s New York: Julian Schnabel, Andy Warhol, David Hockney, Jean-Michel Basquiat, Keith Haring, Kenny Scharf, Francesco Clemente, Sandro Chia, Will Wegman, Tony Shafrazi, and Robert Mapplethorpe, among others. Mapplethorpe, in an interview conducted that year for a Spanish television documentary about him, made an observation so aphoristically true that it is uncanny how little he seemed to apply the lesson to his own activities: "The most important thing about being an artist is to learn about yourself. People today are more obsessed about being an artist then learning about oneself through one's art."[43]

Sam and Robert's relationship remained exceptionally close. "I'm looking for someone to spoil," Sam had said in 1972 just before they met, and certainly in many ways Sam had succeeded all too well in spoiling Robert. Now, once again, perhaps anticipating his own fate and Robert's too, Sam, flush with the resources of his Getty sale, indulged Robert with some choice real estate: He purchased for him a new loft on West 23rd Street for $500,000; Robert quickly turned it into a showcase for his Stickley furniture and his collection of decorative glass, enough to warrant a feature on his new home in *House & Garden*.[44]

Mapplethorpe's name was in the papers regularly and, as if addicted to the public recognition, he seemed eager to perpetuate his fame. Perhaps it was proportional to the dread of a disease that was spread through sex—the very activity that gave him such pleasure and life sustenance. His growing fame distracted him from his terror of dying. Of course, Robert had always had his eye on celebrity, as early as when he and Patti Smith first arrived in Manhattan. It would take a very secure person like Sam not to be seduced by the halo of worship surrounding Warhol and the countless ways the waters came almost magically to part for him—respect, adulation, access to social position as a result of his work as an artist. What an indelible imprint it must have made on the young Mapplethorpe.

Consciously or not, Robert felt like a victim of his humble background as he traversed the most sophisticated precincts of the high-culture world of the Reagan 1980s and the new ostentation promulgated, on the one hand, by the Adolfo-red First Lady and, on the other hand, by the artistic demimonde where the devastating encroachment of AIDS set off its own Weimar-like manic exuberance. There was, there had always been, an insecurity that tangled with his confidence or ambition and turned it, for many who had known him, into something ugly. Now there was also something else—the threat, if not imminence, of a death sentence. Raging against the terrifying specter of the AIDS virus, his behavior became ever more selfish and very harsh.

In May 1985, Mapplethorpe had a show at Jeffrey Fraenkel Gallery in San Francisco. By now he was taking his many exhibitions in stride, but Fraenkel had gone out of his way—even stretching his means—to make it a splashy occasion, throwing an opening night party for Robert at Club 181. For San Francisco, it was a sensational event, and Robert, who had always been drawn to the city, came and enjoyed himself. "The gallery was six years old, and we spent more money on that party than we ever had before," Jeffrey Fraenkel recalled. "It was a big deal for a young gallery." Yet afterward there was no acknowledgment from Robert whatsoever, "no thanks for the show or the party."[45]

"THE NEXT TIME YOU come to the big city I'll show you some exciting silver," Sam wrote to Anne MacDonald in October 1985, by now in the throes of his new obsession. "I thought I was collecting early, classic Paul Revere–type things till I found that was a bore, like spending big bucks for Rembrandt, and I discovered the really special, beautiful, strange, bizarre things made in the second half of the 19th century— Japanesey, Chinesey, Etruscan, Aztec, Russian—very gutsy and not at all 'grandma' as Robert pretends with his love for shmoo-shaped 50s [glass], the art deco for the collectors of the '80s."[46]

Silver objects were occupying more floor space in Sam's apartment than all the furniture combined. Visiting one day, John Waddell was shocked by how all-encompassing the new passion had become, as if Sam was now a hoarder of all things silver. There were silver objects on every surface. "You literally couldn't walk from one side of the room to the other, the path was so narrow," Waddell said.[47]

Swept into Sam's enthusiasm for the individual objects, and perhaps ambushed, his guests would have to endure his discourse on the designer of a silver ice cream spoon with a bowl fashioned into the shape of a smooth maple leaf, its handle made from intertwining stems that resulted in a folded leaf with a tiny beetle on it. He might point out the remarkably detailed lobsters in relief on the handles of his Wendt salad servers. If detractors called the pieces ridiculous, he simply didn't care. These were examples of the aesthetic movement in silver, and Sam would put forward his own delighted, if ironic view of the object as the epitome of camp. When the objects are out of fashion, "it helps you espouse the cause with more determination," Sam told Nicholas Fox Weber. "I don't collect things for any other reason than to please myself," is how he characterized it.[48]

Sam had invited Waddell over that day to make a gesture of friendship. Some years earlier Sam had shown Waddell a picture by Martin Munkacsi called *Liberia* (1931), made when the Hungarian photographer had been on assignment for *Berliner Illustrirte Zeitung*. Waddell was known among art dealers and curators to remain poker-faced when being shown any object or group of photographs. However, when he saw Sam's Munkacsi, a photograph of three African boys running naked into the foamy surf, he blurted out, "This picture is music." It was said to be Cartier-Bresson's favorite picture. "I held it out from the collection for you and I want you to have it," Sam now said, offering it to John as a gift. Then, parsimonious to a fault, he added, "I am only going to charge you what I paid for it."[49]

It was classic Sam, a gesture so affectionate and thoughtful, grounded in his respect for his friend's collection and astute in his sensitivity to the emotion Waddell had allowed in an unguarded moment when first viewing the picture. But he could not bring himself simply to offer the gift without attaching a final set of strings before being released from photography permanently. Indeed, Waddell bought this "gift" from Sam. (Today the picture resides in the Ford Motor Company Collection at the Metropolitan Museum of Art.)

Nevertheless, Sam's tightfistedness had not stopped him from giving Robert $500,000 that year for the new loft. Or, when Jim got sick, spending $300,000 on the house in Oakleyville, where he could spend time convalescing, even if the house was as much a refuge for Sam and his own portentous future as it was for Jim. Like so many gay men at the time, with an AIDS test looming in the near future, Sam lived with a vague sense of the time bomb that might be ticking away inside him.

Fending off the disease, at least symbolically, with gifts of hearth and home for those closest to him was as much a salve as a manifestation of love. And perhaps offering John Waddell a token of respect and friendship with his gesture—regardless of the drop of blood he was compelled to extract in the process—was another symbol of closure on his affair with photography.

In fact, with photography now a vestige of his past, silver collecting became the most urgent of emotional lifelines. Because he had garnered such enormous respect for his prescience, his first-class collection, and his tireless advocacy of photography's significance in art history, one would think he had earned enough credibility from his insight, if not foresight, that his focus on silver would be followed with curiosity. It is not surprising, however, given the vagaries of the art world, that once again people thought that the formidable Sam Wagstaff had lost his marbles. Why would someone so high-minded turn to something so trivial, and ostentatious, as a decorative silver object—never mind spend $65,000 on a single Chinese silver teapot from Shrubsole, Inc., among his first purchases?

A set of tall nineteenth-century silver beakers had been in his family since the days when the Wagstaffs owned a farm in Central Park, and Sam treasured them, boyishly bringing them out for any occasion. "He would serve us champagne in them at all times of the day if something wonderful happened," Anne Ehrenkranz recalled. It was her impression that these beakers had provided the initial impetus for Sam to start collecting silver: "He always associated silver with his family's patrician heritage."[50]

Early on Sam had become enamored of the silver displayed in his childhood home, which would be incorporated into Olga and Peter's dinner parties. He often mentioned to friends that as a child he looked forward to visiting playmates for the sole purpose of ogling the silver in their homes.[51] "If you were born into the world of Edith Wharton and were cultivated by anachronistic characters like Chick Austin [once director of the Wadsworth Atheneum] and you frequented houses that were the last word in style," Barbara Jakobson mused, "deciding to collect silver was not a stretch."[52]

At sixty-four, Sam's life seemed to have come full circle, to the point when halcyon memories can reveal—Proust-like—the arc of one's lifetime almost whole. To some, incongruously, the lover of Mapplethorpe was gravitating back to the "fancy pants" aspects of his life that he had condemned for so long. Having established his identity at a safe distance from the *Social Register*, he could now come out of the closet as a patrician and collect silver if he wanted, and it would not seem predictable at all. Even more amusing for him was the all-too-ironic fact that the particular silver he commenced collecting was now frowned upon by proper members of society as gaudy and déclassé.

The middle-aged man who had once sat half naked at Woodstock with hippies, smoking weed and staring for hours at a tree, now was assiduously polishing silver in his penthouse on lower Fifth Avenue. Klaus Kertess remembered coming to see Sam and finding him with a silver candlestick in his hands. "He was rubbing it with his fingers and explaining you can clean silver with your thumbs. And he was smiling, and he was so happy to have this physical contact with his silver. And there aren't many people whose lives are that visceral with their art. For Sam it was a visceral experience."[53] Richard Tuttle understood that, for Sam, the silver was something yet again to examine closely, well beyond the glimmering surfaces. "Silver is not silver just because it's silver," Tuttle said. For Sam it was about art. "One of the important things is that it's polished, and there are very few people who know how to polish silver in the world. . . . Sam was one of the finest, taught himself to be one of the finest silver polishers."[54]

John Richardson, the British-turned-American art historian, was not exactly scandalized by Sam's turn to silver, but seemed dismissive. "Sam got so interested in early-twentieth-century silver, which I found the most boring thing in the world," he said. "American silver seems to have no quality to it."[55]

Despite the naysayers and the members of his circle who were flummoxed by the obsession, silver gave him a new hunting ground. As he had done with photography a decade earlier, he could haunt obscure little antique shops, go to auctions, and cultivate rare dealers in Manhattan and out of town. He could, as he had amply demonstrated in the past, bargain. And he could get better at recognizing the pieces that had for so long been overlooked and undervalued, as if mining them from the graveyard of history, dusting them off and showing a skeptical world that all along little treasures of civilization itself had been secreted through in plain sight.

Wagstaff's infatuation with and immersion in silver annoyed Robert, especially Sam's disquisitions on all the details about the metalwork on some art nouveau centerpiece or the elaborate flourishes on the handle of a teapot. Robert could not ignore Sam's excitement over his latest acquisitions when he proudly showed his visitors, lecturing them on the significance of each one in the history of silver production in the United States. He was delighted to elaborate on an object's function with the harmonies of ornamentation, and proportion, and the quality of the silver. Dimitri Levas remembered sitting with Sam at lunch at One Fifth when, as if he were a magician, he suddenly pulled a recently purchased silver spoon out of his jacket pocket, just waiting for the perfect moment to share this latest acquisition.[56]

Function was fundamental to silverware producers in America in the late nineteenth century, but the achievement of beauty was essential to the refinement these craftsmen aspired to. Ornamentation was heavily influenced by motifs from other cultures. The industry, mostly situated in the Northeast and consisting of a handful of major companies, positioned silver in a tradition of high art. In promotional materials, the industry was often unabashed in its elevation of silver ornamentation to the realm of Cellini, in particular, the great mannerist artist of the sixteenth century also known for his metalwork in gold.[57]

In contrast to photographs, which Sam helped to elevate in a Herculean endeavor to high art, silver posed an altogether different challenge. He took it upon himself to revivify a once highly regarded form that had fallen into neglect in the late twentieth century. *International Review* in New York had published an article in 1878 entitled "Silver in Art," which compared American silverwork to sixteenth-century Italian:

From the days of restless Benvenuto Cellini until now, no process of presenting designs in metals has been so much esteemed as the repoussé, as the reason is manifest, for none is so clearly the work of man's mind and hand. The artist chaser can send into the pliant metal his very thought, and by the cunning of his hand render it palpable forever. The extreme ductility of silver renders it highly susceptible to treatment by the repoussé process, and it is possible to produce the most delicately finished and expressive repoussé pictures.[58]

Catherine Kurland, a Manhattan dealer who specialized in nineteenth- and twentieth-century decorative arts, observed Sam's extraordinary feeling for quality, citing his purchase of an "aesthetic silver" piece, a Tiffany water pitcher from 1893,[59] described as "baluster-shaped, with a stylized leaf handle, the body in the form of a cluster of deeply repoussé and chased spider chrysanthemums and leaves."[60] Kurland told Nicholas Fox Weber in 1987 that, when Wagstaff first saw it, he couldn't keep his hands off of it. "He fondled it lovingly, as he often does, while comparing it to vermicelli."[61] Echoing a description of Sam by Ann Horton of Sotheby's a decade before, Kurland said that he looked for pieces that were "unusual, exuberant, exotic, and original. He has a truly personal eye. He listens and takes in information, but ultimately it's his decision. Unlike so many collectors, he has confidence—without arrogance."[62]

His collecting then took on a familiar pattern, imprinted in him almost since his youth. Nicholas Fox Weber, while writing about antiques for *House & Garden*, described Sam as a silver collector who "does not seek works of one given movement or era. Nor does he try to round out his collection, fill gaps, or carefully include all the well-known designers or makers." His focus was on gothic and "bright cut" pieces from the 1850s, aesthetic movement objects from the 1870s and '80s and the Arts and Crafts designs that prevailed between 1890 and 1925. "He reveres (the verb is particularly appropriate) a rather traditional pitcher made in Boston circa 1810 and rhapsodizes over a severely modern sugar and cream set from the 1930s," Fox Weber wrote. "On the other hand, he has 'hated Jensen ever since childhood': his taste is his own."[63]

With his own descriptions of the decorative objects he liked and collected ranging from "important" to "bizarre" to "gutsy," silver had never had such an eloquent, sophisticated, and enthusiastic champion as Sam Wagstaff. But perhaps it was another quality of silver—its pure reflectiveness, when skillfully rubbed and polished—that attracted him at a more sensory level. "Mirrors have always existed," Sam had once said, going on to praise the Mayans' volcanic glass and the bronze of the Romans, Chinese, and Egyptians. If only one mirror existed in the world, he believed people from all over would make pilgrimages for a chance to see themselves reflected in it.[64] In silver, Sam may have been seeking nothing less than a perfectly American mirror in which to see himself and his entire life reflected back to him with a sparkling kind of radiance—not only a nostalgia for the luxe pleasures of his youth but perhaps the fading memory and perpetual enigma of his own physical beauty.

G A R D E N I A S,
F R A G R A N T,
F L O A T I N G

My blood and my semen are poison to my species.

—ROBIN HARDY[1]

AS A COLLECTOR IN THE LAST FEW YEARS OF HIS LIFE, Sam had eyes only for silver, but his love for his cats had never wavered. Now he was ready to draft the feline species into a bit of art world mischief. For years he had harbored the idea of organizing an exhibition of photographs of cats. It pleased him to think of shocking those humorless art aficionados with the cliché-addled cat as a subject to be taken seriously. Sam had a willing conspirator in his good friend Ingrid Sischy, then the editor of *Artforum*, who agreed to publish a picture essay on a selection of Sam's cat photographs. Founded in the 1960s as a laboratory of intellectual ponderings about contemporary art, throughout the '70s *Artforum* became home to increasingly abstract writing. Sischy was not yet thirty when, in 1980, she was named editor of the magazine. At *Artforum* she contended with the parallel, if dueling, forces of neo-expressionism and postmodernism admirably enough to warrant a New Yorker profile: "A Girl of the Zeitgeist," written by Janet Malcolm, appeared in late 1986. Earlier that year she had fulfilled Sam's long-standing wish: "I'm so excited about opening the season with your kitty cats," Sischy wrote in an official letter of assignment on *Artforum* stationery that June. "It will be the most beautiful, cuddly, ferocious spread in magazine history." She urged Sam to select the pictures he wanted to use and she would hand them off to the art director. She signed the letter with the sincere affection of a dear friend: "All my love and joy, Ingrid."[2]

Despite the intellectual weight of her position, Sischy, too, was not shy of controversy. Less than two years after becoming editor of the magazine, she had shaken up her audience with a February 1982 cover story about the fashion designer Issey Miyake in which couture was presented as a serious medium in the realm of high art. Now, though, she may have been indulging Sam's whim out of an abiding fondness. By this time, she was all too aware that Sam was sick.

Early that summer of 1986, complaining of chest pains and shortness of breath, Sam was rushed to St. Vincent's Hospital, where he was diagnosed with tuberculosis. St. Vincent's, in the heart of Greenwich Village, had the highest numbers of AIDS patients in the city. The doctors knew perfectly well that the appearance of tuberculosis in a man like Wagstaff, who was gay and had the means to live well enough to maintain his health, indicated an opportunistic infection from the erosion of the immune system—the first visible stage of the AIDS virus. As a matter of protocol they would have tested his blood for the virus and informed him that he had AIDS. Nevertheless Sam explained his cough to friends as nothing more than a mild case of tuberculosis.[3]

It was now five years after the first reports in the papers about the contagious "gay cancer," and the general population was in a state of protracted terror about the disease. In New York and San Francisco, where the largest number of cases had been reported, the stigma of AIDS was compounded for those diagnosed with the illness: not only did they suffer from the resulting opportunistic infections and the knowledge that there was no cure, they had to contend with the sometimes hysterical fears of exposure in the friends and relatives who genuinely cared for them. In fact, the American population had been devastated by fear of the "gay plague," a terror further abetted by media coverage that vilified homosexuals and held them accountable for their fate. "The disease itself was as frightening as anything known to twentieth-century man," Charles Kaiser would later write about AIDS in its first decade. "If it didn't kill you within weeks with a particular virulent strain of pneumonia, it would cover your entire body with sores, sometimes blind you, addle your brain, and force you into diapers with violent diarrhea."[4]

Some gay men who had tested negative for the virus distanced themselves from those who were sick. Many heterosexual men and women not even remotely in the path of potential exposure kept their distance from gay people in general. The madness of people like William F. Buckley suggesting draconian solutions like tattooing those who had been diagnosed, only further stoked an already insidious homophobia. Those suffering with the disease were afraid to reveal their condition, left even further alienated from those who might have been capable of providing comfort or care.

Adding to the climate of homophobia was the Supreme Court decision *Bowers v. Hardwick* in June 1986. Michael Hardwick had been arrested in the privacy of his own Atlanta bedroom while performing fellatio on a sexual partner. He contested his arrest, challenging the Georgia sodomy laws all the way up to the Supreme Court. The Court upheld the laws, issuing a stinging defeat to the civil rights of an entire gay population (this decision was reversed in *Lawrence v. Texas* in 2003).

Political cartoonist Tom Toles captured the prevailing public sentiment even as he lambasted it in an acerbic cartoon syndicated to newspapers around the country. In it, a reporter conducts a man-on-the-street interview, asking: "What do you think about AIDS?" The caption: "It affects homosexual men, drug users, Haitians and hemophiliacs," replies his interviewee. "Thank goodness it hasn't spread to human beings yet."[5]

Both now diagnosed with the AIDS virus, Sam Wagstaff and Jim Nelson would spend most of the summer of 1986 in Oakleyville. Sam's rustic cabin had more of the air of a sleepaway camp than a comfortable beachside home, but it was quiet and peaceful: the clean air, ocean breezes, and tall beach grasses were as close to a natural balm as both men might have hoped to find. Sam was free from social obligations and he talked regularly about fixing up the house, building a deck around the entire perimeter to open up the view to the bay.

Steve Wachlin was there in the summer of 1986. He had grown up in Sayville, across the bay from Fire Island, and spent many a summer in Oakleyville. His grandmother was an Oakley, and his parents, whose cottage was just down the path, took care of the Wagstaff house, which Wachlin now owns. "Sam was very thin," Wachlin recalled. "He was coughing every night, all night long, although he never said anything to anyone about AIDS." Yet because it was such a small community everyone could hear his persistent coughing. They could also see he was losing weight.[6]

Of course, anyone that summer in the Fire Island gay communities of the Pines and Cherry Grove—as well as in Oakleyville, where gay residents such as Peter Hujar had also been diagnosed with AIDS— would have recognized the familiar signs of the disease. Jim, who had been diagnosed the year before, was asymptomatic throughout the summer and had the stamina to take care of Sam. With his worshipful kind of love, Jim never seemed to grow impatient. "Jim and Sam were always together, lying out on the hammock or sitting in the two chairs side by side on the screened-in porch," Wachlin said. "Jim was just the nicest person, always had time for everyone. He would talk to all of us." But Sam was beginning to withdraw. "Sam would just sit on the porch and stare," Wachlin said.[7]

A family named the Grieks lived in a house nearby. Even in the poor soil composed mostly of mineral sand with residual garnet and magnetite, Ency Griek was able to grow a colorful array of flowers. She was generous in offering tips to Jim, who was eager to cultivate a garden that summer. She knew Sam loved flowers, too, and once stopped by to give him one from her garden. When she left, Sam, irritable from being sick, looked at the flower in his hand and snarled under his breath, "Beware of Greeks bearing gifts."[8] Perhaps he was being ungrateful, yet it was with bitter wit that he turned an aphorism from *The Aeneid* about the

Trojan horse at Troy into his own declaration of despondency. Harbingers of death seemed to be closing in on him.

That spring, a meltdown of the Chernobyl nuclear power plant had caused catastrophic levels of radiation to spread across much of the Soviet Union and westward into Europe. Concerns were mounting that the crops would be exposed to the radiation. News coverage of Chernobyl continued to dominate American papers that summer, reporting on the aftereffects of the nuclear accident. In early May the *Times* reported, "Death within weeks or months for people exposed to the heaviest doses of radiation at Chernobyl was predicted by public health specialists in Sweden and Italy."[9] By the sixteenth, six people had died from radiation and burns, and by June 3, the death toll was up to twenty-five. While the world watched anxiously as the tally of deaths rose exponentially, much closer to home the gay community watched the numbers of deaths rise from the "gay cancer." By contrast, the news coverage of AIDS was scant.

Everyone with AIDS who suffered from the opportunistic infections of a suppressed immune system—the persistent coughing, the loss of energy, the nausea, diarrhea, the night sweats, the purple marks on the skin from Kaposi's sarcoma—feared that their condition would only get worse and that the pain, discomfort, and humiliation would never go away. A good day when the discomfort subsided was met with gratitude and trepidation, the return of any symptom with abandoned hope. Sam's irritability and bitterness seemed an appropriate reaction to his hideous condition.

Only a swath of sea grasses separated the house from the ocean. The sea provided a little solace, the consistent rhythms of the waves in the vast expanse of water, as if washing away the daily preoccupations of man on earth, and of his own in the midst of the inevitable. Sam would walk along the beach at dawn and watch the sun-tipped waves as if like golden flames. It still was his habit to search the sand for little nail heads that had washed ashore from the sunken merchant ships of the nineteenth century.

Not surprisingly, Sam had brought his cats to the beach house that summer, and his primary escape was the delight he took in working on his cats essay. No doubt he found inspiration by observing Teenangel and Manny in the wild of that natural habitat, cats doing what they do—watching, hallucinating, stalking, being. Like so many other cat lovers, Sam was not above anthropomorphizing his pets. Having always felt an affinity, he appreciated their improvisational state of being-here-now, the intensity of their focus, their purity of spirit, their almost psychedelic and mystical consciousness.

He and Ingrid Sischy settled on pictures by Munkacsi, Paul Outerbridge, Tony Mendoza, and, of course, Mapplethorpe—one of the few pictures of cats Robert had ever taken. The six-page feature on cats ran in the September issue of *Artforum*, an intellectual risk for the magazine and a kiss from Ingrid to Sam, blown across the art world ethos of detachment. The comical cover photograph showed two cats standing upright, anthropomorphically blasé, beside a miniature toilet. Both cats are dressed in black suits with gold buttons, one of them holding a cigarette to its lips; several cigarette butts litter the floor all around them. It was hardly the sweet and cuddly image of typical domestic feline repose. In fact, the picture was diligently conceptual and held the cover of *Artforum* respectably; it was from a series entitled *Perlorian Cats* (1982), with credit given to Satoru Tsuda for the scenarios and Toshi Wakita for the photographs.

The feature, "Tiger in the House," by Sam Wagstaff, had the cutline, " 'Let dogma eat dogma,' say a few smart cats. Aren't we good enough to join fine photography, too?"[10] Sam's blithe one-page essay was not without intent. He opens with a reference to Jean Paulhan, the esteemed French literary critic, and bolsters his case for the subject of the cat as something above cliché—noble, pure, misunderstood. "The problem is that cats come to us trailing a series of prejudices (ours, not theirs)," Sam wrote. "There are no bad cats, just bad cat photographers. Rightly, perhaps, but unfortunately, this has set good pictures of cats—carefully and intelligently observed cats, cats, shall we say, of exemplary catness—within the same taboo. I believe there are great overlooked pictures, some of which can be seen here, where cats are allowed to exercise their catness." He ends with something of a one-line joke, citing a question the art dealer Betty Parsons used to ask friends: "What's the difference between cats and dogs?" The answer: "Cats aren't afraid for their job."[11]

He may have felt compelled to represent the plight of cats in photography as an underappreciated genre, yet he derived gleeful pleasure from taunting an art world that took itself so seriously with a subject thought to be so clichéd, in a publication they considered a kind of bible. He wanted to show them they were wrong while getting something of the last laugh.

IT HAD TAKEN THE shocking revelation of a movie star's illness from the AIDS virus the previous summer to finally get the attention of the President of the United States. Rock Hudson announced he was sick in July 1985, three months before he died. Hudson was an old Hollywood friend of Ronald and Nancy Reagan, and his illness forced them to acknowledge the disease, although the President himself still remained silent. Hudson's death would destigmatize the disease, in a manner of speaking, softening not only the President's views but forcing the American populace to reconsider its own harsh attitudes. Nonetheless, it would not be until June 1987, almost two years after Hudson's death, that Reagan would deliver his first official speech about the AIDS epidemic. "This is a battle against disease, not against our fellow Americans," he said.[12]

Robert Mapplethorpe was officially diagnosed with AIDS in September 1986. He had been experiencing chills, swollen glands, bouts of diarrhea for weeks before finally submitting to Dimitri Levas's entreaties to go to the hospital. The tests confirmed what he, and those around him, had suspected. Meanwhile, Sam Wagstaff had still not acknowledged the disease to his friends, but he was fully cognizant of his own condition. Jim's health had wavered, too, during the summer, and now Robert, his "little Wumpers," had been diagnosed. AIDS was very much a death sentence in 1986 and enough of a taboo subject that the name alone seemed contagious. It is worth repeating that people with AIDS were still being made to feel like lepers; now all three men were soldiers in a single foxhole, slowly going down from the stealth enemy within.

Five years into the epidemic, the medical establishment was still uncertain about how much and what type of physical contact was required for transmission of the virus. Treatments, including AZT, which had just been introduced, were in such experimental stages that they could not be relied on, despite the willingness by most patients with the disease to try anything. The level of desperation brought about a rigor of its own as those who were ill—as well as those who feared exposure—took it upon themselves to pursue any possible treatment, whether homeopathic, experimental, or mystical. For example, people were eating entire diets of seaweed or raw garlic.

Friends, lovers, and family members were at once heartbroken and terrified. Feeling helpless, they watched in real time as the life visibly drained from their loved ones. Sam succumbed to the usual pattern: the hacking cough; the loss of weight; the slowed-down gait; the empty gaze; features that hollowed out as his skin slowly conformed to the skeletal shape of his face.

In the fall, Sam was again hospitalized. Visitors came and went, including Jane Smith and John Waddell. "They tell me I have tuberculosis" is how Sam continued to explain his hospitalization to Waddell, still not comfortable acknowledging the underlying disease.[13] In her prescient 1978 book, *Illness as Metaphor*, Susan Sontag compares attitudes about tuberculosis in the nineteenth century with cancer in the twentieth century, and challenges the accusation that repressed passion causes the disease. This, she argues, is how the victim is blamed: "With the modern disease (once TB, now cancer), the romantic idea that the disease expresses the character is invariably extended to assert that the character causes the disease—because it has not expressed itself," she writes. "Passion moves inward, striking and blighting the deepest cellular recesses."[14] For Sam, tuberculosis may have been a euphemism for the romanticized illness of the bohemian artist in the nineteenth century, but there was nothing romantic or appealing about the slow withering away of the life force evident in everyone who suffered from AIDS. "But that was his party line," Waddell said.[15]

Medical treatment was still a guessing game. While experimental drug trials were underway, there was not enough support on the government level to fund all of them or to expedite approval for the promising ones. In October, Anne Ehrenkranz sent a check for $500 to Cornell Medical Center at New York Hospital,[16] a meaningful gesture of hope from a caring friend, but hardly enough at a time when major federal funds were required to increase the studies and the trial. Sam's decline proceeded throughout the fall.

Living in Detroit with her husband and children, Patti Smith was made aware that Robert had been hospitalized. After a seven-year silence, she finally worked up the courage to call Sam, who was home from the hospital at that point, to ask how Robert was doing. "He's doing better than I am," he replied, finally acknowledging that what he had—and what they had—was AIDS. "I've got it, Jim's got it, everybody's got it."[17]

Even back in the hospital, however, Sam could not stop thinking about his silver. It made him genuinely happy. It had become his obsession, a kind of disease of its own that permeated Sam's emotional life and rational mind in the same way that the virus had invaded the cells of his body. As he had his entire life, Sam fell in love with an idea for which the object, replaceable over time, provided visual, palpable representation and, ultimately, pleasure. The pleasure was genuine but, again, serial, perhaps the result of a lifetime of shame that began with his inappropriate feelings for other boys and a longing for the consistent warmth and love from his mother, who had so often become more an idea than a presence throughout his childhood. After the collections of regional art, the drawings, and the photographs, perhaps the silver was closer to home.

Since the beginning of the year Sam had been buying silver compulsively, barely making the time to unpack an object before going out and buying something else. "He was like that with anything he collected—totally obsessed," Robert told a reporter. "With the photographs, every day he had another one to show me." At least Robert understood and valued the allure of the photograph, but "he lost me with the silver," he said. Jim Nelson concurred that silver was the top for Sam. "He always told me he'd know he had really made it when he felt ready for the silver."[18]

In Sam's photography-collecting days, John Waddell remembered his saying that he was going to have to "clip some coupons" to come up with the cash for the latest acquisition.[19] Sam's euphemism referred to interest income coupons issued for a type of bond in his financial portfolio; he could trade the coupons for cash in order to buy new work. Now, the furious pace of his pursuit of silver objects was making coupon-clipping ever more necessary. He decided to divest himself of a few remaining photographs, consigning them to Howard Read at Robert Miller Gallery. Among them were a choice F. Holland Day *Nude* (1907), for $27,500; Paul Outerbridge's *Shower for Mademoiselle* (circa 1937), for $15,000; and a Hans Bellmer study (c. 1940), for $4500; The gallery gave him an advance of $15,000 against the sale—funds he immediately put to use for new silver purchases. Replacing his love of photography with silver, he was trading in the old objects for new ones.

That fall, Ron Hoffman called Sam in the hospital to tell him about a match safe he had just acquired. Match safes, which predated the matchbook, were a necessity in the nineteenth century. People always needed matches before the advent of electricity, and these small portable boxes were used to hold matches and strike them. Hoffman's match safe was silver and gold, with other mixed metals, and it came in its own leather case. He told Sam he would put it on reserve for him to come take a look when he got out, but Sam was so excited by the description that he begged Hoffman to bring it to the hospital. Hoffman paid a visit. "He sat there in the bed, and he was so sick," he recalled. "And he just fondled this little piece. He asked if I could leave it there so he could play with it. I was worried one of the nurses would steal it, but he asked me again and I left it with him."[20] Perhaps fearing that this might be the last time he would experience the euphoria of infatuation, Sam bought it for $4300.

"Silver was something he felt was underappreciated," Paul Walter said about Sam. "And then once he got going, every time you'd see him, he'd lecture you on it. If you weren't appreciative enough on why it was so great, he would get all worked up. He was very passionate about it. Look at this! he'd say. Look at this!"[21]

When there was a new history to mine and a new species of object to contemplate, it had always given Sam free rein to exercise his immanent creativity, seeing the glint of beauty, relevance, or meaning beneath the grime of the culturally discarded, and introducing it to his friends and to the public. "All the little-bit things that were marginal, which then economically one could have access to, those things underappreciated in the culture that are important parts of our history," is how Kiki Smith described what she had seen Sam doing with one object or another, and one collection after another, ever since she was a child.[22] With old silver, especially, there was not only so much grime to remove but also so many intricate details and patterns hidden underneath. Sadly, there was no human equivalent for a wraithlike body riddled with disease, no magic to restore within.

Sam was home only for short stretches, between stints in the hospital. One day Daniel Wolf paid a visit to Sam at One Fifth Avenue. Like Pierre Apraxine, Daniel was struck by the very white walls of the apartment and the brilliant reflections on the silver objects that filled the space. Sam—now rail thin, his face etched with deep lines and so gaunt you could see the skeletal structure—sat precariously on the couch with Jim. The room had become a hoarder's paradise, gleaming silver in every shape of domestic service and covering almost every inch of the floor. "He was very frail," Wolf said, "but he would pick a piece up and study it and say, 'Look at this form, this detail, the shape,' just as he would with a photograph. Sam and passion were always the same thing, even at the end. No middle ground."[23]

Moved by Sam's delicate regard for the objects in the final fragile stages of his physical decline and increasingly distraught, Wolf contacted Maria Morris Hambourg, chief curator of photography at the Met, and set up a fund in Sam Wagstaff's name for the museum to acquire photographs.

Peter Coffeen was a young photography collector Sam had met in the mid-1970s at Robert Schoelkopf Gallery when they were both just starting to collect photographs. Over the years Coffeen would see Sam occasionally, and he had facilitated Sam's appearance on *The Dick Cavett Show* in 1980. In late 1986, Coffeen ran into Sam while walking in Greenwich Village. He had heard that Sam might be sick, and now here the man was a ghost of the formidable vitality, a wisp of his former self, resting on a cane, taking his steps slowly. "I've heard some rumors, Sam," he said. "I want to ask you, are you ill or not?" With resignation more than bitterness, Sam nodded. "Sad to say, I am."[24]

Meanwhile, Anne Ehrenkranz, Sam's research assistant and archivist, led an almost paradoxically bifurcated life. She kept an eye on Sam's health while maintaining domestic order and basic hygiene in the apartment. Leaving One Fifth Avenue every day, she had her other, more established existence. As wife and mother in a spacious apartment on the Upper East Side, Anne had a luxurious life, where servants did the tasks that she had deputized herself to do at Sam's. The Ehrenkranzes were philanthropically active, giving money to any number of institutions, among them the New-York Historical Society, where Ehrenkranz had recently become a board member. She proceeded to interest James Bell, the director of the Historical Society, in an exhibition of Sam's silver collection. Then she facilitated an agreement, which Sam happily signed on November 25, 1986, to lend approximately 200 pieces of American silver for an exhibition scheduled to open in March 1987 and run through August. The insurance value placed on the silver was $600,000.[25] Initially and perhaps naïvely, the Historical Society asked Sam to contribute $60,000 to pay for the show and the catalog. Since this would have appeared to be quid pro quo, compromising the ethics and curatorial integrity of the institution, it was anathema to Sam, hinting at self-promotion and tantamount to buying himself a show. Thinking better of it, the Historical Society found another way to subsidize the exhibit.

"It was Sam's dying wish to curate the show himself," Anne Ehrenkranz would tell *The New York Times*, and given his credentials as more than just a collector, the Historical Society agreed.[26] The exhibit became his lifeline in the last months of 1986. Marshaling what little energy he had left, Sam set about selecting the objects, orchestrating the lighting, deciding on the placement, even choosing the right silk moiré to line the display cases, just as he had organized exhibitions as a museum curator in the 1960s in Hartford and Detroit. He also wrote a statement for the show, a manifesto of sorts for the historical and aesthetic importance of American silver.

"I think the last time I saw him was on the streets of Manhattan and he looked like a mountain man," recalled Richard Tuttle. "Hair was flying everywhere, and he was quite gray. His face was very lined, his eyes were blazing away, and he was dressed in a very quickly-put-together way. He was carrying two shopping bags filled with silver." It had surprised Tuttle to see Sam in this physical condition, as well as to see him walking around like a wild eccentric. "He struck me as a man that had really played his fantasy to the limit, and he was enjoying it, and he didn't care who was witnessing it and who wasn't, and in some strange way he was very eternal."[27]

In December, Ron Hoffman called Sam at home to say he had found a unique and wonderful sterling silver and silver gilt Gorham fruit stand. It was a two-tiered object with a rectangular tray over which a layer of crafted silver was draped like soft cloth over the edges. Sam was not strong enough to go to the shop, and asked Hoffman if he would bring it downtown. The potentially lucrative sale was incentive enough for Hoffman to hop in a cab with the heavy object. Anne Ehrenkranz was waiting to greet him at the door, and Jim waited inside. Hoffman walked over to the couch and placed it on the table in front of Sam. "He just sat there and couldn't get over it," Hoffman said. "He kept on touching it. He was so excited."[28]

Supported in all four corners by elaborately detailed elephants, the object was grand indeed, designed in an East Indian variation of the "Moresque style." Named by Tiffany designer Edward C. Moore, in the late nineteenth century, Moresque described his interpretations of the "oriental art" that became popular in the 1870s and '80s.[29] "I want this to be the centerpiece of my exhibit," Sam announced to everyone in the room. "I want gardenias floating in it."[30] Sam wrote a check for $60,558.25 on the spot. He slept with the stand in his bed that night.

Robert Mapplethorpe was much more present in these few final months, visiting Sam at home and in the hospital daily. He was not alone in worrying that the silver dealers were taking advantage of Sam. Nonetheless, the silver brought Sam so much joy that it was hard for anyone to stop them from contacting him, even when he returned to the hospital during the Christmas holidays. By that time, Sam was going in and out of hallucinatory states. "He would fluctuate," Robert later said. "One day he'd be quite coherent, the next completely out of it. You'd think he couldn't possibly make it through the night, but in the morning he'd be buying silver. At some point you wanted him either to get better—or worse."[31]

During this hospital stay, James Bell of the New-York Historical Society presented Sam with a letter of agreement to extend the loan of silver for an additional five years beyond the exhibit. Sam allegedly signed it. However, Robert, unaware of this agreement, was feeling pressure about the fate of the collection and finally asked Sam whether he wanted the Historical Society to have the silver, and later told *New York* magazine that Sam rather indignantly replied, "Oh, not necessarily."[32]

Sam's health continued to decline, the threat to his life measured in his blood count and his breathing. Amid the radiance of the silver and the loss of his strength, he received a letter from Maria Morris Hambourg at the Met that stands as a fitting valedictory: "I want to tell you how much I have always admired you and how I regret having politely kept my distance all these years," she wrote. "What you taught me in just one afternoon about Le Gray has whetted my appetite. So when you get back some strength and have the inclination, let us talk more. I want your help with Fenton, Emerson, and Vroman, for example." She went on to acknowledge the fund Daniel Wolf established at the museum and asked about the kinds of images he would like to see acquired in his name. She concluded, "I need to state what you would never let me say, which is how immeasurably important is what you have done in photography. Without your eye and knowledge, Sam, we'd still be in the Dark Ages."[33]

Pierre Apraxine visited Sam in the last few weeks of his life. During a lucid moment, Sam told Pierre why Robert had meant so much to him. "Robert brought me to photography," Sam said, and Pierre understood from the conversation that Sam would be leaving the bulk of his estate to Robert.[34] Shortly afterward, Patti Smith visited Sam to say good-bye. "I have only loved three things in my life," he told her. "Robert, my mother and art."[35]

During Sam's final stay in the hospital, he received a phone call from his sister, Judith Jefferson. When he hung up, he lamented to a visitor: "There are people who try to do their best, but they always seem to get it wrong."[36] Sam had maintained a cordial, if obligatory, relationship with Judith, making brief appearances at her family Christmas gatherings on East 72nd Street. She was his sister, but they had grown far apart. Judith, conventional and proper, could never quite reconcile her brother's homosexuality, never mind his bohemian manner of living; to Sam, she was the epitome of "fancy pants." She simply was not able to fathom her brother's dissolute life.

It was then common practice, in the last stages of AIDS, to allow patients who could, and wanted to, to go home, to die in familiar surroundings with those closest to them. When Sam was brought home from the hospital in the second week of January, he lapsed into a coma. Anne Ehrenkranz informed Judith Jefferson that she had better come and say good-bye. When she arrived, Anne, Robert, and Jim were sitting vigil around his bed. Judith found herself surrounded by the people closest to Sam—his chosen family. She didn't stay long, but she asserted her rank as the last remaining member of his family of origin. As she was leaving, she said, "We'll probably have a small family service." Robert turned to Anne and whispered, "I'm sure they'll really appreciate having a Jew and two faggots show up."[37]

SAM DIED JUST AFTER midnight on January 14, 1987. Jim Nelson, with traces of his own illness in the pallor of his skin, was holding Sam in his arms. Gorgeous Sam. Art-loving Sam. Educated Sam. Passionate Sam. Glamorous Sam. Generous Sam. Parsimonious Sam. Controlling Sam. Sensitive Sam. Playful Sam. Mystical Sam. Iconoclastic Sam. Witty Sam. Arrogant Sam. Anti-Semitic Sam. Irreverent Sam. Homosexual Sam. The patrician Samuel Jones Wagstaff Jr. and all that that entailed, gone, the mass of particles that constitute life no longer detectable in his body. The expression on his face was vacant, his gaunt features further slackened, the ashen, papery skin now hardened on his long, emaciated frame, all that remained of him in material form.

Sam left a will, and he left a legacy in art history. He left behind the people in the room—Jim, Robert, and Anne Ehrenkranz—as well as an inner circle of people not present who had been deeply touched by him: Jane Smith, Anne MacDonald, Ingrid Sischy, Barbara Jakobson, Pierre Apraxine, Judy Linn, Patti Smith. He also left behind those who benefited from his passion for photography and his company—John Waddell, Paul Walter, Daniel Wolf, Harry Lunn, George Rinhart, Jane Livingston—and another group of people who would always remember his encouragement, mentorship, or support: Richard Tuttle, Michael Heizer, Ray Johnson, Neil Jenney, Gordon Newton, Walter De Maria, Mark di Suvero; and the broader circle of people who admired him for his personal style, elan, and his contribution to art history, which remains largely unknown. And there were those he had once loved romantically—Gerald Incandela, Mark Kaminsky, Chuck Howard—and those with whom he shared passionate afternoons at the beach or in his One Fifth Avenue penthouse.

The bulk of Sam's $5 million estate went to Robert Mapplethorpe; several million dollars of it lay in works of art—Andy Warhol's *Race Riot*, Tony Smith's *Throne*, as well as others that had been on loan to the Metropolitan Museum of Art, the Wadsworth Atheneum, and the Detroit Institute of Arts. Robert would inherit all the remaining photographs, including his own pictures that Sam had kept. And, of course, the silver.

Mapplethorpe, himself wasted, weakened and sick, had to file a lawsuit in order to wrestle the silver back from the New-York Historical Society. In one of the ugliest stories from the worst era of the AIDS epidemic, the court action resulted in considerable media attention and pitted a dying man against a museum that seemed to exploit the advantage of its fine reputation. Since there was little cash in the estate, Robert planned to auction off the silver to pay the estate taxes. But the Historical Society was intent on keeping the silver for the full five-year loan period Sam had agreed to on his deathbed. Sam had been in and out of a disoriented state in the last weeks of his life, and the veracity of Sam's signature was what Robert had challenged. After articles appeared in *The New York Times* and *New York*,[38] the Historical Society, fearing that their reputation would be tarnished, agreed to return the silver.

Jim Nelson, who was already sick, was left 25 percent of the liquid funds from Sam's estate. Knowing that the will would probably be tied up in probate court, Sam had arranged an immediate stipend, as well as ownership of the Fire Island house in Oakleyville. Robert put the penthouse at One Fifth up for sale immediately, to bring in some necessary funds to pay legal fees and taxes, which essentially rendered Jim homeless. While Robert did not care much for Jim (ironically, since Robert had delivered Jim as a present from San Francisco eight years before), they were bonded in the tragic loss of Sam and it was understood that Jim had taken good care of him. So Robert negotiated a fair settlement with Jim: Jim would collect $500,000, a sum that represented the likely outcome of his 25 percent, and relinquish further claims on the money. That, and the Oakleyville house, would leave Jim enough to live comfortably for his remaining days. Jim died a year later.

To his sister, Judith, Sam left the paltry sum of $10,000, as well as several heirlooms from the Wagstaff family. He also left his niece and two nephews $10,000 apiece. Judith, often dressed in tailored suits, was indignant and dumbfounded. She filed a lawsuit that contested the will. "You had a hairdresser with Kaposi's sarcoma all over the place, and an S&M photographer who was always in the gossip sheets—who could blame her?" Michael Stout, Mapplethorpe's lawyer, said, describing how the principal heirs must have looked to her. However, once it became clear that Sam's will was legitimate and that his feelings about Robert and Jim were indisputable, she dropped the suit.[39] In addition, Sam left $100,000 each to the Metropolitan Museum of Art, the Museum of Modern Art, and the New York Public Library.

After a cremation and a small family funeral, Sam's ashes were placed in the family crypt at the Church of Heavenly Rest at Fifth Avenue and 90th Street. But another service took place a few blocks south, at the Met, on March 2, 1987. Sam had been a friend of the Met, sitting for years on the Prints and Photographs Department's advisory board, called the Visiting Committee. And, Daniel Wolf had established the Sam Wagstaff Fund for the acquisition of photographs. After an initial suggestion by John Waddell, Maria Morris Hambourg organized Sam's memorial, with the help of Robert.

That the service was held at the site where Sam's interest in photography had begun, at the museum's 1973 exhibit, "The Painterly Photograph," represented a lovely bookend. Sam had had his revelatory moment precisely there in front of *The Flatiron*, by Edward Steichen. "Sam's collection was certainly something splendid, and what he had done was noteworthy, remarkable, and admirable and should be properly memorialized," Hambourg said about her decision. "I went to the director and said, 'We need to do this,' and he said, 'Fine.'"[40]

On a mild but rainy day, the memorial took place in one of the hushed new galleries of the twentieth-century wing, an intimate carpeted space with walls of fabric; in fact, the gallery was used mostly to exhibit Paul Klee. The gallery was between shows and the walls were bare. Robert had printed some small pictures of Sam, which he handed out to some of the 125 people in attendance.

Perhaps Robert, who spoke first, took his cue from something Sam had written in a letter soon after they met, when they were in love and the seductions of romance, for which Sam would draw on his surprising reservoir of arcane knowledge, were still at play: "The Sufis say that if you hear someone being praised at his funeral, you can be sure he was a hypocrite."[41] Robert's statement was brief but moving:

> I am here—we are here to pay tribute to Sam Wagstaff—a man who was a great master of the art of looking. He loved to educate, most of all himself, but in so doing was an inspiration for many. He knew passion and was able to transfer it to the people around him. Those of us who were fortunate enough to get close to you, Sam, loved you very much.[42]

Then Robert read a poem by Patti Smith that was printed on the memorial program. Her friendship with Sam had begun when he first met Robert and grew from their conversations about literature and poetry, with throwing the I Ching together, with the clandestine portrait sessions in which she posed for Sam wearing Olga's boa and hats, and with Sam's financial help for her pilgrimage to Rimbaud's grave.

Next up was Ingrid Sischy, the consciously, playfully disheveled editor of *Artforum*, her oversized glasses a Dada-like gesture. She spoke with genuine feeling, slowly, deliberately, and with her characteristic originality:

> It always seemed to me that Sam was the handsomest man in the world. It always seemed as though he could have been anything, and done anything, he wanted. He could have and he did. If any human being can be said to have been free, free of the laws that make most of us servants—whether to an institution, a consensus, an order, a stereotype, or a lifestyle—he was the free one. If anyone can be said to have been his own man, he was.[43]

She described a picnic on the beach some years earlier when Sam roamed off by himself, as he was wont to do. Eventually he returned bearing a few native gifts—such as they were on the beaches of eastern Long Island. "Our Poseidon, our Neptune, had collected bark, seaweed, bayberry leaves, beach plums, and other gifts of the sea. Some of them were to eat, and the rest he had tied together with a little bit of help from the discards of industry," Sischy said. "This food that he offered and these sandals that he made rendered it utterly clear that Sam Wagstaff's collecting was so profoundly connected to the rhythms and tides of life itself that it could give us the stuff of survival."[44]

Pierre Apraxine, the elegant curator of the Gilman Collection who had considered Sam an encouraging, if mischievous, older brother, acknowledged his debt to Sam. Not only had Wagstaff introduced him to Richard Tuttle and Tony Smith, and to the work of Agnes Martin and Robert Morris, but his influence in the field of photography was a worthy example for curators and collectors alike:

> Sam told me of his belief that if one looked at things with enough intensity, they could, by passing mystic disciplines or drug-induced trances, hold the key to a heightened state of consciousness, a fuller experience of life. . . .

Collector or beachcomber, Sam taught us all his life that it is

less the object at which we look that gives value to our experience, than the intensity with which we look at it. It is the intensity
of the pure act of seeing which illuminated Sam's life, and which
now reflects ours.[45]

In effect, aside from the small, obligatory family funeral, Sam had
two memorials. The first was this official art world memorial at the
Met. He had hoped to be alive for the second, but "The Wagstaff Collection of American Silver" opened on March 20, 1987, at the New-York
Historical Society, which stood beside land once owned by his great-
grandfather Dr. Alfred Wagstaff. In the statement for the show, which
he finished just weeks before his death, Sam explained how his silver
collection could be understood as a proxy for the entirety of his sensibility. "In the true sense of the word this show is about Americana, which
is not the ordinary way of receiving silver into one's ken—silver the
glamorous, the rare, the elegant. This is not that," he wrote. "This is a
collection sifted through my eccentricity and therefore, hopefully, quite
bizarre as to individual pieces and even more bizarre in its totality."[46]

Even in death, it seemed, Wagstaff had the ability to attract talented
men and provide a kind of mentorship. He could not know that Charles
Venable, a young PhD candidate at Boston University, would come to
New York that March to attend the exhibit and become so influenced by
it, so struck by the collective power of the objects, that he would write
his dissertation on American silver of that period. Two years later, Venable was an assistant curator at the Dallas Museum of Art and attended
the Christie's sale "The Sam Wagstaff Collection of American Silver,"
at which he would buy half a dozen pieces for the museum.[47]

Robert Mapplethorpe's retrospective at the Whitney Museum of Art
in October 1988 would have made Sam profoundly happy, but he did not
witness that celebrity-studded opening, at which his Wumpers appeared
to be, at forty-two, an emaciated old man in a wheelchair, makeup covering the lesions on his face. Robert died on March 9, 1989.

Nor would Sam be able to relish with Wagstaffian glee the national
controversy over "The Perfect Moment," another show of Robert's
work several months later.[48] The exhibit was abruptly canceled by the

Corcoran Gallery of Art (just a decade earlier the site of Sam's triumphant show from his own collection) after Jesse Helms, a conservative Republican from North Carolina, stood on the floor of the United States Senate and labeled Mapplethorpe's work smut. Sam would have savored that controversy—the biggest provocation yet to the puritanical, unenlightened attitudes of a closed-minded establishment. It would have gratified Sam to see that—despite or perhaps in part because of the Corcoran scandal, as well as his own early support and his enlightened vision—the name Robert Mapplethorpe has been elevated in the years since to the artistic pantheon.

It might surprise Sam to learn of the significance of photography today, the museum departments all over the world devoted to it, the number of galleries around the world exclusively representing it, the number of international art fairs in which the photography market thrives, and the high volume of books of photographs published annually. This is one legacy he had not anticipated.

If Wagstaff were to witness the price of his Warhol today—*Race Riot* (1964), which sold for $62.8 million at a 2014 Sotheby's auction—he may very well simply nod knowingly.[49] He already believed Warhol to be one of the greatest artists of the twentieth century.

Only a month before he died, so weak he was barely able to get out of bed, much less even hold anything in his hands, Ron Hoffman had brought the elaborate centerpiece downtown for him to see, and which Sam felt so compelled to hold. Perhaps it was with provocative irony that Sam believed it to be the ultimate reflection of his cultivated sensibility. "Four Elephant Fruit Stand" was the centerpiece of the silver show at the New-York Historical Society. It was his express desire for it to be shown in public so that others would appreciate the wit of the object, its eccentric charm, its playful flourishes, the exquisite craft, and the legacy of aesthetic silver it represented. During the exhibit it was filled with white gardenias, replaced every few days in order to keep them fresh. That was his final wish.

AFTERWORD

ROBERT MAPPLETHORPE DIED OF AIDS AT THE AGE OF forty-two in 1989. He was the primary heir to Sam Wagstaff's estate, and the Christie's catalog of the Mapplethorpe estate sale of October 31, 1989, included several works with the provenance of Wagstaff: James Ensor's *Stilleben* (1896, est. $600,000–800,000); Eduoard Vuillard's *Vue plongeante sur un jardin (Jardin des Nabi)* (c. 1900, est. $200,000–300,000); John Chamberlain's *Ultima Thule* (undated, est. $100,000–200,000); Tony Smith's *Throne* (undated, est. $100,000–150,000); and Andy Warhol's *Race Riot* (1964, four panels, synthetic polymer silk-screened on canvas; est. $700,000–1,000,000).

These works of art constitute a partial representation of the legacy of Sam Wagstaff; equally, his acquisition and relish of Jackson Pollock's *The Deep*, and its later carefully orchestrated sale to the Centre Pompidou in Paris, where it resides today, exemplifies Sam's art historical judgment, personal taste, and curatorial stewardship. Other works that he acquired directly from the artists he knew in the 1960s, whether paintings or drawings, today remain bequests of Sam Wagstaff at the Metropolitan Museum of Art, the Detroit Institute of Arts, or the Wadsworth Atheneum in Hartford. His crowning achievement—the Samuel J. Wagstaff Jr. collection of photographs at the J. Paul Getty Museum—is considered a cornerstone of that museum's photography holdings.

Wagstaff was a thoroughbred in societal terms, a product of class, breeding, and wealth. The arc of his life is drawn on his search for meaningful counterpoints to his privileged, if stultifying, upbringing, those stepping-stones, if you will, into a parallel existence where something approximating enlightenment became his goal. Perhaps his cultivation, in concert with his homosexuality, led him to a less obvious frequency of being, from which he grew to trust his senses, his intuition, and the actuality of his experience. At the same time, he continued to rely on the accumulated knowledge from his fine education to discern what is pure—and what was often overlooked—in civilization, which he would collect in turn, as if to establish new foundations of thinking about culture and other ways of perceiving the world. "Black, White, and Gray," the first museum exhibition of minimalist art, in 1964, was one of his stepping-stones into a portal of expanded consciousness. Sam would follow the artist's frequency to a prescient recognition of minimal art, pop art, fluxus, and earth art, with forays into West Somali Dogon sculpture and Native-American Mimbres pots, before turning to photography.

It is widely understood that John Szarkowski, the legendary curator at the Museum of Modern Art from 1962 to 1990, elevated photography to the realm of the fine arts. The exhibitions he mounted, the photographers he introduced, the music of his language in lectures and essays and books, in addition to the sheer force of his stentorian personality, conspired to redefine photography among curators, critics, and artists themselves, making it an equal among the arts.

Nevertheless, after spending five years of research into the life of Sam Wagstaff—mining the history of the decades through which he was actively involved, discussing his passion for art and artists with those who knew him, assaying his aesthetic and historical choices as a collector with contemporary curators and art historians, tracking his

tireless activities and his advocacy of photography's significance—
there is ample evidence that Wagstaff, too, was instrumental in generat-
ing respect for the medium of photography in the highest precincts of
the art world. His curatorial experience, art historical knowledge, and
profound belief in the medium only underscored the persuasive glamour
of his reputation. Furthermore, almost single-handedly, Wagstaff established the marketplace for photography, for better or worse, spending
unprecedented sums in the auction rooms of London and New York on
a medium to which a second thought had rarely before been given.

I am convinced that Wagstaff's role was equal to Szarkowski's in
securing respect for photography as an art form. Szarkowski, of course,
proceeded from the institutional platform of MoMA—the highest
mountaintop. Indisputably his legacy includes the astute introduction of
Diane Arbus, Lee Friedlander, Garry Winogrand, and William Eggleston into museum canon, and, also, the deification of Eugène Atget,
among a pantheon of photographers. Wagstaff, by contrast, was an
institution of one. He turned to photography when it was still considered an art world bastard, a utilitarian medium. Because of his reputation in the art world and his access to New York society, Wagstaff's
decision to collect photographs changed minds in influential circles,
garnering a regard for photography that even Szarkowski could not
achieve. For example, Sotheby's did not establish an autonomous department of photographs until 1977—a specific result of Wagstaff's acquisition of photographs that they had been following from his early
purchases in the auction houses of London.

Simultaneously, Sam was Mapplethorpe's ardent champion from the
beginning; that Robert's work lives on with such stature (despite Szar-
kowksi's dismissal of it) is one more example of Wagstaff's behind-the-
scenes hegemony. "Sam revolutionized the way we look at photographs,"
Barbara Jakobson told *Vanity Fair* in 1989. "When he sold his collection to the Getty Museum, his position in photography was forever
assured."[1]

Wagstaff had one foot in "society," and one foot defiantly outside it.
In *The Importance of Being Earnest*, Oscar Wilde's ambivalence toward
his homosexuality is "epitomized by the very notion of 'Bunburying,'

the need to lead a double life, into a complex parody of both himself and his society, and thereby creates a masterpiece, perhaps the greatest comedy in the language," writes scholar Claude J. Summers. "He turns Victorian values on their heads and discovers in the comedy of camp a means of covertly attacking his society's prejudices and discreetly defending his own nonconformity." Summers asserts that Wilde occupied a liminal position in relation to his homophobic society, "in it, yet not of it," and that his comedy is fueled by the "desperate desire to be accepted by the very society he lampoons."[2]

The double life of "Bunburying" was native to Wagstaff and speaks directly to his relationship to his own background. Sam had always done what he wanted, but with one eye fastened on maintaining the façade—that which is correct. Through the years, he was able to break the rules with less regard for the social repercussions. Still, he remained tethered to the upper tiers of civilization through art world activities that had cachet in the "fancy pants" world he often dismissed, nodding to the façade while, just as often, thumbing his nose at it.

The profound bond between Wagstaff and Mapplethorpe served each of them in an elegant kind of notoriety. As Carol Squiers said, "Sam gave Robert class and Robert gave Sam sex appeal."[3] In fact, for Sam, already fifty when they met, Robert was the consummate surrogate: he affected the persona of the decadent and the dandy, and Sam benefited without having to compromise his age and his standing to don the costume himself. At the same time, Wordsworth's line, "the child is the father of the man," applied to each of them (as it does to all of us). Individually, they allowed the impulses of childhood free rein, and each responded to the other in kind.

The artworks Wagstaff kept until his death, which were sold as part of the Mapplethorpe estate sale, reflect a particular strain of Sam's sensibility, extending from Vuillard, an oppositional artist of the fin de siècle, to Warhol, who proved revolutionary in art historical terms, and Mapplethorpe, who scandalized the public with homoerotic subject matter in photographs of strict formal resolution and beauty.

It was Wagstaff's wish—and deeper instinct—to leave everything to Robert Mapplethorpe, which in turn made possible the Mapplethorpe

Foundation. Today, Mapplethorpe's reputation hovers in mythic proportion, his name representing at once a manifestation of artistic purity and a defiant challenge to convention—as Wagstaff might have predicted and surely would have savored. To be sure, no heir could better symbolize the sum of Sam Wagstaff's beliefs as a connoisseur and scholar, and his regard of knowing life through the senses.

NOTES

EPIGRAPHS

1. From one of five unpublished draft texts to accompany a volume of Evans's subway portraits. This one, "People Anonymous, People in the Subway, Unposed Portraits Recorded by Walker Evans" published in Jerry Thompson, *Walker Evans at Work* (New York: Harper & Row, 1982), p. 161.

2. Ruth Kligman, "#1–5th–27–107," unpublished poem "for Sam Wagstaff," Robert Mapplethorpe Papers (2011.M.20), J. Paul Getty Trust, Getty Research Institute, Los Angeles. Ruth Kligman (1930–2010) was an artist and writer; she is known primarily as Jackson Pollock's mistress at the time of his death.

PROLOGUE

1. "Black, White, and Gray," Wadsworth Atheneum Museum of Art, Hartford, Conn., January 9–February 9, 1964.

2. "Tony Smith: Two Exhibitions of Sculpture," Wadsworth Atheneum, Hartford, Conn., and the Institute of Contemporary Art, Philadelphia, November 22, 1966–January 6, 1967.

3. Paul Richard, "The Collector the Establishment Trusts," *The Washington Post*, February 3, 1978, p. D-1.

4. Pierre Apraxine, transcript of his eulogy given at the memorial service for Sam Wagstaff at the Metropolitan Museum of Art, New York, March 2, 1987, Archives of the Department of Photography, Metropolitan Museum of Art, New York.

ONE   DRAGGED MASS DISPLACEMENT

1. Interview with Barbara Jakobson, New York, December 16, 2010.

2. "Michael Heizer: Photographic and Actual Work," Detroit Institute of Arts, March 25–April 25, 1971.

3. Samuel J. Wagstaff Jr., interview by Marilyn B. Ghausi, May 21, 1982. Oral History of the Detroit Institute of Arts Project, Research Library and Archives, Detroit Institute of Arts.

4. Ann Perron Spivak, telephone conversation with author, June 8, 2010.

5. Susanne Hilberry, interview by James Crump, Detroit, February 20, 2003.

6. Wagstaff, interview by Ghausi.

7. *Gracehoper* (1962) was issued in an edition of 3, with one artist's proof; the first was fabricated in 1972 and is on the lawn of the Detroit Institute of Arts; the original cardboard maquette, created in 1961, which is also painted black, is also in the DIA's collection.

8. Minuro Yamasaki and Edward Durell Stone are considered to be the master practitioners of New Formalism in architecture. Yamasaki is best known for the Twin Towers of the World Trade Center (1972) in New York.

9. Interview with Anne MacDonald, New York, April 2, 2012.

10. Spivak, telephone conversation.

11. Interview with Judy Linn, Ghent, N.Y., May 25, 2009.

12. Frank Kolbert, telephone conversation with author, November, 2011.

13. Ellen Phelan, telephone conversation with author, September 12, 2011.

14. Ibid.

15. Wagstaff, interview by Ghausi.

16. Mary Jane Jacob, *Kick Out the Jams: Detroit's Cass Corridor, 1963—1977*, p. 20. Catalog to accompany the exhibition of the same name, Detroit Institute of Arts, July 13–September 14, 1980.

17. Ibid., p. 21.

18. Phelan, telephone conversation.

19. Frederick J. Cumming, preface to exhibition catalog, *Kick Out the Jams*, p. 5.

20. Michael Heizer, telephone conversation with author, November 11, 2010.

21. Jim Crawford, telephone conversation with author, September 20, 2011.

22. John Egner, telephone conversation with author, September 7, 2011.

23. Interview with Susanne Hilberry, Detroit, June 3, 2010.

24. Gordon Newton, interview by James Crump, February 20, 2003.

25. Egner, telephone conversation.

26. Newton, interview by Crump.

27. Egner, telephone conversation.

28. Newton, interview by Crump.

29. Egner, telephone conversation.

30. Newton, interview by Crump.

31. Ibid.

32. Phelan, telephone conversation.

33. E. E. Cummings, "somewhere i have never travelled,gladly beyond," *Complete Poems 1904–1962*, ed. George J. Firmage (New York: Liveright, 1991), p. 367.

34. Interview with Gil Silverman, Detroit, June 4, 2010.

35. Wagstaff, interview by Ghausi.

36. Silverman, interview.

37. Spivak, telephone conversation.

38. Linn, interview.

39. Michael Maidenberg, "Art Curator Says Farewell to City," *Detroit Free Press*, October 14, 1971, p. A3.

40. Lee Winfrey, "Arty Rock *Is* Gone—What's Next?" *Detroit Free Press*, May 13, 1971, p. A3.

41. MacDonald, interview.

42. Sam Wagstaff, letter to Anne MacDonald, May 15, 1978, courtesy of Anne MacDonald.

43. *The Deep* (1953) is widely regarded as one of Pollock's most important later paintings. It is currently in the collection of the Centre Georges Pompidou, Paris.

44. Sam Wagstaff to Tony Smith, n.d., box 75, folder 7, Sam Wagstaff Papers (2005.M.46), J. Paul Getty Trust, Getty Research Institute, Los Angeles.

45. Sam Wagstaff to Willis Woods, September 19, 1971, box 9, folder 7, The Samuel J. Wagstaff Jr. Records, 1956–1978, Research Library and Archives, Detroit Institute of Arts.

TWO THE CROSSING

1. "You're the Top," *Anything Goes* (1934), words and music by Cole Porter.

2. Joan Juliet Buck quoting Wagstaff in the documentary *Black, White + Gray* (2007), directed by James Crump.

3. Wagstaff had received the David E. Finley Fellowship, awarded annually by the National Gallery of Art in Washington, D.C., in support of his advanced graduate research in the history, theory, and criticism of art. The first two years of the Finley Fellowship are intended for research and travel in Europe to visit collections, museums, monuments, and sites related to a well-advanced dissertation in Western art.

4. George Butler, telephone conversation with author, November 1, 2011.

5. "Fire Damages Tallaulah [sic]," *The New York Times*, May 13, 1913.

6. Butler, telephone conversation.

7. S. R. Harlow and H. H. Boone, *Life Sketches of the State Officers, Senators, and Members of the Assembly of the State of New York in 1867* (Albany, N.Y.: Weed, Parsons and Company, 1867), p. 381.

8. "S.P.C.A. President Appeals to Mayor," *The New York Times*, March 17, 1911.

9. The Spee Club is an all-male social club at Harvard University. Notable alumni include John F. and Robert F. Kennedy.

10. Cleveland Amory, "The Great Club Revolution," *American Heritage*, 1954.

392 | NOTES TO PAGES 28-42

11. Ibid.

12. Elsie French Vanderbilt was the wife of Alfred Gwynne Vanderbilt, the third son of Cornelius Vanderbilt II.

13. *The New York Times*, August 11, 1911.

14. Ibid.

15. "S. J. Wagstaff, Divorced 2 Weeks, Weds Divorcee," *New York Tribune*, December 23, 1920, p. 11.

16. Wilbur Fawley, "Gala Assemblage Sees Horse Show," *The New York Times*, November 7, 1939.

17. Judy Jefferson, telephone conversation with author, January 2012.

18. See, for example, her advertising illustration "Onyx Hosiery in *Harper's Bazaar* 53 (March 1918), p. 2.

19. "City's Birth Re-lived at Beaux-Arts Ball: Leaders in Drama, Letters and Art Crowd the Waldorf to Honor First President," *The New York Times*, January 23, 1932.

20. "Mrs. Wagstaff Wed to Donald Newhall," *The New York Times*, February 17, 1932.

21. "Noel Coward at 70," *Time*, December 26, 1969.

22. Sam Wagstaff to Olga Newhall, April 29, 1936, box 80, folder 1, Sam Wagstaff Papers (2005.M.46), J. Paul Getty Trust, Getty Research Institute, Los Angeles.

23. "26 Refugees Back with Terror Tales," *The New York Times*, August 5, 1936.

24. The Hotchkiss School yearbook of 1940 lists Wagstaff as president of the Dramat and notes the productions in which he appeared: *Air Raid*, *Front Page*, and *Paths of Glory*.

25. Interview with Anne Ehrenkranz, New York, January 4, 2012.

26. Wagstaff folders, Archives of the Social Register Association, 60 Fifth Avenue, New York.

27. Interview with Thomas L. Jefferson, Los Angeles, October 28, 2011.

28. Ibid.

29. Peter Jefferson, telephone conversation with author, August 23, 2011.

30. Olga Newhall to Sam Wagstaff, n.d., box 80, folder 1, Sam Wagstaff Papers, Getty.

31. Wolf's Head Society, a secret society at Yale University, was founded in 1884 to counter the dominance of Skull and Bones Society.

32. Buck quoting Dominick Dunne *Black, White + Gray*.

33. Interview with Barbara Jakobson, New York, December 16, 2010.

34. Bernard Perlin, introduction to David Leddick, *Intimate Companions: A Triography of George Platt-Lynes, Paul Cadmus, Lincoln Kirstein and Their Circle* (New York: St. Martin's Press, 2000) p. xi.

35. Gerald Ayres, e-mail to author, December 6, 2011.

36. Owen Johnson, with illustrations by F. R. Gruger, *Stover at Yale* (Boston: Little, Brown, 1931).

37. Andrew Delbanco, "Colleges: An Endangered Species?" *The New York Review of Books*, March 10, 2005.

38. http://alumninet.yale.edu/classes/yc1942/Waterbury.htm.

39. "Drama Group at Yale Appears Here December 22: The 'Waterbury Tales' Will Be Given at the Waldorf," *The New York Times*, December 7, 1941.

40. Bob Colacello as quoted in Michael Lobel, "Warhol's Closet," *Art Journal* 55, no. 4 (1996): 44.

41. Jed Johnson as quoted in Sotheby auction catalog of Warhol Estate, 1988.

42. Gerald (John) Palmer, telephone conversation with author, February 19, 2012.

43. Interview with Steven M. L. Aronson, New York, January 4, 2011.

44. www.Vogue.com/voguepedia/Babs_Simpson.

45. Notes from Dickie to Menocal to Sam Wagstaff, n.d., Sam Wagstaff Papers, Getty.

46. Samuel J. Wagstaff Jr., interview by Marilyn B. Ghausi, May 21, 1982. Oral History of the Detroit Institute of Arts Project, Research Library and Archives, Detroit Institute of Arts.

47. James Crump, "Art of Acquisition: The Eye of Sam Wagstaff," *Archives of American Art Journal* 46, nos. 3–4 (2007): 5–11.

48. Laurence Kantor, "The Richard Offner Photo Archives at the Institute of Fine Arts: Seeing Paintings in Black and White," paper delivered at a symposium at the Institute of Fine Arts, New York, March 2011, and reprinted in *Photo Archives and the Photographic Memory of Art History*, ed. Costanza Caraffa (Berlin: Deutscher Kunstverlag, 2011).

49. Transcript of Wagstaff talk to students of photographer William Gedney at Pratt Institute, Brooklyn, N.Y., March 22, 1978, "William Gedney Photographs and Writings, 1940–1989," David M. Rubenstein Rare Book and Manuscript Library, Duke University, Durham, N.C.

50. Interview with Edgar Munhall, New York, January 13, 2010.

THREE BE HERE NOW

1. W. Somerset Maugham, *Of Human Bondage* (New York: Doubleday, 1915).

2. Interview with John Richardson, New York, September 17, 2009.

3. *Gauguin*, exhibition catalog for show at the Metropolitan Museum of Art, April 21–May 31, 1959.

4. Gerald Ayres, e-mail to author, January 30, 2012.

5. Interview with Richard Tuttle, New York, June 2, 2009.

6. Ibid.

7. Ibid.

8. Tom Wolfe, *The Kandy-Kolored Tangerine-Flake Streamline Baby* (New York: Pocket Books, 1966), p. 207.

9. Ad Reinhardt to Sam Wagstaff, n.d., Samuel J. Wagstaff Papers (c. 1932–1985), Archives of American Art, Smithsonian Institution, Washington, D.C.

10. Interview with Mark di Suvero, New York, September 9, 2011.

11. Interview with Billy Name, Poughkeepsie, N.Y., May 24, 2013.

12. Ibid.

13. Charles Moore, "They Fight a Fire That Won't Go Out," *Life*, May 17, 1963.

14. Adam Fairclough, *To Redeem the Soul of America* (Athens: University of George Press, 1987), p. 138

15. Georg Frei and Neil Prints, *Warhol: Paintings and Sculpture 1964–1969, Vol. 2: The Andy Warhol Catalogue Raisonné* (London: Phaidon Press, 2004), p. 357.

16. Brett Gorvy, "Video: Andy Warhol's Race Riot, 1964," Christie's, 2014.

17. Christie's sale no. 2847, May 13, 2014.

18. Judith Thurman, "Dressing Up: How Charles James Elevated American Fashion," *The New Yorker*, May 5, 2014, p. 76

19. Roberta Smith, "Where Elegance Meets Eros," *The New York Times*, May 9, 2014.

20. Harold Koda, "Charles James: Beyond Fashion," exhibition catalog (New York: Metropolitan Museum of Art, 2014).

21. Sam Wagstaff, "Paintings to Think About," *ARTnews*, January 1964.

22. Ibid.

23. Sam Wagstaff to Andy Warhol, n.d. [December 1963], Samuel J. Wagstaff Papers, Wadsworth Atheneum, Hartford, Conn.

24. Sam Wagstaff to Agnes Martin, n.d. [December 1963], ibid.

25. Sam Wagstaff to Jasper Johns, n.d. [December 1963], ibid.

26. Sam Wagstaff to Clement Greenberg, n.d. [December 1963], ibid.

27. Wagstaff to Warhol, ibid. The Warhol *Brillo Boxes* were first exhibited at the Stable Gallery in April 1964.

28. Sam Wagstaff to magazine art critics, n.d. [December 1963], ibid.

29. Sam Wagstaff, interview by Nicholas Fox Weber, September 30, 1974, Oral History of the Wadsworth Atheneum Museum of Art, Research Library and Archives, the Wadsworth Atheneum Museum of Art, Hartford, Conn.

30. Sam Wagstaff quoting Poons, ibid.

31. Gerald (John) Palmer, telephone conversation with author, February 19, 2012.

32. Ibid.

33. Ibid.

34. John C. Parsons to Charles Cunningham, n.d. [1964], Samuel J. Wagstaff Papers, Wadsworth Atheneum.

35. Florence Berkman, "Pop Art on Exhibition Free, Far Out," *Hartford Times*, January 11, 1964, p. 26.

36. Wagstaff, interview by Fox Weber.

37. Frances Beatty in *How to Draw a Bunny* (2002) directed by John W. Walter and produced by Andrew L. Moore.

38. Jill Johnston, "Cunningham in Hartford," *The Village Voice*, April 9, 1964, p. 19.

39. Eugene R. Gaddis, *The Magician of the Modern: Chick Austin and the Transformation of the Arts in America* (New York: Alfred A. Knopf, 2000), p. 5.

40. Charles Kaiser, *The Gay Metropolis* (New York: Houghton Mifflin, 1997), p. 41. Kaiser cites Franz Schulze's *Philip Johnson: Life and Work* (New York: Alfred A. Knopf, 1994) as the source for "impeccable enunciation."

41. Michael Heizer, telephone conversation with author, November 11, 2010.

42. Exhibition catalog: Carl Andre, David Annesley, and Kynaston McShine, *Primary Structures: Younger American and British Sculptors* (New York: Jewish Museum, 1966). The exhibition was at the Jewish Museum, April 27–June 12, 1966.

43. "An Exhibition of Italian Panels and Manuscripts from the Thirteenth and Fourteenth Centuries in Honor of Richard Offner," Wadsworth Atheneum, April 9–June 6, 1965.

44. Sam Wagstaff, introduction to exhibition catalog, *An Exhibition of Italian Panels and Manuscripts from the Thirteenth and Fourteenth Centuries in Honor of Richard Offner* (Hartford, Conn.: Wadsworth Atheneum, 1965).

45. Richard Offner to Sam Wagstaff, April 27, 1965, box 85, folder 1, Sam Wagstaff Papers (2005.M.46), J. Paul Getty Trust, Getty Research Institute, Los Angeles.

46. "Sculpture: Master of the Monumentalists," *Time*, October 13, 1967.

47. Samuel J. Wagstaff, "Talking with Tony Smith," *Artforum*, December 5, 1966, p. 16.

48. Ibid.

49. Richardson, interview.

50. Interview with Steven M. L. Aronson, New York, January 4, 2011.

51. Frances Kiernan, *The Last Mrs. Astor* (New York: W. W. Norton, 2007), pp. 123–25.

52. Aronson, interview.

53. Tuttle, interview.

54. Ibid.

55. Sarah Greenough, *Looking In: Robert Frank's "The Americans,"* (Washington, D.C.: National Gallery of Art, 2008).

56. Allan Kaprow, "The Legacy of Jackson Pollock." *ARTnews*, October 1958.

57. Ibid.

58. The term "snapshot aesthetic" was coined in the early 1970s to define an

evolving style in picture making that combined the unself-conscious look of family snapshots, the authenticity of news photos, and the spontaneity of the documented moment.

59. Sam Wagstaff, exhibition catalog, *Other Ideas* (Detroit Institute of Arts, 1969), p. 2. September 10–October 19, 1969.

60. Allan Kaprow to Sam Wagstaff, n.d. [1966], Sam Wagstaff Papers, Getty.

61. Agnes Martin to Sam Wagstaff, n.d. (c. 1970), Samuel J. Wagstaff Papers (c. 1932–1985), Archives of American Art, Smithsonian Institution, Washington, D.C.

62. Agnes Martin to Sam Wagstaff, n.d. (c. 1971), ibid.

63. $500,000 in 1971 is the approximate equivalent of $3 million in 2014.

64. Samuel J. Wagstaff Jr., interview by Marilyn B. Ghausi, May 21, 1982. Oral History of the Detroit Institute of Arts Project, Research Library and Archives, Detroit Institute of Arts.

65. Steven Watson, "The Art of Max's," in *Max's Kansas City: Art, Glamour, Rock and Roll*, ed. Steven Kasher (New York: Abrams Image, 2010), p. 8.

FOUR   JARDIN DES NABI

1. Thomas Mann, *Confessions of Felix Krull, Confidence Man* (New York: Vintage 1955) p. 79.

2. Sam Green, telephone conversation with author, March 4, 2008.

3. The Tony Smith exhibitions ran at the Wadsworth Atheneum, Hartford, Conn., and the Institute of Contemporary Art, Philadelphia, November 22, 1966–January 6, 1967.

4. "Sculpture: Masters of the Monumentalists," *Time*, October 13, 1967, p. 80.

5. Green, telephone conversation.

6. Guy Trebay, "A Collector of People Along with the Art," *The New York Times*, April 6, 2011, p. E1.

7. Interview with John Richardson, New York, September 17, 2009.

8. Interview with Richard Turley, New York, May 28, 2009.

9. Ibid.

10. Ibid.

11. Green, telephone conversation.

12. Interview with David Croland, New York, April 2008.

13. Patti Smith, *Just Kids* (New York: Ecco/HarperCollins, 2010), p. 77.

14. Croland, interview.

15. Ellen Phelan, telephone conversation with author, September 12, 2011.

16. Croland, interview.

17. Joan Juliet Buck quoting Wagstaff in *Black, White + Gray* (2007), directed by James Crump.

18. Quoted in Ingrid Sischy, "A Society First" in *Robert Mapplethorpe* (exhibition catalog), ed. Richard Marshall (New York: Whitney Museum of American Art, 1988), p. 81.

19. Patti Smith, videotaped public conversation during the Louisiana Literature Festival, Louisiana Museum of Modern Art, Humlebaek, Denmark, August 24–26, 2012.

20. Smith, *Just Kids*, p. 70.

21. Patti Smith, interview by Amy Goodman, *Democracy Now*, April 29, 2010 (www.democracynow.org/2010/4/29/punk_rock_legend_patti_smith_on).

22. Interview with Gerard Malanga, Hudson, N.Y., March 20, 2009.

23. Brice Marden, telephone conversation with author, October 6, 2011.

24. *Robert Having His Nipple Pierced* (1971), directed by Sandy Daley, with commentary by Patti Smith.

25. Interview with Steven M. L. Aronson, New York, January 4, 2011.

26. Smith, *Just Kids* p. 203.

27. Ibid., p. 204.

28. Patricia Morrisoe, *Mapplethorpe: A Biography* (New York: Da Capo Press, 1997), p. 113.

29. Interview with Susanne Hilberry, Detroit, June 3, 2010.

30. Interview with Klaus Kertess, New York, February 24, 2009.

31. Interview with Edmund White, New York, March 3, 2009.

32. Morrisoe, *Mapplethorpe*, p. 111.

33. White, interview.

34. Hilberry, interview.

35. White, interview.

36. Croland, interview.

37. Edouard Vuillard's painting *Downhill View Towards a Garden*, also referred to as *Le Jardin Nabi*, was owned by Wagstaff until his death. It was sold at the Christie's auction of the Robert Mapplethorpe Collection in October 31, 1989, titled in the catalog as *Vue plongeante sur un jardin*, and signed E. Vuillard.

38. *Untitled (Sam Wagstaff)*, 1972, is reproduced in Sylvia Wolf, *Polaroids: Mapplethorpe* (New York: Prestel, 2007) fig. 23, p. 42. Exhibition catalog for the Whitney Museum of American Art show of the same name in collaboration with the Robert Mapplethorpe Foundation, New York, 2007.

FIVE KAMA SUTRA, BABY

1. Charles Baudelaire, "Hymn to Beauty," *Les Fleurs du Mal*, trans. Richard Howard (Boston: David R. Godine, 1984), p. 28.

2. Interview with Steven M. L. Aronson, New York, January 4, 2011.

3. Interview with Edmund White, New York, March 3, 2009.

4. Ibid.

5. Patricia Morrisroe, *Mapplethorpe: A Biography* (New York: Da Capo Press, 1997) pp. 111, 114.

6. Interview with Paul F. Walter, New York, March 10, 2009.

7. John Egner, telephone conversation with author, September 17, 2011.

8. David Croland quoted in Nick Haramis, "Because the Night: Robert Mapplethorpe Remembered," BlackBook, July 22, 2008, accessible at www.bbook.com/because_the_night.

9. Interview with Lynn Davis, Hudson, N. Y., March 2, 2009.

10. Janet Kardon, interview with Robert Mapplethorpe in *Robert Mapplethorpe: The Perfect Moment*, p. 23, catalog published in conjunction with the exhibition of the same name, Institute of Contemporary Art, Philadelphia, December 9, 1988–January 29, 1989.

11. *Race Riot*, Warhol's four silk screens on canvas of the same repeated photograph by the American photographer Charles Moore (1931–2010), published in *Life* magazine, May 17, 1963.

12. Nicholas Cullinan, "To Exist in Passing Time," in *Robert Rauschenberg Photographs: 1949–1962*, ed. David White and Susan Davidson (New York: D.A.P./Schirmer/Mosel, 2011), p. 17.

13. "Street photography" is the term generally applied to photographs made of people or situations on urban streets; Garry Winogrand is regarded as an exemplar of the genre.

14. Lisette Model quoted in Jonathan Green, "Lisette Model," *The Snapshot* (1974), 19, no. 1, p. 6.

15. Hilton Kramer, "125 Photos by Arbus on Display," *The New York Times*, November 8, 1972, p. 52.

16. Kardon, *Robert Mapplethorpe: The Perfect Moment*, p.23-29.

17. White, interview.

18. Hutchinson to Sam Wagstaff, July 31, 1964, box 88, folders, Sam Wagstaff Papers (2005.M.46), J. Paul Getty Trust, Getty Research Institute, Los Angeles.

19. Richard de Menocal to Sam Wagstaff, n.d. (1940s), box 71, folder 2, Sam Wagstaff Papers, Getty Trusts, Getty.

20. John Money, *Lovemaps: Clinical Concepts of Sexual and Erotic Health and Pathology* (Amherst, N. Y.: Prometheus Books, 1986), p. 80.

21. Dan Basen to Sam Wagstaff, November 30, 1967, box 71, folder 1, Sam Wagstaff Papers, Getty.

22. Dan Basen to Sam Wagstaff, n.d. [1970], ibid.

23. Morrisroe, *Mapplethorpe*, p.113.

24. Ibid., p. 117.

SIX FROM MINIMALISM TO MAPPLETHORPE

1. Marcel Proust, *The Fugitive*, trans. C. K. Scott Montcrieff and Terence Kilmartin, ed. D. J. Enright (New York: Modern Library, 1993), p. 343.

2. *The Painterly Photograph, 1890–1914*, the Metropolitan Museum of Art, New York, January 8–March 15, 1973.

3. Aaron Scharf, "The Art of Photography," review of *Creative Photography: Aesthetic Trends 1839-1960* by Helmut Gernsheim, *Burlington Magazine* 105, no. 722 (May 1963).

4. Ibid.

5. Florence Berkman, "Atheneum Curator Explains: Modern Art: A Visual Language," *Hartford Times*, November 25, 1961.

6. Transcript of Wagstaff talk to students of photographer William Gedney at Pratt Institute, Brooklyn, N.Y., March 22, 1978, "William Gedney Photographs and Writings, 1940–1989," David M. Rubenstein Rare Book and Manuscript Library, Duke University, Durham, N. C.

7. Interview with Weston Naef, Los Angeles, April 23, 2009.

8. The most complete history of "The Family of Man" exhibition can be found in John Szarkowski, "The Family of Man," *Studies in Modern Art* 4 (1995): 12–37. See also Hilton Kramer, "Exhibiting the Family of Man, The World's Most Talked About Photographs," *Commentary* 20 (October 1955): 366–67.

9. Weston Naef and Suzanne Boorsch, *The Painterly Photograph, 1890–1914* (New York: Metropolitan Museum of Art, 1973).

10. Interview with Enrico Natali, Ojai, Calif., December 5, 2011.

11. Nancy Barr, "The Pleasure of Looking, The Pleasure of Seeing," *Bulletin of the Detroit Institute of Arts* 83, no. 1/4 (2009). Barr quotes from Sam's oral history interview with Marlyn B. Ghausi.

12. Sam Wagstaff, letter of recommendation for Enrico Natali, January 15, 1971, Archives of the John Simon Guggenheim Memorial Foundation, New York.

13. Video of Spanish television documentary on Robert Mapplethorpe, 1980s, box 196, Robert Mapplethorpe Papers (2011.M.20), J. Paul Getty Trust, Getty Research Institute, Los Angeles.

14. Interview with George Rinhart, Palm Springs, Calif., November 5, 2011.

15. Ibid.

16. Bruce Hainley, "The Eye of Sam Wagstaff: J. Paul Getty Museum—Photographer," *Artforum* (April 1997).

17. Janet Kardon, interview with Robert Mapplethorpe in *Robert Mapplethorpe: The Perfect Moment*, p. 24, catalog published in conjunction with the exhibition of the same name, Institute of Contemporary Arts, Philadelphia, December 9, 1988–January 29, 1989.

18. Interview with Jed Perl, New York, August 2, 2011.

19. Transcript of Wagstaff talk to Pratt students.

20. Interview with Klaus Kertess, New York, February 24, 2009.

21. Interview with Agnes Gund, New York, May 23, 2012.

22. Sam Wagstaff, "Paintings to Think About," *ARTnews* 62, no. 9 (January 1964): 38.

23. John Cage to John Kobler as quoted in Richard Kostelanetz, *Conversing with John Cage* (London and New York: Routledge, 2003), p. 65.

24. Interview with Barbara Jakobson, New York, December 16, 2010.

25. Interview with Jonas Mekas, http://PlanetGroupEntertainment.square space.com/the-jonas-mekas-interview.

26. Gerald (John) Palmer, telephone conversation with author, February 19, 2012.

27. Interview with Gerard Malanga, Hudson, N.Y., March 20, 2009.

28. Victor Bockris, *The Life and Death of Andy Warhol* (New York: Bantam, 1989).

29. *Photopath*, *1967—69* was first shown at the Institute of Contemporary Art, London, in the exhibition "Live in Your Head: When Attitudes Become Form," 1969.

30. John Szarkowski, wall text for the exhibition "New Documents," Museum of Modern Art, New York, February 28—May 7, 1967.

31. Richard Marshall in *Robert Mapplethorpe* (2006), directed by Paul Tschinkel, in association with Art/New York.

32. "Polaroids," an exhibition of Mapplethorpe's photographs, opened at Light Gallery, New York, on January 6, 1973.

SEVEN   TRANSFORMATION

1. R. D. Laing, *The Politics of Experience and the Bird of Paradise* (Harmondsworth, Eng.: Penguin Books, 1967), p. 30.

2. Joan Juliet Buck quoting Olga Newhall in *Black, White + Gray* (2007), directed by James Crump.

3. "Ma's Funeral" photographs, boxes 6 and 45, Sam Wagstaff Papers (2005 .M.46), J. Paul Getty Trust, Getty Research Institute, Los Angeles.

4. Pierre Apraxine and Sophie Schmit, *Photography and the Occult* (New Haven and London: Yale University Press, 2004), p. 12.

5. Sam Wagstaff to Robert Mapplethorpe, June 1973, box 181, folder 1, Robert Mapplethorpe Papers (2011.M.20), J. Paul Getty Trust, Getty Research Institute, Los Angeles.

6. Robert Mapplethorpe to Sam Wagstaff, May 1973, box 181, folder 1, ibid.

7. Sam Wagstaff to Robert Mapplethorpe, May 1973, box 181, folder 1, ibid.

8. Sam Wagstaff to Robert Mapplethorpe, May 1973, box 181, folder 1, ibid.

9. Sam Wagstaff to Robert Mapplethorpe, May 1973, box 181, folder 1, ibid.

10. Patricia Morrisroe, *Mapplethorpe: A Biography* (New York: Da Capo Press, 1997).

11. Sam Wagstaff to Robert Mapplethorpe, May 1973, box 181, folder 1, Robert Mapplethorpe Papers, Getty.

12. Transcript of Wagstaff talk to students of photographer William Gedney at Pratt Institute, Brooklyn, N.Y., March 22, 1978, "William Gedney Photographs and Writings, 1940–1989," David M. Rubenstein Rare Book and Manuscript Library, Duke University, Durham, N.C.

13. Interview with Richard Tuttle, New York, June 2, 2009.

14. Self-portraits, box 16, Sam Wagstaff Papers (2005.M.46), Getty.

15. Morrisroe, *Mapplethorpe*, p. 135.

16. Sam Wagstaff to Robert Mapplethorpe, February 1979, box 181, folder 1, Robert Mapplethorpe Papers, Getty.

19. Thomas Mann, *Death in Venice*, trans. David Luke (New York: Bantam Classics, 1988), p. 340.

20. Interview with Thomas L. Jefferson, Los Angeles, October 28, 2011.

EIGHT   CIRCLES OF INFLUENCE

1. Oscar Wilde, *The Picture of Dorian Gray*.

2. Jack Woody, *George Platt Lynes: Photographs 1931–1955* (Santa Fe, N.M.: Twelve Trees Press, 1980), p. 79.

3. Ibid, p. 105.

4. Interview with Bernard Perlin, Ridgefield, Conn., April 16, 2012.

5. Ibid.

6. Ibid.

7. Sam Wagstaff to Robert Mapplethorpe, January 23, 1974, box 181, folder 1, Robert Mapplethorpe Papers, (2011.M.20), J. Paul Getty Trust, Getty Research Institute, Los Angeles.

8. Ibid.

9. Ibid.

10. Patricia Morrisroe, *Mapplethorpe: A Biography* Da Capo Press, 1997 (New York), p. 136.

11. Robert Mapplethorpe to Sam Wagstaff, February, 1974, box 181, folder 1, Sam Wagstaff Papers (2005. M. 46), J. Paul Getty Trust, Getty Research Institute, Los Angeles.

12. Robert Mapplethorpe to Sam Wagstaff, n.d. [Spring 1974], box 181, folder 1, ibid.

13. Sam Wagstaff to Mark Kaminsky, March 8, 1974; courtesy of Paul F. Walter.

14. Sam Wagstaff to Mark Kaminsky, March 11, 1974; courtesy of Paul F. Walter.

15. Sam Wagstaff to Mark Kaminsky, March 12, 1974; courtesy of Paul F. Walter.

16. Interview with Judy Linn, Ghent, N.Y., May 25, 2009.

17. Ibid.

18. Marge Neikrug, telephone conversation with author, December 7, 2011.

19. Invoice from Neikrug Gallery, September 1, 1974, Sam Wagstaff Papers (2005.M.46), J. Paul Getty Trust, Getty Research Institute, Los Angeles.

20. The exhibition "David Octavius Hill: Portrait Photographs 1843–1848" was held at the Museum of Modern Art, New York, September 9–October 19, 1941, and organized by Beaumont Newhall, who chose the work from the collection of Heinrich Schwarz of Buffalo, New York.

21. J. Craig Annan, "David Octavius Hill, R.S.A., 1802–1870," *Camerwork*, July 1905, p. 17.

22. Ibid.

23. Interview with George Rinhart, Palm Springs, Calif., November 5, 2011.

24. Transcript of Wagstaff talk to students of photographer William Gedney at Pratt Institute, Brooklyn, N.Y., March 22, 1978, "William Gedney Photographs and Writings, 1940–1989," David M. Rubenstein Rare Book and Manuscript Library, Duke University, Durham, N.C.

25. Ibid.

26. Interview with Keith De Lellis, New York, April 27, 2011.

27. Ibid.

28. Daniel Wolf, telephone conversation with author, July 8, 2009.

29. Ibid.

30. Interview with Harvey Shipley Miller, New York, January 25, 2013.

31. The collection of Harvey Shipley Miller and Randell Plummer sold for $1,832,625 at Christie's, New York, on October 8, 2009. Among the more valuable photographs was, Marcus Aurelius Root, which realized $350,500; an Alexander Gardner sold for $92,500; William Henry Fox Talbot's edition of *Sun Pictures* brought $62,500; and an Atget for $56,250.

32. Miller, interview.

33. Ibid.

34. Interview with Klaus Kertess, New York, February 24, 2009.

35. Brice Marden, telephone conversation with author, October 6, 2011.

36. Ibid.

37. Julia Margaret Cameron, Heilbrunn Timeline of Art History, Metropolitan Museum of Art, web site, www.metmuseum.org/toah/hd/camr/hd_camr.htm.

38. Julia Margaret Cameron, Artists, the J. Paul Getty Museum web site, www.getty.edu/art/gettyguide/artMakerDetails?maker=2006.

39. Beaumont Newhall, "Eighteen Thirty-nine: The Birth of Photography," *Photography: Discovery and Invention: Papers Delivered of a Symposium*

Celebrating the Invention of Photography (Los Angeles: Getty Publications 1990), p. 36.

40. Souren Melikian, "Old Photos Making a Hit," *International Herald Tribune*, October 19–20, 1974.

41. Philippe Garner, e-mail to author, March 3, 2012.

42. Interview with Philippe Garner, New York, October 4, 2012.

43. Wolf, telephone conversation.

44. André Jammes, e-mail to author, May 18, 2012.

45. Ibid.

46. Interview with Clark Worswick, Millbrook, N.Y., May 9, 2012.

47. Sam Wagstaff to Anne MacDonald, December 1978; courtesy of Anne MacDonald.

NINE   LUXE, CALME, ET VOLUPTE

1. Wallace Stevens, *The Necessary Angel: Essays on Reality and Imagination*, (New York: Vintage, 1965), p. 138.

2. Interview with Klaus Kertess, New York, February 24, 2009.

3. Sam Wagstaff to Thomas Messer, October 12, 1974, box 85, Sam Wagstaff Papers (2005.M.46), J. Paul Getty Trust, Getty Research Institute, Los Angeles.

4. Thomas Messer to Sam Wagstaff, April 29, 1975, box 85, ibid.

5. Interview with Kiki Smith, New York, May 14, 2009.

6. "Sculpture: Masters of the Monumentalists," *Time*, October 13, 1967.

7. Interview with John Waddell, New York, October 3, 2012.

8. *Die* (1962), Smith's first steel sculpture, was fabricated in an edition of three. In 1998 the Museum of Modern Art in New York acquired one as a gift of Jane Smith, Tony Smith's widow. In 2003 the National Gallery of Art in Washington, D.C., acquired one cast. The third belongs to the Whitney Museum of American Art.

9. *Journal of the Photographic Society* 3 (1857).

10. Interview with Ann Horton, New York, September 24, 2009.

11. Ibid.

12. Daniel Wolf, telephone conversation with author, July 8, 2009.

13. Interview with Clark Worswick, Millbrook, N.Y., May 9, 2012.

14. Ibid.

15. Interview with Paul F. Walter, New York, March 10, 2009.

16. In 1981, at the invitation of John Szarkowski, Wagstaff would organize the exhibition "Photographs by Alfred Capel-Cure" at the Museum of Modern Art, New York, April 3–June 28, 1981. The exhibition consisted of forty-five calotype prints, mostly architectural views in the English countryside from 1853 to 1860.

17. Walter, interview.

18. Wolf, telephone conversation.

19. Interview with Keith De Lellis, New York, April 27, 2011.

20. Worswick, interview.

21. Ibid.

22. Harry Lunn to Sam Wagstaff, August 12, 1975, box 89, folder 5, Harry Lunn Papers (2004.M.17), J. Paul Getty Trust, Getty Research Institute, Los Angeles.

23. Interview with G. Ray Hawkins, Los Angeles, January 10, 2013.

24. Ibid.

25. Waddell, interview.

26. Horton, interview.

27. Bruce Hainley, "The Eye of Sam Wagstaff: J. Paul Getty Museum—photographer," *Artforum* (April 1997).

28. Worswick, interview.

29. Wolf, telephone conversation.

30. Walter, interview.

31. The symposium Collecting the Photograph took place on September 30, 1975. In addition to Peter Bunnell, John Szarkowski, Weston Naef, Harry Lunn, and Sam Wagstaff, the panelists included Nathan Lyons of the Visual Studies Workshop and Eugenia Parry Janis of Wellesley College.

32. *Interview* (November 1975).

33. Ibid.

34. Ibid.

35. Ibid.

36. Patricia Morrisroe, *Mapplethorpe: A Biography* (New York: Da Capo Press, 1997), p. 141.

37. Maxime de la Falaise, "Now Chic: Patti Smith, Rock Star, by Robert Mapplethorpe, Art Photographer." *Interview*, February 1976.

38. Rene Ricard, "Patti Smith and Robert Mapplethorpe at Miller," *Art in America* (September/October 1978).

39. Photos from Majorca and other Balearic Islands, box 27, Sam Wagstaff Papers, Getty.

40. Sam Wagstaff to Robert Mapplethorpe, n.d. [1975], box 181, folder 1, Robert Mapplethorpe Papers (2011.M.20), J. Paul Getty Trust, Getty Research Institute, Los Angeles.

TEN   THE INAMORATO

1. Frank O'Hara, "Steven," *The Collected Poems of Frank O'Hara*, ed. Donald Allen (New York: Alfred A. Knopf, 1972), p. 100.

2. Harold Pfister, Program Management Officer, National Portrait Gallery, Washington, D.C., to Sam Wagstaff, September 20, 1976, box 85, folder

1, Sam Wagstaff Papers (2005.M.46), J. Paul Getty Trust, Getty Research Institute, Los Angeles.

3. Interview with Clark Worswick, Millbrook, N.Y., May 9, 2012.

4. Alexander Shouvaloff, *The Art of Ballets Russes: The Serge Lifar Collection of Theater Designs, Costumes, and Paintings at the Wadsworth Atheneum* (New Haven: Yale University Press, 1977).

5. Interview with John Waddell, New York, March 18, 2009.

6. Interview with Gerald Incandela, Santa Barbara, Calif., April 4, 2009.

7. Ibid.

8. Sam Wagstaff to Gerald Incandela, n.d. [Spring 1976]; courtesy of Gerald Incandela.

9. Ibid.

10. Sam Wagstaff to Gerald Incandela, 1976; courtesy of Gerald Incandela.

11. Ger Osten, to Sam Wagstaff, October 26, 1975, box 80, folder 2A, Sam Wagstaff Papers, Getty.

12. Sam Wagstaff to Gerald Incandela, n.d. [Spring 1976]; courtesy of Gerald Incandela.

13. Interview with Steven M. L. Aronson, New York, January 4, 2011.

14. Ibid.

15. Interview with Paul F. Walter, New York, March 10, 2009.

16. Aronson, interview.

17. Incandela, interview.

18. Douglas Davis to Sam Wagstaff, January 20, 1977, box 85, folder 2, Sam Wagstaff Papers, Getty.

19. Andy Grundberg to Sam Wagstaff, May 24, 1978, ibid.

20. Christopher Phillips, "The Judgment Seat of Photography," *October* 22 (Autumn 1982): 27–63.

21. Interview with Susan Kismaric, New York, August 3, 2012. The museum acquired the Nicholas Nixon print, continued to collect others from the series, and on the twenty-fifth anniversary of their documentation published the collection *The Brown Sisters, 1975–1999*.

22. Interview with Maria Morris Hambourg, New York, September 18, 2012.

23. Harold Edgerton to Sam Wagstaff, January 17, 1975, Sam Wagstaff Papers, Getty.

24. Sam Wagstaff, "The Wagstaff 10," *American Photographer* 16, no. 5 (May 1986): 62.

25. Interview with Ellen Brooks, New York, November 12, 2010.

26. Interview with Lynn Davis, Hudson, N.Y., March 2, 2009.

27. Ibid.

28. Ibid.

29. Ibid.

30. Interview with Elaine Mayes, New York, October 30, 2009.

31. Ibid.
32. Ibid.
33. Walter, interview.
34. Robert Mapplethorpe to Sam Wagstaff, December 22, 1976. box 181, folder 1, Sam Wagstaff Papers, Getty. The men often referred to each other as "Wumper" or "Wumpers."

ELEVEN   LET THE GAMES BEGIN

1. Sam Wagstaff, *A Book of Photographs from the Collection of Sam Wagstaff* (New York: Gray Press, 1978), epigraph.
2. Hilton Als, *The Women* (New York: Farrar Straus Giraux, 1996), p. 113.
3. Ed Shostak, telephone conversation with author, June 2, 2012.
4. Hilton Kramer, "Art: Focus on Photo Shows," *The New York Times*, May 28, 1976, p. 62.
5. Christopher Knight, "Holly Solomon, 68; Art Dealer Who Helped Transform Soho," *Los Angeles Times*, June 11, 2002.
6. David Boyce, "At Home with Robert Mapplethorpe," *The Gay and Lesbian Review*, November 2008.
7. Ibid.
8. Holly Solomon in *Robert Mapplethorpe* (2006), directed by Paul Tschinkel in association with Art/New York.
9. Holly Solomon as quoted by Laura Paulson, international director, postwar and contemporary art, on Christie's web site discussing Andy Warhol's silk screen on canvas, *Holly Solomon* (1966), offered at sale of May 11, 2010, www.christies.com/features/2314_51-560-4.aspx.
10. Carol Vogel, "Second Night of Caution at Auction," *The New York Times*, May 4, 1995.
11. Boyce, "At Home with Robert Mapplethorpe."
12. Ibid.
13. The exhibition "Women of Photography: An Historical Survey," organized by the San Francisco Museum of Modern Art, began its tour there, April 18–May 23, 1975.
14. Solomon in *Robert Mapplethorpe*.
15. "Erotic Pictures," by Robert Mapplethorpe, an exhibition of photographs opened at The Kitchen, New York, on February 4, 1977.
16. Solomon in *Robert Mapplethorpe*.
17. Patricia Morrisroe, *Mapplethorpe: A Biography* (New York: Da Capo Press, 1997), p. 178.
18. Jennifer Blessing, Arkady Ippolitov, Kyoichi Tsuzuki, Germano Celant, *Robert Mapplethorpe and the Classical Tradition* (New York: Guggeheim Museum, 2004).
19. Morrisroe, *Mapplethorpe*, p. 179.

20. Interview with George Rinhart, Palm Springs, Calif., November 5, 2011.

21. Shostak, telephone conversation.

22. Interview with Fran Leibowitz, New York, October 22, 2009.

23. Philippe Garner, e-mail to author, March 3, 2012.

24. Interview with Paul F. Walter, New York, March 10, 2009.

25. Gar Osten to Sam Wagstaff, October 26, 1975, box 80, folder 2A, Sam Wagstaff Papers (2005.M.46), J. Paul Getty Trust, Getty Research Institute, Los Angeles.

26. Jane Livingston, telephone conversation with author, November 8, 2011.

27. Mark Donovan, "You Don't Have to Be an Expert, Says Sam Wagstaff, to Recognize Great Photographs," *People*, April 18, 1978, p. 66.

28. Interview with Arne Lewis, New York, June 21, 2012.

29. Interview with Gerald Incandela, Santa Barbara, Calif., April 4, 2009.

30. Ibid.

31. Ibid.

32. Ibid.

33. Interview with Barbara Jakobson, New York, December 16, 2010.

34. Incandela, interview.

35. Ibid.

36. Ibid.

37. Sam Wagstaff, "The Wagstaff 10," *American Photographer* 16, no. 5 (May 1986): p. 62.

38. Incandela, interview.

39. Gustave Le Gray, Heilbrunn Timeline of Art History, the Metropolitan Museum of Art web site, www.metmuseum.org/toah/hd/gray/hd_gray .htm.

40. Incandela, interview.

41. Wagstaff quoted in Owen Edwards, "The Collector Who Would Be King," *American Photographer*, September 1978, p. 20.

42. Incandela, interview.

43. Livingston, telephone conversation.

44. Lewis, interview.

45. Ibid.

46. Incandela, interview.

47. Walter, interview.

48. Interview with John Waddell, New York, March 18, 2009.

49. Jared Bark, telephone conversation with author, December 20, 2013.

50. Ibid.

51. Rinhart, interview.

52. The song "Native New Yorker," by Odyssey, was written by Sandy Linzer and Denny Randell.

53. Incandela, interview.

54. *Tulips, New York* by Robert Mapplethorpe, which appeared on the cover of

A Book of Photographs from the Collection of Sam Wagstaff, was acquired by the Museum of Modern Art in 1981.

55. Interview with Judy Linn, Ghent, N.Y., May 25, 2009.

56. Incandela, interview.

57. Sam Wagstaff, inscription to Gerald Incandela, in Wagstaff, *A Book of Photographs from the Collection of Sam Wagstaff*; courtesy of Gerald Incandela.

TWELVE   APPLAUSE

1. Wagstaff quoted in Owen Edwards, "The Collector Who Would Be King," *American Photographer* (September 1978), p. 20.

2. Stephanie Mansfield, "A Flashy Opening Night for Gallerygoers," *The Washington Post*, February 4, 1978, p. E5.

3. Susan Sontag, *On Photography* (New York: Farrar Straus Giroux, 1977). The essays in *On Photography* were first published, beginning in 1973, in slightly different form in *The New York Review of Books*. The influence of her essays on the photographic intelligentsia, the academic community, and those who appreciate photography has been significant.

4. Paul Richard, "Sam Wagstaff, The Collector the Establishment Trusts," *The Washington Post*, February 3, 1978, p. D1.

5. Ibid.

6. Jane Livingston, telephone conversation with author, November 8, 2011.

7. Transcript of Wagstaff talk to students of photographer William Gedney at Pratt Institute, Brooklyn, N.Y., March 22, 1978, "William Gedney Photographs and Writings, 1940–1989," David M. Rubenstein Rare Book and Manuscript Library, Duke University, Durham, N.C.

8. Ibid.

9. Interview with Gerald Incandela, Santa Barbara, Calif., April 4, 2009.

10. Transcript of Wagstaff talk to Pratt students.

11. Ibid.

12. Ibid.

13. Ibid.

14. Richard, "Sam Wagstaff," p. D1.

15. Livingston, telephone conversation.

16. Ibid.

17. Transcript of Wagstaff talk to Pratt students.

18. Livingston, telephone conversation.

19. Ibid.

20. Mary Swift, telephone conversation with author, August 2, 2012.

21. Incandela, interview.

22. Livingston, telephone conversation.

23. The symposium Photography: Where We Are was held at the Corcoran Museum of Art auditorium on February 25, 1978, a two-day affair. The first day began at 10:00: Morning speakers included Peter Bunnell, director of the Princeton Art Museum, and photographers Frederick Sommer and Alex Jamison. The afternoon panel about collecting was moderated by Jim Enyeart, then director of the archives at the Center for Creative Photography and included Van Deren Coke, curator of photography at the San Francisco Museum of Modern Art; Alan Fern, head of the National Portrait Gallery, André Jammes, the French collector, and Sam Wagstaff. The second-day speakers included Susan Sontag, Rosalind Krauss, Hilton Kramer, and Joel Snyder, professor at the University of Chicago. A transcript of the symposium is in the archives of the Corcoran Gallery of Art, Washington, D.C.

24. Ibid.

25. Ibid.

26. Ibid.

27. Ibid.

28. Ibid.

29. Ibid.

30. Ibid.

31. Ibid.

32. In 1974, Clement Greenberg quipped to his student Rosalind Krauss: "Spare me smart Jewish girls with their typewriters." She would use a picture of her younger self at a typewriter on the cover of her book of essays and include Greenberg's line on the back of the book: *Perpetual Inventory* (Cambridge, Mass.: MIT Press, 2010).

33. Ibid.

34. Ibid.

35. After its run at the Corcoran Gallery of Art, "Photographs from the Collection of Sam Wagstaff" traveled to sixteen other museums, including those in New York City, St. Louis, Seattle, and Berkeley. The show opened at New York University's Grey Art Gallery in June 1978.

36. Sam Wagstaff to Anne MacDonald, May 15, 1978; courtesy of Anne MacDonald.

37. Gene Thornton, "The Wagstaff Collection," *The New York Times*, July 2, 1978, pp. D19–20.

38. Edwards, "The Collector Who Would Be King," p. 20.

39. John Szarkowski to Sam Wagstaff, March 7, 1978, files of the Department of Photographs, the Museum of Modern Art, New York.

40. Richard, "Sam Wagstaff," p. D1.

41. Richard Avedon to Sam Wagstaff, May 5, 1978, Sam Wagstaff Papers (2005.M.46), J. Paul Getty Trust, Getty Research Institute, Los Angeles.

THIRTEEN   BACK TO POMPEII

1. Larry Kramer, *Faggots* (New York: Random House, 1978), p. 238.

2. Marcuse Pfeiffer, *The Male Nude: A Survey in Photography* (New York: Marcuse Pfeiffer Gallery, 1979). The catalog includes an essay by Shelley Rice. The exhibition at the Marcuse Pfeiffer Gallery in New York was held June 13–July 28, 1978.

3. Ibid.

4. Gene Thornton, "From the Ideal to the Erotic," *The New York Times*, June 18, 1978, pp. D27–28.

5. Ben Lifson quoted in Allen Ellenzweig, *The Homoerotic Photograph: Male Images from Durieu/Delacroix to Mapplethorpe* (New York: Columbia University Press, 1992), p. xvi.

6. John Ashbery quoted in ibid.

7. Rene Ricard quoted in ibid.

8. Vicki Goldberg quoted in ibid.

9. Interview with Paul F. Walter, New York, March 10, 2009.

10. Frank Rich, "The Gay Decades," *Esquire*, November 1987, pp. 87–99.

11. National Park Service web site: www.nps.gov/fiis/index.htm.

12. Elsa Bulgari [Carol Squiers], "Interview with Robert Mapplethorpe," *Fire Island Tide*, July 3, 1979.

13. Mark Donovan, "You Don't Have to Be an Expert, Says Sam Wagstaff, to Recognize Great Photographs," *People*, April 18, 1978.

14. Owen Edwards, "The Collector Who Would Be King," *American Photographer*, September 1978, p. 20.

15. Clive Barnes, "Revue: Bette Midler. 'Clams on Half Shell' Opens at Minskoff," *The New York Times*, April 18, 1975.

16. Interview with Barbara Jakobson, New York, December 16, 2010.

17. Ibid.

18. Robert Sherman, speaking at Working with Mapplethorpe, a panel held at The Getty Center, Los Angeles, January 9, 2013. The panel, moderated by the author, included Brian English, Judy Linn, and Robert Sherman.

19. *Black Beauty* (1979), by Gerald Incandela, a view of the Metropolitan Life Building in Manhattan, was acquired by the Museum of Modern Art in 1984.

20. Janet Kardon, interview with Robert Mapplethorpe in *Robert Mapplethorpe: The Perfect Moment*, p. 26, catalog published in conjunction with the exhibition of the same name, Institute of Contemporary Art, Philadelphia, December 9, 1988–January 29, 1989.

21. Sylvia Wolf, *Polaroids: Mapplethorpe* (New York: Prestel, 2007). Published in conjunction with the exhibition of the same name at the Whitney Museum of American Art, New York in collaboration with the Robert Mapplethorpe Foundation, Inc., 2007, p. 51.

22. Video of Spanish television documentary on Robert Mapplethorpe, 1980s, box 196, Robert Mapplethorpe Papers (2011.M.20), J. Paul Getty Trust, Getty Research Institute, Los Angeles.

23. Sam Wagstaff to Anne MacDonald, December 11,1978; courtesy of Anne MacDonald.

24. Robert McDonald, "Censored," *The Advocate*, June 28, 1978.

25. Ibid.

26. Interview with Anne MacDonald, New York, April 2, 2012.

27. Interview with William Ewing, New York, October 4, 2012.

28. Ibid.

29. Ibid.

30. Interview with Lynn Davis, Hudson, N.Y., March 2, 2009.

31. Ibid.

32. Ibid.

33. "Trade off: Lynn Davis and Robert Mapplethorpe," an exhibition of portraits of the same individuals taken by both photographers, was mounted at the International Center of Photography, New York, March 17–April 22, 1979.

34. Carol Squiers, unpublished essay; courtesy of Carol Squiers.

35. Interview with Carol Squiers, New York, January 26, 2011.

36. Holly Solomon quoted in *Robert Mapplethorpe* (2006), directed by Paul Tschinkel in association with Art/New York.

37. "Contact" was shown at Robert Miller Gallery, New York, March 21–April 18, 1979.

38. Ben Lifson, quoted in Ellenzweig, *Homoerotic Photograph*, p. xvi.

39. Hilton Kramer, "Art: Jean Dubuffet at Pace Gallery" *The New York Times*, April 6, 1979, p. C21.

40. Vicki Goldberg quoted in Patricia Morrisroe, *Mapplethorpe: A Biography* (New York: Da Capo Press, 1997), p. 218.

41. Bulgari, "Interview with Robert Mapplethorpe."

42. Squiers, interview.

43. Ibid.

44. Ibid.

45. Ibid.

46. Ewing, interview.

47. Ibid.

48. Sam Green quoted in Morrisroe, *Mapplethorpe*, p. 208.

FOURTEEN THE ARRIVISTE

1. Quoted in Philip Gefter, "Henry Wessel: Capturing the Image, Transcending the Subject," *The New York Times*, May 21, 2006.

2. *The Dick Cavett Show*, October 17, 1980, PBS; DVD transfer of the video-taped show courtesy of John Waddell.

3. Interview with John Waddell, New York, October 3, 2012.

4. "Walker Evans and Robert Frank: An Essay on Influence" was presented at the Yale University Art Gallery, New Haven, January 21–March 15, 1981, and at the Daniel Wolf Gallery, New York, March 31–April 25, 1981. Tod Papageorge, professor and director of photography of the Yale University School of Art, organized the exhibition and wrote the accompanying catalog essay.

5. *American Photographs* was first published in 1938 by the Museum of Modern Art to accompany an exhibition of Walker Evans's photographs of the same title. It was subsequently reissued by MoMA in 1962; by the East River Press, New York, in 1975; and again by MoMA in 1988. A seventy-fifth-anniversary edition appeared in 2013.

6. Tod Papageorge, *Walker Evans and Robert Frank: An Essay on Influence* (New Haven: Yale University Art Gallery, 1981), pp. 6–7.

7. Robert Frank's *The Americans* (New York: Grove Press, 1959) was originally published the year before in France as *Les Americains*.

8. Interview with Carol Squiers, New York, January 26, 2011.

9. Belinda Rathbone and Clark Worswick, *Walker Evans: The Lost Work* (Santa Fe, N.M.: Arena Editions, 2000), p. 11.

10. Sam Wagstaff to Bob Bishop, September 4, 1978, The Samuel J. Wagstaff Jr. Records, 1956–1978, Research Library and Archives, Detroit Institute of Arts.

11. John Szarkowski, *The Photographer's Eye* (Garden City, N.Y.: Museum of Modern Art/Doubleday, 1966).

12. Interview with George Rinhart, Palm Springs, Calif., November 5, 2011.

13. Ibid.

14. The full contract between George Rinhart and Walker Evans is reprinted in Rathbone and Worswick, *Walker Evans*, pp. 22–23. The contract that was drawn up states, "Specifically, you and I agree that we [Rinhart Galleries] will purchase all photographic prints owned by you, including portfolios and books or mock-ups of books, either by you or illustrated by you or containing illustrations of your works, excepting, of course, one copy each of your personal library, and excepting your personal letters and correspondence. . . . We have also agreed that the negatives of any of these photographic prints are not presently included in our purchase agreement."

15. Several people interviewed by the author have raised questions about the authenticity of Evans's signatures on the individual works of art.

16. Judy Keller, "Circa 1970: The Invention of the Photography Market" (lecture, Art Beijing Forum, Beijing, September 8, 2008).

17. Jane Livingston, telephone conversation with author, November 8, 2011.

18. Edmund White, introduction, *Black Males* (Amsterdam: Galerie Jurka, 1980).

19. Interview with Betsy Wittenborn Miller, New York, October 2, 2012.

20. Waddell, interview.

21. Patricia Morrisroe, *Mapplethorpe: A Biography* (New York: Da Capo Press, 1997), p. 251.

22. The four exhibitions, organized by John Szarkowski, on view at the Museum of Modern Art were "The Work of Atget: Old France (Atget I)," October 3, 1981–January 3, 1982; "The Work of Atget: The Art of Old Paris (Atget II)," October 14, 1982–January 4, 1983; "The Work of Atget: The Ancien Regime (Atget III)," March 14–May 14, 1985; and "The Work of Atget: Modern Times (Atget IV), "March 1–May 14, 1985. Catalogs accompanied each exhibition.

23. Interview with Susan Kismaric, New York, August 3, 2012.

24. John Szarkowski and Maria Morris Hambourg, *The Work of Atget: Old France* (New York: Museum of Modern Art, 1981), p. 11.

25. John Szarkowski to Sam Wagstaff, May 27, 1977, correspondence files of the Department of Photographs, the Museum of Modern Art, New York.

26. Morrisroe, *Mapplethorpe*, p. 230.

27. Waddell, interview.

28. Interview with Paul F. Walter, New York, March 10, 2009.

29. Interview with Anne MacDonald, New York, April 2, 2012.

30. Interview with Pierre Apraxine, New York, December 22, 2010.

31. Rinhart, interview.

32. Morrisroe, *Mapplethorpe*, p. 252.

33. Douglas Crimp, "The Museum's Old/The Library's New Subject," *Parachute* 22 (Spring 1981): 32–37.

34. Sam Wagstaff to John Szarkowski, February 13, 1980, correspondence files of the Department of Photographs, the Museum of Modern Art, New York.

35. Lawrence K. Altman, "Rare Cancer Seen in 41 Homosexuals," *The New York Times*, July 3, 1981.

36. Lawrence Mass, "Disease Rumors Largely Unfounded," *New York Native*, May 18, 1981.

37. Altman, "Rare Cancer Seen in 41 Homosexuals."

38. Charles Kaiser, *The Gay Metropolis* (New York: Houghton Mifflin, 1997), p. 279.

FIFTEEN   THE PICTURES GENERATION

1. Rainer Maria Rilke, *Letters to a Young Poet* (New York: W. W. Norton, 1993), p. 41.

2. Paul Richard, "Sam Wagstaff, the Collector the Establishment Trusts," *The Washington Post*, February 3, 1978, p. D1.

3. Lynn Zelevansky, newsletter of the Carnegie Museum, Pittsburgh, Winter 2009.

4. Interview with Paula Cooper, New York, December 6, 2012.

5. Ibid.

6. Frank Di Giacomo, "Bright Lights, Big '80's, Live from Tribeca," *Vanity Fair*, November 2005.

7. Anthony Haden-Guest, "The New Queen of the Art Scene," *New York*, April 17, 1982.

8. Ibid.

9. Robert Hughes, *The Shock of the New* (New York: Alfred A. Knopf, 1980), p. 9.

10. Hilton Kramer, "Art: Two Painters Explore New Wave," *The New York Times*, April 17, 1981.

11. Interview with David Hockney, New York, October 30, 2009.

12. André Jammes and Eugenia Parry Janis, *The Art of French Calotype* (Princeton N.J.: Princeton University Press, 1983).

13. Abigail Solomon-Godeau, "Calotypomania: The Gourmet Guide to Nineteenth-Century Photography," *Afterimage*, nos. 1–2 (Summer 1983): 27.

14. Margaret Loke, "Collecting's Big Thrill Is the Chase," *The New York Times Magazine*, March 17, 1985, p. 41.

15. Andy Grundberg, "Photography View: A Renewed Vitality in the Face of Economic Hard Times," *The New York Times*, April 11, 1982.

16. Michael Lobel, "We're Here: Gay and Lesbian Presence in Art and Art History," *Art Journal*, 55, no. 4 (1996): pp. 42–50.

17. Sam Wagstaff to Robert Mapplethorpe, n.d. [Spring, 1982], box 181, folder 1, Robert Mapplethorpe Papers (2011.M.20), J. Paul Getty Trust, Getty Research Institute, Los Angeles.

18. Daniel Wolf, telephone conversation with author, July 8, 2009.

19. Bruce Chatwin, "An Eye and Some Body" in Robert Mapplethorpe, *Lady Lisa Lyon*, (New York: Viking, 1983), p. 12.

20. Patricia Morrisroe, *Mapplethorpe: A Biography* (New York: Da Capo Press, 1997), p. 231.

21. *Robert Mapplethorpe* (2006), directed by Paul Tschinkel in association with Art/New York.

22. Morrisroe, *Mapplethorpe*, p. 233.

23. Sam Wagstaff, foreword to *Lady Lisa Lyon*, p. 8.

24. Sam Wagstaff to Patti Smith, September 1, 1982, box 86, folder 1, Sam Wagstaff Papers (2005.M.46), J. Paul Getty Trust, Getty Research Institute, Los Angeles.

SIXTEEN   WHISPERS OF THE MUSE

1. Holland Cotter, "Images That Preserve History, and Make It," *The New York Times*, September 20, 2012, p. C27.
2. John Russell, "Boston Museum Curator Named Director of Getty," *The New York Times*, March 4, 1983.
3. Daniel Wolf, telephone conversation with author, July 8, 2009.
4. Ibid.
5. Ibid.
6. Barbara Eisenberg, "Photography: A Guy Who's Sharply Focused," *Los Angeles Times*, December 11, 1994.
7. Maria Morris Hambourg, e-mail to author, February 25, 2014.
8. Eisenberg, "A Guy Who's Sharply Focused."
9. Wolf, telephone conversation.
10. Ibid.
11. Ibid.
12. Interview with John Waddell, New York, October 3, 2012.
13. Ibid.
14. Harris Fogel, e-mail to author, January 28, 2012.
15. Interview with Dimitri Levas, New York, November 10, 2012.
16. Patricia Morrisroe, *Mapplethorpe: A Biography* (New York: Da Capo Press, 1997), p. 283.
17. Interview with Anne Ehrenkranz, New York, January 4, 2012.
18. Waddell, interview.
19. Interview with Philippe Garner, New York, October 4, 2012.
20. Ibid.
21. Interview with George Rinhart, Palm Springs, Calif., November 5, 2011.
22. Eisenberg, "A Guy Who's Sharply Focused."
23. Andy Grundberg, "Photography View: The Getty Shifts the Focus Westward," *The New York Times*, June 17, 1984.
24. Suzanne Muchnic, "Getty Museum Acquires Major Photo Collection," *Los Angeles Times*, June 8, 1984.
25. Ibid.
26. Interview with Judy Keller, Los Angeles, November 11, 2011.

SEVENTEEN   THE GLIMMER AND THE GLOOM

1. Friedrich Nietzsche, "Apophthegms and Interludes," *Beyond Good and Evil*, (Mineola, N.Y.: Dover Thrift Editions 1997), p. 46.
2. Interview with Pierre Apraxine, New York, December 22, 2010.
3. Ibid.
4. Ibid.

5. After the Metropolitan Museum of Art purchased the Gilman Collection, it mounted a show, "The Waking Dream: Photography's First Century; Selections from the Gilman Paper Company Collection," which appeared March 25–July 4, 1993. The exhibition was accompanied by a catalog with essays by Maria Morris Hambourg, Pierre Apraxine, Malcolm Daniel, Jeff. L. Rosenheim, and Virginia Heckert.

6. Randy Kennedy, "Met Museum Acquires Gilman Trove," *The New York Times*, March 17, 2005.

7. Ibid.

8. Ibid.

9. "A Personal View: Photography in the Collection of Paul F. Walter" appeared at the Museum of Modern Art, New York, May 23–August 12, 1985.

10. After the Metropolitan Museum of Art purchased Waddell's collection, it mounted a show, "The New Vision: Photography Between the Wars; Ford Motor Company Collection at the Metropolitan Museum of Art, New York," which appeared September 22–December 31, 1989. The accompanying catalog by Maria Morris Hambourg included essays by Christopher Phillips.

11. "Met Acquires Collection of Historical Photos," *The New York Times*, April 17, 1987.

12. Interview with John Waddell, New York, October 3, 2012.

13. "Photographs from the Sam Wagstaff Collection at the J. Paul Getty Museum" was on view at the International Center of Photography, New York, March 29–May 12, 1985.

14. Margaret Loke, "Collecting's Big Thrill Is the Chase," *The New York Times Magazine*, March 17, 1985, p. 41.

15. Inscription on invitation to Dimitri Levas by Sam Wagstaff; courtesy of Dimitri Levas.

16. Loke, "Collecting's Big Thrill Is the Chase," p. 41.

17. Ibid.

18. Ibid.

19. Interview with Barbara Jakobson, New York, December 16, 2010.

20. Bruce Hainley, "The Eye of Sam Wagstaff, J. Paul Getty Museum—Photographer," *Artforum* (April 1997).

21. Interview with Paul F. Walter, New York, March 10, 2009.

22. Sam Wagstaff Papers (2005.M.46), J. Paul Getty Trust, Getty Research Institute, Los Angeles, California.

23. Charles Venable, telephone conversation with author, December 19, 2012.

24. Interview with Ronald Hoffman, New York, December 12, 2012.

25. Ibid.

26. Nicholas Fox Weber, "Silver Futures," *House & Garden*, March 1987, pp. 42–48.

27. Jakobson, interview.

28. James Crump, "Art of Acquisition: The Eye of Sam Wagstaff," *Archives of American Art Journal* 46, no. 3–4 (2007): 4–13.

29. Interview with Richard Tuttle, New York, June 2, 2009.

30. Jonathan Weinberg, "Boy Crazy: Carl Van Vechten's Queer Collection," *Yale Journal of Criticism* (1994).

31. Ibid.

32. Interview with Edmund White, New York, March 3, 2009.

33. Interview with Judy Linn, Ghent, N.Y., May 25, 2009.

34. Christopher Bram, *Eminent Outlaws: The Gay Writers Who Changed America* (New York: Twelve Grand Central, 2012), p. 51; citing Mailer's *Advertisements for Myself*, p. 407.

35. Hans Johnson and William Eskridge, "The Legacy of Falwell's Bully Pulpit," *The Washington Post*, May 19, 2007.

36. William F. Buckley Jr., "Crucial Steps in Combating the AIDS Epidemic: Identify All the Carriers," *The New York Times*, March 18, 1986.

37. Peter Gay, *Weimar Culture: The Outsider as Insider* (New York: W.W. Norton, 2001), p. xiv.

38. Armistead Maupin, "The First Couple: Don Bachardy and Christopher Isherwood," *The Village Voice*, July 2, 1985.

39. Dan Sullivan, "Stage Review: 'Normal Heart': Aids Crisis [*sic*]," *Los Angeles Times*, December 13, 1985.

40. Interview with Fran Lebowitz, New York, October 22, 2009.

41. Patricia Morrisroe, *Mapplethorpe: A Biography* (New York: Da Capo Press, 1997), p. 294.

42. Ibid., p. 299.

43. Video of Spanish television documentary on Robert Mapplethorpe, 1980s, box 196, Robert Mapplethorpe Papers (2011.M.20), J. Paul Getty Trust, Getty Research Institute, Los Angeles.

44. Martin Filler, "Robert Mapplethorpe," *House & Garden*, June 1988.

45. Interview with Jeffrey Fraenkel, San Francisco, February 4, 2009.

46. Sam Wagstaff to Anne MacDonald, October 13, 1985; courtesy of Anne MacDonald.

47. Waddell, interview.

48. Nicholas Fox Weber, "Silver Futures," *House & Garden*, March 1987, pp. 47–48.

49. Waddell, interview.

50. Interview with Anne Ehrenkranz, New York, January 4, 2012.

51. Glen Hopkins, "Silver Rush: The Bitter Battle for a Collector's Trove," *New York*, July 11, 1988, p. 30.

52. Jakobson, interview.

53. Interview with Klaus Kertess, New York, February 24, 2009.

54.   Tuttle, interview.

55.   Interview with John Richardson, New York, September 17, 2009.

56.   Levas, interview.

57.   Charles L. Venable, *Silver in America, 1840–1940: A Century of Splendor* (New York): Harry N. Abrams, 1995).

58.   *International Review*, (New York: A.S. Barnes, 1879), Vol. 7.

59.   The pitcher was purchased by Charles L. Venable, assistant curator of decorative arts at the Dallas Museum of Art, Dallas, at the Christie's auction of Wagstaff's silver collection, January 20, 1989.

60.   Catalog for the Sam Wagstaff Collection of American Silver, Christie's sale, January 20, 1989.

61.   Weber, "Silver Futures," p. 45.

62.   Ibid.

63.   Ibid.

64.   Francesco Scavullo, "Sam Wagstaff," in *Scavullo on Men* (New York: Random House, 1977), p. 174.

EIGHTEEN   GARDENIAS, FRAGRANT, FLOATING

1.   Robin Hardy with David Groff, *The Crisis of Desire: AIDS and the Fate of Gay Brotherhood* (New York: Houghton Mifflin, 1999), p. 1.

2.   Ingrid Sischy to Sam Wagstaff, June 11, 1986, box 96, folder 2, Sam Wagstaff Papers, (2005.M.46), J. Paul Getty Trust, Getty Research Institute, Los Angeles.

3.   Interview with John Waddell, New York, October 3, 2012.

4.   Charles Kaiser, *The Gay Metropolis, 1940–1996* (New York: Houghton Mifflin, 1997), p. 282.

5.   Tom Toles, cartoon, *The Buffalo News*, c. 1982–1985.

6.   Interview with Steve Wachlin, Oakleyville, N.Y., August 5, 2011.

7.   Ibid.

8.   Ibid.

9.   "News Summary," *The New York Times*, May 3, 1986, p. A5.

10.   Sam Wagstaff, "Tiger in the House," *Artforum* (September 1986), p. 96.

11.   Ibid.

12.   Ronald Reagan, speech (written by Landon Parvin) given at a fund-raising gala for the American Foundation for AIDS Research (amfAR), Washington, D.C, May 31, 1987. Reagan was invited to speak by Elizabeth Taylor, founding national chairman of the organization.

13.   Waddell, interview.

14.   Susan Sontag, *Illness as Metaphor* (New York: Picador, 2001), p. 46.

15.   Waddell, interview.

16. Sanford Ehrenkranz to Cornell Medical Center, New York, October 30, 1986. Sam Wagstaff Papers, Getty.

17. Patricia Morrisroe, *Mapplethorpe: A Biography* (New York: Da Capo Press, 1997), p. 310.

18. Ellen Hopkins, "Silver Rush: The Bitter Battle for a Collector's Trove," *New York*, July 11, 1988, p. 30.

19. Waddell, interview.

20. Interview with Ronald Hoffman, New York, December 12, 2012.

21. Interview with Paul F. Walter, New York, March 10, 2009.

22. Interview with Kiki Smith, New York, May 14, 2009.

23. Daniel Wolf, telephone conversation with author, July 8, 2009.

24. Interview with Peter Coffeen, New York, June 3, 2009.

25. Douglas McGill, "Suit Seeks the Return of AIDS Victim's Silver," *The New York Times*, May 28, 1988.

26. Rita Reif, "Antiques: From American Sideboards," *The New York Times*, March 29, 1987.

27. Richard Tuttle, interview by James Crump, Abiquiu, N.M. December 21, 2003; courtesy of James Crump.

28. Hoffman, interview.

29. Charles L. Venable, *Silver in America, 1840–1940: A Century of Splendor* (New York: Harry N. Abrams, 1995), p. 163.

30. Hoffman, interview.

31. Hopkins, "Silver Rush," p.31.

32. Ibid.

33. Maria Morris Hambourg to Sam Wagstaff, December 18, 1986, Archives of the Department of Photography, Metropolitan Museum of Art, New York.

34. Interview with Pierre Apraxine, New York, December 22, 2010.

35. Morrisroe, *Mapplethorpe*, p. 315.

36. Anonymous source, conversation with author, New York, 2012.

37. Morrisroe, *Mapplethorpe*, p. 316.

38. McGill, "Suit Seeks the Return of AIDS Victim's Silver"; Reif, "Antiques: From American Sideboards"; Hopkins, "Silver Rush," p. 28–33

39. Morrisroe, *Mapplethorpe*, p. 318.

40. Interview with Maria Morris Hambourg, New York, September 18, 2012.

41. Sam Wagstaff to Robert Mapplethorpe, n.d. [c. 1973], box 181, folder 1, Robert Mapplethorpe Papers (2011.M.20), J. Paul Getty Trust, Getty Research Institute, Los Angeles.

42. Robert Mapplethorpe, eulogy given at memorial service for Sam Wagstaff at the Metropolitan Museum of Art, New York, March 2, 1987, Archives of the Department of Photography, Metropolitan Museum of Art, New York.

43. Ingrid Sischy, transcript of eulogy given at memorial service for Sam Wagstaff, March 2, 1987, ibid.

44. Ibid.

45. Peire Apraxine, transcript of eulogy given at memorial service for Sam Wagstaff, March 2, 1987, ibid.

46. Sam Wagstaff, statement for brochure, *The Wagstaff Collection of American Silver Chosen by the Late Samuel J. Wagstaff, Jr.*, published by the New-York Historical Society in conjunction with the exhibition of the same title, which opened there March 20, 1987.

47. The Sam Wagstaff Collection American Silver, Christie's Sale, January 20, 1989.

48. "The Perfect Moment" was mounted at the Institute of Contemporary Art, Philadelphia, December 9, 1988–January 29, 1989. Exhibition catalog: Janet Kardon, *Robert Mapplethorpe: The Perfect Moment* Philadelphia: Institute of Contemporary Art, 1988).

49. Carol Vogel, "Asian Collectors Give Christie's a High-Yield Night," *The New York Times*, May 14, 2014, p. A22.

AFTERWORD

1. Dominick Dunne, "Robert Mapplethorpe's Proud Finale," *Vanity Fair*, February 1989.

2. Claude J. Summers, "Oscar Wilde," *The Gay and Lesbian Literary Heritage* (New York: Routledge, 2002), 2nd edition.

3. Interview with Carol Squiers, New York, January 26, 2011.

ACKNOWLEDGMENTS

The list of individuals to whom I am indebted, and equally grateful, for their observations about Sam Wagstaff is long; for their memories, expertise, or scholarship; for their encouragement, support, or assistance. At the top, however, is James Crump, who generously brought to my doorstep his own comprehensive research materials for *Black, White + Gray*, his documentary about Wagstaff—I relied consistently on this invaluable trove throughout my own research.

Without an editor, a writer is left to become his own worst enemy. Robert Weil, my editor at Liveright, provided focused insight and the kind of rigorous dialogue on the page that every author welcomes. Trent Duffy, an exacting surgeon of the manuscript, not only smoothed grammatical wrinkles and trimmed narrative fat but also held me to the facts with finesse.

Several other editors provided early and meaningful guidance along the way, and I am grateful to each one of them: Samuel Douglas, for his elegance and tone; Maria Russo, who nudged me to trust my intuition; and Craig Seligman, who encouraged me from the beginning.

I appreciate the efforts of Ira Silverberg, the most literary of agents, who first brought the project to Bob Weil, and to Jim Rutman, who continues my representation with a steady hand.

I thank Susan Kismaric, my good friend, for our ongoing, lifelong conversation about photography, as well as for her expertise, keen discernment, and practical assistance. I welcomed the lunches with my good friend Bill Goldstein became a ritual of commiseration about the labor of writing, researching, and making order out of so much—and so little—information.

At the J. Paul Getty Museum, Judy Keller not only made possible my museum scholar residency but also generously shared her knowledge and provided access to the museum's collection of photographs. I also am grateful for the help of her curatorial staff: Virginia Heckert, Paul Martineau, and Amanda Maddox. At the Getty Research Institute, Marcia Reed, Fran Terpak, and Alexa Sekyra provided kind support; Raquel Zamora, worthy research; and Michelle Brunnick, collegial assistance.

At the Detroit Institute of Arts, Nancy Barr generously shared her notable scholarship and made introductions to people who had known Wagstaff there; at the Wadsworth Atheneum Museum of Art, Gene Gaddis unearthed valuable material from the museum's archives.

At the Mapplethorpe Foundation, Joree Adilman and Michael Stout provided unfettered access to their holdings.

To the people I had the pleasure of interviewing about Sam, a genuine—if collective—thank you, in particular for the numerous conversations, personal materials, and recollections: Pierre Apraxine, Ellen Brooks, Lynn Davis, Anne Ehrenkranz, Susanne Hilberry, Gerald Incandela, Barbara Jakobson, Judith Jefferson (Sam's niece), Peter and Tom Jefferson (Sam's nephews), Judy Linn, Anne MacDonald, Maria Morris Hambourg, Weston Naef, Ellen Phelan, George Rinhart, Carol Squiers, John Waddell, Paul Walter, Daniel Wolf, and Clark Worswick.

Several individuals were helpful in idiosyncratic ways and I owe them my gratitude: Vince Aletti, Chris Bollen, Malcolm Daniel, James Danziger, Allen Ellenzweig, Monica Espinel, Megan Feingold, Peter Galassi, Perrin Lathrop, Dimitri Levas, Peter MacGill, Edward Mapplethorpe, Will Menaker, Jeff Rosenheim, John Solomon, and Colin Westerbeck.

Finally, I wish to express my delight to the others from whom I draw inspiration, and not only on the weekend: Franklin Tartaglione, Dave King, Richard Friedman, Robert Hughes, Carey Lebowitz, Simon Lince, Robert Flynt, Jeff MacMahon, Patterson Scarlett, Taylor Mac, Bill Jacobson, Josh Gosfield, Camille Sweeney, Peter Franck, Kathleen Triem, and, across the country and over the years, Kelly Sultan. And, of course, Richard Press, my husband, my inspiration, the perpetual song in my heart.

INDEX

Page numbers in *italics* refer to illustrations.

ABOUT THE AUTHOR

PHILIP GEFTER was on staff at *The New York Times* for over fifteen years, where he wrote regularly about photography. His book of essays, *Photography After Frank* (Aperture), was published in 2009. He also produced the documentary film *Bill Cunningham New York* (2010). He lives in New York City.